History beyond apartheid

Manchester University Press

History beyond apartheid

New approaches in South African historiography

Edited by Thula Simpson

MANCHESTER UNIVERSITY PRESS

Copyright © Manchester University Press 2023

While copyright in the volume as a whole is vested in Manchester University Press, copyright in individual chapters belongs to their respective authors, and no chapter may be reproduced wholly or in part without the express permission in writing of both author and publisher.

Published by Manchester University Press
Oxford Road, Manchester M13 9PL

www.manchesteruniversitypress.co.uk

British Library Cataloguing-in-Publication Data
A catalogue record for this book is available from the British Library

ISBN 978 1 5261 5907 6   hardback
ISBN 978 1 5261 7897 8   paperback

First published 2023

The publisher has no responsibility for the persistence or accuracy of URLs for any external or third-party internet websites referred to in this book, and does not guarantee that any content on such websites is, or will remain, accurate or appropriate.

Typeset
by New Best-set Typesetters Ltd

Contents

List of illustrations	*page* vii
Contributors	viii
Editor's preface	x
Abbreviations	xiv

1. Towards a school of their own: the varieties of South African historiography — 1
   Thula Simpson
2. Beasts of the southern world: multispecies history and the Anthropocene — 25
   Sandra Swart
3. Black academics matter: history and antiblackness at South African universities — 55
   Janeke Thumbran
4. Black mothering, 'maids' and mixed methods in women's history: Zanele Muholi's contemporary art and Sindiwe Magona's short stories — 76
   Mandisa Mbali
5. Vernacular traditions as counter-hegemonic archives in Eastern Cape historiography — 102
   Nomalanga Mkhize
6. The revolution in South African historiography — 119
   Thula Simpson
7. From grand narratives to complicated subjects: biography in the postapartheid era — 142
   Lindie Koorts
8. Whiteness must fall: whiteness, whites and insurgent history writing — 177
   Neil Roos

9. Bringing white workers back in: new histories of race and class in South Africa 198
Danelle van Zyl-Hermann
10. The transnational nation: South African history beyond and across borders 227
Rob Skinner

Index 256

Illustrations

4.1 *Minah VI*, © Zanele Muholi, 2008   *page* 90
4.2 *'Massa' and Maids, IV, Hout Bay*, © Zanele Muholi,
     2009   91
4.3 *Bester I, Mayotte*, © Zanele Muholi, 2015   93

Contributors

Lindie Koorts is a historian and biographer affiliated to the University of the Free State. She is the author of *DF Malan and the Rise of Afrikaner Nationalism* (2014), which was shortlisted for the Sunday Times Alan Paton Prize, as well as the KykNet-Rapport Prys, and is a regular media contributor.

Mandisa Mbali is Senior Lecturer in Historical Studies at the University of Cape Town. Her work deals with South African and global health policy and activism, with a particular focus on HIV/AIDS. She has also written on race and medical humanitarianism and new approaches to historicising COVID-19.

Nomalanga Mkhize is a historian based at the Nelson Mandela University in the city of Gqeberha, South Africa. Her research interests are in African language historical literatures and their historiographical contributions.

Neil Roos is Professor of History and Dean of Social Sciences and Humanities at the University of Fort Hare. His research focuses on social histories of race, and he has a book forthcoming from Indiana University Press entitled *Ordinary Whites in Apartheid Society: Social Histories of Accommodation*.

Thula Simpson is a historian based at the University of Pretoria and is the author of *Umkhonto we Sizwe: The ANC's Armed Struggle* (2016), and *History of South Africa: From 1902 to the Present* (2021). His chapters in this book are based on research supported by the National Institute for the Humanities and Social Sciences.

Rob Skinner is Senior Lecturer in Modern History at the University of Bristol. He has written extensively on South Africa, including *The Foundations of Anti-Apartheid* (2010) and *Modern South Africa in Global History* (2017) and recently coedited *A Global History of Anti-Apartheid* (2019) with Anna Konieczna.

Sandra Swart is Professor and Chair of the Department of History, Stellenbosch University. She received her DPhil in history from Oxford University in 2001, with a simultaneous MSc in environmental change and management, also at Oxford. She studies (and supervises doctoral students from Botswana, Malawi, South Africa, Tanzania, Uganda and Zimbabwe in the area of) socioenvironmental histories of southern Africa, with her own focus on animals.

Janeke Thumbran is Senior Lecturer in the History Department at Rhodes University. She has a PhD in African history from the University of Minnesota. Her research is on the history of universities and social disciplines in South Africa.

Danelle van Zyl-Hermann is a social historian of Southern and East Africa at the University of Basel, Switzerland. She is author of *Privileged Precariat: White Workers and South Africa's Long Transition to Majority Rule* (2021) and coauthor of *Rethinking White Societies in Southern Africa: 1930s–1990s* (2020).

Editor's preface

In his review of the Hans Erik Stolten edited *History Making and Present Day Politics: The Meaning of Collective Memory in South Africa* (2007), André du Toit disputed the claim advanced by many contributors that South African historiography had slumped into a general 'crisis' after apartheid. Du Toit argued that these claims overlooked the many ways in which the field remained productive and vibrant, and mistook for a crisis the decline of the 'radical' or 'revisionist' approach that had dominated the field in the 1970s and 1980s. He called for more self-reflection among historians of South Africa about their discipline's intellectual trajectory.[1]

Du Toit's review appeared in 2010, and the pertinence of the points he raised was underscored when the *Cambridge History of South Africa* appeared in two volumes, in that year and in 2012. In their introduction, the *Cambridge History*'s editors acknowledged that the volumes were 'based to a great degree on scholarship that preceded the fall of apartheid', but they argued that this was unavoidable, because 'as yet there have been limited signs of a blooming of new historiographies'. In introducing the second volume, Robert Ross, Anne Kelk Mager and Bill Nasson identified two conditions as being necessary to remedy the situation: first, the ranks of the profession would have to be refreshed by new entrants – and particularly black Africans – who could offer fresh perspectives; second, the postapartheid era would have to generate its own controversies capable of stimulating original efforts at historicisation.[2]

These characterisations of the state of the field were challenged by some reviewers, whose rebuttals echoed Du Toit. Helena Pohlandt-McCormick argued that the *Cambridge History*'s editors had overlooked the 'considerable historiographical work since the early 1990s that has not only addressed the "legacies" of apartheid and colonialism' but had also challenged the 'concepts, chronologies, and turning points' of radical/revisionist historiography. Keith

Breckenridge meanwhile insisted that this new scholarship had not only raised many 'questions about the paradoxical effects of the segregationist state and Apartheid', but had also long since transcended the limits of the radical/revisionist problematic by exploring a wide variety of themes in realms as diverse as intellectual, scientific, medical and ecological history. Jon Soske insisted that black academics had been full participants in this process – he in fact argued that the *Cambridge History* could have been filled entirely with contributions by them.[3]

The present collection seeks to explore the abovementioned themes. It is the outcome of a project launched early in 2018, when invitations were sent to a number of historian colleagues to contribute to a publication on 'History and Decolonisation: Perspectives on Transformation in South African Historiography'. The original working title reflected a desire to frame the initiative around the implications for the discipline of the debates that had embroiled South African universities from 2015 onwards, but that idea was soon revised for the simple reason that the themes explored by historians of South Africa extend far beyond 'decolonisation' and 'transformation', as the paper proposals soon showed. That being said, readers will find traces of the original framing in some of the chapters that follow, and there can be little doubt that decolonisation and transformation are here to stay as themes in South African historiography, given their prominence among the postapartheid controversies that the *Cambridge History*'s editors predicted would emerge to shape the research agenda within the discipline in the future.

The title was revised to 'Future Directions in South African Historiography', which reflected an aspiration to link past, present and future approaches. Beyond this, there was no further prescription. In advancing with an 'open' historiographical agenda, there was no preconceived notion of proclaiming any particular 'turn' in the literature, or of excluding from sight any sphere of active inquiry. This includes radical/revisionist historiography – readers will find that many chapters in the collection (including my own) focus on the continuing consequences of that powerful strand in the tradition.

Some justification may be needed for including the future in a project focused on historiography. The first consideration was my concurrence with those who have argued that South African historiography has expanded in multiple directions since the 1990s, and that it has in the process established numerous areas of overlap with other disciplines, but that there has been relatively little sustained engagement among historians about the historiographical implications of the work. The present collection seeks to bring the discipline's frontiers into closer contact with its midlands, by fostering discussion about the historiographical significance of the new work, and thus identifying leads for future research by indicating unresolved questions, novel conceptual frameworks, and fresh methods of empirical attack. The second consideration was my agreement with Ross, Mager and Nasson that historiographical innovation owes both to demographic shifts within the guild and to the willingness of historians to apply their research to emerging societal challenges. If this reading is correct, then the discipline's continued flourishing rests to a considerable extent on the preparedness of each successive generation of scholars to make the case anew for the tradition's continued relevance in times of change. This process is an endless one, with the consequence that no collection can pretend to be complete for all time – the chapters that follow were all written during the COVID-19 lockdown, for example, and the fallout of that crisis will undoubtedly cast a fresh aspect on the country's historiography, as will the reverberations of the present war in Europe.

In short, the book's objectives will be achieved to the extent that the collection furthers engagement between historians of South Africa about their craft, and the degree to which from that engagement fresh lines of inquiry emerge capable of providing an impetus for the work of the next generation of researchers to enter the field.

I have accumulated numerous debts of gratitude during the course of this project. Professor Dawne Curry helped to develop the initial call for papers, in which capacity she served as both a source of and a sounding board for ideas, and a mobiliser of funding from her institution, the University of Nebraska-Lincoln. Further funding for the project was obtained from the National Institute for the Humanities and the Social Sciences and the Andrew W. Mellon Foundation. Within the University of Pretoria, Professors Karen Harris, Vasu Reddy and Maxi Schoeman offered invaluable assistance on numerous occasions in their respective capacities at departmental and faculty level, while the Administrator of the Department of Historical and Heritage Studies, Zimkhitha Tsotso, expedited the many administrative processes. The support of Emma Brennan, Meredith Carroll, Paul Clarke, Lianne Slavin and Laura Swift at Manchester University Press has been indispensable for bringing this project through to publication. Further thanks are owed to Maia Vaswani for her copy-editing of the typescript, and to Christine Love-Rodgers and Elizabeth Williams for aiding us with tracking down some elusive references during this process. Finally, I must thank Cathy Burns, David Fig, Linda Chisholm and, once again, Dawne Curry, whose contributions at a work-in-progress seminar at an early stage of the process have greatly strengthened the contributions that follow.

Thula Simpson Pretoria
December 2022

Notes

1 A. du Toit, 'The Owl of Minerva and the Ironic Fate of the Progressive Praxis of Radical Historiography in Post-apartheid South Africa', *History and Theory*, 49 (2) May 2010, 266, 268, 269.
2 'Editors' Introduction', in C. Hamilton, B.K. Mbenga and R. Ross (eds), *The Cambridge History of South Africa*, vol. 1, *From Early Times to 1885* (Cambridge: Cambridge University Press, 2010), xiv; R. Ross, A. Kelk Mager and B. Nasson, 'Introduction', in R. Ross, A. Kelk Mager and B. Nasson (eds), *The Cambridge History of South Africa*, vol. 2, *1885–1994* (Cambridge: Cambridge University Press, 2012), 12, 16.
3 H. Pohlandt-McCormick, *African Studies Review*, 55 (3) Dec. 2012, 180; K. Breckenridge, *South African Historical Journal*, 66 (4) 2014, 723; J. Soske, 'The Striking Minority of Black Contributors', *Africa Is a Country*, 29 Nov. 2012, https://africasacountry.com/2012/11/why-does-south-african-history-continue-to-be-written-primarily-by-white-scholars (accessed 29 Mar. 2022).

Abbreviations

ANC	African National Congress
CHBE	*Cambridge History of the British Empire*
ICS	Institute of Commonwealth Studies
LGBTIQ	lesbian, gay, bisexual, transgender, intersex and queer
MWU	Mineworkers' Union
NP	National Party
SOAS	School of Oriental and African Studies
TRC	Truth and Reconciliation Commission
UCT	University of Cape Town
UN	United Nations
UP	University of Pretoria
UWC	University of the Western Cape
Wits	University of the Witwatersrand

1

Towards a school of their own: the varieties of South African historiography

Thula Simpson

Towards the end of 1991, Floors van Jaarsveld completed a chapter on the past, present and future of history writing in Afrikaans. He was deeply concerned about the future. Based on a self-conducted survey of the *South African Historical Journal* and various international periodicals, he argued that works on South African history in English already far outstripped those in Afrikaans. But his concerns were also qualitative, and drawing on the *Archives Yearbook*, Potchefstroom University's *Gesamentlike Katalogus van Proefskrifte en Verhandelinge*, the University of South Africa's *South African History and Historians – A Bibliography*, and a further sample of journals, he concluded that the output of Afrikaans historians had since the 1960s remained focused on political themes, and particularly the role of 'great' leaders.[1]

Van Jaarsveld's concern was that Afrikaans historiography risked obsolescence as a consequence of developments that had transformed its English-language counterpart over the previous generation. In the 1950s, Monica Wilson and Leonard Thompson respectively headed the University of Cape Town's Social Anthropology and History departments. By the mid-1960s, Thompson had relocated to the University of California, Los Angeles, where he was visited by Wilson, who was on sabbatical. Over lunch they discussed the volume of the *Cambridge History of the British Empire* focused on South Africa, of which a new edition was published in 1963, minimally revised from the 1936 original. They were both highly critical of it, and turned to considering what they would do differently. They agreed that they would treat Africans as agents rather than mere recipients of colonial influence, and would challenge racist framings of events. The discussion birthed a joint project to deliver such a publication.[2]

Thompson was involved in a parallel initiative in the late 1960s that had a similar objective. His partner was the white South African head of the University of Zambia's History Department, John Omer-Cooper, and they aimed to bring historians, archaeologists and social anthropologists together to achieve for southern Africa what scholars of tropical Africa were accomplishing by using interdisciplinary methods to uncover indigenous agency in the continent's past. As part of this second project, a conference was held in Lusaka in July 1968 where the presenters included Martin Legassick, who was Thompson's doctoral student, and Shula Marks, a lecturer attached to the School of Oriental and African Studies (SOAS) and the Institute of Commonwealth Studies (ICS) in London. Legassick and Marks had first met in London in 1966–67 during the former's doctoral research, and they shared similar perspectives on the precolonial period, as was reflected in their respective conference papers on the 'Sotho-Tswana' and 'Nguni', in which they argued that the peopling of southern Africa had unfolded gradually over many centuries, involving multiple layers of migration.[3]

Both projects involving Thompson resulted in publications in 1969 – namely, the first volume of the *Oxford History of South Africa* (which he coedited with Wilson) and *African Societies in Southern Africa*. Monica Wilson had attended the Lusaka conference, and Legassick later recalled her having been highly critical, with Thompson's support, of the employment of the concept of historical layering in Marks's paper. Marks used a review of the *Oxford History* to renew the controversy: she claimed Wilson's four chapters were 'purely synchronic and ahistorical', those of an anthropologist considering the past 'for the sake of extracting static conclusions from moving elements'. As examples, she cited Wilson's failure to comprehend that the Khoikhoi band was 'a changing social institution', and her habitual use of the terms 'Sotho' and 'Nguni' in ways that overlooked oral, archaeological and literary evidence that South Africa had been peopled over a millennium 'by little trickles of peoples ... who intermingle and proliferate ... to produce new amalgams'. While allowing that Wilson at one point appeared to concede 'a layering of peoples', Marks argued that on the whole: 'We are still given a picture of a way of life that has been static from time immemorial.'[4]

Marks had an equally strong interest in the modern period – her appointment to SOAS earlier in the 1960s had been to lecture on 'African people and European rule in Southern Africa from 1890 to 1924', and she had launched an ICS seminar series in 1969 on 'Societies of Southern Africa in the Nineteenth and Twentieth Centuries'. Through the latter, she became a pivotal figure in developing the critique of the *Oxford History*'s second volume, which appeared in 1971, covering events since the 1860s. This was because while presenters were invited from a range of disciplines, the overarching goal of the seminar series remained – as Marks later put it in a paper coauthored with her SOAS colleague Anthony Atmore – 'to get beyond the limitations of the liberal "problematic"'.[5]

The seminars followed the tradition set by the ICS's first director, Keith Hancock, of precirculating written papers to facilitate discussion, and the

Collected Papers of the series eventually ran to twenty volumes. The contributions of three early seminar presenters proved particularly influential in forging the critique of the prevailing scholarship. The first volume of the Collected Papers, published in 1971, contained an essay by Frederick Johnstone, a Canadian DPhil candidate at Oxford. Johnstone's paper used the controversy over the colour bar during the 1922 Rand Revolt to illustrate the larger claim of his doctoral research, that racial discrimination in South Africa historically owed less to a desire to achieve separate development than to procure the supplies of cheap labour on which white prosperity – and the profitability of the mining industry in particular – depended.[6]

The second volume of the Collected Papers included 'The Frontier Tradition in South African Historiography' by Martin Legassick, who completed his thesis at the University of California, Los Angeles, in 1969 on 'The Griqua, the Sotho-Tswana and the Missionaries, 1780–1840: The Politics of a Frontier Zone'. Legassick's paper challenged the convention that contemporary South African racial attitudes were traceable to frontier conflict, and it did so by marshalling evidence that racial distinctions on the frontier were more fluid than most scholars had assumed, before concluding with the question: 'If the stereotype of the African as enemy cannot be traced to the eighteenth century, when and why did it in fact come into existence?' Legassick left the question open, but he proposed an answer in another 1972 publication, a review of the *Oxford History*'s second volume (as well as *South Africa: Sociological Perspectives*, edited by Heribert Adam), in which he echoed Johnstone by characterising the African reserves as a 'sub-subsistence sector' that effectively cross-subsidised starvation wages paid by white employers to migrant labourers. He faulted the two books under review for failing to understand that economic exploitation was the point of racist legislation.[7]

The year 1972 also saw Harold Wolpe publish 'Capitalism and Cheap Labour in South Africa: From Segregation to Apartheid' in the journal *Economy and Society*. Wolpe concurred with Johnstone and Legassick about racism's economic function, but he added the argument that as the twentieth century developed, segregation had been plunged into crisis as Africans migrated to the cities in growing numbers to escape the poverty generated by the cheap labour system. For Wolpe, the social strains created by rapid urbanisation had fostered the emergence of a new, radical black politics, and he attributed the shift from segregation to apartheid to the need for greater state repression to preserve the edifice of white supremacy.[8]

As Shula Marks noted approvingly in her 1973 review of the second *Oxford History* volume, the crux of the argument advanced by Johnstone, Legassick, Wolpe and others was that 'the pattern of race relations in South Africa was not simply inherited ready-made from the agrarian societies of the seventeenth and eighteenth centuries ... but is structurally linked to the process of industrialisation'.[9]

In challenging the liberal paradigm, the radical critique simultaneously erected a new one, centred on exploring the role of capitalism and industrialisation in shaping South Africa's racial order. The new questions proved hugely successful in stimulating intellectual engagement: the ICS seminar's Friday 5 p.m. sittings attracted guests from across Britain and beyond, while similar forums sprouted elsewhere, notably at Oxford under Stanley Trapido's aegis.[10]

But the process of exploring the new problems quickly exposed important differences among the participants. A group of students at Sussex University was developing a perspective rooted in the traditions of French structuralism, drawing on Louis Althusser and Nicos Poulantzas; by contrast, Belinda Bozzoli and Charles van Onselen (two South African DPhil candidates at Sussex and Oxford respectively) regularly attended meetings of the History Workshop that was established at Ruskin College in Oxford in 1967 and had pioneered a 'social history' approach of which the two key tenets were a focus on 'ordinary' people, rather than Great Men, and addressing research to broader audiences than just fellow academics.[11]

Legassick later recalled that the 'theoreticist' Poulantzians and 'empiricist' social historians soon fell out. He dated the schism to a September 1974 conference on South African social and economic history that he co-organised with Stanley Trapido at Oxford. By his account, the trigger came during a paper by Mike Morris on agriculture, when Charles van Onselen interjected: 'I would rather write about donkey-fucking than what you're writing about.'[12]

South African social history

The new perspectives being pioneered in England soon percolated to South Africa itself, both surreptitiously through dog-eared copies of papers delivered at Oxford, Sussex and London, but also openly as graduates began returning to fill posts in South Africa's white English-speaking universities, which were expanding rapidly from the bounty of the economic boom of the 1960s. Numerous initiatives followed within South Africa to further explore the problems of the new paradigm, including an Oral History Project at the University of Cape Town, a Worker History Project at the University of Natal, and a History Workshop that was established at the University of the Witwatersrand (Wits) in 1977 by a cluster of scholars including Belinda Bozzoli, Charles van Onselen, Phil Bonner, Eddie Webster, Tim Couzens, Peter Kallaway and Luli Callinicos.[13]

As its name suggested, the Wits History Workshop sought to develop a South African social history tradition. It held an inaugural conference in 1978, which followed the pattern set by its Oxford counterpart by offering both scholarly papers that sought to reinterpret the Witwatersrand's history from the perspective of its working-class population and 'nonacademic' events that were open to the public, including slide and tape shows, a film, and even a theatre production of Van Onselen's essay 'Randlords and Rotgut'. Bozzoli explained the rationale behind this approach in her introduction to the subsequent publication of conference papers: 'what kind of blind academicism would it be to adopt a "grassroots" academic perspective without making some attempt to communicate it beyond the seminar room and conference table'?[14]

That being said, the organisers were disappointed by the yield: most of the approximately one hundred conference attendees were white, and the majority of black participants were middle class. There was a conscious effort to remedy those demographics for the workshop's second conference in 1981, but while working-class Africans formed a much higher proportion of the thousand attendees, the organisers remained dissatisfied. This was because their ambitions extended beyond the mere communication of their research to working class audiences. As Bozzoli put it in the publication of the 1981 conference papers, they also sought to 'encourage and stimulate the writing of *their own history* and the recovery of their *own cultural past* by people drawn from the poorest classes'. It was in that regard that the conference was felt to have fallen short. Bozzoli noted that 'worker audience participation in most events was extensive. But audience participation is not sufficient – it runs against the emphasis of the Workshop on the *production*, rather than *consumption*, of historical work.' She lamented the fact that 'stimulating this kind of production has not been easy in a hostile and often shallow cultural milieu; the temptation to take on the role of "sponge" – of absorbing and squeezing out anything it happens to encounter – has been difficult to resist'.[15]

As the 1980s progressed, the radical paradigm faced further difficulties on the purely theoretical terrain. In a 2006 interview Martin Legassick recalled that the radical historians had initially sought 'to situate the mineral revolution as a decisive moment in South African history, as opposed to the frontier for the liberals and conquest for the nationalists', but he added that in so doing, they were 'not saying that conquest is not important, because social relations that were established in the mineral revolution depended on those of conquest. Nevertheless, we situated the mineral revolution as central.'[16]

Acknowledging that capitalism built on relations that it inherited from the frontier raised the question of how it could simultaneously be credited with having been 'decisive' and 'central' in establishing those relations. Political reforms within South Africa during the 1980s posed a further challenge, by offering credence for the liberal contention that the nexus between capitalism and racism was not nearly as tight as the radicals had claimed. Harold Wolpe addressed the implications of these political developments in 'Class Concepts, Class Struggle and Racism', a 1986 chapter that advanced a revised position whereby 'social classes are simultaneously economically, politically and ideologically shaped', meaning relations of production would no longer be considered the sole *determinant* of the concrete'. It was a concession, not a capitulation, on Wolpe's part, for he added that the 'mode of production' would remain 'privileged' within the new framework. This was because, he claimed, productive relations 'provide a context for, post issues for and set limits to struggle' elsewhere.[17]

With its greater flexibility, this 'non-reductionist Marxist conception of class' (as Wolpe put it) closed much of the difference that had once existed between radical historiography's 'theoreticist' and 'empiricist' variants, but in the process it illuminated a difficulty that they shared. This was because a focus on relations of production lay at the heart of the 'class'-based approach that both had sought to advance. Wolpe's admission that political and ideological factors as often as not shaped the formation of classes called into question the rationale for continuing to privilege productive relations for analytical purposes.

The underlying issue was highlighted well by events towards the end of the 1980s. In *Towards Socialist Democracy* (2007), his academic memoirs, Legassick wrote of the seismic events in Eastern Europe and the Soviet Union between 1989 and 1991, that the 'collapse of the Stalinist states and the restoration of capitalism in them transformed the balance of forces on a world scale'. Then, in perhaps his last work (published in a 2019 festschrift for Harold Wolpe), Legassick argued that these international developments profoundly affected the course of the antiapartheid struggle, for they 'disoriented the active layer of South African workers and stood in the way of the mass rejection of a negotiated compromise that we had anticipated' (he was referring to the position that he and other radical historians had long advanced, that capitalism and apartheid had become so closely intertwined in the collective mind of the country's black proletariat that African workers would reject any settlement that failed to overthrow both orders).[18]

Whatever else one makes of the claim that black workers were disoriented by geopolitical developments during the transition to majority rule, in advancing it as an explanation of the apartheid denouement, Legassick essentially accepted as uncontroversial the notion that political and ideological factors were capable of overwhelming economic ones in shaping historical outcomes. If he was correct, there was no good reason for historians to continue privileging the 'mode of production' as the 'determinant of the concrete'.

Killing Kas Maine

'Structure and Experience in the Making of Apartheid' was the theme of the History Workshop's fifth triennial conference, which was held at Wits University on 6–10 February 1990. A record five thousand people attended the open day, but the proceedings fell directly between the unbanning of the African National Congress (ANC) and Nelson Mandela's release,[19] and the impending shakeup of the country's racial order raised a question about the workshop's future direction, given the attention that the centre had hitherto devoted to exploring the making of apartheid, and identifying itself politically with the system's opponents.

An important landmark in the workshop's repositioning came in 1992, when at Cynthia Kros's instigation it hosted a conference on 'Myths, Monuments, Museums: New Premises?' with the aim of fostering engagement by academics with discussions that had begun in museums and the broader heritage sector about how public representations of history might change following Mandela's release.[20]

Public history became a central component of the workshop's activity after the 1994 elections that brought the ANC to power, as it partnered with the incoming authorities in a series of commemorative projects that included the creation of Johannesburg's Apartheid Museum, and the establishment of the Alexandra Heritage Trail.[21]

The workshop soon found itself the target of a critique emanating from the University of the Western Cape (UWC), which had positioned itself during the 1980s as the 'intellectual home of the left'. In 1986, UWC's History Department launched a 'People's History' project that fell squarely within the country's social history tradition: undergraduates were trained to operate as 'barefoot historians' and employ oral history to recover the hidden histories of local communities, while an inaugural open day in 1987 featured films, exhibitions, music, poetry and workshops for schoolchildren.[22]

Among the presenters at the History Workshop's 1990 conference were Gary Minkley and Ciraj Rassool, who were then junior lecturers in UWC's History Department, and Leslie Witz, the Coordinator of African History at Khanya College in Johannesburg. Witz had published *Write Your Own History* in 1988, a book that resulted from an initiative launched by the History Workshop and the South African Committee for Higher Education two years earlier to advance the former's longstanding goal of stimulating the production of historical works by nonacademics. In the late 1990s,

Witz joined UWC, where he would partner with Minkley and Rassool in a self-styled 'Troika' that aimed to critically interrogate the practices of the social history tradition in which they had hitherto operated. The trio later recalled that they remained 'in some measure in accord with the objectives of the History Workshop (particularly in the employment of oral history methodology and the historical materialist framework)'. The problem they sought to unpack concerned why – despite having embraced that methodology and that framework – South African social historians had failed in their objective of enlisting a broad lay public as partners in developing a true 'people's history'.[23]

The trio used the UWC History Department's seminar (which subsequently expanded to become an interdisciplinary 'South African and Contemporary History and Humanities' seminar) to collectively explore this question. The essence of the answer that they developed was that the key shortcoming lay in the continued fealty among South African social historians to practices that privileged the perspectives of academics over those of nonspecialists. As a remedy they called for a renewed focus on the issue that had originally animated the tradition, that of the *production* of history.[24]

Perhaps the best-known exposition of the position came in 'Orality, Memory, and Social History in South Africa', a 1998 chapter by Minkley and Rassool that included a critique of *The Seed Is Mine*, Charles van Onselen's biography of the black sharecropper Kas Maine, which had appeared two years earlier. Minkley and Rassool argued that Van Onselen's use of interviews reflected the two dominant perspectives among South African social historians regarding the uses of orality and memory: one was that personal recollections offered a supplementary source capable of filling 'black holes' in the official and documentary record; the second was that they could 'stand for collective ones, sifted, checked, ordered, cross-referenced, evaluated, and processed by the historian'. They insisted that this fixation on 'dredging personal and public memories … into a "body of historically verifiable facts"' obscured how reminiscences conveyed their 'own story of remembrance, forgetting, and narrativity', and they contended that a consequence of this oversight was that *The Seed Is Mine* was not a biography at all, for 'the narrative voice that emerges is Van Onselen's'.[25]

The Troika's critique was supplemented by another from UWC early in the twenty-first century. Its author, Premesh Lalu, had completed his DPhil at the University of Minnesota in 2003, before publishing a series of articles and a 2009 book, *The Deaths of Hintsa*. It was another critique from within the family of radical historiography – Lalu wrote that he considered it to be a 'continuation' of the 'Marxist scholarship of the 1970s', one that 'supplements the unravelling of apartheid in terms of race and class' that Legassick, Wolpe and others had begun to perform. Lalu sought to interrogate why, despite adopting a Marxist approach, radical scholarship had failed to complete that unravelling.²⁶

He probed the issue by considering the case of Nicholas Tilana Gcaleka, who had returned to South Africa from Scotland in 1996 claiming to have recovered the skull of the nineteenth-century Xhosa King Hintsa, only to suffer ridicule after archaeologists demonstrated that the relic was that of a white woman. Lalu declined to join the chorus, and instead interpreted the affair as continuing a longer tradition of scholarly complicity in the maintenance of racial oppression in South Africa. He argued that this complicity was rooted partly in the colonial origins of most disciplines, with this dependence being manifested among historians in the privileging of archival research. Lalu noted that even radical historians had based their accounts of Hintsa's death on material sourced from colonial repositories. Lalu insisted that such borrowings inevitably contributed to racist framings, while he dismissed as inadequate the method that many had identified as offering a corrective to the biases of the colonial archive, for he insisted that the employment of oral history had led only to an uncritical embrace of 'nationalist narratives.'²⁷

This last argument converged with one that Minkley and Rassool had advanced in their 1998 chapter, where they argued that South Africa's social historians had habitually misidentified as 'voices from below' the perspectives of leaders of nationalist movements, with the result that their scholarship became 'mobilized in support of building a national movement on the basis of the dominant resistance politics of the 1950s' (with the History Workshop's postapartheid partnership with the ANC offering an illustration of this). Lalu insisted that nationalism was incapable of unravelling race and class oppression, and he turned to the South Asian Subaltern Studies Collective for insights as to how historians might escape their profession's heritage of subordination to political power. He latched on to two claims in particular: one was the Collective's questioning of the criteria conventionally used to demarcate historians from nonhistorians; the other was its criticism of the employment of disciplinary protocols to limit what was expressible about the past. He invoked both claims to defend Gcaleka's right to use his imagination as a resource in reconstructing the past.²⁸

The critiques emanating from UWC met with a mixed reception within the profession. The History Workshop hosted a colloquium on 3–5 April 2009 to reflect on its 'thirty odd' years of existence. Ciraj Rassool was invited to contribute, and he used the opportunity to restate the Troika's critique of the workshop's supposedly hierarchical approach. He also offered the District Six Museum, which had been launched in 1994, as an example of how the shortcomings could be overcome. As a museum trustee, Rassool had collaborated with activists, public intellectuals, academics, and former residents in developing the venue, and he explained that they had opted to develop spaces as forums where the perspectives of different knowledge creators would meet on terms of strict equality.[29]

But his claim to have thereby succeeded in flattening hierarchies between academic and nonacademic knowledge producers was challenged by the colloquium's keynote speaker, Professor Neeladri Bhattacharya of Jawaharlal Nehru University, who countered that 'Orchestrating disruption is a narrative choice,' and one that was in fact conventional among academics and curators, who often sought to juxtapose conflicting voices. The mere act of juxtaposing perspectives was insufficient to subvert hierarchies, Bhattacharya argued, for it failed to address the factors that bestowed ultimate power, such as: 'Who makes the final curatorial decision to create an open space? Who allocates spaces for different forms of exhibits? Who provides the wall where the memories of forced removals are to be inscribed? Who structures the way the building is designed and things are displayed?' Bhattacharya claimed Rassool had failed to specify how the District Six Museum had resolved such issues.[30]

Lalu's 'postcolonial critique of apartheid' also faced criticism. In his review of *The Deaths of Hintsa*, Brian Rutledge argued that if the book's advice were accepted and Hintsa reduced to a 'colonial statement' or 'figure of speech' (owing to the alleged impossibility of retrieving impartial knowledge from colonial archives), then African historical figures risked being relegated to mere 'victims of colonial narrative techniques'. Hlonipha Mokoena meanwhile flagged the implications of another dimension of the critique – namely, Lalu's suggestion that he would remain opposed to writing about figures such as Hintsa, even if his epistemic objections to archival research were resolved. As Mokoena put it, whereas other historians had considered Hintsa 'as a leader of a people suffering and resisting the consequences of imperial expansion, Lalu veers away from any such narrative lest he be accused of writing "nationalist history"'. The consequence of this reticence, she claimed, was that *The Deaths of Hintsa* 'kills Hintsa once more'.[31]

These points bore relevance to Minkley and Rassool's criticism of *The Seed Is Mine*, for in their chapter they had acknowledged that in a 1993 article, 'The Reconstruction of a Rural Life from Oral Testimony', Van Onselen had reflected extensively on the challenges he faced in writing Kas Maine's biography, including how differences in age, colour, class, gender and language mediated interactions between interviewer and interviewee, and how subjectivity and the passage of time qualified the accuracy of recollections, while he also freely acknowledged that 'the resulting product will in itself partly determine the voice and style in which the final presentation is made'.[32]

Hence it was *not* the case that Van Onselen failed to reflect on how remembrance, forgetting and narrativity affected the process of biographical writing. The critical difference was that he was *also* interested in the insights that Maine could offer on matters as diverse as (to quote Minkley and Rassool) 'prices, markets, contracts, and agreements, about weather, movement, and family'.[33] In short, Van Onselen was no more willing to strip social history of its social content than Mokoena was to eschew inquiry into 'nationalist' themes. He may also have agreed with her that for historians to restrict their engagement with black voices to discussions of the vagaries of remembrance, forgetting and narrativity would be to kill Kas Maine too.

Volksgeskiedenis

In a 1992 interview, the liberal historian Rodney Davenport noted, with irritation: 'we have had all kinds of people's history in the past. We've had *Volksgeschichte* in Nazi Germany, we've had *volksgeskiedenis* in this country. There are many different kinds of people – when are people not people?'[34]

Volksgeskiedenis was a major strand in twentieth-century Afrikaans historiography, and its fortunes were closely tied to those of the broader Afrikaner nationalist movement. When Victoria College became the University of Stellenbosch in April 1918, it capped a struggle dating to the late nineteenth century to avoid being merged with the English-medium South African College in Cape Town. Victoria College had possessed an autonomous History Department since 1904. The first chair, Everhard C. Godeé-Molsbergen, was a Dutchman who had graduated from Leiden under P.J. Blok's supervision, and he was succeeded in 1911 by Willem Blommaert, who obtained his degree from Ghent under Henri Pirenne's guidance. Through its two founding chairs, the department was exposed to French, German and Dutch influences, and the 'Stellenbosch School' came to be characterised by its 'objective-scientific' approach, involving meticulous archival research and the detailed narration of the facts thereby obtained. But while the school's methodological approach was informed by its continental European connections, Afrikaner nationalism provided its subject matter. Blommaert was replaced as department head in 1937 by H.B. Thom, whose DPhil he had supervised to completion seven years previously. In a 1943 essay, Thom proclaimed that 'the spirit of the volk must ring through' historical research, which had to 'be rooted in the same cultural soil as the people'. This commitment to cross-fertilising scholarship and popular culture was the conviction that lay behind *volksgeskiedenis*, and Thom's commitment to that ideal was reflected in his participation in numerous cultural organisations, including the Historical Monuments Commission, the Simon van der Stel Foundation and the Stellenbosch Museum.[35]

Stellenbosch exercised the predominant influence on the development of Afrikaans historical writing. Its preeminence owed largely to its status as the oldest Afrikaans history department, which placed it in the position of producing graduates who filled positions elsewhere.[36] The University of Pretoria (UP) – which had been known as the Transvaal University College from its establishment in 1908 until it gained its independence from the University of South Africa in 1930 – became the second fully fledged Afrikaans university in 1932, when it phased out English as a medium of instruction. The institution's Afrikanerisation had profound implications for its History Department, which had been led since its founding in 1909 by Leo Fouché, an outspoken proponent of the bilingual policy. The UP Senate appointed a committee in 1933 to 'strengthen' the department. The committee recommended revising the curriculum to include more material on the Voortrekkers and South Africa's Dutch heritage, and it seconded two professors to teach the material. The appointees were made autonomous of Fouché, who promptly resigned in 1934 to take the history chair at Wits University.[37]

Fouché's replacement at Pretoria, Isak Bosman, placed the department wholly at the service of Afrikaner nationalism. Bosman was an unproductive researcher and according to contemporaries was also an uninspired teacher, but he achieved lasting impact by overseeing the revision of the department's curriculum in a nationalist direction. The changes proved hugely popular among students, with the resulting increase in numbers feeding through to postgraduate level, and it was under Bosman that the foundations were laid for research in Afrikaans in a department in which most original scholarship had hitherto been delivered, in English, by J.A.I. Agar-Hamilton.[38]

Bloemfontein and Potchefstroom joined the network of Afrikaans-medium universities in 1950 and 1951.[39] The flourishing of Afrikaans historiography inside and outside academe reflected the fact that the professional historians involved were able to operate within the broader nationalist movement without encountering the kinds of linguistic, class and other social barriers that bedevilled the efforts of their neo-Marxist successors to accomplish a similar feat with African workers a generation later. But while this enabled Afrikaans historians to obtain a much richer understanding of the possibilities of 'people's history', the triumphs of *volksgeskiedenis* also alerted them to important limitations of the genre, and by the 1970s some leading practitioners had begun questioning whether the impressive historical industrial complex that they had helped to bring into being remained fit for purpose.

Francois du Toit Spies took over as head of UP's History Department in 1970, replacing A.N. Pelzer, who had followed the tradition set by Bosman (who died in 1947) of using scholarship to further nationalist goals. Though

Spies was a member of many cultural organisations, he was growing increasingly concerned about the state of historical scholarship in the country, and he used an article in the *South African Historical Journal* in 1971 to articulate his objections. The article *inter alia* faulted South African historical writing for its archive centrism, its political orientation and its preference for local over international subject matter, while it called for greater engagement with developments that were transforming the discipline internationally, including the work of the French Annales School and the 'New History' from America. Spies also made it clear that his criticisms were targeted specifically at Afrikaans historians, for he acknowledged that the changes he was recommending were beginning to be seen among historians of South Africa based in England, and others in South Africa's white English-speaking universities.[40]

Spies's tenure as department head was brief, ending with his resignation in 1972. His successor, Floors van Jaarsveld, shared many of his concerns about the ossification of Afrikaans historiography, and began the process of revising the department's curriculum: socioeconomic and contemporary history were introduced as themes, while Louis Changuion has argued that Pretoria in 1975 became the first department in the country to incorporate content on black Africans into every year of undergraduate study.[41]

Yet there was one important difference in the motives guiding Spies and Van Jaarsveld – namely, that while Spies's concerns were largely limited to the academic sphere, Van Jaarsveld had embroiled himself during the 1960s in public debate over the future of the Afrikaner people. *Die Verlede Spreek* in 1965 and *Afrikaner Quo Vadis?* in 1971 offered compilations of Van Jaarsveld's interventions on the question. In both, he denounced communism and liberalism and called for the racial partitioning of South Africa, but events in the mid-1970s – above all the collapse of Portugal's African Empire and the Soweto uprising – induced him to doubt whether apartheid was capable of securing Afrikaner survival. By the end of the decade the content of his articles, lectures and newspaper columns had shifted to exhorting Afrikaners to change their conceptions of the past for the sake of progress.[42]

The new directions in Van Jaarsveld's public advocacy saw him become a lightning rod for right-wing hostility, which took the forms of hate mail, threatening phone calls, even treason accusations from students, and led to perhaps the most notorious incident in South African historiography. Van Jaarsveld was invited to deliver a keynote address at the opening day of a conference held at the University of South Africa from 28 to 30 March 1979, on 'The Meaning of History: Problems in the Interpretation of History with Possible Reference to Examples from South African History such as the Battle of Blood River'. He used his presentation, titled the 'Historical

Mirror of Blood River', to reprise his warning about the danger of history developing into an obstacle to progress if it was ever allowed to crystallise into a petrified image. On the Battle of Blood River itself, he said that though Afrikaners could observe the 16 December anniversary as they wished, they ought to no longer try to make it an obligatory Sabbath for all. For its impiety to the established civic religion, his oration was interrupted by Afrikaner Weerstandsbeweging members, who tarred and feathered him, while their leader, Eugene Terre'Blanche, apologised to the audience for the interruption and explained that his men were protesting the 'desecration and degradation of everything holy to Afrikaners.'[43]

At the time of Van Jaarsveld's retirement in 1985, the situation was largely unchanged, and the issue became the subject of the inaugural address that Johan Bergh, his successor at Pretoria, delivered on 23 April 1987. Bergh echoed his two immediate predecessors in the chair by faulting Afrikaans historians for having failed to take critical distance from nationalism, or to embrace new methodological approaches. To illustrate the field's parochialism, he cited a report published earlier that year which indicated that no serving history lecturer at any Afrikaans university had obtained their main qualifications abroad, versus seventeen at just two of South Africa's white English universities, and that no historian from an Afrikaans university had published in foreign journals during the previous five years, versus twenty-two such publications by scholars at just two of the English institutions. Bergh flagged similar disparities in appointments of foreign lecturers and courses delivered abroad, before calling for urgent action to ensure that Afrikaans historians kept pace with global trends within the discipline.[44]

In their different ways, the concerns articulated by Spies and Van Jaarsveld raised questions about the role of professional historians in popular movements, and thus bore relevance to the postapartheid debates between radical historians about South African history's future in the public realm. Afrikaans historiography had received a tremendous initial impetus from its links with continental Europe and its associations with Afrikaner nationalism. These connections provided the methodology and subject matter that came to define the field, but Spies argued that scholarly renewal in the 1970s would require professional historians to engage more deeply among themselves and with foreign peers about technical aspects of their craft, while Van Jaarsveld in effect sought to leverage his professional credentials to position himself as a critic of popular conceptions of the past, based on his fear that the existing preoccupation with nationalist themes was preventing Afrikaners from responding creatively to emerging social challenges that were rooted, essentially, in the rise of new nationalisms. Their calls largely fell on deaf ears, but the pertinence of their interventions was highlighted by the crisis that John Bergh and others identified in the 1980s, because the issues were closely implicated in the productivity gap that was increasingly evident between the Afrikaans and English literatures at the time. Specifically, it was not that talented Afrikaans-speaking historians had ceased to emerge, rather it was that for those seeking to explore new methodological approaches, or to focus their research to pressing societal problems, English had by default become the lingua franca of the scholarly communities engaged in furthering inquiry in those fields.

There was, in short, a baby in the bathwater of the ancient professional ideals that South African historians ought not to sacrifice lightly in pursuit of the (critically important) task of popularising their craft.

Beyond apartheid

The chapters in this collection build on the abovementioned strands in South African historiography in numerous ways.

Sandra Swart argues that creating a 'usable past' in the era of the Anthropocene and the Sixth Extinction will require South African historians to broaden their focus beyond the frames of race, class and nation that have hitherto dominated the field. After reflecting on the lessons that the unfolding COVID-19 crisis offers regarding the porous boundaries between species, she uses the long entanglement between baboons and humans to explain how a 'more than human history' might be written. She explains that the new approach would involve fusing South African environmental historians' utilisation of findings from the fields of ethnoprimatology, palaeontology and paleoecology with the sense of the *longue durée* that South African social historians have obtained through their dialogue with archaeologists and anthropologists about precolonial themes.

The chapters by Janeke Thumbran and Mandisa Mbali respectively grapple with South African historiography's gender problem. Thumbran uses the arguments of Premesh Lalu and Windsor Leroke about the colonial bias of the existing historiographical canon as a basis for reflecting on the implications that this literature has for lecturers of colour tasked with employing it to teach South African history. Drawing on her experiences as a lecturer during the student protests that roiled South African universities in the mid-2010s, she notes the irony that in an institutional context shaped by the rise of consumer-based education, her students would often use 'woke' terminology (borrowed out of context from its American origins) to offer critiques of her as a lecturer that reprised the gendered and racialised tropes contained in the historiographical literature.

Mbali meanwhile argues that nurturing a new generation of queer and black female academics will require developing historiographical multivocality.

Her chapter outlines what this would entail, and she identifies the key obstacle as being the discipline's continued reliance on conventional archives, which typically marginalise female and queer perspectives. She argues, however, that there are many alternative resources 'hiding in plain sight', such as creative literature and the fine arts, that are capable of addressing this deficit, and she offers Zanele Muholi's *'Massa' and Mina[h]* and Sindiwe Magona's *Mother to Mother* to illustrate how such sources might be harnessed by historians.

Nomalanga Mkhize discusses another alternative archive – namely, vernacular accounts of the history of the Xhosa peoples, which she argues should be considered 'indigenous classics'. These vernacular accounts include literary products by late-nineteenth/early-twentieth-century figures such as H.I.E. Dhlomo and A.C. Jordan, who were responding to the works of white historians such as George Theal and George Cory, but Mkhize also considers the arguments provided by the likes of Ntongela Masilela and Nomathamsanqa Tisani, concerning how Xhosa oratures might be utilised as historical sources. Mkhize contends that engagement with the vernacular archive would yield fresh perspectives on aspects of Xhosa social and cultural history, such as ritual, descent, ethnic identification, and totemic practices, and in the process contribute to transforming our understanding of the Cape-centric founding narrative of South African history.

My chapter explores English-language South African historiography in the twentieth century. It challenges the conventional interpretation that developments from the 1960s onwards represented a 'historiographical revolution', by demonstrating that the previous scholarship was much more innovative than has been conceded, and that this includes its employment of interdisciplinary methodology and exploration of Africanist subject matter, which are often upheld as the two key pillars of the disciplinary revolution. The chapter concludes with an exploration of possible future lines of inquiry that such a revision of historiographical classifications might facilitate.

Political biography forms the subject matter of Lindie Koorts's chapter, which considers how the genre has changed after apartheid. She identifies the most conspicuous shift to be an alteration of focus from heroes of Afrikaner nationalism to stalwarts of the liberation struggle, but she also considers biographers whose work has fallen outside those parameters, and whose contributions have begun to challenge the long hegemony of the liberation struggle narrative. This includes those who have discussed apartheid collaborators, and others who have taken inspiration from the Fallist critique that emerged from the university protests of the mid-2010s.

The chapters by Neil Roos and Danelle van Zyl Hermann call for renewed attention to the history of white South Africans. Roos attributes the decline in such studies to demands for the decolonisation of the discipline and to scepticism about the analytical merits of the concept of 'whiteness'. He uses his chapter to outline methodological principles capable of meeting such objections. The chapter explains that this would involve supplementing the insights of the social history tradition with the arguments of those members of the Subaltern Studies Group who have questioned the analytical primacy that radical historians have habitually accorded to class. Hermann meanwhile notes that whereas white people featured prominently in early studies by radical historians of late-nineteenth/early-twentieth-century industrialisation, there have been few similar studies of late-apartheid developments. She calls for 'bringing whites back in', not only to enhance our understanding of the origins of the new South Africa but also to permit the country's reinsertion into global and comparative history, given the resurgence of white identity politics internationally during the early twenty-first century.

The global rise of populist and xenophobic discourses against migrants and 'citizens of nowhere' forms the departure point of Rob Skinner's chapter, which considers the potential of transnational history to offer a corrective to them. The chapter considers what a transnational turn in South African historiography might entail, and it discusses, *inter alia*, the potential for centring discourses of humanitarianism and antiracism in accounts of colonialism and segregation, and for inserting international solidarity into antiapartheid histories.

As mentioned in the 'Editor's preface', the hope is that the collective consideration of these past and present developments in South African historiography will provide a lead to future lines of inquiry among the next generation of historians to enter the field.

Notes

1 F.A. van Jaarsveld, 'Afrikanergeskiedskrywing: Verlede, Hede en Toekoms', in H.C. Bredekamp (ed.), *Afrikaanse Geskiedskrywing en Letterkunde: Verlede, Hede en Toekoms* (Bellville: Universiteit van Wes-Kaapland se Instituut vir Historiese Navorsing, 1992), 128–9.
2 L. Berat, interview with L. Thompson, *South African Historical Journal*, 30, May 1994, 23–4.
3 L. Thompson, 'The Forgotten Factor in Southern African History', M. Legassick, 'The Sotho-Tswana Peoples before 1800', and S. Marks, 'The Traditions of the Natal "Nguni": A Second Look at the Work of A. T. Bryant', in L. Thompson (ed.), *African Societies in Southern Africa* (London: Heinemann, 1969), 6, 86–125, 126–44; C. Rassool, 'History Anchored in Politics: An Interview with Martin Legassick', *South African Historical Journal*, 56 (1) 2006, 23–4; P. Delius, 'E. P. Thompson, "Social History", and South African Historiography, 1970–90', *Journal of African History*, 58 (1) 2017, 5.

4 Rassool, 'History Anchored in Politics', 27; S. Marks, 'Review Article: African and Afrikaner History', *Journal of African History*, 11 (3) 1970, 441, 443, 445–6.
5 S. Marks and A. Atmore, 'Introduction', in S. Marks and A.Atmore (eds), *Economy and Society in Pre-industrial South Africa* (London: Longman, 1980), 1; Ndifuna Ukwazi Dare to Know, 'Shula Marks – A Life in History', YouTube, 7 May 2012, https://www.youtube.com/watch?v=OANIbgdhwxM (accessed 31 Mar. 2022); S. Friedman in collaboration with J. Hudson, *Race, Class and Power: Harold Wolpe and the Radical Critique of Apartheid* (Pietermaritzburg: UKZN Press, 2015), 48; S. Marks, 'The Societies of Southern Africa Seminar at the Institute of Commonwealth Studies', 1, University of London School of Advanced Study, https://sas-space.sas.ac.uk/3557/ (accessed 31 Mar. 2022).
6 F.A. Johnstone, 'White Prosperity and White Supremacy in South Africa Today', *African Affairs*, 69 (275) Apr. 1970, 126–8; F.A. Johnstone, 'Class Conflict and Colour Bars in the South African Gold Mining Industry – 1910–26', Institute of Commonwealth Studies, *Collected Seminar Papers*, 10, 1971, 112–26; Ndifuna Ukwazi Dare to Know, 'Shula Marks'; Marks, 'Societies of Southern Africa', 1.
7 M. Legassick, 'The Dynamics of Modernization in South Africa', *Journal of African History*, 13 (1) Jan. 1972, 146–7; M. Legassick, 'The Frontier Tradition in South African Historiography', Institute of Commonwealth Studies, *Collected Seminar Papers*, 12, 1972, 1–33, reprinted in Marks and Atmore, *Economy and Society*, 44–79.
8 H. Wolpe, 'Capitalism and Cheap Labour Power in South Africa: From Segregation to Apartheid', *Economy and Society*, 1 (4) 1972, 425–56.
9 S. Marks, 'Liberalism, Social Realities and South African History', *Journal of Commonwealth Political Studies*, X, 1972, 246.
10 C. van Onselen and I. Phimister, 'In Commemoration of Stanley Trapido (1933–2008): Obituary and Introduction', *Historia*, 53 (1) May 2008, 8; Ndifuna Ukwazi Dare to Know, 'Shula Marks'; Friedman and Hudson, *Race, Class and Power*, 48.
11 P. Delius and S. Marks, 'Rethinking South Africa's Past: Essays on History and Archaeology', *Journal of Southern African Studies*, 38 (2) June 2012, 248; J. Hyslop, 'E. P. Thompson in South Africa: The Practice and Politics of Social History in an Era of Revolt and Transition, 1976–2012', *International Review of Social History*, 61 (1) 2016, 98, 101; B. Bozzoli in 'Wits History Workshop', YouTube, 30 May 2017, https://www.youtube.com/watch?v=5s3eM5KX5K8&list=TLPQMjUwNTIwMjBtItkSRdn9Ug&index=12 (accessed 31 Mar. 2022); Delius, 'E. P. Thompson', 10.
12 Rassool, 'History Anchored in Politics', 33; M. Legassick, 'Recollections of Bernard ("Ben") Magubane', *Safundi: Journal of South African and American Studies*, 16 (2) 2015, 225.
13 B. Bozzoli and P. Delius, 'Radical History and South African History', in J. Brown, P. Manning, K. Shapiro, J. Wiener, B. Bozzoli and P. Delius (eds), *History from South Africa: Alternative Visions and Practices* (Philadelphia, PA: Temple University Press, 1991), 12; P. Bonner, 'New Nation, New History: The History

Workshop in South Africa, 1977–1994', *Journal of American History*, 81 (3) Dec. 1994, 980; C. Rassool, 'Power, Knowledge and the Politics of Public Pasts', *African Studies*, 69 (1) Apr. 2010, 82; S.P. Lekgoathi, 'The History Workshop, Teacher Development and Outcomes-Based Education over the Past Seven Years', *African Studies*, 69 (1) Apr. 2010, 105; Marks, 'Societies of Southern Africa', 4.
14 B. Bozzoli, 'Popular History and the Witwatersrand', in B. Bozzoli (ed.), *Labour, Townships and Protest: Studies in the Social History of the Witwatersrand* (Johannesburg: Ravan, 1979), 4; B. Bozzoli, 'Intellectuals, Audiences and Histories: South African Experiences, 1978–88', in Brown et al., *History from South Africa*, 215.
15 B. Bozzoli, 'History, Experience and Culture', in *History Workshop 2: Town and Countryside in the Transvaal: Capitalist Penetration and Popular Response* (Johannesburg: Ravan, 1983), 6–7; Bozzoli, 'Intellectuals, Audiences and Histories', 216–17.
16 Rassool, 'History Anchored in Politics', 29.
17 H. Wolpe, 'Class Concepts, Class Struggle and Racism', in J. Rex and D. Mason (eds), *Theories of Race and Ethnic Relations* (Cambridge: Cambridge University Press, 1986), 120–3.
18 M. Legassick, *Towards Socialist Democracy* (Scottsville: University of KwaZulu-Natal Press, 2007), 430; M. Legassick, 'Colonialism of a Special Type and the Approach of the Marxist Workers' Tendency of the African National Congress to the National Question', in J. Reynolds, B. Fine and R. van Niekerk (eds), *Race, Class and the Post-apartheid Democratic State* (Scottsville: University of KwaZulu-Natal Press, 2019), 65–6.
19 P. Bonner, 'Keynote Address to the "Life after Thirty" Colloquium', *African Studies*, 69 (1) 2010, 21.
20 C. Kros, 'Twenty Years of Heritage Studies – the Showbiz of History?', *Social Dynamics*, 43 (3) 2017, 360, 362.
21 Rassool, 'Power, Knowledge', 85.
22 A. Odendaal, 'Developments in Popular History in the Western Cape in the 1980s', in Brown et al., *History from South Africa*, 366; L. Witz, G. Minkley and C. Rassool, 'The Troika: A Preface', in L. Witz, G. Minkley and C. Rassool (eds), *Unsettled History: Making South African Public Pasts* (Ann Arbor: University of Michigan Press, 2017), vii.
23 L. Witz, 'The Write Your Own History Project', in Brown et al., *History from South Africa*, 369; L. Witz, G. Minkley and C. Rassool, 'South Africa and the Unsettling of History', in *Unsettled History*, 6–7.
24 Witz, Minkley and Rassool, 'Troika', xii, and 'South Africa', 7–8.
25 G. Minkley and C. Rassool, 'Orality, Memory, and Social History in South Africa', in S. Nuttall and C. Coetzee (eds), *Negotiating the Past: The Making of Memory in South Africa* (Cape Town: Oxford University Press, 1998), 90, 97, 98; see also G. Minkley, C. Rassool and L. Witz, 'Oral History in South Africa: A Country Report', in Witz, Minkley and Rassool, *Unsettled History*, 27–51.

26 P. Lalu, *The Deaths of Hintsa: Post-apartheid South Africa and the Shape of Recurring Pasts* (Cape Town: HSRC Press, 2009), x–xiii, 15–16.
27 P. Lalu, 'When Was South African History Ever Postcolonial?', *Kronos*, 34 (1) 2008, 271–2; Lalu, *Deaths of Hintsa*, 1–13.
28 Minkley and Rassool, 'Orality, Memory', 91–2; Lalu, 'South African History', 279–80; Lalu, *Deaths of Hintsa*, 15–16, 18–22, 254–6.
29 A. Lissoni, N. Nieftagodien and S. Ally, 'Introduction: "Life after Thirty" – a Critical Celebration', *African Studies*, 69 (1) 2010, 1; Rassool, 'Power, Knowledge', 80–1, 86–7.
30 N. Bhattacharya, 'Some Reflections on "Life after Thirty"', *African Studies*, 69 (1) 2010, 134–5.
31 B. Rutledge, 'Premesh Lalu's Post-colonial Push: Is It Time to Dismantle the Discipline?', *South African Historical Journal*, 63 (1) 2011, 160; H. Mokoena, 'The Frontier Mix', *History and Theory*, 50 (1) 2011, 118.
32 C. van Onselen, 'The Reconstruction of a Rural Life from Oral Testimony: Critical Notes on the Methodology Employed in the Study of a Black South African Sharecropper', *Journal of Peasant Studies*, 20 (3) 1993, 494–514; Minkley and Rassool, 'Orality, Memory', 96.
33 Minkley and Rassool, 'Orality, Memory', 97.
34 N. Southey, interview with R. Davenport, *South African Historical Journal*, 26, 1992, 33.
35 *Rand Daily Mail*, 3 Apr. 1918; D.J. Kotzé, 'Historikus', in D.J. Kotzé, B. Booyens, J.J. Oosthuysen, G.P.J. Trümpelmann and P.J. Lombard (eds), *Professor H.B. Thom* (Stellenbosch: University of Stellenbosch, 1969), 17, 20; F.A. van Jaarsveld, 'Geskiedenis van die Departement Geskiedenis, Universiteit van Stellenbosch, 1866–1979', in *Die Afrikaners se Groot Trek na die Stede en Ander Opstelle* (Johannesburg: Perskor, 1982), 228–9, 233–6, 244, 249; J. du Bruyn, 'F A Van Jaarsveld Afrikanerhistorikus en Vernuwer', *Historia*, 27 (1) May 1982, 56; A. Grundlingh, 'Politics, Principles and Problems of a Profession: Afrikaner Historians and Their Discipline, c. 1920–c. 1965', paper presented at University of the Witwatersrand History Workshop conference, 6–10 Feb. 1990, 3, 11–12; P.H. Kapp, *Verantwoorde Verlede 'n Historiografiese Studie: Die Verhaal van die Studie van Geskiedenis aan die Universiteit Stellenbosch, 1866–2000* (Somerset West: Mediator Publishers, 2004), 15–16, 22, 26–7; N. Southey and F.A. Mouton, '"A Volksvreemde Historian": J.A.I. Agar-Hamilton and the Production of History in an Alien Environment', in F.A. Mouton (ed.), *History, Historians & Afrikaner Nationalism: Essays on the History Department of the University of Pretoria* (Vanderbijlpark: Kleio, 2007), 57.
36 Kotzé, 'Historikus', 19.
37 F.A. Mouton, 'Professor Leo Fouché, the History Department and the Afrikanerisation of the University in Pretoria', in *History, Historians*, 15–16, 31–7.
38 University of Pretoria, *Ad destinatum: Gedenkboek van die Universiteit van Pretoria* (Johannesburg: Voortrekkerpers, 1960), 113; Van Jaarsveld, 'Geskiedenis van die Departement Geskiedenis', 229–30; L.A. Changuion, 'Die Universiteit van Pretoria se Departement Geskiedenis, 'n Afrikaanse stem uit die noorde',

Historia, 49 (2) Nov. 2004, 154–5; Southey and Mouton, 'Volksvreemde Historian', 57.
39 Van Jaarsveld, 'Geskiedenis van die Departement Geskiedenis', 231.
40 F.J. du T. Spies, 'Leemtes in die Suid-Afrikaanse Geskiedskrywing', *South African Historical Journal*, 3, Nov. 1971, 82–92; Changuion, 'Universiteit van Pretoria', 156; F.A. Mouton, 'A.N. Pelzer: A Custodian of Afrikanerdom', in *History, Historians*, 89, 98; F.A. Mouton, 'F.J. du Toit Spies, Afrikaner Nationalism and Volksgeskiedenis at the University of Pretoria', in *History, Historians*, 218–19, 222–5.
41 Changuion, 'Universiteit van Pretoria', 159–60; Mouton, 'F.J. du Toit Spies', 225.
42 F.A. Mouton, 'Professor F.A. van Jaarsveld (1922–1995): A Flawed Genius?', in *History, Historians*, 236–7; P. de Klerk, 'Afrikaanse Historici as Politieke Kritici en Koers-Aanduiders', *Journal for Contemporary History*, 37 (1) 2012, 51–2.
43 *Rand Daily Mail*, 29 Mar. 1979 and 30 Mar. 1979; G. Allen, 'The Case of the Volkscustodian and the Professor: Heritage versus History', *Historia*, 47 (2) 2002, 407–8, 412–13, 416; Mouton, 'Professor F.A. van Jaarsveld', 237.
44 J.S. Bergh, 'Uitdagings vir die Afrikaanse historikus', *Historia*, 32 (2) 1987, 21–2.

Bibliography

Allen, G. (2002). 'The Case of the Volkscustodian and the Professor: Heritage versus History', *Historia*, 47 (2).

Berat, L. (1994) Interview with L. Thompson, *South African Historical Journal*, 30.

Bergh, J.S. (1987) 'Uitdagings vir die Afrikaanse historikus', *Historia*, 32 (2).

Bhattacharya, N. (2010) 'Some Reflections on "Life after Thirty"', *African Studies*, 69 (1).

Bonner, P. (1994) 'New Nation, New History: The History Workshop in South Africa, 1977–1994', *Journal of American History*, 81 (3).

Bonner, P. (2010) 'Keynote Address to the "Life after Thirty" Colloquium', *African Studies*, 69 (1).

Bozzoli, B. (1979) 'Popular History and the Witwatersrand', in B. Bozzoli (ed.), *Labour, Townships and Protest: Studies in the Social History of the Witwatersrand*. Johannesburg: Ravan.

Bozzoli, B. (1983) 'History, Experience and Culture', in B. Bozzoli (ed.), *History Workshop 2: Town and Countryside in the Transvaal: Capitalist Penetration and Popular Response*. Johannesburg: Ravan.

Bozzoli, B. (1991) 'Intellectuals, Audiences and Histories: South African Experiences, 1978–88', in Brown et al., *History from South Africa*.

Bozzoli, B., and P. Delius (1991) 'Radical History and South African History', in Brown et al., *History from South Africa*.

Brown, J., P. Manning, K. Shapiro, J. Wiener, B. Bozzoli and P. Delius (eds) (1991) *History from South Africa: Alternative Visions and Practices*. Philadelphia: Temple University Press.

Changuion, L.A. (2004) 'Die Universiteit van Pretoria se Departement Geskiedenis, 'n Afrikaanse stem uit die noorde', *Historia*, 49 (2).

De Klerk, P. (2012) 'Afrikaanse Historici as Politieke Kritici en Koers-Aanduiders', *Journal for Contemporary History*, 37 (1).

Delius, P. (2017) 'E. P. Thompson, "Social History", and South African Historiography, 1970–90', *Journal of African History*, 58 (1).

Delius, P., and S. Marks (2012) 'Rethinking South Africa's Past: Essays on History and Archaeology', *Journal of Southern African Studies*, 38 (2).

Du Bruyn, J. (1982) 'F A Van Jaarsveld Afrikanerhistorikus en Vernuwer', *Historia*, 27 (1).

Friedman, S., in collaboration with J. Hudson (2015) *Race, Class and Power: Harold Wolpe and the Radical Critique of Apartheid*. Pietermaritzburg: UKZN Press.

Grundlingh, A. (c. 1990) 'Politics, Principles and Problems of a Profession: Afrikaner Historians and Their Discipline, c. 1920–c. 1965', paper presented at University of the Witwatersrand History Workshop conference, 6–10 Feb. 1990.

Hyslop, J. (2016) 'E. P. Thompson in South Africa: The Practice andPolitics of Social History in an Era of Revolt and Transition, 1976–2012', *International Review of Social History*, 61 (1).

Johnstone, F.A. (1970) 'White Prosperity and White Supremacy in South Africa Today', *African Affairs*, 69 (275).

Johnstone, F.A. (1971) 'Class Conflict and Colour Bars in the South African Gold Mining Industry – 1910–26', Institute of Commonwealth Studies, *Collected Seminar Papers*, 10.

Kapp, P.H. (2004) *Verantwoorde Verlede 'n Historiografiese Studie: Die Verhaal van die Studie van Geskiedenis aan die Universiteit Stellenbosch, 1866–2000*. Somerset West: Mediator Publishers.

Kotzé, D.J. (1969) 'Historikus', in D.J. Kotzé, B. Booyens, J.J. Oosthuysen, G.P.J. Trümpelmann and P.J. Lombard (eds), *Professor H.B. Thom*. Stellenbosch: University of Stellenbosch.

Kros, C. (2017) 'Twenty Years of Heritage Studies – the Showbiz of History?', *Social Dynamics*, 43 (3).

Lalu, P. (2008) 'When Was South African History Ever Postcolonial?', *Kronos*, 34 (1).

Lalu, P. (2009) *The Deaths of Hintsa: Post-apartheid South Africa and the Shape of Recurring Pasts*. Cape Town: HSRC Press.

Legassick, M. (1969) 'The Sotho-Tswana Peoples before 1800', in Thompson, *African Societies*.

Legassick, M. (1972) 'The Dynamics of Modernization in South Africa', *Journal of African History*, 13 (1).

Legassick, M. (1972) 'The Frontier Tradition in South African historiography', Institute of Commonwealth Studies, *Collected Seminar Papers*, 12.

Legassick, M. (2007) *Towards Socialist Democracy*. Scottsville: University of KwaZulu-Natal Press.

Legassick, M. (2015) 'Recollections of Bernard ("Ben") Magubane', *Safundi: Journal of South African and American Studies*, 16 (2).

Legassick, M. (2019) 'Colonialism of a Special Type and the Approach of the Marxist Workers' Tendency of the African National Congress to the National Question', in J. Reynolds, B. Fine and R. van Niekerk (eds), *Race, Class and the Post-apartheid Democratic State*. Scottsville: University of KwaZulu-Natal Press.

Lekgoathi, S.P. (2010) 'The History Workshop, Teacher Development and Outcomes-Based Education over the Past Seven Years', *African Studies*, 69 (1).

Lissoni, A., N. Nieftagodien and S. Ally (2010) 'Introduction: "Life after Thirty" – a Critical Celebration', *African Studies*, 69 (1).

Marks, S. (1969) 'The Traditions of the Natal "Nguni": A Second Look at the Work of A. T. Bryant', in Thompson, *African Societies*.

Marks, S. (1970) 'Review Article: African and Afrikaner History', *Journal of African History*, 11 (3).

Marks, S. (1972) 'Liberalism, Social Realities and South African History', *Journal of Commonwealth Political Studies*, X.

Marks, S. (2012) 'The Societies of Southern Africa Seminar at the Institute of Commonwealth Studies', 1. University of London School of Advanced Study, https://sas-space.sas.ac.uk/3557/ (accessed 31 Mar. 2022).

Marks, S., and A. Atmore (eds) (1980) *Economy and Society in Pre-industrial South Africa*. London: Longman.

Marks, S., and A. Atmore (1980) 'Introduction', in *Economy and Society*.

Minkley, G., and C. Rassool (1998) 'Orality, Memory, and Social History in South Africa', in S. Nuttall and C. Coetzee (eds), *Negotiating the Past: The Making of Memory in South Africa*. Cape Town: Oxford University Press.

Minkley G., C. Rassool and L. Witz (2017) 'Oral History in South Africa: A Country Report', in Witz et al., *Unsettled History*.

Mokoena, H. (2011) 'The Frontier Mix', *History and Theory*, 50 (1).

Mouton, F.A. (2007) 'A.N. Pelzer: A Custodian of Afrikanerdom', in *History, Historians*.

Mouton, F.A. (2007) 'F.J. du Toit Spies, Afrikaner Nationalism and *Volksgeskiedenis* at the University of Pretoria', in Mouton, *History, Historians*.

Mouton, F.A. (ed.) (2007) *History, Historians & Afrikaner Nationalism: Essays on the History Department of the University of Pretoria*. Vanderbijlpark: Kleio.

Mouton, F.A. (2007) 'Professor F.A. van Jaarsveld (1922–1995): A Flawed Genius?', in Mouton, *History, Historians*.

Mouton, F.A. (2007) 'Professor Leo Fouché, the History Department and the Afrikanerisation of the University in Pretoria', in Mouton, *History, Historians*.

Ndifuna Ukwazi Dare to Know (2012) 'Shula Marks – A Life in History', YouTube, 7 May, www.youtube.com/watch?v=OANIbgdhwxM (accessed 31 Mar. 2022).

Rassool, C. (2006) 'History Anchored in Politics: An Interview with Martin Legassick', *South African Historical Journal*, 56 (1).

Rassool, C. (2010) 'Power, Knowledge and the Politics of Public Pasts', *African Studies*, 69 (1).

Rutledge, B. (2011) 'Premesh Lalu's Post-colonial Push: Is It Time to Dismantle the Discipline?', *South African Historical Journal*, 63 (1).
Southey, N. (1992) Interview with R. Davenport, *South African Historical Journal*, 26.
Southey, N., and F.A. Mouton (2007) '"A Volksvreemde Historian": J.A.I. Agar-Hamilton and the Production of History in an Alien Environment', in Mouton, *History, Historians*.
Spies, F.J. du T. (1971) 'Leemtes in die Suid-Afrikaanse Geskiedskrywing', *South African Historical Journal*, 3.
Thompson, L. (ed.) (1969) *African Societies in Southern Africa*. London: Heinemann.
Thompson, L. (1969) 'The Forgotten Factor in Southern African History', in Thompson, *African Societies*.
University of Pretoria (1960) *Ad destinatum: Gedenkboek van die Universiteit van Pretoria*. Johannesburg: Voortrekkerpers.
Van Jaarsveld, F.A. (1965) *Die Verlede Spreek*. Johannesburg: Voortrekkerpers.
Van Jaarsveld, F.A. (1971) *Afrikaner Quo Vadis?* Johannesburg: Voortrekkerpers.
Van Jaarsveld, F.A. (1982) 'Geskiedenis van die Departement Geskiedenis, Universiteit van Stellenbosch, 1866–1979', in *Die Afrikaners se Groot Trek na die Stede en Ander Opstelle*. Johannesburg: Perskor.
Van Jaarsveld, F.A. (1992) 'Afrikanergeskiedskrywing: Verlede, Hede en Toekoms', in H.C. Bredekamp (ed.), *Afrikaanse Geskiedskrywing en Letterkunde: Verlede, Hede en Toekoms*. Bellville: Universiteit van Wes-Kaapland se Instituut vir Historiese Navorsing.
Van Onselen, C. (1993) 'The Reconstruction of a Rural Life from Oral Testimony: Critical Notes on the Methodology Employed in the Study of a Black South African Sharecropper', *Journal of Peasant Studies*, 20 (3).
Van Onselen, C., and I. Phimister (2008) 'In Commemoration of Stanley Trapido (1933–2008): Obituary and Introduction', *Historia*, 53 (1).
'Wits History Workshop' (2017) YouTube, 30 May, www.youtube.com/watch?v=5s3eM5KX5K8&list=TLPQMjUwNTIwMjBtItkSRdn9Ug&index=12 (accessed 31 Mar. 2022).
Witz, L., G. Minkley and C. Rassool (2017) 'South Africa and the Unsettling of History', in Witz, *Unsettled History*.
Witz, L., G. Minkley and C. Rassool (2017) 'The Troika: A Preface', in Witz, *Unsettled History*.
Witz, L., G. Minkley and C. Rassool (eds) (2017) *Unsettled History: Making South African Public Pasts*. Ann Arbor: University of Michigan Press.
Wolpe, H. (1972) 'Capitalism and Cheap Labour Power in South Africa: From Segregation to Apartheid', *Economy and Society*, 1 (4).
Wolpe, H. (1986) 'Class Concepts, Class Struggle and Racism', in J. Rex and D. Mason (eds), *Theories of Race and Ethnic Relations*. Cambridge: Cambridge University Press.

2

Beasts of the southern world: multispecies history and the Anthropocene

Sandra Swart

It is a strange new world: baboons and humans have swapped places. It is like a twenty-first-century remake of *Macbeth*, with the earth feverous, the humans feverish and the natural world out of kilter. Or perhaps it is more like some improbable Freaky Friday 'body swap' movie from the 1980s. Either way, in the Cape, on some streets the only pedestrians are baboons. Suddenly, in a reversal of fortune, the *humans* are locked down, caged in, forbidden to roam freely, and pursued by law enforcement for venturing across boundaries. This is because we write this book during unprecedented times: we are all watching the victorious progression of a microbe – coronavirus disease 2019 (COVID-19). Perhaps a third, or even up to half, of the earth's eight billion people are in confinement or under curfew to help stop the rapid spread of this little bit of genetic code gone rogue. The final drafts of our chapters are written on a mandatory lockdown by the South African state in order to try to contain the disease in our own country by 'flattening the curve' of infection.

The virus seems to have come to us from the animal kingdom, from a so-called 'wet market' in China. First reports suggested that the trade in wildlife triggered this virus spillover, with it jumping from animals to humans. Such leaps are likely when human exploitation and habitat destruction threaten wild animals, but in point of fact domesticated mammals (our companion animals and livestock) host most of the viruses likely to be passed to us. So humans are compelled to think afresh about zoonoses in this time of crisis.[1] We reconsider our relationships with the animals close to us *physically* (like pets, many of whom have been abandoned or killed by their owners as panic rises, and livestock, whose mass production in industrial agriculture poses massive environmental problems) and close to us *physiologically* (especially our close cousins, the primates). This latter concern – the 'primate as proxy' or the 'baboon as almost-human' – has a complicated history, as this chapter will contend. For example, when fifteen monkeys mysteriously died in a village in India, probably from insecticide poisoning, locals immediately feared it was from COVID-19.[2] This is not a foolish view: primates catch the virus as we do. Just like us, they get a high fever, a tight cough and chest congestion.

Indeed, this shared epidemic is not the first: a century ago, when the so-called 'Spanish flu' hit South Africa in the wake of World War One, it claimed not only human victims. People suddenly started stumbling upon baboon corpses. In the Magaliesburg, whole troops of baboons were found lying in the veld and along the side of the road, dead from 'pneumonic complications'. Even in the high ranges of the Drakensberg, reports filtered in of baboon bodies filling the *kloofs*.[3] Primates are family, and we share diseases. In fact, as the global pandemic gains terrifying momentum, primate sanctuaries all over Africa – for chimpanzees and gorillas – are closed to prevent the retransmission of this zoonosis back to animals from people. Great apes are being protected by being under lockdown – just like us.

In stark contrast, baboons are being pressed into service on the frontlines of fighting the virus. They are dragooned into drug testing because they offer researchers an ideal subject for complex human diseases owing to their genetic and physiological similarities to humans.[4] In fact, many hopes for a vaccine are pinned on a colony of a thousand baboons who were captured in Africa eight baboon generations (two human generations) ago and now live in exile in Texas. At the Texas Biomedical Research Institute in San Antonio (known as Texas Biomed or, more simply, 'The Institute'), baboons live in cages, with access to a recreational yard for inmate exercise. No living internees may leave the premises, but their bodies escape in other ways: for example, some were used to test Ebola medicines now deployed in Africa. For COVID-19, baboons are enlisted (by being inoculated with a heavy dose of the virus) to start the process of finding a cure modelled on our fellow primates.[5] The mid-twentieth century saw the rise of this brand new way of thinking about baboons as a 'proxy' or 'stand in' for us – with the invention of the 'medical primate', as monkeys, macaques and baboons were circulated in the human body and the body politic.[6] The first baboon was used in a laboratory in the United States in 1956. An international group of scientists eagerly adopted the idea and the first symposium was organised by The Institute in 1963. South African scientists embraced using baboons experimentally – after all, they were cheap, in large supply, and were in the main regarded as 'pests' or worse domestically. Such was their enthusiasm that by the mid-1970s, the Director of Nature Conservation in the Cape Province declared that 'large-scale live trapping of baboons for medical research ha[d] largely eliminated the baboon problem in certain areas'.[7] They could no longer be regarded as 'useless mountain-dwelling primates'. The Institute was willing to pay up to $250 for an adult male baboon delivered alive in Texas.[8] Stellenbosch University responded to this new market by drawing on expertise from The Institute to build its own baboon colony on campus in 1967, with the help of American academic allies.[9] Baboon colonies started popping up in unexpected places in far-flung parts of the globe. In fact, as far back as 1929, the Soviet Union had established the Institute of Experimental Pathology and Therapy at Sukhumi, which provided the Russian medical community with primate models for testing – primarily baboons. As the little carceral colony in Texas illustrates, baboons were not only colonised by humans in this new way but also compelled to colonise in their own right, spreading across the world in medical networks as a new trade in baboon bodies developed.

Of course, baboons were not always compliant bodies – they sometimes refused to conform to the role of model laboratory specimen. Occasionally baboons even made their own history, although not in circumstances of their own choosing.[10] An event from just a few years ago at the Texas Institute illustrates this. After the incident, a spokesperson for the facility explained it away as an 'animal perimeter breach'. But to tell it another way, four incarcerated baboons made a determined and daring bid for freedom. They strategically positioned a two-hundred-litre drum (an 'enrichment' tool unwisely provided by their guards), using it to jump the fence. Three of them were apprehended, while the fourth appeared to get cold feet and returned to captivity by itself. (As *The Shawshank Redemption* reminds us, 'These walls are funny. First you hate 'em. Then you get used to 'em. Enough time passes, you get so you depend on them. That's institutionalized.') The three fugitives fled down Military Drive, feeling – perhaps – the excitement 'only a free man can feel … at the start of a long journey whose conclusion is uncertain'. But they were recaptured just short of the treeline. While their capture was underway, I like to think the other baboons barked and grunted, their voices soaring 'higher and farther than anybody in a gray place dares to dream'.[11] Perhaps for the briefest of moments, every last baboon in The Institute felt free.

This brings us back to the mandatory lockdown under which we write. We already know that the world after the pandemic will be a different place. Now is a good time for historians to help revisit the past in order to rethink the future. In order to mitigate future pandemics, we will need to rethink our relationships with animals on a global and a local level. In this time of global crisis, what can historians do in and about the Anthropocene?[12] What kind of history do we write for the Apocalypse? Of course, a hundred historiographical flowers may bloom and the only things to avoid are a prescriptive normativity or a coalescence of orthodoxy – as this very book indicates. So this essay adopts an unashamed embrace of usefulness – creating a 'useable past' for unusual times.[13] Moreover, it contends that one way to render the past edifyingly unfamiliar in these strange times is to reconstruct histories of the ultimate Others – to tell a 'more than human history'. In essence, this answers a call issued twenty years ago by *biologists* for sharing data between conservation biologists and environmental historians.[14] Since then, history has been integrated into some conservation efforts in the global North – but not (yet) widely in Africa.

Thus this chapter makes a bid for a new kind of freedom, much like the baboons at the Texas Institute. After all, environmental history as a sub-discipline has (like the fourth baboon) become institutionalised. Over the last generation, it lost its outlaw status and became part of the discipline's establishment.[15] Environmental history has established the reciprocal influences of a mutable nature and a shifting society, offering a sustained critique of colonialism, capitalism, and apartheid through this new lens. But, in doing so, it also frequently settled into existing historiographic paradigms and lost the iconoclastic ferality of its earlier incarnations. So in this essay, history escapes. It heads for the treeline, scampering across the boundaries between the precolonial and colonial periods, beyond disciplinary boundaries between history and the other disciplines (especially ethology and ecology – the former focusing on studying behaviour of animals mainly within their natural environment; the latter on the relations of organisms/species to one another and to their physical surroundings), and past the once ostensibly 'natural' frontier between the 'human' and the 'animal'. The limits and challenges of this kind of history are exposed in the process, but equally its possibilities emerge into view. To rewild the approach, a synanthropic species that adapts to living closely with humans is chosen: a creature equally poised between wild and tame – the baboon.[16]

Ethology, ecology, conservation – and the *longue durée*

There have been efforts to bring biology and history into conversation, with explorations into 'deep history' both internationally and, more tentatively, locally.[17] Histories that take animals seriously have flourished in recent years globally,[18] and in southern Africa.[19] Recently, some engagements have begun to focus specifically on animals in the Anthropocene.[20] The coevolution of *Homo sapiens* with other organisms has started to receive historical analysis.[21] Moreover, a few historians have also started to address historical research to conservation initiatives.[22] After all, history answers but also challenges the assumptions upon which conservation programs are predicated, while also addressing 'landscape amnesia', the social disremembering of how different landscapes looked a mere generation ago, let alone a hundred or a thousand years ago. Moreover, to return to our opening concerns about COVID-19 and the wildlife trade: how do we challenge the emerging discourse on pandemics that is frequently and ahistorically premised on the notion that people and wildlife were hermetically sealed from each other prior to the late-modern period? This idea flattens the complex contours of human–wildlife interaction that are evinced, for example, in shifting nonlinear relationships between humans and wild animals among hunter-gatherers, transhumant agriculturalists, sedentary farmers and peri-urban dwellers in fragmented landscapes.

A conservation initiative that has called for an increased interaction between the social and natural sciences is ethnoprimatology.[23] It looks at the interconnections between humans and primates as more than just disruptions of a 'natural' state, and instead accepts that anthropogenic contexts must be considered as part of the 'new natural'. Serious study has gone into understanding specific human societies and local baboon societies, such as in the interspecies conflict between humans and baboons in the Cape.[24] As generalist foragers, baboon species can survive (even sometimes thrive) as human populations increase.[25] Moreover, their responses to increasing proximity to humans (through eating human foods and food waste) often accelerate retributive attacks against them.[26] Studies have so far included attempts to understand the belief structures underlying human perceptions of primates, crop conflict and urban interfaces.[27] This has so far drawn in anthropologists (and some academics from cognate disciplines) but could benefit from historians' inclusion – an effort I make in this chapter. Recent studies have highlighted the need to understand the relationship between the species from a historical perspective that investigates the deeply embedded sociocultural baggage humans bring to interactions: 'A better understanding of the factors that contribute to high threat perception associated with baboons is important for effective management and education schemes.' Moreover, interviewees who perceived baboons as 'threatening' were also more likely to support a lethal solution.[28] Here I think historians can be useful, having the power to link apparently singular events to larger narratives of continuity and change. Historians are also able to access primary sources unknown to natural scientists – such as antique maps, travellers' accounts, colonial archives, indigenous knowledge systems (including myths, folklore, songs, and rock art), photographs, and oral history – and integrate them with other sources to reach more nuanced narrative understandings covering longer periods. We can use history to evaluate conflicting evidence, integrate data from different time periods and explain the findings to a range of different audiences – including those who make the decisions that shape our world.

Environmental history, which as a subdiscipline has tended to neglect precolonial pasts, needs to be pushed to not only understand the deeper history but also challenge static and stagnant representations of the precolonial period.²⁹ Here this chapter makes a strong case for new environmental history that draws on cognate disciplines like palaeontology, paleoecology, archaeology and the study of rock art, hitherto largely neglected by historians. Fossil evidence suggests that humans and baboons have lived in close proximity for hundreds of millennia. In fact, the Plio-Pleistocene fossil record suggests that hominin ecology and habitats were closer to those of ur-baboons than to those of the other great apes, despite the latter's genetic propinquity to us. (Indeed, hominin fossils are so closely associated with baboon fossils that bones of early baboons are an index species in searching for early fossil hominins: where their remains are, ours are likely to be also.) In an example that highlights our long overlapping of territories and diets, the bones of a now extinct ur-baboon (*Parapapio broomi*) and an early hominin (*Australopithecus prometheus*) female have lain intermingled at the bottom of a cave for over 3.67 million years. It seems this female ancestor of ours and a large male proto-baboon both fell down a crevice to their doom – while tussling over food.³⁰

Long-term investigations may lead to a further understanding of the affiliative relationship between us. In fact, I contend that early in our shared history, living in proximity had strong advantages for both species – possibly resulting in coevolution for close sympatric living. Firstly, mutual benefit would have ensued from alarm calls raising awareness about (jointly feared) predators like leopards and snakes. Studies from the field suggest baboons are cautiously watchful, showing increased vigilance in heavy bush or in areas where they have encountered predators before. Baboons may avoid a particular area or become hypersensitive to danger signals in an area as a result of a recent experience with a predator, and repeated experiences may result in longer-term shifts in habitat preference and avoidance.³¹ Our ancestors may have found the presence of baboons in a particular area to be a useful proxy for safety for themselves. Moreover, warning barks alert the troop to any danger – with evidence to suggest possible different alarms for different predators, which would scatter the troop to safety in trees and *krantzes*. Some troops encircle and overwhelm predators – there are documented killings of leopards, and there is more contentious evidence of joint operations to rout lions.³² From the baboon's perspective, when at first our hominin ancestors were unarmed and physically slower than baboons, we might simply have been useful to them as fall guys for any predator. But later, with our tool use improving into weapons over time – by 280,000 years before the present in some places we already had stone-tipped spears and projectile weapons – we would have been security guards against the predators to which baboons alerted us.

Secondly, baboon usage of plants was certainly valued by some indigenous groups, while indigenous and settler groups both benefitted from baboons' ability to locate water. Baboons teach each other what is good: for example, once a novel foodstuff is discovered the news disseminates rapidly through the troop.[33] Equally, baboons teach one another what is bad: for example, in an experiment adults prevented young baboons from eating fruit laced with an anaesthetising drug until they learned to avoid it themselves.[34] This is a form of cultural knowledge transfer – be it finding water and new edible plants or avoiding poisonous plants and insects. It was certainly useful to other baboons, but probably also useful to our own ancestors. We can extrapolate that for early hominins and later nonfarming humans, living near and learning from baboons was an advantage and a sensible decision for them. Baboons could be good neighbours.

We cannot know how *all* Africans felt about baboons in precolonial or indeed colonial times, but we can analyse oral tradition and the traces left behind in the oldest archive: rock art. This analysis suggests – following the points made above – that there was no blanket or inevitable hostility between baboons and humans.[35] Indeed, some groups chose baboons as constitutive of their own personal identities through their totem animals.[36] Baboons were afforded a quasi-human position in the cosmology of the Bushmen or San, the indigenous hunter-gatherer groups, and there is evidence of belief in therianthropic shapeshifting between human and baboon.[37] Some believed baboons were to be admired – even emulated – because of their association with certain root medicines.[38] This root medicine was believed to make them invulnerable to illness and invincible to enemies, as discussed extensively below. This was likely a belief consequent to millennia of humans having witnessed baboons choosing certain plants and avoiding poisonous ones, as explained earlier. The idea was also that medicine gave the baboons uncanny foreknowledge of approaching danger – again, probably a belief consequent to millennia of humans benefitting from baboon alarm calls warning of specific predators and observing the uncanny way baboons knew before them of the predator's presence. In exploring these older histories, we again see that baboons and humans were not always enemies and that their relationships were complex – although it is hard to generalise over regions and dangerous to speculate over long stretches of time. Beliefs were almost certainly variable, individual and mutable. Nevertheless, we can see that, over time, some shared points in different demographic groups' cosmologies helped connect them – and connect them with the baboon. Baboons were both totemic and apotropaic, crossing cosmological boundaries between peoples. For example, the /Xam considered the baboon almost-human: baboons sang and spoke their own language, they understood human speech and would refer to people by their names. They lived as men do, with their wives, and they were even said to 'smell of people'. It was said that 'its actions are still like a man's, although it is a baboon'. It was risky to hunt a baboon as its 'death would live in the hunter's bow'. Baboons were not killed for meat but very occasionally, despite the risks, for the powerful medicine they could offer'.[39] As noted, they were associated with a kind of root medicine called *so-/oa* by the /Xam and *U-mabophe* by the Nguni.[40] These shielded one against attack – so one could defeat foes in the day and raid their cattle by moonlight.[41] The /Xam believed 'root medicines' could treat quotidian problems like pains in the head and belly or extraordinary problems like needing to avoid an enemy – both actions associated with being 'well' and 'safe'. The baboon, because it also self-medicated with such plant roots was, therefore, understood as protection incarnate. I would argue that the /Xam San connected the baboon with such protection for precisely the two 'good neighbour' hypotheses sketched above.

As a /Xam man explained, the baboon keeps a special stick of medicine in its mouth, which does three things – it allows them to know things beyond what could be 'naturally' known, teaches them caution and prevents sickness:[42]

> My grandfather told me that a baboon holds a stick of so:-/a in its mouth; this little stick tells it about things which it does not know. That is why it seems to understand them well, because that stick of so:-/a has talked to it about them. ... For its body does not feel as it usually feels, it does not feel comfortable at that time. The so:-/a is doing this to its body, in order to teach it to know. Therefore the baboon is a thing that does not want to die.[43]

This reflects very clearly the 'special magic' baboons would have been seen to possess by hunter-gatherers living near them – and the very advantages from which humans could also benefit by proximity to and close observation of baboons. They noted that 'medicine' also teaches the baboon 'fear' – a nod to the wary watchfulness so useful to baboons (and neighbouring humans). But, equally, Nguni agriculturalists (who suffered baboon raids of their crops and small livestock) would have noted only too well how baboons also evaded farmers and avoided their wrath. So understandably there arose a Janus-faced baboon in the human imagination – a creature capable of being both natural and unnatural, good and evil, helpful and harmful. The natural animal was 'good' – associated with mountains and also with the ancestors, even sometimes a benevolent spirit guide of particular Nguni diviners.[44] In Nguni tellings, the unnatural baboon was not just a trickster figure – as in many Bushman stories – but more sinister, understandable in an agropastoralist society that experienced baboon depredations on crops and small livestock.[45] Their unnatural baboons were understood to work as so-called 'witches' familiars',[46] or even occasionally to be 'witches' themselves.[47] These *imfene* (baboon familiars)[48] remain enduringly linked with unnatural 'wrongness' even up to the present.[49] It is difficult to write the history of such subterranean beliefs (especially as these were further driven underground by colonial-era antiwitchcraft laws, which have persisted until the late twentieth century). Periodisation of belief (of both ruptures and continuities) is always hard, but especially so when the beliefs are palimpsestic and syncretic. Two schools of thought arose, for example, in some parts of Zululand: those who thought zombie slaves, or *umkhovu*, were male baboons tamed with dark magic, and those who thought that all baboons were potentially able to operate as a familiar '*imfene*' in their own forms. A possible historical explanation suggests that the untrustworthy trickster baboon could have emerged from oral tradition concerning the human sedentary transition. The shift from positive relations (as sketched above) to enmity with baboons came with the shift to agropastoralism and sedentism. This 'trickster' ambiguity of baboons may have stemmed from oral tradition filtering through in the cosmology of those making the transition to crop growing from hunting and gathering. In essence, long memories of a once good neighbour becoming a bad neighbour.

In any event, there was a porous boundary between belief systems, evidenced by Nguni borrowing from San/Bushman beliefs that, as Hammond-Tooke argued, 'added a potent element of further supernatural power to that of the ancestors, by explicitly harnessing the "primordial" intuitions of an animal-haunted pre-agropastoralist world to use in a predominantly pastoral society.'[50] An example of diachronic and syncretic belief patterns may be found by looking closely at a small group of people who developed new ideas about baboon–human relations very rapidly and in very particular circumstances.

The circumstances of nineteenth-century colonisation led to the creation of a curious little group of men who came together in order to survive on the frontier.[51] Their historical record was at first wildly misunderstood: they left behind rock paintings, in the Drakensberg, depicting men with guns on horses, not unusual depictions by Bushmen/San victims of genocidal white commandos. But these images were puzzling: they were all mixed up somehow. On the weaponry front, some horsemen bore spears, some knobkerries, and some bows and arrows. On the sartorial side, some wore wide-brimmed hats but others sported dashingly plumed headdresses. They also occasionally appeared to be engaged in trance dances – a pursuit not normally associated with Boer farmers. This warranted a closer look, and it transpired that this group were drawing pictures not of their oppressors but of *themselves*. These were the self-portraits of a cosmopolitan little group – the AmaTola, as they came to be known – composed not only of Bushmen but also Khoe, Africans and some deserting white soldiers, who all came together to form a ragtag raiding band operating between the 1830s and 1860s. They devised new lifeways, predicated on swooping down on the agriculturalists below the escarpment and then returning to their mountain fastness for safety – a modus operandi that modelled that of the baboon, whose identity they not unnaturally adopted as totem. They initially brought horses to the Drakensberg from the Eastern Cape frontier and raided cattle from Africans and poor white *trekboers* (nomadic or migratory graziers or pastoralists descended from Dutch settlers) and then wealthier white farmers below the escarpment. This new lifeway needed a new way of understanding the world. So they proceeded to forge a fresh identity using a combination of symbols – so evident in the residue of their religion remaining behind in rock paintings. The ritual dances were used to harness power through new identifications with animals: the dancing humans were depicted transforming therianthropically into baboons and horses. This enabled the assumption of their protective powers to keep the AmaTola safe on their mounted forays. They built syncretically on the existing Bushman belief that baboons had powerful protective medicine to allow them to raid homesteads with impunity.[52] They added new ideas linking horses and baboons in their vernacular cosmology, hanging 'baboon root medicine' around their necks to render them invisible and turn enemy bullets to water.[53] As Challis notes: 'For the AmaTola, the most powerful and binding symbol was the baboon – the manifestation of protective powers derived from the medicinal plants with which it was associated. The baboon is depicted in the rock art imagery of a creolised cosmos that is new and unique to the nineteenth century.'[54] Thus human–baboon relationships shifted and evolved over time. In tracing these older histories, we see that baboons and humans were not always enemies, and possibilities of further change may be embraced by tracing a more accurate and nuanced history of the relationship between humans and baboons over the *longue durée*.

Inventing the killer ape

Arguably the most important historical shift – certainly the worst rupture – in the baboon–human relationship came with the really dramatic change in human history: the shift from hunter-gatherer lifeways to sedentary crop farming and livestock keeping.[55] As agriculture developed over time, crop raiding became a 'natural' part of many baboons' survival strategy. It was clearly an evolutionary boon as it meant less time lost on foraging, and more time for leisure and socialising.[56] Farmers battled the baboon raiders, who were a real threat to human food security. This was especially after the big predators – of both humans and baboons – were extirpated. As noted in this example from 1877:

> The [African farmer] dreads the baboon more than anything else, and there is a regular organised system of warfare between them, in which the baboons by no means get the worst. I heard a sickening story of how only last season ... a local kraal, infuriated by their losses managed to catch an old baboon, leader of his troop, and skinned him alive and let him go again in the woods.[57]

This illustrates the consequences of the first fundamental rupture in the relationship between humans and baboons, precipitated by the transition to sedentary crop farming and livestock rearing. This is tellingly echoed, for example, in the praises of the baboon-totem people in Shona and Ndebele totemism, which reflect an unequivocally agriculturalist point of view: *vadyi vezvekuba/Abaphila ngokutshontsha* (Shona/Ndebele) meaning 'those who survive on stealing'.[58] Thus the new sedentary crop-farming context saw the very start of the making of the baboon as enemy.

Baboons certainly posed a serious agricultural threat and were the scourge of farmers. They were shot for the state bounty (not for trophy hunting or meat). In the Cape, for example, the bounty system ran until the mid-twentieth century. In the long internecine war between the two primate species, it was not easy to ensure a victory for humans – battles could be won, but not the war. After all, baboons had developed alongside irate farmers for hundreds of generations, so they had evolved the ability to recognise human threat in basic form. This is illustrated by the desperate measures the hunters had to deploy:

> The older methods of [baboon] control consisted of organized shooting, trapping and poisoning, and were of limited efficacy as the animals are extremely wary. The latest technique consists of prebaiting an area with maize or fruit, and then treating this with Thallium ... [But] we consider that lethal doses of sodium cyanide in small gelatin capsules which could easily be inserted into fruit would be better and more humane. ... A peculiar method, which is said to be employed with good effect in the dry regions of the Province, is to set out large basins of sweet wine in areas frequented by baboons. It is claimed that they become so intoxicated that they can be dispatched without difficulty.[59]

At the same time, while baboons were perceived as materially useless, a social use was found for them. Under the segregationist and apartheid states, white people often likened Africans to baboons as part of policing the racist social order of the time. Such comparisons were integral to a toxic taxonomy that classified Africans as nearer the other primates in a crude interpretation of the 'Great Chain of Being' and, from the late nineteenth century, in a crude *mis*interpretation of Darwinism. Such comparisons (ranging from the 'scientific' to personal insults) operated not merely on the quotidian, individual level, but more profoundly as instruments of social control. Certain human groups have been more closely linked (by other groups – especially by those in a position of socioeconomic or political power above them) to a 'state of animality'.[60] This social Darwinism was to evolve into something very different by the 1920s and also thousands of miles away from the African veld, in London Zoo.

In 1924, the Zoological Society of London announced a spanking new baboon display called 'Monkey Hill', an open-air rocky cage replete with extra heaters to replicate the sunny expanse of the animals' natural habitat. The zoo ordered delivery of about a hundred sacred baboons from the Horn of Africa. They had specified males only, thinking that the males, long-toothed and brightly bottomed, would draw paying punters far more than would the frumpier-rumped females. But through some unforgivable bureaucratic error, some of the consignment were female.[61]

The result was a baboon bloodbath. Almost immediately, with the sex imbalance and the confined space, a massacre began. Caught in a literal tug-of-war between the larger males, most of the females were killed in the first few months. Even then, the males fought over their corpses. The brutality frightened even the zookeepers, who sometimes had to wait days for a ceasefire before bolting into no man's land – like the Red Cross – to recover the bodies. But rather than remove the few surviving females, the zoo thought that it could buy peace by adding more females. So the war broke out again, and the deaths continued, most by shockingly brutal means. By 1931, two-thirds of all the males and more than 90 per cent of the females that had been brought to Monkey Hill had died. The zoo authorities eventually removed the surviving females. As the violence waned, so did the public's interest in the exhibit.

But the interest of Solly Zuckerman, born in South Africa and a new graduate in anatomy from the University of Cape Town, was piqued. Growing up in a place where baboons were regarded as vermin, in his youth he had shot them for the state bounty. He was now employed to study and explain the carnage at the zoo. The developing 'morality tale' was entrenched by Zuckerman in the book he wrote on the Monkey Hill massacre. Published in 1932, this book was titled *The Social Life of Monkeys and Apes*. Zuckerman firstly started the scientific trend of comparing baboons to humans and, secondly, popularised the idea that all primate society is built on violence and sexual dominance. His work on the Monkey Hill massacre helped establish the very foundations of primatology. This was the start of a new phase in the relationship between baboons and humans.

Zuckerman's grand metanarrative covered all primate society. In his view, all 'subhuman' primate societies are modelled on male-dominated pecking orders maintained through covert coercion and overt violence. In the aftermath of World War One and with another world conflict seeming increasingly inevitable as the 1930s progressed, social theorists and politicians (and ordinary people) embraced Monkey Hill as an allegory of how humanity behaves if unfettered by law and the niceties of convention. Zuckerman was to become enormously influential – he became scientific advisor to Whitehall, particularly on defence matters. The image he created of primates was of an affluent society, supplied by the zookeepers with more than enough food for all. Yet violence continued to predominate, Zuckerman contended, because rank and territory mattered so much – and rank could be secured only by aggression. It was a cruel and terrible world that Zuckerman witnessed. His reports read like contemporary war despatches.

But Zuckerman had forgotten one small point: *the carceral is never the normal*. Baboons do not normally butcher one another in their usual habitats, nor do all primates share anything like the societal structure of sacred baboons. The acute gender disproportion and their tiny encaged territory were far from anything that might occur naturally. Moreover, Hamadryas baboons are the only primate species (besides the gentle gorilla) that maintain so-called harems. But for the rest of the twentieth century, the 'lessons' of the Monkey Hill massacre defined primatology, political theory and psychology, and baboons became intimately and enduringly connected with aggression in the public mind.

Thus, baboons started to be a model for human society. Subsequent studies saw what they wanted to see, so the 'dominance paradigm' predominated.[62] Moreover, there was a transition from focusing on baboons as a means of understanding humans in the present to studying baboons as a key to comprehending the evolutionary origins of humankind. Even when social Darwinism was refuted – especially after World War Two – the hunger for biological explanations of human behaviour remained as strong as ever. From the early 1950s, South Africa's palaeontologist Raymond Dart proposed that violence in modern-day humans was an innate trait inherited from our earliest hunting hominin ancestors.[63] Just as the wider world started accepting that humans first evolved in Africa, *Australopithecus* was co-opted into the 'killer ape theory' – arguing that *Homo sapiens* was the end result of millions of years of an evolutionary propensity for violence. This explains why, just as some primate experts started abandoning the baboon model, the popular press and academics from other disciplines, keen to explain human evolution, championed that increasingly outdated view of primate society. For example, Robert Ardrey – an American playwright and journalist who had moved to apartheid South Africa – drew heavily on Dart's work. He popularised the 'killer ape' hypothesis with his 1961 book *African Genesis* and subsequent bestsellers.[64] He described his bad-boy baboon as a 'born bully, a born criminal, and a born candidate for the hangman's noose'. His baboon was a 'thief who loved killing … with the yellow amber eyes that one associates with the riverboat gambler'.[65] The baboon model of human nature was based on naturalising nationalism and aggrandising aggression – validating the existing social hierarchy of race, class and gender. These male scientists, public intellectuals and populist culture brokers were able to deploy the baboon model in order to insist on the inevitability, longevity and naturalness of the sociopolitical status quo. In essence, *boys will be boys, because boys will be baboons.*

Academic and popular science books had enormous cross-over audiences. Desmond Morris's 1967 bestseller *The Naked Ape*, which sold twenty million copies, further popularised the idea of the human as a 'hunting ape'. Richard Lee and Irven DeVore's *Man the Hunter* (1968) affirmed that the hunting way of life had made up 99 per cent of human history and was thus the 'natural' prototype of a thing they called 'human nature'.[66] A series of books (including Lionel Tiger's 1969 *Men in Groups* and Tiger and Robin Fox's 1971 *The Imperial Animal*) all deployed the baboon analogy for human society. But by then, after a reign of three decades, Zuckerman's grand theory was defied by a new cohort of primatologists in the late 1960s and 1970s. Thelma Rowell, Shirley Strum and others, basing their challenge on fieldwork rather than the zoo, started to argue that primate behaviour is not a rigid dominance hierarchy based on violence, but rather flexible and influenced by shifting environments.[67] They pointed out also that female baboons played much more significant roles than had previously been believed. We had radically misunderstood baboons – and then deployed them to misunderstand ourselves. But the damage had been done. The public was convinced and human society remained modelled on the 'killer male baboon', ensconced in many popular works of the new field of sociobiology and ersatz popular science books about modern masculinity and aggression.

From vermin to gangsta?

There would in time be another major challenge to the alpha ape model. This is because there was a dawning perception that baboons vary – certainly by species and perhaps by 'culture'. Evidence from the field was appearing, suggesting significant ethological or indeed cultural change in baboon societies. South African baboons had been studied for the first time at length in the early twentieth century, with the results published from the 1920s, by amateur naturalist Eugene Marais.[68] He recorded what can be described as cultural differences between those he observed in the (then) Transvaal and a local troop whose behaviour had changed because of the effects of the 1899–1902 South African War. In broader southern Africa, several studies of the chacma baboon were carried out from the 1950s onwards in the Cape and Natal, and in (then) South West Africa and Rhodesia; work on olive and yellow baboons was undertaken in Kenya and on hamadryas baboons in Ethiopia.[69] Douglas Hey, Director of Nature Conservation in the Cape Province, recorded changes in baboon culture: '[They] search for] food in the form of fruit and seeds, and tender shoots. They also feed on bulbs and roots, eggs, nestlings, and insects ... Recently it has been claimed that they have taken to killing young sheep and lambs and are becoming carnivores.'[70] Ten years later (and as mentioned at the opening of this chapter), Hey noted that while the trapping of baboons for medical research had removed the baboon problem in some places, they remained a significant threat, and that during an 'abnormal drought in the Northern Cape Province, one farmer alone claimed to have lost 364 goats to the depredations of baboons in a seven month period'.[71]

If one thing was clear by the 1960s and 1970s, it was that it was a mistake to generalise about baboons.[72] Later studies have borne this out. Baboons have evinced a variety of responses to different environments, and vernacular or local variances are evident. For example, even if one looks only at dietary preferences (rather than more nuanced aspects of their social lives): in some communal lands in Zimbabwe, baboons were found to be responsible for over half of the livestock killed; in contrast, in some communities next to the Serengeti in Tanzania and next to the Masai Mara in Kenya, baboons killed less than 1 per cent of livestock or were not blamed for any livestock deaths at all.[73] Cultural change is evident in baboons at the Cape.[74] For example, it has been reported that some specific baboons at Cape Point will watch a picnic being set up and then casually, almost insouciantly, grab a human youngster. Ear-splitting chaos ensues from the baboon, the parents and – no doubt, given how prone they are to intemperate outbursts – the child. When the outraged human parents spring to their progeny's rescue, they leave the delicious high-calorie picnic treats unattended on a blanket. So the rest of the troop swoops in to demolish the cucumber sandwiches and what is left of simian-human relations. This kind of innovation often begins with specific inventor but spreads rapidly to an entire troop, just like information about new food sources or predators.

A long-term study of baboons in Kenya offered similar evidence of cultural-historical change over time. This study started in the 1970s, but in the early 1980s tuberculosis led to the death of a large proportion of the local troop. The disease stemmed from tainted food dumped on a tourist lodge's rubbish heap. The big males got most access to the contaminated food, and so they were the ones who perished. One by one, they died. The scientists departed disheartened; the research was abandoned. However, after nearly a decade that specific troop received scientific attention again and it became startlingly obvious that something remarkable had happened.

Suddenly, members of the troop were sitting closely together, males were grooming each other and even grooming females. The higher-ranking baboons did not vent their spleen very violently on subordinates. Life had become better for ordinary baboons; they no longer had either the classic stress markers or elevated stress hormones. So what was going on here? It seems that, over the several generations that had elapsed since the terrible tragedy, the troop was maintaining a radically altered, more peaceful society.[75]

It is helpful and hopeful to know that baboon cultures can *change*, because – to move back to the place where we started, here in the Cape – to many it seems that baboon–human relations have changed for the worse in the last few decades. This period has seen the animals move from the mountains to the suburbs, or rather the suburbs have encroached into their territory. Interestingly, in some areas their numbers have increased – unlike every other great ape and most monkeys. But the myth of the naturally aggressive baboon stayed strong in the public mind, however, and has had tangible and terrible consequences. This was key to the next phase in the long relationship between humans and baboons.

'Fred', a notorious Cape gangster, was executed by South African state authorities in March 2011.[76] Fred started small, but eventually became leader of his own gang, responsible for a series of escalating crimes. His band was linked to terrorising tourists, theft, robberies, damage to property and even assaults. Fred had a legendary ability to break into cars: when he heard motorists unlock their vehicles with a remote control, he would open the door and dash inside before the owner even reached the vehicle. Well-built, rugged – some even thought him handsome – Fred was certainly an alpha male. He defended his gang's turf above the naval port centre of Simon's Town. Anyone standing in his way faced intimidation and aggression. Yet, famously, when he broke into a car in which a baby was strapped, he gently avoided harming the infant. His public loved him for it. Fred became a celebrity – the media reported his exploits, and newspaper readers came to know him by his first name only, like any other top-tier celebrity. He was aided by a perhaps misguided but sympathetic public, who indulged him as they once indulged the charismatic Scotty Smith, André Stander and later other popular gangsters. A Facebook page was started by admirers, who celebrated his outrages against society. But his lifestyle came to mean his inevitable death. Fred was caught and killed by lethal injection. Many people mourned his passing. Some missed his gallant defiance of authority, his ability to live with panache outside the law. Others lamented the unnecessary nature of his death – without a supportive but misguided public to fuel his addictions, he would never have become a successful criminal. A community wake and candlelit vigil was held for him in Simon's Town, attended by strangers who knew only the legend and had never even spoken to Fred before.

Fred was a baboon. In fact, he was one of several charismatic gangster baboons. There was William, the stalker of Scarborough, the terror of that sleepy coastal hamlet. Then there was Jimmy, who was executed for his sugar addiction, which saw him break into homes in the middle of the night. Here baboons are 'unnatural' once more – not as tricksters, diviners or witches – but rather in a new form as 'criminal' in a country obsessed by crime. Of course, perceptions of primates are influenced by their similarity to humans, creating anthropomorphised expectations about conforming to a human social code. When animals violate the anthropomorphic social order, they are measured unconsciously against the same moral, even legal, code as humans. This shapes how people perceive baboons, and their willingness to tolerate coexistence.

One may track a curious history in suburbia, one of cruelty. Over the last two decades, public rage towards primate invasions is often disproportionate. Testimonies from primate NGO volunteers and welfare organisations suggest that the rage is not really just about the baboons, but about societal anxiety more generally, with baboons acting as proxies for humans, just as they have so often in the past. One volunteer argued that people had spent a lot of money creating their 'own environments' behind high walls, razor-wire fences and security systems and therefore resent any kind of intrusion. Another volunteer noted: 'They dread burglars, they resent the people who hang around begging at traffic lights and outside shops and they want them removed. But it's a New South Africa and they cannot just be removed – so they take their rage out on the baboons.'[77] There is serious evidence of extreme violence towards baboons, using real guns, pellet guns, paintball guns and poison. The aged and elderly baboons, with their broken teeth, are reduced to scavenging our dustbins – perhaps they live too long, as their natural predators have been exterminated. Except for us, of course.

South Africa is no country for old baboons. When Fred was finally executed, it was discovered through an autopsy that that he had seventy-two bits of metal and birdshot and buckshot pellets. He carried a deeply embedded signature of conflict with people on his body – a visceral archive of hate. And I wonder from where this violence must stem – surely either from fear or from rage, but is it the fear of the invader, the burglar staring in through the window? Or is it the rage of Caliban seeing his own face in the glass?

Conclusion

This chapter opened with the pandemic that has closed the world down. To paraphrase Lenin, there are certain historical events that light up reality like a flash of lightning across a dark sky. They illuminate all kinds of things that you would not otherwise see – like the baboons enlisted on the front lines to help end an animal disease that has become a human disease. Let us hope that in this time of COVID-19 we can begin to see the other living creatures around us and understand the depth and length of our shared past. For example, the deeper timescales of environmental historians who draw on palaeontology and paleoecology enable us to see ourselves not just as a civilisations or societies but as a species alongside others. After all, an important strength of historians is the ability to take an apparently immutable and 'natural' order and show that 'it was not always so', exposing the seemingly 'natural order' for just how 'unnatural', how anthropogenically constructed, it is. This empowers further challenges to the existing order that might otherwise seem 'natural' or 'inevitable'. Sometimes we need a different history in order to create a different future.

Environmental history has long rejected the idea that humans are separate from natural ecosystems. There is no 'natural' world – only 'the' world. To extend this now, this chapter has explored the notion suggested by ethnoprimatology that there are no ecosystems utterly free from human influence, and that studying primates in less-impacted 'natural' settings gives us 'better' knowledge than studying those primates who live alongside us. So this chapter has represented an attempt at recognising the subjective agency of two primate species, their entanglements with each other's lives and landscapes, and has highlighted the complementary roles of the humanities, the social sciences and the natural sciences in integrating history with research from palaeontology, paleoecology, rock art, conservation biology, ecology and ethology. It has drawn on ethnoprimatology to emphasise that interconnections between humans and primates should be viewed as more than just disruptions of a 'natural' state. Rather than sticking to the human past, as history normally does, rather than focusing on only behaviour and ecology, as in conventional primatology, or only on the symbolic meanings, as in anthropology, an environmental history sensitive to the animal may merge these perspectives into a more integrative approach. Our relationship with baboons is both extended and enduring. However, it needs to be understood diachronically not synchronically. This is where historians, drawing on various disciplines, can be helpful in synthesising from each to produce a cohesive narrative that accounts for and elucidates change over time, while insisting on the importance of idiographic context.

This chapter has argued that our relationships with baboons are powerfully shaped by shifting human lifeways, as well as international academic trends and local knowledge. You cannot tell merely a 'Global North' story of ape–human connections from the classical period to the rise of twentieth-century primatology and deem it to be the full story. After all, 'baboon' has meant different things to different people in different periods: good neighbours (alarm systems and safety providers, teachers and diviners), bad neighbours (witches and thieves, vermin and gangsters), models for our own society and – now, maybe – good neighbours again. If it has changed before, it may change again – which offers hope for future conservation efforts. One thing we should think about is that in conservation programmes, perhaps we must also undertake a different kind of fieldwork – back through time. We should consider that before we can achieve real change, before present-day conservation can be successful, we need to fathom the dark ecology of the human heart. Another point to consider is if specific animal groups have particular cultures, it may change how we should think about conservation – not in terms of 'species' or even individuals, but in terms of preserving cultures. If a local baboon troop is destroyed, do we lose only individual animals, do we lose only genetic diversity, or is it possible that we also lose something like a culture? Should that also be conserved?

We also see how biological determinism has been unconsciously or even strategically deployed to understand but also to legitimise the sociopolitical status quo. It is a salient reminder that we remain sceptical of any sort of biological determinism, even in our fellow animals. We have moved away from determinism in the human world since World War Two, and we have come to champion flexibility and resilience as humanity's essential characteristics. Perhaps it is really this resilience and flexibility that we should see when we seek the baboon in the mirror? Like us, and unlike most other primate species, they are survivors of modernity – perhaps even of climate change. Baboons help us cling to the wild in our domesticated spaces. Their ability to flourish alongside us, if given a chance to do so, is remarkable – as the long history of the two species reveals. Including baboons in our urbanising world may be a southern form of rewilding. Surely we need to see them for themselves too, and not as simply cruder versions of ourselves, living dioramas of our early ancestors or medical proxies for our own bodies?

The key thing to remember is that there is no such thing as *the* baboon, or at least no such thing as a model baboon – organically essential, unchanging and homogeneous. Baboons are as historical as we are ourselves. They, like us, are products of their (and perhaps partly our) own biology and evolutionary pasts, but also products of their changing environments and their shifting sociopolitical present, within cultures that change over time and which contain individuals who do not conform to stereotype. In short, they both experience change and effect change – *they have history*. Where once Zuckerman could speak blithely of a universal primate society, we now know that differences exist between and indeed within subspecies, between different troops, between lineages and between individuals. Baboon cultures change and individuals behave anomalously. Think of the hippy baboons who disavowed war and discovered their own (endless) summer of love. Think of the hostage-taking picnic gatecrashers. Finally, think of the four baboons who staged a breakout from The Institute, despite eight generations of captivity and exile in a foreign land. It is a reminder to us of the individuality of baboons. Biology is not destiny – not even for baboons.

Notes

1 Zoonoses are infectious diseases spread from animals to humans.
2 *India News*, 8 Apr. 2020; 'Amid Corona Outbreak, 15 Monkey Deaths Create Alarm in UP', *Tribune*, 9 Apr. 2020, www.tribuneindia.com/news/nation/amid-corona-outbreak-15-monkey-deaths-create-alarm-in-up-67338 (accessed 31 Mar. 2022).
3 *Lancet*, 29 Mar. 1919, 520; *Rand Daily Mail*, 31 Oct. 1918, 7 Nov. 1918 and 8 Nov. 1918; *Rhodesia Herald*, 13 Dec. 1918; *The Times* (London), 5 Nov. 1918. Thanks to Thula Simpson for alerting me.
4 S. Warren, 'Texas Baboon Troop Enlisted in Humankind's War on Coronavirus', Bloomberg, 7 Mar. 2020, www.bloombergquint.com/onweb/texas-baboon-troop-enlisted-in-humankind-s-war-on-coronavirus (accessed 10 Apr. 2020).
5 J.A. Drewe, M.J. O'Riain, E. Beamish, H. Currie and S. Parsons, 'Survey of Infections Transmissible between Baboons and Humans, Cape Town, South Africa', *Emerging Infectious Diseases*, 18 (2) Feb. 2012, 298–301; E.J. van Rensburg et al., 'Simian Immunodeficiency Viruses (SIVs) from Eastern and Southern Africa: Detection of a SIVagm Variant from a Chacma Baboon', *Journal of General Virology*, 79 (7) July 1998, 1809–14.
6 H. Vagtborg, *The Baboon in Medical Research* (Austin: University of Texas Press, 1965); J. Van de Berg, S. Williams-Blangero and S.D. Tardif (eds), *The Baboon in Biomedical Research* (Springer, 2009).
7 D. Hey, 'Keynote Address – Vertebrate Pest Animals in the Province of the Cape of Good Hope, Republic of South Africa', *Proceedings of the 6th Vertebrate Pest Conference* (1974), 5.
8 L.P. Stoltz and M.E. Keith, 'A Population Survey of Chacma Baboon in the Northern Transvaal', *Journal of Human Evolution*, 2 (3) May 1973, 195–212.
9 Stellenbosch University had support from the University of the Witwatersrand, which had long possessed a colony, and Johns Hopkins University. J.N. de Klerk, J.J. van Zyl, H.D. Brede, H.W. Weber, J.A. van Zyl, F.D. van Zijl, A.J. Brink, G.P. Murphy, W.W. Scott and E.C. Melby, 'A Primate Research Colony: The Stellenbosch-Johns Hopkins Baboon Facility', *South African Medical Journal*, 42 (19) May 1968, 459–62; J.H. Groenewald, 'Preview of the Experimental Projects Supported by the University of Stellenbosch Primate Colony', *Journal of the South African Veterinary Association*, 41 (3) 1970, 167–70.
10 *Washington Post*, 17 Apr. 2018; 'Baboons Prop up Barrels to Escape Texas Research Centre', *BBC News*, 17 Apr. 2018, www.bbc.com/news/world-us-canada-43794906 (accessed 31 Mar. 2022).

11 Quotes from F. Darabont's *The Shawshank Redemption* (Beverley Hills: Castle Rock Entertainment).
12 L. Robin and W. Steffen, 'History for the Anthropocene', *History Compass*, 5 (5) 2007, 1694–1719.
13 For recent analysis of the possibilities of the phrase 'useable past' in South Africa, see C. Burns, 'A Useable Past: The Search for a History in Chords,' in H.E. Stolten (ed.), *History Making and Present Day Politics: The Meaning of Collective Memory in South Africa* (Uppsala: Nordiska Afrikainstitutet, 2007), 351–62.
14 C. Meine, 'It's about Time: Conservation Biology and History', *Conservation Biology*, 13 (1) Feb. 1999, 1–3.
15 J. Carruthers, 'Tracking in Game Trails: Looking Afresh at the Politics of Environmental History in South Africa', *Environmental History*, 11 (4) Oct. 2006, 804–29.
16 Synanthropy refers to undomesticated species living alongside humans and benefiting from the proximity.
17 D.L. Smail, *On Deep History and the Brain* (Berkeley: University of California Press, 2008); S. Dubow, 'Global Science, National Horizons: South Africa in Deep Time and Space', Inaugural Lecture, Smuts Professor of Commonwealth History, Magdalene College, Cambridge, 28 Nov. 2018.
18 H. Ritvo, 'On the Animal Turn', *Daedalus*, 136 (4) Fall 2007, 118–22.
19 S. Swart, 'Writing Animals into African History', *Critical African Studies*, 8 (2) 2016; S. Swart, 'Animals in African History', in *Oxford Research Encyclopaedia of African History*, 2019, https://oxfordre.com/africanhistory/view/10.1093/acrefore/9780190277734.001.0001/acrefore-9780190277734-e-443 (accessed 31 Mar. 2022).
20 A. Guerrini, 'Deep History, Evolutionary History, and Animals in the Anthropocene', in B. Bovenkerk and J. Keulartz (eds), *Animal Ethics in the Age of Humans* (Cham: Springer, 2016).
21 E. Russell, *Evolutionary History: Uniting History and Biology to Understand Life on Earth* (Cambridge: Cambridge University Press, 2011), 145; H. Ritvo, *The Platypus and the Mermaid and Other Figments of the Classifying Imagination* (Cambridge, MA: Harvard University Press, 1997), and *Noble Cows and Hybrid Zebras: Essays on Animals & History* (Charlottesville: University of Virginia Press, 2010); D. Haraway, *Primate Visions: Gender, Race, and Nature in the World of Modern Science* (New York: Routledge, 1989).
22 J. Sheail, 'Nature Conservation and the Agricultural Historian', *Agricultural History Review*, 34 (1) 1986, 1–11; H. Wels, M. Spierenburg and J.B. Gewald (eds), *Nature Conservation in Southern Africa: Morality and Marginality: Towards Sentient Conservation?* (Leiden: Brill, 2018); P. Locke, 'Multispecies Methodology, Transdisciplinary Collaboration, and Human-Elephant Relations', New Zealand Centre for Human–Animal Studies Conference, University of Canterbury, 5–6 Nov. 2015.
23 A. Fuentes and K. Hockings, 'The Ethnoprimatological Approach in Primatology', *American Journal of Primatology*, 72 (10) Aug. 2010, 841–7.

24 B. Kaplan, 'In Pursuit of a Panacea: Mitigating Human-Baboon Conflict in the Cape Peninsula' (DPhil thesis, University of Cape Town, 2013); T. Hoffman and M.J. O'Riain, 'The Spatial Ecology of Chacma Baboons (*Papio ursinus*) in a Human-Modified Environment', *International Journal of Primatology*, 32 (2) Apr. 2011, 308–28; R. Kansky and D. Gaynor, *Baboon Management Strategy for the Cape Peninsula* (Cape Town: Table Mountain Fund, 2000); S. Strum, 'The Good, the Bad and the Smart – What Makes Baboons So Difficult to Manage?', Baboon Expert Workshop, Cape Town, University of Cape Town, 2012; A. van Doorn, 'The Interface between Socioecology and Management of Chacma Baboons (*Papio ursinus*) in the Cape Peninsula, South Africa' (DPhil thesis, University of Cape Town, 2009).

25 L. Swedell, 'African Papionins: Diversity of Social Organization and Ecological Flexibility', in C.J. Campbell, A. Fuentes, K.C. MacKinnon, S. Bearder and M. Panger (eds), *Primates in Perspective* (Oxford: Oxford University Press, 2011), 241–77.

26 S. Hurn, '"Like Herding Cats!" Managing Conflict over Wildlife Heritage on South Africa's Cape Peninsula', *Ecological and Environmental Anthropology*, 6, 2011, 39–53.

27 C. Hill, 'Conflict of Interest between People and Baboons: Crop Raiding in Uganda', *International Journal of Primatology*, 21 (2) 2000, 299–315.

28 J. Mormile and C. Hill, 'Living with Urban Baboons: Exploring Attitudes and Their Implications for Local Baboon Conservation and Management in Knysna, South Africa', *Human Dimensions of Wildlife*, 22 (2) 2017, 99–109 (quote at 108).

29 S. Swart, 'History Eats Its Young: The Perils of Short-Termism in Understanding the Past', in G. Cederlöf and M. Rangarajan (eds), *At Nature's Edge* (Oxford: Oxford University Press, 2018), 120–41.

30 C. Barras, 'Hominin v Monkey Deathmatch Ended in a Draw When They Fell Down a Hole', *New Scientist*, 21 Dec. 2018, www.newscientist.com/article/2189192-hominin-v-monkey-deathmatch-ended-in-a-draw-when-they-fell-down-a-hole/ (accessed 31 Mar. 2022).

31 A.S. Altmann and J. Altmann, *Baboon Ecology: African Field Research* (Chicago: University of Chicago Press, 1970).

32 R. Estes, *The Behavior Guide to African Mammals: Including Hoofed Mammals, Carnivores, and Primates* (Berkeley: University of California Press, 1991), 512.

33 J.P. Camberfort, 'A Comparative Study of Culturally Transmitted Patterns of Feeding Habits in the Chacma Baboon *Papio ursinus* and the Vervet Monkey *Cercopithecus aethiops*', *Folia Primatologica*, 36 (3–4) 1981, 243–63.

34 J.R. Fletemeyer, 'Communication about Potentially Harmful Foods in Free-Ranging Chacma Baboons, *Papio ursinus*', *Primates*, 19, 1978, 223.

35 S. Marks, 'Khoisan Resistance to the Dutch in the Seventeenth and Eighteenth Centuries', *Journal of African History*, 13 (1) 1972, 55–80.

36 T. Mangena and S. Ndlovu, 'Figurative and Symbolic Function of Animal Imagery in Packaging Human Behaviour in Ndebele and Shona Cultures', *South African Journal of African Languages*, 36 (2) 2016, 251–6, 255.

37 P. Jolly, 'Therianthropes in San Rock Art', *South African Archaeological Bulletin*, 57 (176) Dec. 2002, 85–103. For specifics, see S. Challis, 'Taking the Reins: The Introduction of the Horse in the Nineteenth-Century Maloti-Drakensberg and the Protective Medicine of Baboons', in P. Mitchell and B. Smith (eds), *The Eland's People: New Perspectives in the Rock Art of the Maloti-Drakensberg Bushmen* (Johannesburg: Witwatersrand University Press, 2009), 104–7.
38 J. Holleman (ed.), *Customs and Beliefs of the /Xam Bushmen* (Johannesburg: Witwatersrand University Press, 2004), 10–13.
39 D.F. Bleek. 'Customs and Beliefs of the /Xam Bushmen, Part 1, Baboons', *Bantu Studies*, 5 (1) 1931, 174, 168. See also Holleman, *Customs and Beliefs*, 10–12; M.G. Guenther, *Tricksters and Trancers: Bushman Religion and Society* (Bloomington: Indiana University Press, 1999), 74.
40 W.D. Hammond-Tooke, 'Divinatory Animals: Further Evidence of San/Nguni Borrowing?' *South African Archaeological Bulletin*, 54 (170) Dec. 1999, 128–32.
41 Bleek, 'Customs and Beliefs', 167–70.
42 S. Challis, 'Creolisation on the Nineteenth-Century Frontiers of Southern Africa: A Case Study of the AmaTola "Bushmen" in the Maloti-Drakensberg', *Journal of Southern African Studies*, 38 (2) 2012, 265–80, 276.
43 Bleek, 'Customs and Beliefs', 167–8.
44 W.D. Hammond-Tooke, 'The Symbolic Structure of Cape Nguni Cosmology', in M.G. Whisson and M. West (eds), *Religion and Social Change in Southern Africa: Anthropological Essays in Honour of Monica Wilson* (Cape Town: David Philip, 1975), 26–7.
45 H. Callaway, *Nursery Tales, Traditions, and Histories of the Zulus* (Springvale, Natal: J.A. Blair, 1868), 351.
46 *City Press*, 14 May 1995; *Natal Witness*, 11 Mar. 1997; *Star*, 29 Feb. 2000; *Sunday Tribune*, 9 Sept. 2007; Truth and Reconciliation Commission, amnesty hearing, 28 Feb. 2000, Hendrik Rakgotho, application AM0647/97, matter: killing of Violet Masomela, https://sabctrc.saha.org.za/documents/amntrans/johannesburg/54054.htm (accessed 31 Mar. 2022).
47 I. Niehaus, 'Witches of the Transvaal Lowveld and Their Familiars: Conceptions of Duality, Power and Desire', *Cahiers d'études africaines*, 35 (138–9) 1995, 513–40.
48 University of the Witwatersrand, Historical Papers Research Archives, South African Institute of Race Relations Archive, Collection AD843, A.B. Xuma Papers, 'The African Concept of Disease'.
49 H. Callaway, *The Religious System of the Amazulu: Izinyanga Zokubula; Or, Divination, as Existing among the Amazulu, in Their Own Words* (Springvale, Natal: J.A. Blair, 1870, 1884), 348.
50 Hammond-Tooke, 'Divinatory Animals', 128–32 (quote at 131); M. Guenther, '(S)animism and Other Animisms', in *Human-Animal Relationships in San and Hunter-Gatherer Cosmology*, II (Cham: Palgrave Macmillan, 2020).
51 Challis, 'Taking the Reins', 104–7; S. Swart, *Riding High: Horses, Humans and History* (Johannesburg: Witwatersrand University Press, 2010), 42–3, 208.

52 Challis, 'Creolisation', 265–80, 270; J.B. Wright, *Bushman Raiders of the Drakensberg, 1840–1870* (Pietermaritzburg: University of Natal Press, 1971), and 'Bushman Raiders Revisited', in P. Skotnes (ed.), *Claim to the Country: The Archive of Lucy Lloyd and Wilhelm Bleek* (Johannesburg: Jacana Press, 2007), 118–29.
53 Estes, *Behavior Guide to African Mammals*, 513.
54 Challis, 'Creolisation', 270.
55 Much of this part of the chapter comes from my inaugural address: 'The Lion's Historian: Animal Histories from the South', Stellenbosch University, Oct. 2017.
56 Y. Warren, J.P. Higham, A.M. Maclarnon and C. Ross, 'Crop-Raiding and Commensalism in Olive Baboons: The Costs and Benefits of Living with Humans', in V. Sommer and C. Ross (eds), *Primates of Gashaka: Developments in Primatology: Progress and Prospects* (Cham: Springer, 2011).
57 M. Barker, *A Year's Housekeeping in South Africa* (London: Macmillan, 1877), 327.
58 Thembani Dube, 15 Apr. 2020, personal communication.
59 D. Hey, 'Keynote Address – Vertebrate Pest Animals in the Province of the Cape of Good Hope, Republic of South Africa', *Proceedings of the 2nd Vertebrate Pest Conference* (1964), 66.
60 Caricatured in parodies, working-class Irish were depicted as monkey-men in the 1860s and 1870s.
61 J. Burt, 'Solly Zuckerman: The Making of a Primatological Career in Britain, 1925–1945', *Studies in History and Philosophy of Science*, 37 (2) 2006, 295–310, esp. 299; Swart, 'Lion's Historian', 6; S. Zuckerman, *The Social Life of Monkeys and Apes* (New York: Harcourt, Brace, 1932).
62 S.L. Washburn and I. DeVore, 'The Social Life of Baboons', *Scientific American* 204 (6) June 1961, 62–71.
63 R. Dart, 'The Predatory Transition from Ape to Man', *International Anthropological and Linguistic Review*, 1 (4) 1953, 201–17.
64 R. Ardrey, *African Genesis: A Personal Investigation into Animal Origins and Nature of Man* (New York: Athenium, 1961).
65 R. Ardrey, *The Territorial Imperative: A Personal Inquiry into the Animal Origins of Property and Nations* (New York: Dell, 1966), 227.
66 R. Lee and I. DeVore (eds), *Man the Hunter* (Chicago: Aldine, 1968).
67 T. Rowell, *Social Behaviour of Monkeys* (Harmondsworth: Penguin Books, 1972); T. Rowell, 'The Concept of Social Dominance', *Behavioral Biology*, 11 (2) 1974, 131–54; S. Strum, *Almost Human: A Journey into the World of Baboons* (Chicago: University of Chicago Press, 2001).
68 E. Marais, *My Friends the Baboons* (London: Methuen, 1939) and *The Soul of the Ape* (London: Penguin, 1969).
69 I. DeVore and S.L. Washburn, 'Baboon Ecology and Human Evolution', in F.C. Howell and F. Bourliere (eds), *African Ecology and Human Evolution* (Abingdon: Routledge, 2017), 335–67; N. Bolwig, 'A Study of the Behaviour of the Chacma Baboon, *Papio ursinus*', *Behaviour*, 14, 1959, 136–62; K.R.L. Hall, 'Numerical Data, Maintenance Activities and Locomotion of the Wild Chacma

Baboon, *Papio ursinus*', *Proceedings of the Zoological Society of London*, 139 (2) 1962; H. Kummer and F. Kurt, 'Social Units of a Free-Living Population of Hamadryas Baboons', *Folia primatologica*, 1, 1963, 4–19.
70 Hey, 'Keynote Address' (1964), 57–70, quote at 66.
71 Hey, 'Keynote Address' (1974), 3.
72 L.P. Stoltz and G.S. Saayman, 'Ecology and Behaviour of Baboons in the Northern Transvaal', *Annals of the Transvaal Museum*, 26 (5) 1970, 99–143.
73 G. Pahad, 'Social Behaviour and Crop Raiding in Chacma Baboons of the Suikerbosrand Nature Reserve' (MSc thesis, University of the Witwatersrand, 2010), 8.
74 Hoffman and O'Riain, 'Spatial Ecology'; Van Doorn, 'Interface between Socio-ecology and Management'.
75 As adolescents, males migrate from natal troops, but females normally stay in their birth troops – so they probably upheld the new cultural behaviour given them serendipitously by this quirk of history. By reacting receptively to novel, less-aggressive behaviour, the matriarchs were able to guide group behaviour. This nonviolent approach survived the individuals who established it – and that is *culture*.
76 From Swart, 'Lion's Historian'; for more on Fred, see J.B. Gewald, 'Brothers in Arms: Baboon-Human Interactions, a Southern African Perspective', in H. Wels, M. Spierenburg and J.B. Gewald (eds), *Nature Conservation in Southern Africa: Morality and Marginality: Towards Sentient Conservation?* (Leiden: Brill, 2018), 48–66.
77 Interview with primate NGO worker (anonymous at their request), Cape Town, 27 Apr. 2018.

Bibliography

Altmann, A.S., and J. Altmann (1970) *Baboon Ecology: African Field Research*. Chicago: University of Chicago Press.
Ardrey, R. (1961) *African Genesis: A Personal Investigation into Animal Origins and Nature of Man*. New York: Athenium.
Ardrey, R. (1966) *The Territorial Imperative: A Personal Inquiry into the Animal Origins of Property and Nations*. New York: Dell.
Barker, M. (1877) *A Year's Housekeeping in South Africa*. London: Macmillan.
Barras, C. (2018) 'Hominin v Monkey Deathmatch Ended in a Draw when They Fell Down a Hole', *New Scientist*, 21 Dec., www.newscientist.com/article/2189192-hominin-v-monkey-deathmatch-ended-in-a-draw-when-they-fell-down-a-hole/ (accessed 31 Mar. 2022).
Bleek. D.F. (1931) 'Customs and Beliefs of the /Xam Bushmen, Part 1, Baboons', *Bantu Studies*, 5 (1).
Bolwig, N. (1959) 'A Study of the Behaviour of the Chacma Baboon, *Papio ursinus*', *Behaviour*, 14.

Burns, C. (2007) 'A Useable Past: The Search for a History in Chords,' in H.E. Stolten (ed.), *History Making and Present Day Politics: The Meaning of Collective Memory in South Africa*. Uppsala: Nordiska Afrikainstitutet.

Burt, J. (2006) 'Solly Zuckerman: The Making of a Primatological Career in Britain, 1925–1945', *Studies in History and Philosophy of Science*, 37 (2).

Callaway, H. (1868) *Nursery Tales, Traditions, and Histories of the Zulus*. Springvale, Natal: J.A. Blair.

Callaway, H. (1870, 1884) *The Religious System of the Amazulu: Izinyanga Zokubula; Or, Divination, as Existing among the Amazulu, in Their Own Words*. Springvale, Natal; J.A. Blair.

Camberfort, J.P. (1981) 'A Comparative Study of Culturally Transmitted Patterns of Feeding Habits in the Chacma Baboon *Papio ursinus* and the Vervet Monkey *Cercopithecus aethiops*', *Folia primatologica*, 36 (3–4).

Carruthers, J. (2006) 'Tracking in Game Trails: Looking Afresh at the Politics of Environmental History in South Africa,' *Environmental History*, 11 (4).

Challis, S. (2009) 'Taking the Reins: The Introduction of the Horse in the Nineteenth-Century Maloti-Drakensberg and the Protective Medicine of Baboons', in P. Mitchell and B. Smith (eds), *The Eland's People: New Perspectives in the Rock Art of the Maloti-Drakensberg Bushmen*. Johannesburg: Witwatersrand University Press.

Challis, S. (2012) 'Creolisation on the Nineteenth-Century Frontiers of Southern Africa: A Case Study of the AmaTola "Bushmen" in the Maloti-Drakensberg', *Journal of Southern African Studies*, 38 (2).

Darabont, F. (director) (1994) *The Shawshank Redemption*. Based on Stephen King's 1982 novella *Rita Hayworth and Shawshank Redemption*. New York: Viking Press.

Dart, R. (1953) 'The Predatory Transition from Ape to Man', *International Anthropological and Linguistic Review*, 1 (4).

De Klerk, J.N., J.J. van Zyl, H.D. Brede, H.W. Weber, J.A. van Zyl, F.D. van Zijl, A.J. Brink, G.P. Murphy, W.W. Scott and E.C. Melby (1968) 'A Primate Research Colony: The Stellenbosch-Johns Hopkins Baboon Facility', *South African Medical Journal*, 42 (19).

DeVore, I., and S.L. Washburn (2017) 'Baboon Ecology and Human Evolution', in F.C. Howell and F. Bourliere (eds), *African Ecology and Human Evolution*. Abingdon: Routledge.

Drewe, J., M.J. O'Riain, E. Beamish, H. Currie and S. Parsons (2012) 'Survey of Infections Transmissible between Baboons and Humans, Cape Town, South Africa', *Emerging Infectious Diseases*, 18 (2).

Dubow, S. (2018) 'Global Science, National Horizons: South Africa in Deep Time and Space', inaugural lecture, Smuts Professor of Commonwealth History, Magdalene College, Cambridge.

Estes, R. (1991) *The Behavior Guide to African Mammals: Including Hoofed Mammals, Carnivores, and Primates*. Berkeley: University of California Press.

Fletemeyer, J.R. (1978) 'Communication about Potentially Harmful Foods in Free-Ranging Chacma Baboons, *Papio ursinus*', *Primates*, 19.

Fuentes, A., and K. Hockings (2010) 'The Ethnoprimatological Approach in Primatology', *American Journal of Primatology*, 72 (10).

Gewald, J.B. (2018) 'Brothers in Arms: Baboon-Human Interactions, a Southern African Perspective', in H. Wels, M. Spierenburg and J.B. Gewald (eds), *Nature Conservation in Southern Africa: Morality and Marginality: Towards Sentient Conservation?* Leiden: Brill.

Groenewald, J.H. (1970) 'Preview of the Experimental Projects Supported by the University of Stellenbosch Primate Colony', *Journal of the South African Veterinary Association*, 41 (3).

Guenther, M. (2020) '(S)animism and Other Animisms', in *Human-Animal Relationships in San and Hunter-Gatherer Cosmology*, II. Cham: Palgrave Macmillan.

Guenther, M.G. (1999) *Tricksters and Trancers: Bushman Religion and Society*. Bloomington: Indiana University Press.

Guerrini, A. (2016) 'Deep History, Evolutionary History, and Animals in the Anthropocene', in B. Bovenkerk and J. Keulartz (eds), *Animal Ethics in the Age of Humans*. Cham: Springer.

Hall, K.R.L. (1962) 'Numerical Data, Maintenance Activities and Locomotion of the Wild Chacma Baboon, *Papio ursinus*', *Proceedings of the Zoological Society of London*, 139 (2).

Hammond-Tooke, W.D. (1975) 'The Symbolic Structure of Cape Nguni Cosmology', in M.G. Whisson and M. West (eds), *Religion and Social Change in Southern Africa: Anthropological Essays in Honour of Monica Wilson*. Cape Town: David Philip.

Hammond-Tooke, W.D. (1999) 'Divinatory Animals: Further Evidence of San/Nguni Borrowing?', *South African Archaeological Bulletin*, 54 (170).

Haraway, D. (1989) *Primate Visions: Gender, Race, and Nature in the World of Modern Science*. New York: Routledge.

Hey, D. (1964) 'Keynote Address – Vertebrate Pest Animals in the Province of the Cape of Good Hope, Republic of South Africa', *Proceedings of the 2nd Vertebrate Pest Conference*.

Hey, D. (1974) 'Keynote Address – Vertebrate Pest Animals in the Province of the Cape Of Good Hope, Republic of South Africa', *Proceedings of the 6th Vertebrate Pest Conference*.

Hill, C. (2000) 'Conflict of Interest between People and Baboons: Crop Raiding in Uganda', *International Journal of Primatology*, 21 (2).

Hoffman, T., and M.J. O'Riain (2011) 'The Spatial Ecology of Chacma Baboons (*Papio ursinus*) in a Human-Modified Environment', *International Journal of Primatology*, 32 (2).

Holleman, J. (ed.) (2004) *Customs and Beliefs of the /Xam Bushmen*. Johannesburg: Witwatersrand University Press.

Hurn, S. (2011) '"Like Herding Cats!" Managing Conflict over Wildlife Heritage on South Africa's Cape Peninsula', *Ecological and Environmental Anthropology*, 6.

Jolly, P. (2002) 'Therianthropes in San Rock Art', *South African Archaeological Bulletin*, 57 (176).

Kansky, R., and D. Gaynor (2000) *Baboon Management Strategy for the Cape Peninsula*. Cape Town: Table Mountain Fund.

Kaplan, B. (2013) 'In Pursuit of a Panacea: Mitigating Human-Baboon Conflict in the Cape Peninsula'. DPhil thesis, University of Cape Town.

Kummer, H., and F. Kurt (1963) 'Social Units of a Free-Living Population of Hamadryas Baboons', *Folia primatologica*, 1.
Lee, R., and I. DeVore (eds) (1968) *Man the Hunter*. Chicago: Aldine.
Locke, P. (2015) 'Multispecies Methodology, Transdisciplinary Collaboration, and Human-Elephant Relations', New Zealand Centre for Human–Animal Studies Conference, University of Canterbury.
Mangena, T., and S. Ndlovu (2016) 'Figurative and Symbolic Function of Animal Imagery in Packaging Human Behaviour in Ndebele and Shona Cultures', *South African Journal of African Languages*, 36 (2).
Marais, E. (1939) *My Friends the Baboons*. London: Methuen.
Marais, E. (1969) *The Soul of the Ape*. London: Penguin.
Marks, S. (1972) 'Khoisan Resistance to the Dutch in the Seventeenth and Eighteenth Centuries', *Journal of African History*, 13 (1).
Meine, C. (1999) 'It's about Time: Conservation Biology and History', *Conservation Biology*, 13 (1).
Mormile, J., and C. Hill (2017) 'Living with Urban Baboons: Exploring Attitudes and Their Implications for Local Baboon Conservation and Management in Knysna, South Africa', *Human Dimensions of Wildlife*, 22 (2).
Morris, D. (1967) *The Naked Ape: A Zoologist's Study of the Human Animal*. London: Jonathan Cape.
Niehaus, I. (1995) 'Witches of the Transvaal Lowveld and Their Familiars: Conceptions of Duality, Power and Desire', *Cahiers d'études africaines*, 35 (138–9).
Pahad, G. (2010) 'Social Behaviour and Crop Raiding in Chacma Baboons of the Suikerbosrand Nature Reserve'. MSc thesis, University of the Witwatersrand.
Ritvo, H. (1997) *The Platypus and the Mermaid and Other Figments of the Classifying Imagination*. Cambridge, MA: Harvard University Press.
Ritvo, H. (2007) 'On the Animal Turn', *Daedalus*, 136 (4).
Ritvo, H. (2010) *Noble Cows and Hybrid Zebras: Essays on Animals & History*. Charlottesville: University of Virginia Press.
Robin, L., and W. Steffen (2007) 'History for the Anthropocene'. *History Compass*, 5 (5).
Rowell, T. (1972) *Social Behaviour of Monkeys*. Harmondsworth: Penguin.
Rowell, T. (1974) 'The Concept of Social Dominance', *Behavioral Biology*, 11 (2).
Russell, E. (2011) *Evolutionary History: Uniting History and Biology to Understand Life on Earth*. Cambridge: Cambridge University Press.
Sheail, J. (1986) 'Nature Conservation and the Agricultural Historian', *Agricultural History Review*, 34 (1).
Smail, D.L. (2008) *On Deep History and the Brain*. Berkeley: University of California Press.
Stoltz, L.P., and M.E. Keith (1973) 'A Population Survey of Chacma Baboon in the Northern Transvaal', *Journal of Human Evolution*, 2 (3).
Stoltz, L.P., and G.S. Saayman (1970) 'Ecology and Behaviour of Baboons in the Northern Transvaal', *Annals of the Transvaal Museum*, 26 (5).
Strum, S. (2001) *Almost Human: A Journey into the World of Baboons*. Chicago: University of Chicago Press.

Strum, S. (2012) 'The Good, the Bad and the Smart — What Makes Baboons So Difficult to Manage?', Baboon Expert Workshop, Cape Town, University of Cape Town.
Swart, S. (2010) *Riding High: Horses, Humans and History*. Johannesburg: Witwatersrand University Press.
Swart, S. (2016) 'Writing Animals into African History', *Critical African Studies*, 8 (2).
Swart, S. (2017) 'The Lion's Historian: Animal Histories from the South', Inaugural Address, Stellenbosch University.
Swart, S. (2018) 'History Eats Its Young: The Perils of Short-Termism in Understanding the Past', in G. Cederlöf and M. Rangarajan (eds), *At Nature's Edge*. Oxford: Oxford University Press.
Swart, S. (2019) 'Animals in African History', in *Oxford Research Encyclopaedia of African History*, https://oxfordre.com/africanhistory/view/10.1093/acrefore/9780190277734.001.0001/acrefore-9780190277734-e-443 (accessed 31 Mar. 2022).
Swedell, L. (2011) 'African Papionins: Diversity of Social Organization and Ecological Flexibility', in C.J. Campbell, A. Fuentes, K.C. MacKinnon, S. Bearder and M. Panger (eds), *Primates in Perspective*. Oxford: Oxford University Press.
Tiger, L. (1969) *Men in Groups*. London: Nelson.
Tiger, L., and R. Fox (1971) *The Imperial Animal*. London: Secker and Warburg.
Truth and Reconciliation Commission (2000) Amnesty hearing, 28 Feb., Hendrik Rakgotho, application AM0647/97, matter: killing of Violet Masomela, https://sabctrc.saha.org.za/documents/amntrans/johannesburg/54054.htm (accessed 31 Mar. 2022).
University of the Witwatersrand, Historical Papers Research Archives, South African Institute of Race Relations Archive, Collection AD843, A.B. Xuma Papers, 'The African Concept of Disease'.
Vagtborg, H. (1965) *The Baboon in Medical Research*. Austin: University of Texas Press.
Van de Berg, J., S. Williams-Blangero and S.D. Tardif (eds) (2009) *The Baboon in Biomedical Research*. Cham: Springer.
Van Doorn, A. (2009) 'The Interface between Socioecology and Management of Chacma Baboons (*Papio ursinus*) in the Cape Peninsula, South Africa'. DPhil thesis, University of Cape Town.
Van Rensburg, E.J., et al. (1998) 'Simian Immunodeficiency Viruses (SIVs) from Eastern and Southern Africa: Detection of a SIVagm Variant from a Chacma Baboon', *Journal of General Virology*, 79 (7).
Warren, S. (2020) 'Texas Baboon Troop Enlisted in Humankind's War on Coronavirus', Bloomberg, 7 Mar., www.bloombergquint.com/onweb/texas-baboon-troop-enlisted-in-humankind-s-war-on-coronavirus (accessed 10 Apr. 2020).
Warren, Y., J.P. Higham, A.M. Maclarnon and C. Ross (2011) 'Crop-Raiding and Commensalism in Olive Baboons: The Costs and Benefits of Living with Humans', in V. Sommer and C. Ross (eds), *Primates of Gashaka: Developments in Primatology: Progress and Prospects*. Cham: Springer.

Washburn, S.L., and I. DeVore (1961) 'The Social Life of Baboons', *Scientific American* 204 (6).

Wels, H., M. Spierenburg and J.B. Gewald (eds) (2018) *Nature Conservation in Southern Africa: Morality and Marginality: Towards Sentient Conservation?* Leiden: Brill.

Wright, J.B. (1971) *Bushman Raiders of the Drakensberg, 1840–1870*. Pietermaritzburg: University of Natal Press.

Wright, J.B. (2007) 'Bushman Raiders Revisited', in P. Skotnes (ed.), *Claim to the Country: The Archive of Lucy Lloyd and Wilhelm Bleek*. Johannesburg: Jacana Press.

Zuckerman, S. (1932) *The Social Life of Monkeys and Apes*. New York: Harcourt, Brace.

3

Black academics matter: history and antiblackness at South African universities

Janeke Thumbran

> I am first and foremost your professor. It is my duty to remind you that academics matter too.[1]

The debates that emerged in the wake of the 2015–17 student protests at South African universities raised several questions of historiographical importance: who produces historical knowledge, for what purposes, and which narratives ought to set the scholarly agenda? These questions informed the invitation for participants in this collection, to reexamine key debates within the historiographical tradition, to explore different methodologies, to think through new forms of curricula and pedagogical practice, and to explore the kinds of historical narratives and resources that are harnessed by contemporary political and social movements.

This chapter aims to think through the challenges of teaching history in the wake of the emergence of these movements. More particularly, it examines how student 'wokeness' in the aftermath of the protests, alongside the rise of consumer-based education, has served to reproduce black women's illegitimacy in the front of the lecture hall. Viewed in the context of the troubling history of South Africa's universities, and South African historiography's complicity with the colonial and apartheid order, black women's everyday experiences of teaching can only be described as an uphill battle. As a young black woman historian, teaching at a historically white university, I believe it is necessary to ask a set of critical questions about the intersections of race, gender, class and sexuality within South African historiography, and the process of the production and dissemination of knowledge within the discipline.

Unless otherwise stated, 'black' in this chapter refers to all nonwhite South Africans: Africans, 'coloureds' and Indians. The term 'coloured' will be accompanied by single quotes to signify the historically problematic and contested nature of that racial category.

Teaching while black

In the edited volume *Stories from the Front of the Room: How Higher Education Faculty of Color Overcome Challenges and Thrive in the Academy*, black academics at historically white and black universities in the United States document their experiences. Their contributions highlight how encounters with students inside the classroom constitute some of the greatest obstacles to promotion and tenure, and contribute to an overall dissatisfaction with their choice of profession. Their papers reveal that black academics are considered to lack scholarly credibility by students, who undermine their authority and expertise in subtle and not-so-subtle ways. Students often directly challenge their credentials and intellect and engage in problematic behaviours, including disrespectful or dismissive speech, and bypassing them in reporting grievances to authorities higher up in the university system.[2]

The authors highlight how course evaluations – where students evaluate a lecturer's effectiveness, course organisation and forms of assessment – affect hiring, promotions, pay rises and opportunities for awards. Yet a growing body of research suggests that a lecturer's race, gender, age and accent affect how they will be evaluated.[3] In the context of the rise of 'client-based' education, the weighting given to teaching evaluations has placed black academics in an invidious position. Cast as product suppliers who are expected to cater to students' expectations, evaluations are likely to reflect the biases of students as much as – if not more than – the performance of the lecturer, or the knowledge gained by the student. *Stories from the Front of the Room* also highlights that mentoring represents another fraught area of the lecturer/student interaction. Black academics have reported that they are often the last to be approached to serve as supervisors and mentors, based on the assumption that white academics are more qualified. Yet despite having fewer formal supervisees, black academics mentor many marginalised students on campus through informal means, helping them navigate the same isolating institutional cultures from which the academics themselves suffer.[4]

The chapters chime with my own experience at Rhodes University, where I am usually the last to be approached by students to supervise their work, yet I am usually the first lecturer they will approach concerning racial or sexual harassment and discrimination. Disrespectful and dismissive speech and the consistent undermining of my knowledge and expertise – which contrasts with an unquestioning deference towards my white and older colleagues – form part of my daily encounters with students. One of the most frequent ways in which students undermine my qualifications is to consistently refer to me as 'Miss', despite the fact that the sign on my office door, my course outlines and contact information, all indicate that I hold a DPhil. That I am the only black woman, and the youngest academic in my department (and the only one at the rank of 'lecturer'),[5] along with the fact that my colleagues are mostly white and middle-aged, helps reinforce students' perception that I am not fully qualified to teach them. Although perhaps not intentional on their part, students' refusal and/or inability to acknowledge my academic credentials speaks to a system that downplays the achievements of black women and their hard-earned place at the front of the classroom.[6]

While my age, gender and race do not constitute me as an *intellectual authority* in the classroom, the trope of the 'angry Black woman'[7] has instead positioned me as an *authoritarian* figure to some students. In *Stories from the Front of the Room*, Delores Mullins discusses some of the dominant stereotypes black women academics encounter in the classroom:

> Antiblack racism shapes the discourse of my position as a black woman teacher who is said to have 'high expectations', which results in certain failure for students; I am 'a hard marker', which means that I 'don't give A's'; my toughness drives students to tears; and my unapproachability invokes fear among students, staff, and faculty.[8]

In addition to being seen as inordinately 'strict',[9] my unwillingness to compromise my academic integrity and accept incomplete or incoherent work has placed me at odds with several students. I am often blamed for their academic challenges – despite offering critical feedback and demonstrating my commitment to supporting those who are prepared to do the work. I have also been accused of 'colluding' with the institution and upholding 'colonial' standards of education. These charges call into question both my ethical and political commitment to support and mentor black students, and my credibility as an academic. However, there are also a variety of additional factors that shape these interactions with students.

Since 1994, black student enrolment at Rhodes has steadily increased. By 2014, the total black enrolment (African, 'coloured' and Indian) stood at 64 per cent, with female enrolment just under 60 per cent.[10] Many of the students are working class and are among the first in their families to attend university, while others form part of what is now an established black middle class.[11] Black students also make up the majority of the 18 per cent of the overall student population who are international students.[12] Rhodes's white student population has also historically shown diversity in terms of national origin. In 1945, a number of 'Rhodesian' ex-servicemen enrolled at the institution, and by 1976, 'predominantly conservative white Rhodesian students' constituted as much as 30 per cent of the student body.[13] Based on my own observations, it is not uncommon for white students from Zimbabwe, Namibia and Kenya to enrol at Rhodes.

This cultural diversity within the student corps also shapes the experience of black women academics at Rhodes. For instance, it is not surprising for a black woman academic to be challenged or undermined by male students who have had little exposure to women in positions of authority (or for students who hold specific religious or patriarchal ideas to harass queer and/or trans academics).[14]

Problematic behaviours from students speak to a broader range of challenges that black academics have encountered since the restructuring of South Africa's institutions at the end of apartheid. These challenges have been highlighted in a number of publications. Magubane and Mabokela's *Hear Our Voices*, published in 2004, aimed to expose the racist and sexist practices of institutions and to gauge their impact on black scholars, and women particularly. The essays sought to both give voice to the varied experiences of black women academics and explore alternative theoretical and methodological frameworks through which to analyse the politics of teaching and research in South African universities.[15] In one essay, Cheryl-Ann Potgieter and Anne-Gloria Senkgane Moleko discuss the experiences of black women at historically white institutions. They found that in addition to not being taken seriously as academics and being blamed for students' academic challenges, black women were often expected to conform to historical patterns of stereotyping that had traditionally cast black people – and especially women – as the caregivers for (white and black) children. To illustrate the pervasiveness of this practice in historically white institutions, Potgieter and Moleko drew on the late bell hooks's observation that:

> Racist and sexist assumptions that black women are somehow 'innately' more capable of caring for others continues to permeate cultural thinking about Black female roles. As a consequence, Black women in all walks of life, from corporate professionals and university professors to service workers, complain that colleagues, co-workers and supervisors, etc. ask them to assume a multipurpose caretaker role … to be the nurturing breast – to be the mammy.[16]

The expectation that black women academics should serve as 'nurturers' rather than knowledge producers is largely supported by the fact that most are concentrated on the lower rungs of higher education ladder. This was highlighted by the 2008 report of the Ministerial Committee on Transformation in Higher Education, which was tasked with investigating discrimination in public institutions. It found that while women constituted just under 50 per cent of academic staff, they were primarily concentrated at the levels of junior lecturer or lecturer, with few in the professoriate.[17] In addition to documenting women's lack of representation at higher levels in institutions, the report also found that black academics in general were not accorded the same respect as white lecturers. Black lecturers reported that students would tell them to 'go and learn to speak English properly'. When challenged about these attitudes, students accused the black lecturers of being 'oversensitive'.[18] The report also claimed that white academics – including women

– did not experience the same challenges. In fact, white academics were, on the whole, 'optimistic about the state of transformation, and there was a general feeling amongst them that racial tension had receded'.[19]

Dismissive behaviour from white academics is a common thread in the literature on black women's experiences in academia, but Matseliso Mokhele's 2013 case study of a black woman academic's journey to the professoriate suggests that resistance and a lack of support from black male counterparts also form a major obstacle.[20] Pryah Mahabeer, Nomkhosi Nzimande and Makhosi Shoba pointed out in a 2018 article that female academics of colour also participate in the exclusion and marginalisation of other black women through a form of internalised and horizontal oppression, whereby they collude in supporting dismissive and infantilising behaviours from male colleagues.[21]

These intricate connections between race and gender were an important theme in *Black Academic Voices: The South African Experience*, a volume which appeared in 2019. The contributors to the book were mostly black women, and they used their own experiences to provide a contemporary analysis of the state of race relations in the country's tertiary institutions. Allison Geduld and Edith Phaswana reflected on the classroom as a space that held possibilities for creating radical change, despite the fact that teaching was becoming increasingly undervalued owing to financial incentives being tied to 'research outputs'.[22] They were, however, also frank about the labour that black women are expected to perform as tokens of demographic transformation, especially in historically white institutions. Geduld wrote that *doing* the work of transformation involves challenging students to grapple critically with antiblackness and its intersection with gender, sexuality, age and nationality.[23] Failure to do so means that black academics are often undermined and questioned by white students, while they are also expected to manage the expectations of black students who have never encountered black authority in an educational context.[24]

Despite a number of development and mentorship programmes aimed at increasing the presence and advancement of black women at historically white universities,[25] the picture painted by Geduld and Phaswana mirrors my own experience in the classroom of a historically white institution. These experiences are symptomatic of an institutional history and culture that still privilege whiteness and class-based elitism.[26] The fact that these institutional cultures formed part of everyday experience at the so-called liberal universities (of Rhodes, University of Cape Town (UCT), Witwatersrand (Wits) and, by some definitions, Natal) calls into question what these particular institutions have already 'foreclosed' for black women academics in terms of the possibilities of them being recognised as legitimate teachers and knowledge producers in those spaces.

Like the other English-language institutions, Rhodes University was established in tandem with the emergence of the modern South African state at the turn of the twentieth century, but those years also saw the colonial authorities face the question of how to meet the labour demands of an industrialising economy centred on the extraction of mineral wealth. A solution was found in the coercion and exploitation of black African labour. The profits extracted by those means were used to fund the establishment of the liberal universities. UCT was established through the bequest of mining magnate Otto Beit, while Randlords such as Alfred Beit and Julius Wernher also made significant contributions.[27] Similarly, Wits University's origins lie in the South African School of Mines, which was established in Kimberley before moving to Johannesburg.[28] As far as Rhodes is concerned, in the 1890s educationalists began issuing calls to establish a university in the Eastern Cape, with Grahamstown the preferred location. In 1903, a subcommittee tasked with the founding of the university decided that it should be named in honour of Cecil John Rhodes, and that the Rhodes Trust should be approached for funding. One of the trustees of Rhodes's estate, Leander Jameson (known for his involvement in the Jameson Raid of 1895–96) was instrumental in founding the university through the provision of a grant of £50,000 in the form of De Beers shares. Rhodes University enrolled its first students in 1904, and though the naming of the institution was motivated initially by the desire to draw on the estate of the Cape Colony's former Prime Minister, the university would in time enthusiastically embrace the 'Imperial idea in South Africa'.[29]

While they were funded, in effect, by the blood, sweat and toil of black mineworkers, the 'liberal' institutions never envisioned themselves to be spaces for black students, teachers and/or knowledge producers. In "A Pigment of Imagination?", Zine Magubane traces Rhodes's beliefs about the place of educated black people in a 'white man's Africa'. In an 1894 speech proposing that hut taxes be used for building industrial training schools,[30] Rhodes warned against rearing a 'native intelligentsia' grounded in liberal education:

> I have travelled through the Transkei and I have found some excellent establishments where natives are taught Latin and Greek. They are turning out Kaffir parsons, most excellent individuals, but the thing is overdone. I find that these people cannot find congregations for them. There are Kaffir parsons everywhere – these institutions are turning them out by the dozen. They are turning out a dangerous class ... [T]he country is overstocked with them. These people will not go back and work, and that is why I say that the regulations of these industrial schools should be framed by the Government; otherwise these Kaffir parsons would develop into agitators against the Government.[31]

Rhodes's opinions on the place of 'educated natives' were shared by white policymakers. Magubane cites the South African Native Races Committee's 1908 report on 'The South African Natives: Their Progress and Present Condition', which concluded that 'the instruction given in many of the schools is ill adapted to the needs of native children. The education has generally been too bookish.'[32]

From such discourses emerged the figure of the 'school Kaffir' – an effeminate, work-shy drifter. Magubane suggests that this discourse rendered the figure of the educated 'native' as biologically male but sociologically female (it coincidentally rendered inconceivable the possibility of the existence of black African intellectuals).[33]

It is clear that at the time of the creation of the South African university, the state's priority was to filter black Africans into the 'appropriate' sectors of the economy, where their exploitation would finance higher education, which would produce the brains trust for the state and its institutions. Such a system would foreclose the possibility of academics such as myself being seen as legitimate knowledge producers. When the National Party came to power in 1948, the exclusion of black people (and women in particular) from white institutions became even more firmly entrenched. The Extension of University Education Act of 1959 not only ended the enrolment of black students at the liberal English-language universities like Rhodes,[34] but also created separate universities for black Africans, 'coloureds' and Indians. By the early 1990s, twenty-two universities existed in South Africa, all divided along racial, ethnic and linguistic lines.[35] Ten of these twenty-two were white universities, all of which reflected existing divisions between Afrikaners and English speakers: Stellenbosch, Pretoria, the Orange Free State and the Rand Afrikaans University all became incubators of Afrikaner nationalism, while Wits, UCT, Rhodes and Natal were designated 'liberal' institutions, with the bilingual Port Elizabeth and University of South Africa lying in between. Black universities were also divided along racial and ethnic lines: the University of the Western Cape for 'coloureds', the University of Durban Westville for Indians, the University of Zululand for Zulus, the University of the North for Sothos, Vendas, Tsongas and Tswanas, and the oldest historically black university in South Africa, Fort Hare, being repurposed as an institution for Xhosas.[36] The establishment of these universities was specifically tied to the project of separate development: while the black 'ethnic' institutions were expected to produce the professional class (teachers, social workers, nurses, etc.) that would serve the Bantustans, the 'coloured' and Indian universities had the task of producing graduates to assume positions in coloured and Indian affairs departments.[37]

Given its colonial history, I was never intended to be a student at Rhodes University, much less a lecturer. Under the apartheid system, my rightful place would have been as a consumer of racially coded knowledge at the University of the Western Cape. It is perhaps unsurprising, given this context, that I would encounter such resistance in the space of the classroom.

Antiblackness and South African historiography

However, it is not merely the history of Rhodes University, or the history of colonial and apartheid education in general, that renders me as an illegitimate presence in the front of the classroom. It is within the space of the *history* classroom, and from my position as a young black woman *historian*, that I have had challenging encounters with students. What has the discipline of history already foreclosed? What are the possibilities for black women historians to be constituted not only as legitimate teachers in that disciplinary space but also as knowledge producers?

In thinking through these questions, I draw on two texts, which were published more than twenty years apart, that critically reflect on the means by which South African historiography has been produced in the past – namely, Premesh Lalu's *The Deaths of Hintsa* and Windsor Leroke's 'Koze Kube Nini'.

In *The Deaths of Hintsa*, Lalu takes a highly publicised event from 1996 as the point of departure for his investigation. A few years after the end of formal apartheid, a healer named Nicholas Gcaleka claimed to have recovered the skull of the early nineteenth-century Xhosa leader Hintsa in an unlikely location: Scotland. Though Gcaleka believed his discovery and the repatriation of Hintsa's skull would unite the country, attempts were immediately launched by journalists and scientists to prove that his claims were false. In doing so, they drew on evidence sourced from the colonial archive, and they succeeded in rendering the healer a public laughing stock. Lalu, however, interpreted the incident as a demonstration of how colonial modes of evidence continued to dominate discussions about the past. He asked: 'how could a form of evidence once used to cover up acts of violence be depended on to offer us an escape from the violence of the apartheid past?'[38]

Lalu explicitly framed his own work as an attempt to take Gcaleka seriously, arguing that the healer offered an alternate way of thinking about the past. Thus, the book's overall argument was that ideas and practices related to the epistemic privileging of archival research have produced and reproduced forms of subjection which continue to haunt the present. Against powerful historiographical currents in the South African academy (such as social history) that have claimed to unearth African agency, Lalu argued that the archive had already foreclosed such possibilities. He added that by analysing the traditional archive and its rootedness in colonial epistemology, historians could, alternatively, trace the subjection of agency and in that manner develop emancipatory practices. In his words: 'we need more histories of concepts, discourses, representations, narratives and formations of subjectivities which might eventually lead us to the rupture we desire'.[39]

Lalu's intervention has been influential in my own research, particularly my DPhil, which examined the appropriation by the University of Pretoria (UP) of the 'coloured' township of Eersterust as a site for the institution's research and community outreach.[40] My sources consisted of the curricula in UP's Social Work and Sociology departments from 1932 to 1990, the published output of its sociologists and the engagement performed by its students in the township. By reading this archive as an apparatus that produced and reproduced subjection through its discourses, my DPhil shifted its historiographical focus away from 'coloured' identities, towards the ways that the community was constituted over time through the disciplines of social work and sociology at institutions like UP. That this archive consisted primarily of Afrikaans sources also demanded a close and critical engagement. Not only do the majority of 'coloureds' in South Africa claim Afrikaans as their mother tongue, but this was also ironically the very language through which 'coloured' subjection was conceived and executed under apartheid. By paying close attention to the significance of Afrikaans terms such as *kleurling* (coloured), *voogdyskap* (trusteeship/guardianship) and *self-beskikking* (self-reliance), my project drew heavily on Lalu's call to question and scrutinise how the colonial and/or apartheid archive *itself* has been assembled.

More than twenty years before the publication of *The Deaths of Hintsa*, Windsor Leroke presented a seminar paper, '*Koze Kube Nini*: The Violence of Representation and the Politics of Social Research in South Africa', which pointed to various ways in which approaches to social sciences research – including the production of South African historiography – have reproduced racial domination. Leroke's initial presentation was to the Wits History Workshop in 1994. He argued that while most disciplines within the social sciences acknowledged to varying degrees the social context of their research, very few questioned their methodology or disciplinary claims of 'objectivity' and 'rationality'. Moreover, this research was not seen by social scientists to be linked to apartheid structures. For Leroke, this obliviousness overlooked the extent to which the guiding concepts of social research reflected practices that were linked to social domination. Consequently, while social research had often critiqued certain aspects of apartheid, it had typically ignored disciplinary complicity in the perpetuation of racial inequality.[41]

In order to substantiate these claims, Leroke outlined the two primary trajectories along which social research developed in South Africa in the

1970s and 1980s. The first involved 'apartheid research' as produced at Afrikaans-speaking institutions in explicit support of the system, while the second, referred to as 'radical research', emerged within the English-speaking 'liberal' institutions. Leroke argued, however, that liberal scholarship advanced political agendas through similar, even complementary, research methodologies to its conservative counterparts, without interrogating the implications of these commonalities. What was truly distinctive about radical research, according to Leroke, was its vocal preoccupation with 'the African oppressed', the marginalised and 'history from below'. Against these presumptions, he argued that despite radical scholarship's contributions and its attempts to 'demarginalise the silent African presence', this scholarship produced a rigid dualism of the subject and object. For instance, when black Africans were not the objects of research, they served as informants and assistants rather than as the producers of knowledge. Radical research developed within this frame, in which the object/source of social research has been (and continues to be) black people, and the researcher/writer, the white intellectual. As such, not only did this reproduce the dominance of white historians, but it perpetuated the subjugation of black South Africans.[42]

Leroke concluded his paper with the following questions: how could the politically legitimate concerns of radical research be achieved through this kind of social research, which is founded on the problematic of subject/object dualism? To what extent are such researches a challenge to apartheid social relations? To what extent is there an attempt to subvert apartheid relations through these research acts? Who really speaks in such texts? Who writes? In short, what is happening to the African object in these texts?[43]

Leroke's paper has resonated with the experiences and concerns of a number of black female academics. In Sharon Welsh and Jon Soske's 2016 volume *Ties That Bind: Race and the Politics of Friendship in South Africa*, contributors Mosa Phadi and Nomancotsho Phakade took up Leroke's discussion of the subject/object dualism and described their own experiences as 'native informants – as research objects which are both represented and which have to learn the skills of representing themselves' in white academia.[44] Phadi and Phakade's assertion that contemporary forms of knowledge production render black women as research objects demonstrates how the effects produced by the premises of social research – including forms of historical research – continue to linger in South African institutions. Both the reliance on the colonial archive – which according to Lalu already foreclosed the possibilities for a recovery of black (and female) agency – and the constitution of black people (women) as research objects account for the discipline's complicity in rendering black women as illegitimate teachers and knowledge producers.[45]

In 2012, Jon Soske raised the question of why South African history continued to be written primarily by white scholars. He referred specifically to the *Cambridge History of South Africa*, which appeared in two volumes in 2010 and 2012. A work of enormous labour, the *Cambridge History*'s one-thousand-page summation of radical/revisionist scholarship was notable for a striking minority of black contributors – an oddity after over forty years of self-consciously progressive praxis. The editors were mostly left-leaning historians, belonging to what Leroke called the tradition of 'radical research', and all had long and unquestionable commitments to writing antiracist history. While this deficit might be attributed to the toxic heritage of South African white supremacy, the economic challenges faced by many black students and the institutional crisis of the postapartheid university, Soske suggested that to so argue would be to gloss over the fact that a large and diverse body of historical writing already existed by black scholars, many of whom had made important contributions over many decades. In fact, he argued that if one included all university-employed academics doing historical work in other fields (sociology, art history, literary studies included) black intellectuals could have predominated. Soske suggested that the ultimate reason might lie in the criteria used for deciding who counts as a historian in the South African context.[46]

Soske argued that the shortage of black writers in the volumes offered an opportunity to raise uncomfortable questions regarding race within South African historiography. He wrote that although such discussions raged in spaces like conference-organising and hiring committees, there rarely seemed to be a robust public conversation on the overall whiteness of the field. Instead, dominant historiographical approaches, underwritten as they were by 'liberal scripts of voice giving and racial atonement', had foreclosed such conversations. For Soske, these prevailing historiographical approaches were often accompanied by the expectation that emerging black scholars would continue working within the moulds created by radical scholarship. This presumption meant that the work of black scholars situated in, for instance, postcolonial theory, was often missing not only from edited volumes that constitute the historiography of this field but also from course outlines and curricula.[47]

'Woke' but antiblack?

Some of the critical issues that Soske raised have been echoed by students in the various movements that have emerged over the last few years – particularly those demanding the 'decolonisation' of South African universities. The upsurge also reignited conversations about the shortage of black academics in the country. Jacob Dlamini estimated that after over forty years of self-consciously progressive South African history, there were only about thirty professional historians of African, 'coloured' and Indian descent in South Africa, and only about twelve of them were women.[48]

I argue that the reasons for the marginalisation of black female academics are explicable in part when considering the performative 'wokeness' that has informed these student movements, because both processes were ultimately nourished in the same intellectual soil. By 2015, when students attempted to resist the commodification of education by calling for free, quality and 'decolonised' education, the demographics of universities – particularly at historically white institutions like UCT, Rhodes, UP and Stellenbosch – had changed significantly since 1994. Yet black students argued that their campus experience remained alienating. They argued that universities continued to cater for white, middle-class, heterosexual men, especially at the level of the professoriate, where white men continued to hold the most power and influence. In critiquing the status quo, student movements drew on arguments from the Black Consciousness and pan-Africanist traditions.[49]

The student protest wave began in March 2015 with the emergence of the '#RhodesMustFall' movement at UCT. Students at UCT centred their protest around the statue of the imperialist Cecil John Rhodes, which sat in a position of prominence on the university's upper campus. They also articulated a range of demands around the inadequate transformation of staff components and curricula, and inadequate funding for poor students. By October 2015, the student ferment had expanded across the country, while simultaneously narrowing its focus to the theme of fee increases, which were unaffordable for the majority of black students. Nationwide protests initiated by '#FeesMustFall' that month managed to secure zero fee increases for 2016. The focus of the protests expanded again in 2016, to include the outsourcing of labour and the medium of instruction at former Afrikaans institutions,[50] while black women students at Rhodes University protested both rape culture and the institution's inadequate responses to it.[51]

Although a new cohort of students enters the universities every year, the claims made by the students between 2015 and 2017 continue to resonate today. But given the broad focus of the demands, the continuing lack of credibility and legitimacy afforded to black academics by many students can only be interpreted as ironic. It is by no means unusual, for example, for students to on the one hand call for decolonisation, while on the other hand offering little reflection on how their dismissals of black academics – and young black female academics in particular – reinforce the power structures established by colonialism that they claim to want to dismantle.

I teach a third-year course titled 'The University in South Africa: Past and Present', which provides students with an overview of how universities developed, how they were intertwined with the project of colonialism and apartheid, and how they continue to be shaped by these legacies in the present day. The decision to design and teach this course stemmed from my doctoral research. Eersterust is also the very township to which my family was forcibly removed in the 1960s, and where I was born and raised. The course and its contents articulate, in part, some of my own experiences as a black and working-class undergraduate student at UP between 2004 and 2007. It is precisely in teaching such courses, where students are asked to use the methodological skills of history (*inter alia*, to think critically about the university as an institution, its disciplines, its forms of knowledge production, and its forms of antiblackness and xenophobia),[52] that students have challenged my knowledge and expertise. This has often been done in the context of the classroom by drawing on a vocabulary of 'wokeness'. For example, several students will challenge my selection of course readings on the basis that the language of the text is 'triggering' or that the author's argument lacks 'intersectionality'. Not only does this demonstrate an unwillingness to engage with my intellectual and pedagogical reasons for selecting the readings, it also undermines my ability to design and structure the course. This kind of opposition to course readings – premised on language and the identity politics of wokeness – forms the basis from which students can claim that I am upholding 'colonial' forms of knowledge.

This raises the question of wokeness, its meaning and potential import. According to Abas Mirzaei, the term 'woke' was first used in 1942 in the first volume of the *Negro Digest*, where J. Saunders Redding used it in an article about labour unions.[53] In literal terms, it refers to being 'awake' in the sense of being alert to social and political injustice. In the twenty-first-century context, wokeness reemerged through social movements like #BlackLivesMatter, whose followers committed themselves to challenge the deeply entrenched white supremacist ideologies that underpinned the brutalisation and killing of African American males in the United States.[54] Contemporary far-right movements such as the Alternative Right (or Alt-Right), by contrast, deride wokeness as merely the latest iteration of 'political correctness', a term of abuse dating from culture wars a generation previously.[55]

Wokeness, according to Hussein Badat, has morphed into a North American 'cultural behemoth' that subsumes local political discourse and praxis. Enabled by the wide penetration – at least amongst the new middle class – of social media platforms such as Twitter, Facebook and Instagram, wokeness adopts products of US popular culture. However, as expressed in universities in the South African periphery, it tends to ignore important material differences between the two contexts. The result is a largely symbolic wokeness, represented by the policing of speech and thought through 'call-out' or 'cancel' culture.[56] This performativity of wokeness – when not displayed in classroom discussions – is often reflected in course evaluations. Paul Gilroy, one of the most critical black scholars on race and empire, has reflected on his own encounters with students by writing: 'One recent evaluation I received included a passing comment saying that one of my classes wasn't "a safe space" for black students ... I think it means that I wasn't offering the scripted responses warranted by internet racial politics. I wasn't, for example ... saying, "intersectionality" to mean the same thing they mean'. He added, 'this updated language of identity politics is spread, virally, via the computer. If you don't follow the resulting doxa you are likely to become an object of the "call-out culture" – which is where people get told off and bullied either into silence or agreement.'[57]

Course evaluations, following the example set in North America, where mobile apps allow one to 'rate' a service, form part of the same neoliberal commodification of higher education that student movements have targeted through protest. However, in the aftermath of these movements, course evaluations, as well as interactions with students in the classroom, have become an arena in which students can undermine knowledge and expertise by policing academics' language, calling them out, or even reporting them to authorities higher up in the system with the aim of cancelling them, when we don't follow 'the scripted responses of internet racial politics'. Combined with the historical illegitimacy of black women as teachers at historically white universities and their position as research objects in the field of South African history, wokeness produces tenuous conditions for us to teach under, while ironically reinforcing the pervasive antiblackness at work in our institutions and disciplines.

Many black academics remain deeply passionate about teaching, despite their often-negative experiences with students. Many more remain silent about these experiences for fear of student backlash or that they may be seen as 'sell-outs'. While I believe that the history classroom is a space in which radical change can be enacted, I do not believe that it should come at the expense of black women, who have fought long and hard battles simply to be able to stand in the front of the classroom. Until universities are willing to grapple with the ways in which the legacy of colonialism and apartheid has converged with contemporary neoliberal practices – and until the field of South African history is prepared to dismantle its antiblack gatekeeping – I do not foresee a future in which black women academics will matter to students.

Notes

1 V. Ng, 'In Solidarity, Dear Student', in M. Harris, S.L. Sellers, O. Clerge and F.W. Gooding Jr (eds), *Stories from the Front of the Room: How Higher Education*

Faculty of Color Overcome Challenges and Thrive in the Academy (Lanham, MD: Rowman and Littlefield, 2017), 58–60.
2 See Harris et al., *Front of the Room*.
3 A. Boring, K. Ottoboni and P.B. Starks, 'Student Evaluations of Teaching Are Not Only Unreliable, They Are Significantly Biased against Female Instructors', London School of Economics (LSE) *Impact Blog*, 4 Feb. 2016, https://blogs.lse.ac.uk/impactofsocialsciences/2016/02/04/student-evaluations-of-teaching-gender-bias/ (accessed 17 July 2019).
4 Harris et al., *Front of the Room*, 44–5.
5 More than half of all academic staff at Rhodes University are white, and black African women account for only 7 per cent of the institution's 105 professors/associate professors. Rhodes University, *Institutional Development Plan* (2018–22), 27.
6 Harris et al., *Front of the Room*, 57.
7 M. Adhikari, '"God Made the White Man, God Made the Black Man…": Popular Racial Stereotyping of Coloured People in Apartheid South Africa', *South African Historical Journal*, 55, 2006, 142–64.
8 Harris et al., *Front of the Room*, 52.
9 According to first- and third-year course evaluations.
10 P. Maylam, *Rhodes University, 1904–2016: An Intellectual, Political and Cultural History* (Grahamstown: ISER, 2017), 340–1.
11 R. Southall, *The New Black Middle Class in South Africa* (Auckland Park: Jacana, 2016), 43.
12 Rhodes University, *Institutional Development Plan*, 16.
13 S.A. Greyling, 'Rhodes University during the Segregation and Apartheid Eras, 1933–1990' (MA thesis, Rhodes University, 2007), 29 (quote), 124.
14 For instance, in 2009, Natalie Donaldson, lecturer in the Department of Psychology at Rhodes at the time, was harassed by a student after presenting a conference paper on lesbian representation in the media. See her 'What about the Queers? The Institutional Culture of Heteronormativity and Its Implications for Queer Staff and Students', in P. Tabensky and S. Matthews (eds), *Being at Home: Race, Institutional Culture and Transformation at South African Higher Education Institutions* (Scottsville: University of KwaZulu-Natal Press, 2015), 130–46.
15 Z. Magubane, 'Introduction', in R. Mabokela and Z. Magubane (eds), *Hear Our Voices: Race, Gender and the Status of Black South African Women in the Academy* (Pretoria: University of South Africa Press, 2004), 1–9.
16 C. Potgieter and A.S. Moleko, 'Stand Out, Stand Up, Move Out: Experiences of Black South African Women at Historically White Universities', in Mabokela and Magubane, *Hear Our Voices*, 80–95.
17 Department of Education, *Report of the Ministerial Committee on Transformation and Social Cohesion and the Elimination of Discrimination in Public Higher Education Institutions* (2008), 53, https://ukzn.ac.za/wp-content/miscFiles/publications/ReportonHEandTransformation.pdf (accessed 31 Mar. 2022).
18 Department of Education, *Report*, 56. See also S. Matthews, 'White Privilege and Institutional Culture', in Tabensky and Matthews, *Being at Home*, 72–95.
19 Department of Education, *Report*, 59.

20 M. Mokhele, 'Reflections of Black Women Academics at South African Universities: A Narrative Case Study', *Mediterranean Journal of Social Sciences*, 4 (3) 2013, 611–19.
21 P. Mahabeer, N. Nzimande and M. Shoba, 'Academics of Colour: Experiences of Emerging Black Women Academics in Curriculum Studies at a University in South Africa', *Agenda*, 32 (2) 2018, 28–42.
22 E.D. Phaswana, 'The Limits of Being and Knowledge in the Academy', in G. Khunou, H. Canham, K. Khoza-Shangaze and E.D. Phaswana (eds), *Black Academic Voices: The South African Experience* (Pretoria: HSRC Press, 2019), 157–77.
23 A. Geduld, 'Belonging to Oneself', in Khunou et al., *Black Academic Voices*, 195–213.
24 Phaswana, 'Limits of Being', 174.
25 D. Z. Belluigi and G, Thondhlana, '"Why Mouth All the Pieties?" Black and Women Academics' Revelations about Discourses of "Transformation" at an Historically White South African University', *Higher Education*, 78, 2019, 947–63.
26 T. Njovane, 'The Violence beneath the Veil of Politeness: Reflections on Race and Power in the Academy', in Tabensky and Matthews, *Being at Home*, 72–95.
27 H. Phillips, *The University of Cape Town, 1918–1948: The Formative Years* (Cape Town: University of Cape Town Press, 1993), 2.
28 B.K. Murray, *Wits – the Early Years: A History of the University of the Witwatersrand, Johannesburg, and Its Precursors, 1896–1939* (Johannesburg: University of the Witwatersrand Press, 1982), 7, 11.
29 P. Maylam, *The Cult of Rhodes: Remembering an Imperialist in Africa* (Claremont: David Phillip, 2005), 64–6 (quote at 65).
30 Z. Magubane, 'A Pigment of Imagination? Race, Subjectivity, Knowledge and the Image of the Black Intellectual', in Mabokela and Magubane, *Hear Our Voices*, 41–58.
31 *Ibid.*; F. Verschoyle, *Cecil Rhodes: His Political Life and Speeches, 1881–1900* (London: Chapman Hall, 1900), 382.
32 South African Native Races Committee, *The South African Natives: Their Progress and Present Condition* (London: John Murray, 1908), 177.
33 Magubane, 'Pigment of Imagination?', 49–50.
34 B.K. Murray, 'Wits as an "Open" University, 1939–1959: Black Admissions to the University of the Witwatersrand,' *Journal of Southern African Studies*, 16 (4) 1990, 649–76.
35 R.O. Mabokela and K.L. King, 'Introduction', in R.O. Mabokela and K.L. King (eds), *Apartheid No More: Case Studies of Southern African Universities in the Process of Transformation* (Westport, CT: Greenwood, 2001), xi–xxiii.
36 *Ibid.*, xiv.
37 S. Badat, *Black Student Politics: Higher Education and Apartheid from SASO to SANSCO, 1968–1990* (New York: Routledge Falmer, 2002), 61–3.
38 P. Lalu, *The Deaths of Hintsa: Postapartheid South Africa and the Shape of Recurring Pasts* (Cape Town: HSRC Press, 2009), 7.
39 *Ibid.*, 258–9.

40 J.D. Thumbran, 'The "Coloured Question" and the University of Pretoria: Separate Development, Trusteeship and Self Reliance, 1933–2012' (DPhil thesis, University of Minnesota, 2018).
41 W. Leroke, '*Koze Kube Nini*? The Violence of Representation and the Politics of Social Research in South Africa', University of the Witwatersrand History Workshop, 13–15 July 1994, 9, https://wiredspace.wits.ac.za/bitstream/handle/10539/7896/HWS-246.pdf?sequence=1&isAllowed=y (accessed 31 Mar. 2022).
42 *Ibid.*, 13.
43 *Ibid.*, 21–2.
44 M. Phadi and N. Phakhade, 'The Native Informant Speaks Back to the Offer of Friendship in White Academia', in S. Welsh and J. Soske (eds), *Ties That Bind: Race and the Politics of Friendship in South Africa* (Johannesburg: University of the Witwatersrand Press, 2016), 288–307 (quote at 289).
45 C. Potgieter, *Black Academics on the Move: How Black South African Academics Account for Moving between Institutions or Leaving the Academic Profession* (Pretoria: Centre for Higher Education Transformation, 2002), 24.
46 J. Soske, 'Why Does South African History Continue to Be Written Primarily by White Scholars?', *Africa Is a Country*, 29 Nov. 2012, https://africasacountry.com/2012/11/why-does-south-african-history-continue-to-be-written-primarily-by-white-scholars (accessed 31 Mar. 2022).
47 *Ibid.* H. Pohlandt-McCormick, '*The Cambridge History of South Africa*: "We Live in Tragic Times"', *African Studies Review*, 55 (3) 2012, 183.
48 J. Dlamini, 'What Does the Decolonisation of Knowledge Mean for Black Historians?', Stellenbosch Institute for Advanced Study, 15 Sept. 2017, https://stias.ac.za/2017/09/what-does-the-decolonisation-of-knowledge-mean-for-black-historians-fellows-seminar-by-jacob-dlamini/ (accessed 31 Mar. 2022).
49 L. Naidoo, 'Contemporary Student Politics in South Africa: The Rise of the Black-Led Student Movements of #RhodesMustFall and #FeesMustFall in 2015', in A. Heffernan and N. Nieftagodien (eds), *Students Must Rise: Youth Struggle in South Africa before and beyond Soweto '76* (Johannesburg: University of the Witwatersrand Press, 2016), 181.
50 *Ibid.*,181–3.
51 J. Bradbury and J. Clark, '"Everything and the Kitchen Sink": Being "at Home" in South African Universities', in R. Pattman and R. Carolissen (eds), *Transforming Transformation in Research and Teaching at South African Universities* (Stellenbosch: SUN Press, 2018), 217–30.
52 C. Sehoole, 'The Bleak Side of Studying in South Africa', *Mail and Guardian*, 3 July 2015, https://mg.co.za/article/2015-07-03-the-bleak-side-of-studying-in-south-africa (accessed 26 Nov. 2019); K. Batizai, 'Black and Foreign: Negotiating Being Different in South Africa's Academy', in Khunou et al., *Black Academic Voices*, 81–102.
53 A. Mirzaei, 'Where "Woke" Came From and Why Marketers Should Think Twice before Jumping on the Social Activism Bandwagon', *Conversation*, 8 Sept. 2019, https://theconversation.com/where-woke-came-from-and-why-marketers-should-think-twice-before-jumping-on-the-social-activism-bandwagon-122713 (accessed 31 Mar. 2022).

54 K. Gatwiri, 'Ayishat Akanbi: Is Wokeness Robbing Us of Our Compassion?', Special Broadcasting Service (SBS), 7 Mar. 2019, www.sbs.com.au/topics/voices/culture/article/2019/02/28/ayishat-akanbi-wokeness-robbing-us-our-compassion (accessed 31 Mar. 2022).

55 O. van Heerden, 'Wokeness, the Political Economy of Racism and Who Can Lay Claim to Being Black', *Daily Maverick*, 3 June 2020, www.dailymaverick.co.za/opinionista/2020-06-03-wokeness-the-political-economy-of-racism-and-who-can-lay-claim-to-being-black/ (accessed 14 Jan. 2021).

56 H. Badat, 'Wokeness and the Professional Outrage Machine', *Africa Is a Country*, 3 Apr. 2018, https://africasacountry.com/2018/04/wokeness-and-the-professional-outrage-machine (accessed 31 Mar. 2022).

57 P. Gilroy, 'Paul Gilroy in Search of a Not Necessarily Safe Starting Point...', Open Democracy, 1 May 2016, www.opendemocracy.net/en/paul-gilroy-in-search-of-not-very-safe-starting-point/#.V0r1DOonY3Y.twitter (accessed 31 Mar. 2022).

Bibliography

Adhikari, M. (2006) '"God Made the White Man, God Made the Black Man...": Popular Racial Stereotyping of Coloured People in Apartheid South Africa', *South African Historical Journal*, 55.

Badat, H. (2018) 'Wokeness and the Professional Outrage machine', *Africa Is a Country*, 3 Apr. 2018, 3, https://africasacountry.com/2018/04/wokeness-and-the-professional-outrage-machine (accessed 31 Mar. 2022).

Badat, S. (2002) *Black Student Politics: Higher Education and Apartheid from SASO to SANSCO, 1968–1990*. New York: Routledge Falmer.

Batizai, K. (2019) 'Black and Foreign: Negotiating Being Different in South Africa's Academy', in Khunou et al., *Black Academic Voices*.

Belluigi, D.Z., and G. Thondhlana (2019) '"Why Mouth All the Pieties?" Black and Women Academics' Revelations about Discourses of "Transformation" at an Historically White South African University', *Higher Education*, 78.

Boring, A., K. Ottoboni and P.B. Starks (2016) 'Student Evaluations of Teaching Are Not Only Unreliable, They Are Significantly Biased against Female Instructors', London School of Economics (LSE) *Impact Blog*, 4 Feb., https://blogs.lse.ac.uk/impactofsocialsciences/2016/02/04/student-evaluations-of-teaching-gender-bias/ (accessed 17 July 2019).

Bradbury, J., and J. Clark (2018) '"Everything and the Kitchen Sink": Being "at Home" in South African Universities', in R. Pattman and R. Carolissen (eds), *Transforming Transformation in Research and Teaching at South African Universities*. Stellenbosch: SUN Press.

Department of Education (2008) *Report of the Ministerial Committee on Transformation and Social Cohesion and the Elimination of Discrimination in Public Higher Education Institutions*, https://ukzn.ac.za/wp-content/miscFiles/publications/ReportonHEandTransformation.pdf (accessed 31 Mar. 2022).

Dlamini, J. (2017) 'What Does the Decolonisation of Knowledge Mean for Black Historians?', Stellenbosch Institute for Advanced Study, 15 Sept., https://stias.ac.za/2017/09/what-does-the-decolonisation-of-knowledge-mean-for-black-historians-fellows-seminar-by-jacob-dlamini/ (accessed 31 Mar. 2022).

Donaldson, N. (2015) 'What about the Queers? The Institutional Culture of Heteronormativity and Its Implications for Queer Staff and Students', in Tabensky and Matthews, *Being at Home*.

Gatwiri, K. (2019) 'Ayishat Akanbi: Is Wokeness Robbing Us of Our Compassion?', Special Broadcasting Service (SBS), 7 Mar., www.sbs.com.au/topics/voices/culture/article/2019/02/28/ayishat-akanbi-wokeness-robbing-us-our-compassion (accessed 31 Mar. 2022).

Geduld, A. (2019) 'Belonging to Oneself', in Khunou et al., *Black Academic Voices*.

Gilroy, P. (2016) 'Paul Gilroy in Search of a Not Necessarily Safe Starting Point...', Open Democracy, 1 May, www.opendemocracy.net/en/paul-gilroy-in-search-of-not-very-safe-starting-point/#.V0r1DOonY3Y.twitter (accessed 31 Mar. 2022).

Greyling, S. (2007) 'Rhodes University during the Segregation and Apartheid Eras, 1933–1990'. MA thesis, Rhodes University.

Harris, M., S.L. Sellers, O. Clerge and F.W. Gooding Jr (eds) (2017) *Stories from the Front of the Room: How Higher Education Faculty of Color Overcome Challenges and Thrive in the Academy*. Lanham, MD: Rowman and Littlefield.

Khunou, G., H. Canham, K. Khoza-Shangaze, and E.D. Phaswana (eds) (2019) *Black Academic Voices: The South African Experience*. Pretoria: HSRC Press.

Lalu, P. (2009) *The Deaths of Hintsa: Postapartheid South Africa and the Shape of Recurring Pasts*. Cape Town: HSRC Press.

Leroke, W. (1994) '*Koze Kube Nini?* The Violence of Representation and the Politics of Social Research in South Africa,' University of the Witwatersrand History Workshop, 13–15 July, https://wiredspace.wits.ac.za/bitstream/handle/10539/7896/HWS-246.pdf?sequence=1&isAllowed=y (accessed 31 Mar. 2022).

Mabokela, R., and Z. Magubane (eds) (2004) *Hear Our Voices: Race, Gender and the Status of Black South African Women in the Academy*. Pretoria: University of South Africa Press.

Mabokela, R.O., and K.L. King (2001) 'Introduction', in R.O. Mabokela and K.L. King (eds), *Apartheid No More: Case Studies of Southern African Universities in the Process of Transformation*. Westport, CT: Greenwood.

Magubane, Z. (2004) 'Introduction', in Mabokela and Magubane, *Hear Our Voices*.

Magubane, Z. (2004) 'A Pigment of Imagination? Race, Subjectivity, Knowledge and the Image of the Black Intellectual', in Mabokela and Magubane, *Hear Our Voices*.

Mahabeer, P., N. Nzimande and M. Shoba (2018) 'Academics of Colour: Experiences of Emerging Black Women Academics in Curriculum Studies at a University in South Africa', *Agenda*, 32 (2).

Matthews, S. (2015) 'White Privilege and Institutional Culture', in Tabensky and Matthews, *Being at Home*.

Maylam, P. (2005) *The Cult of Rhodes: Remembering an Imperialist in Africa*. Claremont: David Phillip.

Maylam, P. (2017) *Rhodes University, 1904–2016: An Intellectual, Political and Cultural History*. Grahamstown: ISER.
Mirzaei, A. (2019) 'Where "Woke" Came from and Why Marketers Should Think Twice before Jumping on the Social Activism Bandwagon', *Conversation*, 8 Sep., https://theconversation.com/where-woke-came-from-and-why-marketers-should-think-twice-before-jumping-on-the-social-activism-bandwagon-122713 (accessed 31 Mar. 2022).
Mokhele, M. (2013) 'Reflections of Black Women Academics at South African Universities: A Narrative Case Study', *Mediterranean Journal of Social Sciences*, 4 (3).
Murray, B.K. (1982) *Wits – the Early Years: A History of the University of the Witwatersrand, Johannesburg, and Its Precursors, 1896–1939*. Johannesburg: University of the Witwatersrand Press.
Murray, B.K. (1990) 'Wits as an "Open" University, 1939–1959: Black Admissions to the University of the Witwatersrand,' *Journal of Southern African Studies*, 16 (4).
Naidoo, L. (2016) 'Contemporary Student Politics in South Africa: The Rise of the Black-Led Student Movements of #RhodesMustFall and #FeesMustFall in 2015', in A. Heffernan and N. Nieftagodien (eds), *Students Must Rise: Youth Struggle in South Africa before and beyond Soweto '76*. Johannesburg: University of the Witwatersrand Press.
Ng, V. (2017) 'In Solidarity, Dear Student', in Harris et al., *Front of the Room*.
Njovane, T. (2015) 'The Violence beneath the Veil of Politeness: Reflections on Race and Power in the Academy', in Tabensky and Matthews, *Being at Home*.
Phadi, M., and N. Phakhade (2016) 'The Native Informant Speaks Back to the Offer of Friendship in White Academia', in S. Welsh and J. Soske (eds), *Ties That Bind: Race and the Politics of Friendship in South Africa*. Johannesburg: University of the Witwatersrand Press.
Phaswana, E.D. (2019) 'The Limits of Being and Knowledge in the Academy', in Khunou et al., *Black Academic Voices*.
Phillips, H. (1993) *The University of Cape Town, 1918–1948: The Formative Years*. Cape Town: University of Cape Town Press.
Pohlandt-McCormick, H. (2012) '*The Cambridge History of South Africa*: "We Live in Tragic Times"', *African Studies Review*, 55 (3).
Potgieter, C. (2002) *Black Academics on the Move: How Black South African Academics Account for Moving between Institutions or Leaving the Academic Profession*. Pretoria: Centre for Higher Education Transformation.
Potgieter, C., and A.S. Moleko (2004) 'Stand Out, Stand Up, Move Out: Experiences of Black South African Women at Historically White Universities', in Mabokela and Magubane, *Hear Our Voices*.
Rhodes University (2018–22). *Institutional Development Plan*.
Sehoole, C. (2015) 'The Bleak Side of Studying in South Africa', *Mail and Guardian*, 3 July, https://mg.co.za/article/2015-07-03-the-bleak-side-of-studying-in-south-africa (accessed 26 Nov. 2019).
Soske, J. (2012) 'Why Does South African History Continue to Be Written Primarily by White Scholars?', *Africa Is a Country*, 29 Nov., https://africasacountry.com/2012/11/

why-does-south-african-history-continue-to-be-written-primarily-by-white-scholars (accessed 31 Mar. 2022).
South African Native Races Committee (1908) *The South African Natives: Their Progress and Present Condition*. London: John Murray.
Southall, R. (2016) *The New Black Middle Class in South Africa*. Auckland Park: Jacana, 2016.
Tabensky, P., and S. Matthews (eds) (2015) *Being at Home: Race, Institutional Culture and Transformation at South African Higher Education Institutions*. Scottsville: University of KwaZulu-Natal Press.
Thumbran, J. (2018) 'The "Coloured Question" and the University of Pretoria: Separate Development, Trusteeship and Self Reliance, 1933–2012'. DPhil thesis, University of Minnesota.
Van Heerden, O. (2020) 'Wokeness, the Political Economy of Racism and Who Can Lay Claim to Being Black', *Daily Maverick*, 3 June, www.dailymaverick.co.za/opinionista/2020-06-03-wokeness-the-political-economy-of-racism-and-who-can-lay-claim-to-being-black/ (accessed 14 Jan. 2021).
Verschoyle, F. (1900) *Cecil Rhodes: His Political Life and Speeches, 1881–1900*. London: Chapman Hall.

4

Black mothering, 'maids' and mixed methods in women's history: Zanele Muholi's contemporary art and Sindiwe Magona's short stories

Mandisa Mbali

How might we 'read' and 'see' black women in South African history – other than through the dominant themes of African nationalist women's organising, or as disempowered mothers and maids? I argue that it is imperative for feminist historians to use new approaches to excavate the emotions and the consciousness of black women, and I use the contemporary art of Zanele Muholi and the literary fiction of Sindiwe Magona as examples of primary sources that can be utilised to that end.

The chapter outlines this approach in the following directions. First, I describe the contemporary social context in which women's history is written, focusing particularly on black women historians' underrepresentation in history departments, especially in the upper echelons of the profession. I argue that in order for there to be adequate knowledge production in relation to women's history (understood as the history of women) it is imperative to have more female historians. Then I discuss how we can interpret black women's 'shameful' experiences of motherhood by juxtaposing Sindiwe Magona's short stories in *Living, Loving and Lying Awake at Night* (2003), which describes domestic workers' experiences, and Zanele Muholi's artworks – namely *Minah VI* (2008) and *'Massa' and Maids, IV, Hout Bay* (2009) from the *'Massa' and Mina[h]* series, and their *Bester I, Mayotte* (2015) from the *Somnyama Ngonyama* series, which I argue can be mined as a rich source for historical writing on the intimate, gendered kinship experiences of transgender, gender nonconforming and nonbinary people in the past.

I also discuss changing types of identities, activism and cultural forms associated with gender-oppressed black people in the past. I move through and between historiographical debates over how to imaginatively describe black experiences of gender oppression (and resistance to it) with reference to terms and concepts such as 'feminism', 'women' and 'womxn' and diverse articulations of queer identities. Throughout, the category LGBTIQ (lesbian, gay, bisexual, transgender, intersex and queer) is used to describe the full spectrum of people who experience sexual-orientation and gender-identity oppression. I also refer to Muholi using the terms 'they/their/them' in accordance with the artist's queer, gender nonbinary identity.[1] Nonbinary people are those who do not identify as either male or female.[2] I point to some shifting and finely grained debates over identities and activisms within the field of gender and history that are complex, but must be engaged with in order to produce narratively rich, sociological descriptions of the operation of gender-based power and resistance over time.

Sexism, racism and the discipline of history at South African universities

The premises of this essay are that the output of historical research on women can expand only if it is conducted by more black women, using well-resourced archives capable of answering their research questions. This is so for the following reason: strategic African feminist activism requires advanced understandings of past advocacy for gender equality on the continent. It is not possible for African feminists to develop visions of a gender-equal future without them obtaining insight into women's experiences in the past produced by black women themselves.

In this regard, one can note that there is a dramatic underrepresentation of black women in academic history departments at South African universities. There is also an absence of data on transgender and gender nonbinary historians. In 2018, the Council on Higher Education published a report entitled 'History Departments at South African Universities', which was based on 'public information provided by [historical studies] departments' and sought to assess the extent to which 'calls for Africanisation and/or decolonisation are reflected in the topics taught and in the staff composition of departments'.[3] This 'monitoring brief' was based on information provided in faculty, school or department handbooks in August 2017, and it offered a clear illustration of the underrepresentation of black women in tertiary institutions: of the historians named in the report, only 11.84 per cent (15 of 76) were black women, and there were only two black women history professors in the country.[4]

According to the programme of the 2017 Southern African Historical Society conference, there were only three black women presenters (excluding the author). For the purposes of writing this chapter, I conducted an analysis of the staff composition of history departments at the universities of Pretoria, the Witwatersrand, the Western Cape, Fort Hare and Johannesburg, which revealed only three further black women employed as historians in these institutions.[5] In terms of our own department at the University of Cape

Town, where there are three black women, there is a strong desire to increase equity in relation to gender and race – that is, to ensure that black women historians who we deem to exhibit research and teaching excellence are sought and developed as postgraduate students and colleagues.

To cement the future of the history of women and LGBTIQ people in Africa, it is incumbent upon our professional associations, such as the Southern African Historical Society and the Historical Association of South Africa, to explore the reasons for their continued exclusion at our universities. I would propose that the study should consist of two parts. First, there needs to be a survey of all black women, transgender and gender nonbinary historians registered for postgraduate and postdoctoral programmes and who are currently employed at South African universities. Second, there should be interviews with a representative sample of black South African women, transgender and gender nonbinary historians to analyse their experiences of gender oppression and racism within the discipline. The study should examine socioeconomic barriers, women's disproportionate engagement in reproductive labour (such as domestic work and child-rearing), the pressure many face to obtain lucrative work outside academia following graduation owing to the legacy of familial poverty, and sexist and transphobic attitudes within departments (one manifestation being 'women teaching "the gender course"') and in the curriculum.

A further matter which requires attention are gaps and silences within the archives. As we know, there is a generalised crisis in relation to the state of many archives in South Africa, but there are particular issues in relation to the development of women's archives. In my own institutional context, the devastating University of Cape Town African Studies' library fire on 18 April 2021 destroyed several rare books and archival collections in its Special Collections, many of which contained material where black women described their own experiences. This loss is all the more tragic in view of the fact that, as Verne Harris has written, in the state archives created during the apartheid era, 'Black experiences were … poorly documented, and in most cases were seen through white eyes. Similarly, the voices of *women* [emphasis added] … and other marginalised people were seldom heard.'[6]

Those of us who teach gender history will have noted that some of our students wish to refer to women in the past as 'womxn'. This reflects both a rejection of the definition of 'women' as an extension of men, and the contemporary feminist adoption of the concept/identity of 'womxn' as one that includes transgender people and women of colour. There are, however, potential pitfalls to the adoption of a 'womxn's' history approach – namely, that it is not necessarily how the women concerned saw themselves. Many historians typically refer to events in the past as historical actors did: this approach would justify using the term 'women' to describe females in the past. Additionally, many African women's rights activists and scholars in the past did not identify as feminists: for instance, some organised as mothers and woman healers; others identified as womanists.[7] Those who did call themselves feminist often identified as such using additional adjectives such as African nationalist, postcolonial, pan-African, Marxist, socialist, black consciousness, environmentalist and queer. African feminist thinkers and historians of Africa have also deployed different ideas of the identities and statuses of women in precolonial and colonial pasts.[8]

This acceptance of past diversity would chime with the idea of intersectionality that has been influential in black feminist scholarly and activist networks.[9] The concept of intersectionality must, in turn, be situated in the longer trajectory of black feminist intellectuals' reading of gender as deeply shaped by the politics of race and capital.[10] Yet, intersectionality bears important resemblances to older African feminist ideas about black women's experiences of oppression on the grounds of gender, race, class and sexual orientation. In a South African context, feminism has been wracked by divisions over white women's dominance in leadership positions and agenda setting.[11] Examining the history of women's feminist organising and research in this manner can help scholars and practitioners gain insights into potentially successful strategies to advance women's rights today.

When we explore intersectionality, it is also incumbent upon us to recognise that South African feminisms have emerged in a pan-African context. Examining South African feminist pasts in this way can help us to move towards an Afro-cosmopolitanism, and here we can note that there is much outstanding work to be done in relation to pan-African and black diasporic feminisms.[12]

The concept of intersectionality is especially applicable in relation to the history of domestic work in South Africa. For instance, in a seminal 1983 article, Belinda Bozzoli developed the concept of South Africa as having had a 'patchwork quilt' of patriarchies that were determined by differing cultural norms in different cultural groups, the penetration of capital, and the development of racist ideologies and institutions.[13] She argued that it was:

> through the employment of domestic labour [that the white woman] was able to defend herself against the isolating and unrewarded labour which her kin would otherwise expect her to perform; and against the double-shift [of paid work and unpaid reproductive labour]. Her victory was at the expense of the subordination and oppression within the white family of the black male domestic worker and in later years, of the black female.[14]

In order to advance women's history in an African context, a number of theoretical and methodological challenges need to be addressed. Firstly, women have been 'hidden from history' and their experiences and perspectives seldom recorded because of sexist biases that predominated in previous ages.[15] This means that women have had to build their own archives and oral histories, often in the vernacular, in endeavours that have been severely underfunded and under-recognised within both the discipline and wider society.

A particular challenge that African women historians face today concerns how to research and write about neglected groups such as LGBTIQ women, disabled women, sex workers and women living with sexually transmitted infections. Some strides have, however, been made in research dealing with lesbians, bisexual women and women living with HIV.[16] However, far more work is required on other gender-marginalised people. For example, there were gender nonconforming people in the past who would probably, today, be identified as transgender and/or gender nonbinary. An approach which has been influential in trans studies and activism is that of self-definition, which has sometimes involved the use of gender-neutral pronouns such as 'they', 'their' and 'them'. However, there are lively debates within transgender studies as to the historical applicability of these terms.[17] These debates are ripe for examination in relation to the intersections between African transgender and women's history. Similarly, contemporary women have adopted the term 'sex workers' as an advocacy tool to challenge the gender oppression of women who have commonly been termed 'prostitutes'. At issue is which term may be best used by historians to describe the women who exchanged their sexual labour for money in the past.

As noted, women historians have to contend with 'source scarcity', and the obstacles that exist are reflected in the extensive theorisation that has been undertaken within the literature on gaps and silences in the archives.[18] Antoinette Burton's work is particularly useful in this regard. Focusing on the memories/histories of three twentieth-century Indian women (Janaki Majumdar, Cornelia Sorabji and Attia Hosain) who used memories of home 'to claim a place in history at the intersection of the public and the private, the personal and the political, the national and the post-colonial', Burton has called for scholars to read archives 'ethnographically' as cultural artefacts 'with systems of logic and representation'.[19] I think this is a very important insight, as anthropologists are especially interested in the fictional, including myth-based rituals.

Women's history can assume multiple forms: family histories, memoires, letters, official reports, oral histories and novels. Women's writings about the past have often been designated as literature, with men's being understood as history. Fiction reveals things to us about the past as it was understood by readers (working with metaphors they could comprehend, characters they could relate to, events they viewed as worthy of remembrance, and so on). The need to challenge crude positivism in relation to our treatment of the archives is a concern not only in relation to women's history: it is also important to get at under-recognised histories of racist oppression in apartheid South Africa. In his aforementioned article, Verne Harris characterised then-active debates about the role of imagination in transforming the archives:

> For over a decade now, in the academy, in memory institutions, school classrooms, courtrooms, the media, people's living rooms, and, crucially, the TRC [Truth and Reconciliation Commission], South Africans have been searching for meanings in a myriad narratives of the past. For some, the meanings are borne by 'facts;' the 'truth' of what happened. For others *'fact' and 'fiction,' 'history' and 'story,' coalesce in imaginative space.*[20]

In some instances there are sources pertaining to women's history, but they are scarcely utilised. To demonstrate a potential approach to harnessing such archives, the rest of this essay considers an interlinked set of short stories and works of contemporary African art.

Fiction and contemporary art as neglected sources in women's history

Fiction and contemporary art can be excellent sources for examining gender in history, and among their potential services is that they can help us think through a different kind of politics, one that falls outside the dominant framing of it as being driven chiefly by African nationalist commitments.

Before moving on to a discussion of Sindiwe Magona's work, it is necessary to offer a synopsis of her biography. She was born in 1943 and spent her early childhood in the Eastern Cape village of Gungungulu. At the age of five, she and her mother moved to Cape Town to live with her father in a shack in Blaauvlei location. Owing to the Group Areas Act, her family was then forcibly removed to Gugulethu. She returned to the Eastern Cape and later trained as a teacher. She taught at a school in Nyanga, but lost her job after becoming pregnant. She then became a maid for four years until 1962, when she lost her job, after which her husband left her and their three children. As sole breadwinner, she turned to cooking and selling sheep heads. After returning to teaching, and then working for Cape Town City Council's Department of Social Welfare, she moved to the United States without her children and lived in New York for over two decades, returning to South Africa only in 2003.

Magona used her literary fiction to describe hidden aspects of black women's history. Given the rich, descriptive nature of her work, it is unsurprising that there have been numerous texts that offer literary and even historical studies of her fiction and biographical work. For instance, Ena Jansen's

Like Family: Domestic Workers in South African History and Literature (2019) contains a detailed discussion of Magona's 1990 memoir, *To My Children's Children*, which is written in the style of a letter from a Xhosa grandmother to her grandchildren.[21] In particular, while *To My Children's Children* offers Magona's life story, it also contains imaginative elements, including the 'Preface: From a Xhosa Grandmother', which begins:

> When I am old, wrinkled, and grey, what shall I tell you, my great-granddaughter? What memories will stay with me of days of yesteryear? ... How will you know who you are if I do not or cannot tell you the story of your past?[22]

The way in which this memoir blends fact and fiction offers evidence that the author is imagining being 'old, wrinkled, and grey' and wondering what she will tell her great-granddaughter. She is imagining her future in a stylistic literary device: this future is inherently speculative and fictive, yet the historical facts laid out in the memoir are, indeed, true to her past life story.

Magona's short story collection, *Living, Loving and Lying Awake at Night* (1991), has also gathered the attention of literary scholars, who have noted its profound sociological insights into the lived experiences of domestic workers in South Africa.[23] The collection offers an interlinked set of short stories detailing the lives of seven domestic workers (Atini, Stella, Sheila, Virginia, Joyce and Lilian), all of whom are 'live-in' maids. The work considers domestic workers' experiences of having had to leave their children behind in rural areas in order to find work. One of the stories is entitled 'Atini': in it a maid tells her story of moving to the city to become a domestic worker. In the story Atini stays illicitly in town with Nombini, who she knows from her village. When another maid, named Imelda, has to return to the village of Malenge in Mzimkhulu because a member of the family is ill, Atini takes over from her and works for the 'madam' – Mrs Reed. When Imelda returns after eleven weeks, Mrs Reed decides to sack her based on her preference for Atini's work. Magona describes Atini's agony in deciding to keep the job:

> What could I do? I had stayed put and worked for my starving children whom I'd deserted while they trustingly slept. I kept reminding myself that my children woke up to find me gone one morning; that they hadn't known where I was or what had happened to me until I sent word when I found someone returning to the village.[24]

In this short story, Magona describes the tug between a black woman's need to provide for her children and her desire to express solidarity with other maids, in instances where they are played off against each other by a madam.

Similar dilemmas are reflected in the stories of 'Sophie' and 'Sheila'. Sophie calls a meeting at her madam's house – Sheila describes Sophie's madam as 'the crazy one who lets us use her house for our meetings'.[25] Sheila suggests that Sophie's madam is perhaps involved in antiapartheid resistance as 'she is always in trouble with the government'.[26] The difficulties in attending such meetings are also expressed in Sheila's version of events: she urges the maid she is talking to 'tell her early in the morning [of the meeting], before she comes with her own nonsense about what she wants you to do for her in the evening, tell her you have to take food money to your baby as soon as you have done the dishes'.[27]

The isolation of the maids is indicated when Sheila hatches a plan to phone her interlocutor in the morning, pretending to be her childminder and asking for her to come over to bring her baby food. The goal of this subterfuge is to clandestinely attract the madam's attention via a phone call, as 'they [madams] always want to know who that was when you get a phone [call]'.[28] This convoluted approach was required for the maid to attend the maids' meeting that evening. It also indicates the extent to which the maid's personal life and access to the outside world were monitored through surveillance of phone calls and control over independent excursions. In Sophie's account (the next story, set the next day) she asks her interlocutor (another maid) why she did not attend the meeting. She also says that her rather paternalistic and controlling madam had been asking her 'about that the whole morning' and warning that if Sophie failed to uncover the issue, she would find out herself.[29] This is a fascinating description of white women's paternalism and appropriation of leadership in relation to black women's resistance. Sophie's irritation at the inquiry is also reflected in her observation: 'That is how she ends up asking me things I don't want to talk to her about; and she gets me into trouble with the medems [madams] of these women. You would think an *mlungu* [white] woman wouldn't worry herself about maid gossip.'[30]

In relation to these two interlinked stories, as Loflin has noted: 'Despite the common circumstances in which they find themselves, the maids in these stories find it difficult to act collectively' owing to their isolated circumstances when sleeping in at their employers' houses, the precarity entailed in working in a low-skill sector at a time of high unemployment, and wide variations in their relationships with their employers and working conditions.[31] For Loflin, these stories are 'a perfect illustration' of the challenges that unions have faced in organising domestic labour; above all the 'isolation, lack of education, jealousies, and fear' which prevent them 'seeing themselves as a collective workforce'.[32]

Magona also explores issues of sexual abuse. One of the other short stories concerns a maid called Virginia. At two points in the story, Virginia mentions that while her madam is 'always reminding me how she got my pass right', this service had been used by her madam as justification for docking her pay. Virginia reflects ruefully: 'Now, in her eyes, I will die on my knees scrubbing floors.'[33] She adds that her madam does not acknowledge the sexual harassment involved in obtaining her pass: 'ONE DAY! One day I will remind her it was not her who had to spread her legs for that white dog, the Bantu inspector who made my pass right. I think she forgets that.'[34]

She then moves on to discuss the issue of (white) 'masters' sexually abusing maids who 'stayed in', reflecting that while families 'pay well' for live-in maids: 'If you can't do it, remember: Virgie – Ever Ready. I know the girls say a lot of nonsense about your master. They say he tries tricks on the maids.'[35] Here it is unclear whether Virginia is imagining talking to another maid about their master or discussing her own master, as it is unclear who she means by 'you' when she says 'If you can't do it'. This is ambiguous, especially as she addresses herself in the next part of the sentence ('Virgie [a nickname for herself] – Ever Ready'). Perhaps this obscurity indicates the issue of shame in relation to sexual harassment; perhaps it indicates a disassociation from the events at hand.

Magona, through Virginia, adds that 'people should be careful what they say [about sexual harassment and assault]. They shouldn't say things if they have no proof.'[36] The unclarity around what constitutes 'proof' is significant in indicating the disempowerment of black women by suggesting the dangers associated with not being able to provide evidence. The protagonist adds, 'they'll go to jail, lying about white people. And there is a law about what they say a man is doing.'[37] She continues: 'You go around saying a person is breaking the law'; here, I would argue that the text can almost certainly be read as describing sexual assault because of the reference to the accusation of illegal behaviour on the master's part. This is a powerful statement about the intersection of class, race and gender oppression – silence here does not imply acceptance, merely self-preservation, for 'your mouth is your policeman. It can take you to jail.'[38]

This story highlights black women's lived experiences of violations of maids' physical autonomy, and in this regard the issue of medical coercion is also suggested. At one point, Sophie divulges to Atini the concerns of her (Sophie's) 'medem' that Atini's '*mlungu* woman will mess you up the same way she messed up Imelda'.[39] Sophie mentions that 'Imelda can't take [become pregnant]', but had 'been pregnant before'.[40] What happened was that 'the doctor her medem had taken her to when she had stopped, that doctor cleaned up Imelda. Cleaned her up not only for what was inside her then – but for all those that would have lain inside her in time to come.'[41]

Here, it is unclear whether Imelda requested her madam to take her for an abortion, but it is evident that she had not consented to being sterilised (the 'cleaning up' of 'all those ... to come'). This indicates an even more tangible transgression of black women's reproductive capacities: in Imelda's case, her employer stripped her of her fundamental right to bear children.[42]

To return to Jansen's *Like Family*, in addition to drawing upon the second volume of Magona's autobiographical trilogy (*To My Children's Children*), it also considers Zanele Muholi's contemporary art. Jansen explains her objective, as an author, in the following terms:

> My aim was to examine what Stuart Hall describes as the 'cycle of representation', and recent works [by Mary Sibande and Zanele Muholi] suggest that the representation of domestic workers continues to be of interest to writers as well as artists.[43]

Jansen explains that Sibande's work involves 'large sculptures modelled on herself' that are used 'to critique stereotypical depictions of domestic workers', and which have been internationally exhibited and 'even been projected onto tall buildings in Johannesburg's city centre'.[44] Muholi's work, by contrast, involved the artist producing 'photographic portraits of herself [*sic*] playing the role of a maid in the "Massa and Minah" series'.[45] Sibande and Muholi both had mothers and grandmothers who had been domestic workers, and their respective work 'confronts viewers from the "madam" class with the attitudes they hold towards these women'.[46]

Muholi is the artist whose work I will focus on, and I believe that their work needs to be considered in the broader context of their life. The artist is a black, nonbinary, LGBTIQ artist-activist, and their work not only biographically describes their experience of having had a mother who was a domestic worker, it also unsettles African nationalist, traditionalist and religious-conservative notions of same-sex desire and gender diversity (as unmotherly or antimotherly, or antifamily).

What I want to suggest is that we can more systematically (than Jansen does) bring Magona's literary work *into conversation* with the art of Muholi in order to show two different subjectivities within the history of women in South Africa. In particular, I argue that we can mine both sets of sources to examine black people's lived experiences of motherhood examined from the perspectives of mother and child. A concern I have which I wish to highlight is what I believe can be termed 'texto-centrism', in relation to the primary sources that historians privilege. There is, I would argue, an alternative lens, which I will call 'picto-centrism'. What happens when we bring the two creative forms (literature and art) together to understand women's life histories? We cannot and should not leave the consideration of women's pictures and visual imaginations to art historians.

What does really looking at contemporary African artworks as historical sources entail? This can be demonstrated through a close interpretation of

Zanele Muholi's work. The artist's work documents queer life in South Africa, from within. Muholi was born into a township family, and trained at the Market Photo Workshop established by David Goldblatt in the late 1980s.[47] This late-apartheid training ground for photographers was specifically set up to develop the craft among emerging photographers who were otherwise excluded from the educational institutions of the day.

Muholi's work has been shown as part of numerous group and solo exhibitions, both domestically and internationally, where it has become highly sought after in the global contemporary art market.[48] Muholi aims to document queer people's experiences and lives, including intimate spaces such as lesbian weddings, trans women and survivors of homophobic hate crimes, including sexual assault. Giving visibility to those who have been historically silenced, the artist provides us with a source repository of lived black queer experiences.

The comparison between Magona and Muholi takes on a particular resonance when we consider that the artist cites the novelist as a source of inspiration for their photographs. For instance, one essay written by Muholi in a volume celebrating their art begins by quoting Magona's poem 'Please, Take Photographs!'.[49]

> Please, take photographs!
>
> Go to the nearest or cheapest electronic goods store.
> Hurry! Go! Go! Go!
> Then come home; gather your family and
> Take photographs of them all
> Especially the children, especially, the young,
> Hurry! Take photos of them all
> Before it is too late
> ...
> Please hurry! Take photographs of all the children, now!
> Take photos for tomorrow they will be gone.

Muholi states in their essay that they first became aware of the poem at a conference convened by the Goethe Institute in Johannesburg in 2011, and it 'felt as if it was speaking directly to me, because I feel a similar imperative to visualize the realities of Lesbian Gay Bisexual Transgender Intersex (LGBTI) communities in South Africa and beyond'.[50] Muholi adds that for themself as an artist, 'photography is not a luxury but *visual activism* [emphasis added]'.[51] Here we can see that as a gender- and sexuality-marginalised artist Muholi uses their own photography to promote their 'political agenda', which is to challenge the 'invisibility of LGBTI communities in the mainstream media' and to 'rewrite/re-visualize/re-present queer bodies in an amicable way'.[52]

This is a different kind of gender activism. It challenges gender and sexual-orientation discrimination in ways which have often been overlooked by women politicians operating in African nationalist traditions – including those in the postapartheid government. Here it would be remiss to overlook a controversy in which Lulu Xingwana (then Minister of Arts and Culture) labelled Muholi's contribution to the Innovative Women Art Exhibition at Constitution Hill in 2010 as 'offensive'.[53] Xingwana was especially 'revolted' to see a work called *Self-rape*, which she said depicted 'a sexual act with nature as a backdrop', because:

> The notion of self-rape trivialises the scourge of rape in this country. ... To my mind, these were not works of arts [*sic*] but crude misrepresentations of women (both black and white) masquerading as artworks rather than engaged in questioning or interrogating – which I believe is what art is about. Those particular works of art stereotyped black women.[54]

Kylie Thomas has described Xingwana's condemnation of the works as demonstrating that 'she had been powerfully affected by her brief immersion into the field of black lesbian art', and was apparently particularly disoriented by Muholi's challenging of conventional gender distinctions.[55] Thomas has argued, however, that Xingwana 'did not see what she describes, nor is she quite sure of what she saw', because 'turning away' based on an 'inability to look' foreclosed engagement with 'how certain images might serve to challenge and even overturn the conventions that govern our gaze'.[56]

While the Minister's statement denied that she was homophobic, it also mentioned her lifelong struggle for 'liberation and women's rights' and her support for the constitutional rights of children.[57] This reprised the classic homophobic trope of same-sex-practising people being 'antifamily'. Xingwana added that Muholi's artworks were not suitable for a family audience, while noting the 'children as young as three years old in the room', and that this 'is why we have laws in this country that protect children against exposure to pornographic material'.[58]

As we have seen, women's role as mothers was – and remains – central to their efforts to claim leadership and political legitimacy in the African National Congress. Unfortunately, homophobia on the part of African nationalist women is nothing new. It has often been based on ideas that same-sex sexuality is antimaternal and against reproduction itself. For example, in a notorious interview with the British publication *Capital 1987*, African National Congress National Executive Committee member Ruth Mompati said, 'Tell me, are lesbians and gays normal? It is not normal. If everyone was like that the human race would come to an end.'[59]

In their works, Muholi revisualises themself as their own mother, who was a domestic worker. Given the history of African nationalist women claiming their particular political authority as mothers, while denigrating LGBTIQ people as antimaternal, this is a radical political act. The respective oeuvres of Magona and Muholi both radically destabilise the dominant 'mother of the nation' tropes of the politics of black motherhood. While Magona uses the medium of memoire, poem and literary fiction, Muholi is a contemporary artist, and in exploring this issue I will focus on a few photographs in their *'Massa' and Mina[h]* series.

In the artist's statement for the exhibition, Muholi frames the project as follows:

> In my latest project 'Massa' and Mina(h) (2008), I turn my own black body into a subject of art. I allow various photographers to capture my image as directed by me. I use performativity to deal with the still racialized issues of female domesticity – black women doing house work for white families. The project is based on the life and story of my mother. I draw on my own memories, and pay tribute to her domesticated role as a [domestic] worker for the same family for 42 years. The series is also meant to acknowledge all domestic workers around the globe who continue to labour with dignity, while often facing physical, financial, and emotional abuses in their place of work. There continues to be little recognition and little protection from the state for the hard labour these women perform to feed and clothe and house their families.[60]

By stating that 'the project is based on the life and story of my mother' and that the artist will 'draw on my own memories', Muholi is making it clear that they are inscribing their own *lived historical experiences* as the child of a black domestic worker.[61] In that sense, we can consider the works as offering a primary source (i.e., material produced by historical actors who lived at the time the events they described took place).

Irene Bronner has argued that we must primarily understand Muholi's work through the lens of the artist's querying of 'the cultural circulation of heteronormative tropes of "maids" and "madams/masters"'.[62] Here she is arguing against the notion that the artist represents 'women employed as domestic workers' and rejects the notion that it is an example of Muholi's 'social-documentary work' which is 'prominent' in the artist's 'oeuvre' and 'critical discussion of … [their] work'. In particular, Bronner emphasises the ways in which the *'Massa' and Mina[h]* series shows cross-racial same-sex desire, or a 'Queer gaze' between maid and madam, and also explores themes of sadomasochism.[63] While I find Bronner's overall interpretation of Muholi's work persuasive, based on the artist's statement quoted above we can observe that there is a social history dimension to the work, focused on the life of their mother. Perhaps at issue is how we should weight the relative importance of the two sets of elements of *'Massa' and Mina[h]* as a body of work in relation to the artist's life: one is that it is art-activism challenging heteronormativity and enabling the self-representation of same-sex desire between gender-marginalised people; the other is that it is art-activism drawing on their own biography to illustrate the intersectional oppression of domestic workers. While it is not within the scope of this chapter to settle these issues, I do think it important for historians of domestic work to consider the artworks as being of relevance to those questions.

Muholi goes further still and offers 'an archive of the self'

To turn to *Minah VI* (2008; Figure 4.1), what we can see is that Muholi, dressed as a maid, is staring out of a window in what would appear to be the 'madam's house'. In the photograph, the artist's longing gaze is directed outside the window, which has net curtains. My interpretation is that the gaze indicates alienation or boredom in a place, a desire to escape and a longing for the outside world. In turn, the net curtains obscure and render the inside, and the artist-as-maid, invisible except to those who are in the interior of the house. What I find particularly interesting is the way in which the artist-turned-maid's arms are positioned. The left arm touches the clavicle and is rounded with an empty space. There a person could hold another very small person close to them – perhaps a young child. The other arm also clutches a pillow close to the torso, which is a fundamental part of the self and a space associated with digestion, sexual pleasure and even reproduction. The torso is a space where a person can hold those intimate to them close to them, including lovers, close friends and children. As we have seen in the case of Imelda in Magona's story 'Sophie', black women domestic workers were sometimes sterilised against their will. Moreover, in Magona's story 'Virginia', a maid describes sexual harassment and assault by white 'masters'.

In the face of black women maids having limited control over their bodies, reproductive capacities and intimate lives, I would argue that Muholi's representation of a maid-mother engaging in a gesture of self-soothing, expressing a desire for the comfort and rest afforded by a bed, is indicative of an oft-neglected element of resistance to gender oppression – self-care. But it also indicates the high barriers to black maids enjoying self-care. In an exploitative workplace context (where they often lived in the employer's premises), the only bed on which they could rest and process their trauma was one that was not their own, and often one that they cleaned for the madam.

The artist who had a maid as a mother could be, at least partly, imagining a maid-mother's loneliness, isolation and distance from her children while at work. If we return to Magona's short story 'Atini', sleep and rest could

Figure 4.1 *Minah VI* by Zanele Muholi, 2008. This work is part of the artist's *'Massa' and Mina[h]* series. In it, Muholi (who was mothered by a 'maid') is rendered as invisible to the outside world, hidden behind net curtains. The placement of their hands suggests the barriers to self-care faced by maids.

have unpleasant connotations for the oppressed domestic worker. While the bedroom was a place where the madam obtained sleep and rest, the room often had more troubling connotations for the maid. Sleep cannot be viewed as divorced from the broader realities of the life of the domestic worker, above all her poverty. Another version of this type of alienation is evident when Atini ascribes her decision to stay working for her madam to her need to provide for her 'starving children whom I'd deserted while they

Black mothering, 'maids' and women's history

Figure 4.2 *'Massa' and Maids, IV, Hout Bay*, by Zanele Muholi, 2009. In this work the artist (centre) and two of their subjects are dressed as maids. These subjects' positioning in relation to the 'master' (bottom left) and their unapologetic gaze at the viewer demonstrates their bodily agency and solidarity in resistance.

trustingly slept.'[64] As we can see when we examine *'Massa' and Maids, IV, Hout Bay* (2009) and bring it into conversation with Magona's work, loneliness itself was related to women's political oppression and served as a barrier to maids organising.

To turn to this further work in the *'Massa' and Mina[h]* series – *'Massa' and Maids, IV, Hout Bay*, reproduced in Figure 4.2 – it shows interesting parallels with some of the stories in *Living, Loving and Lying Awake at Night*. As we saw in Virginia's story, maids were silenced in terms of speaking out about, or lodging police reports in relation to, sexual harassment and rape. If we look closely at *'Massa' and Maids, IV, Hout Bay*, we note that the artist-as-maid and their subjects (also depicted as maids) are in control of their sexuality in relation to the master. Unlike Virginia, who describes sexual harassment in Magona's story, their mouths do not have to be their 'policemen'. They are in control of both his body and their own, and do not fear going 'to jail' in relation to sexual events in their place of work.[65] Instead, they gaze directly – and unapologetically – at the viewer. Muholi touches themself with their right hand close to, but not on, their breast. They also rest their hand above, but not on, the master's genitals. As Bronner states:

> Louche shoulders roll, lips curl, here a sexuality is portrayed that is arguably both consciously harnessed by each player yet simultaneously unpredictable to the 'master/massa'.[66]

Bronner has also noted that the artist and their queer subjects dressed as female maids 'seem to complicate the still racialised South African employer-employee and madam-maid relationship by representing the servants as mimicking, rather than maintaining, the assuredness, decadence and indolence that may be read into a plush domestic interior'.[67]

Furthermore, the artwork can be seen as celebrating maids' solidarity in defiance. As we have seen from Magona's interlinked stories of Sheila and Sophie, the mere act of domestic workers gathering was remarkable and required much effort. In their artist's statement (as quoted above), Muholi stipulates their concern around the limited 'recognition' and 'protection from the state for the hard labour these women perform'.[68] Changing the state to advance gender justice for domestic workers needs solidarity in defiance: this is something that the subjects who are dressed as maids demonstrate.

If we move on to consider *Bester I, Mayotte* (2015; Figure 4.3) from Muholi's *Somnyama Ngonyama* series, which consists of photographs taken from 2014 to 2017 in Europe, Asia, North America and Africa, we see that it draws on forms such as classical portraiture, fashion photography and ethnographic imagery to challenge racism, sexism, homophobia, transphobia and xenophobia. One of the things I found interesting when looking at this work is its reflection of minstrelsy (i.e., the artist's exaggeration of their own features in the post-production process, where they have made themself darker, and the use of white paint on their lips and eyes).

The use of pegs is also very interesting: they are holding their hair and blanket together. Pegs are everyday objects used by women to perform domestic work, but in the artwork, the pegs are transformed into adornments clipped on to the artist's head and ears and holding a blanket around their shoulders. The blanket is textured in a manner redolent of a mat or carpet, which also suggests domestic work. The background is mottled in a way which is, in my view, otherworldly, in the sense that it almost appears to be like the surface of the moon (which has also been symbolically linked to the menstrual cycles, gravity and tides). Another way of looking at the background involves noting that it appears uneven and suggestive of peeling paint, combined with a sense of decay and squalor that is reimagined as, in its own way, luminous and almost impressionistic.

Black mothering, 'maids' and women's history   93

Figure 4.3 *Bester I, Mayotte*, by Zanele Muholi, 2015. This work was conceived by Muholi as a tribute to their mother, who was a maid. The artist is adorned with pegs and their shoulders are covered with a mat/blanket, all of which suggest domestic work. The mottled background suggests, simultaneously, decay and cosmic beauty.

In terms of our central interest in Muholi's piece as a primary source descriptive of the history of women, we can note that the piece also offers a homage to their mother. To be more precise, in an article written for the art blog *CultureType* dealing with an exhibition of the artist's work in Seattle, Victoria Valentine describes it as follows: 'For a portrait paying homage to their mother, who was employed as a domestic worker, the artist dons a crown and earrings made from clothes pins.'[69]

Art and historical inquiry: some concluding reflections

Particia Hill Collins has argued that the history of black feminist thought

> as critical social theory involves including the ideas of Black women not previously considered intellectuals – many of whom may be working-class women with jobs outside academia – as well as those ideas emanating from more formal, legitimated scholarship ... *Musicians, vocalists, poets, writers, and other artists* constitute another group from which Black women intellectuals have emerged.[70]

Reading the contemporary art of Zanele Muholi against the fiction of Sindiwe Magona can be related to the task of theoretically repositioning both as gender-marginalised social theorists whose work partly deals with documenting and interpreting the past. As we have already seen in the first section of this chapter, black women, transgender and gender nonbinary historians are marginalised and oppressed in the South African academy. We can draw on several different strands of black feminist thinking to make the case for both Muholi and Magona to be considered as intellectuals who offer us general models for change over time in the South African past in ways that destabilise dominant patriarchal, heteronormative and white-dominated notions of who has the intellectual authority to describe the past.

Clearly, the imperative of reconsidering the creative works of black female-identifying and LGBTIQ people as sources on women's history is not limited to South Africa, as the quote by Collins above indicates. Perhaps, the approach of using interdisciplinary methods to examine cognitively diverse, creative sources produced by black women and gender nonbinary literary authors and artists can help us both to recover their conceptions about South African society in the past and present and to contribute to thinking within the black and African diasporas about how to bring into dialogue historical sources and voices that can be read against each other in ways which have been *hiding in plain sight*.

It is imperative for literary and artistic primary sources produced by black women and gender nonbinary people to be used by historians to document the history of gender oppression in the past. These visual and literary primary sources should not be considered in cognitive silos: historians should interpret (by 'reading' and 'seeing') the works alongside each other.

As we have seen in relation to the history of women's history internationally, the number of gender-oppressed historians and their power and seniority matter, if 'hidden histories' of women are ever to be uncovered. This is particularly acute in relation to black women historians who experience intersectional oppression as historians in postapartheid South Africa. In addition, the history of the exclusion of the experiences of black women from South African archives needs to be addressed. While it is clear that more oral histories of black women need to be gathered, dominant narratives of 'source scarcity' can successfully be challenged if we look at creative sources dealing with black female experiences.

Generally speaking, histories of women's roles in African nationalist movements have been emphasised, often to the exclusion of the more everyday social histories of women. Motherhood was also deployed by women in these movements to claim political legitimacy. However, under the political and economic racial oppression of apartheid, black motherhood often involved experiences of shame, guilt, isolation and alienation. Creative approaches to self-representation of the history of domestic workers from the perspective of mothers and children can be valuable to get at these painful emotional elements of black women's gender and racial oppression.

There is much outstanding conceptual work to be done in terms of understanding intersectionality and generationality or 'waves' in gender justice activism and creative forms produced by women and LGBTIQ people. While it is widely accepted that there were racial tensions and different understandings of gender justice in the field of South African women's history, newer vocabularies and identities have emerged in recent years. An example of this is the emergence of the self-described identity of gender nonbinary. In a patriarchal, homophobic and transphobic society, gender nonbinary people are subversive as they reveal the fragile nature of the dominant norms of gender identity.

In the interests of gender justice, just as the rigid man/woman dimension must be challenged, so must the concomitant fact/fiction notion of sources. There is an imaginative element to the writing of history, in general, especially in relation to people's experiences of emotions in the past, and particularly where these were hidden, shameful or taboo. To 'get at' the experiences of black women and gender nonbinary people in the past, we need to move beyond disciplinary evidentiary silos – such as art for art historians, literature for literary scholars and archival records for historians, and so on. We must continually violate conventional conceptual borders and criss-cross between cognitively diverse sources. Like a prism or kaleidoscope held up to the sun, the overlapping, unstable and divergent experiences of black women and gender nonbinary people in the past are there: we just have to look for them together in their creative writing and art.

Notes

1 This is described in many places, including Tate Modern's description of the artist's work: 'Zanele Muholi is rewriting visual history and challenging the

way we think about art. The Black, queer, non-binary artist (who uses the pronouns they/them/their) documents the disconnect at the heart of South African society – where marginalised communities face violence, prejudice and bigotry despite the country's liberal constitution'. See Tate Modern, 'Exhibition Guide: Zanele Muholi', 2020, tate.org.uk/whats-on/tate-modern/exhibition/zanele-muholi (accessed 6 Oct. 2021). Victoria Valentine also mentions Muholi's personal pronouns: 'The artist, who prefers the gender-neutral pronouns they/them, adopts various archetypes and personas in the images, accessorizing with props and objects to reflect their personal experiences and certain cultural and historic narratives.' See Valentine's 'Hail the Dark Lioness: Zanele Muholi's Exhibition of Striking Self-Portraits Opens at the Seattle Art Museum Tomorrow', *Culture Type*, 9 July 2019, www.culturetype.com/2019/07/09/hail-the-dark-lioness-zanele-muholis-exhibition-of-striking-self-portraits-opens-at-the-seattle-art-museum-tomorrow/ (accessed 6 Oct. 2021).
2. Gender Dynamix, 'A Guide to LGBTQIA+ Terms', 2021, www.genderdynamix.org.za/ (downloadable via 'Download Guide' icon; accessed 6 Oct. 2021).
3. Council on Higher Education (CHE), 'History Departments at South African Universities', *Speaking CHE*, 4, Jan. 2018, 1.
4. To produce this figure, I counted all the black female historians listed as employed at South African universities.
5. Southern African Historical Society, *Disputed Pasts, Fractured Futures and the Work of History*, SAHS 26th Biennial Conference Programme, held at the University of the Witwatersrand, 21–23 June 2017.
6. V. Harris, 'The Archival Silver: Power, Memory, and Archives in South Africa, *Archival Science*, 2, 2002, 73.
7. C. Burns, 'Louise Mvemve: A Woman's Advice to the Public on the Cure of Various Diseases', *Kronos*, 23, Nov. 1996, 108–34; C. Walker, 'Conceptualising Motherhood in Twentieth Century South Africa', *Journal of Southern African Studies*, 21 (3) Sept. 1995, 417–37; M.P. Eboh, 'The Woman Question: African and Western Perspectives', in C. Eze (ed.), *African Philosophy: An Anthology* (Oxford: Blackwell, 1998), 333–47; I. Berger, 'African Women's Movements in the Twentieth Century: A Hidden History', *African Studies Review*, 57 (3) 2014, 1–19; M. Healy-Clancy, 'The Family Politics of the Federation of South African Women: A History of Public Motherhood in Women's Antiracist Activism', *Signs: Journal of Women in Culture and Society*, 42 (4) 2017, 843–66.
8. See O. Oyěwùmí, *The Invention of Women: Making an African Sense of Western Gender Discourses* (Minneapolis: University of Minnesota Press, 1997); S. Hanretta, 'Women, Marginality and the Zulu State: Women's Institutions and Power in the Early Nineteenth Century', *Journal of African History*, 39 (3) 1998, 389–415; R. Stephens, *A History of African Motherhood: The Case of Uganda, 700–1900* (New York: Cambridge University Press, 2013).
9. K. Crenshaw, 'Demarginalizing the Intersection of Race and Sex: A Black Feminist Critique of Antidiscrimination Doctrine, Feminist Theory and Antiracist Politics', *University of Chicago Legal Forum*, 1989, art. 8; P.H. Collins, *Black Feminist Thought: Knowledge, Consciousness, and the Politics of Empowerment* (New York: Routledge, 2000).

10 A. Davis, *Women, Race and Class* (New York: Random House, 1981); b. hooks, 'Black Women: Shaping Feminist Theory', in Eze, *African Philosophy*, 338–45.
11 C. de la Rey, 'South African Feminism, Race and Racism', *Agenda*, 13 (32) 1997, 6–10; S. Hassim, *Women's Organisations and Democracy in South Africa* (Madison: University of Wisconsin Press, 2006).
12 C. Boyce Davies, 'Pan-Africanism, Transnational Black Feminism and the Limits of Culturalist Analyses in African Gender Discourses', *Feminist Africa*, 19, 2014, 78–93.
13 B. Bozzoli, 'Marxism, Feminism and South African Studies', *Journal of Southern African Studies*, 9 (2) 1983, 159.
14 *Ibid.*, 149.
15 Davis, *Women, Race and Class*; S. Rowbotham, *Hidden from History: 300 Years of Women's Oppression and the Fight against It* (London: Pluto Press, 1973).
16 For relevant research, see, for example, R. Morgan and S. Wieringa (eds), *Tommy Boys, Lesbian Men and Ancestral Wives: Female Same-Sex Practices in Africa* (Sunnyside: Jacana, 2013); H. MacGregor and E. Mills, 'Framing Rights and Responsibilities: Accounts of Women with a History of AIDS Activism', *BMC International Health and Human Rights*, 11 (3) 2011, 53–7; M. Mbali and S. Mthembu, 'Introduction: The Politics of Women's Health in South Africa', *Agenda*, 26 (2) 2012, 4–12; M. Mbali, *South African AIDS Activism and Global Health Politics* (New York: Palgrave Macmillan, 2013).
17 J. Meyerowitz, *How Sex Changed: A History of Transsexuality in the United States* (Cambridge, MA: Harvard University Press, 2002).
18 Rowbotham, *Hidden from History*; Harris, 'Archival Silver'.
19 A. Burton, *Dwelling in the Archive: Women Writing House, Home, and History in Late Colonial India* (Oxford: Oxford University Press, 2003), 27.
20 Harris, 'Archival Silver', 82 (emphasis added).
21 E. Jansen, *Like Family: Domestic Workers in South African History and Literature* (New York: New York University Press, 2019); S. Magona, *To My Children's Children* (Claremont: David Phillip, 1990).
22 Magona, *To My Children's Children*, i.
23 C. Loflin, 'White Women Can Learn Not to Call Us Girl? Linked Short Stories by a New South African Writer Sindiwe Magona', *Journal of Modern Literature*, 20 (1) 1996, 109–14.
24 S. Magona, *Living, Loving and Lying Awake at Night* (Claremont: David Phillip, 1991), 16.
25 *Ibid.*, 28.
26 *Ibid.*, 28.
27 *Ibid.*, 28–9.
28 *Ibid.*, 29.
29 *Ibid.*, 30.
30 *Ibid.*, 29–30.
31 Loflin, 'White Women', 112.
32 *Ibid.*, 112.
33 Magona, *Living, Loving*, 38.

34 *Ibid.*, 38.
35 *Ibid.*, 39.
36 *Ibid.*, 39.
37 *Ibid.*, 39.
38 *Ibid.*, 39.
39 *Ibid.*, 30.
40 *Ibid.*, 30.
41 *Ibid.*, 30–1.
42 *Ibid.*, 30–1. There is an extensive literature on the violation of black women's sexual and reproductive rights. See: Z. Essack and A. Strode, '"I Feel Like Half a Woman All the Time": The Impacts of Coerced and Forced Sterilisations on HIV-Positive Women in South Africa', *Agenda*, 26 (2) 2012, 24–34; R. Hodes, 'The Medical History of Abortion in South Africa, c.1970–2000', *Journal of Southern African Studies*, 39 (3) 2013, 527–42; S. Klausen, *Abortion under Apartheid: Nationalism, Sexuality, and Women's Reproductive Rights in South Africa* (Oxford: Oxford University Press, 2015).
43 Jansen, *Like Family*, 266.
44 *Ibid.*, 266.
45 *Ibid.*, 266.
46 *Ibid.*, 266–7.
47 S. Maunac and M. Santos, 'Fragmentos de una nueva historia/Fragments of a New History', in *Zanele Muholi*, Fotógrafas Africanas/African Women Photographers no. 1 (Las Palmas, Canary Islands: Casa África, [c.2012]).
48 K. Thomas (2010) 'Zanele Muholi's Intimate Archive: Photography and Post-apartheid Lesbian Lives', *Safundi*, 11 (4) 2010, 421–36; Brodie/Stevenson, 'Zanele Muholi: Faces and Phases 9 July–8 August 2009', Stevenson gallery, www.archive.stevenson.info/exhibitions/muholi/index.html (accessed 1 Apr. 2021).
49 S. Magona, 'Please, Take Photographs', in *Please, Take Photographs* (Athlone: Modjaji Books, 2009), 45–6.
50 Z. Muholi, 'Ngibonile-Yo He Visto/Ngibonile – I Have Seen', in *Zanele Muholi*, Fotógrafas Africanas/African Women Photographers no. 1 (Las Palmas, Canary Islands: Casa África, [c. 2012]),
51 Magona, 'Please, Take Photographs', p. 45.
52 *Ibid.*, 45.
53 L. Xingwana, 'Statement by the Minister of Arts and Culture, Ms Lulu Xingwana, on Media Reports around the Innovative Art Exhibition', South African Government, 4 Mar. 2010, www.gov.za/statement-minister-arts-and-culture-ms-lulu-xingwana-media-reports-around-innovative-art-exhibition (accessed 1 Apr. 2022).
54 Xingwana, 'Statement by the Minister'; Thomas, 'Zanele Muholi's Intimate Archive', 425.
55 Thomas, 'Zanele Muholi's Intimate Archive', 425.
56 *Ibid.*, 425; Xingwana, 'Statement by the Minister'.
57 Xingwana, 'Statement by the Minister'.
58 *Ibid.*

59 M. Gevisser, 'A Different Fight for Freedom: A History of South African Lesbian and Gay Organisation from the 1950s to the 1990s', in M. Gevisser and E. Cameron (eds), *Defiant Desire: Gay and Lesbian Lives in South Africa* (New York: Routledge, 1995), 70.
60 Z. Muholi, 'So They Have "Eyes to See"', artist's statement, Stevenson gallery, 2009, http://archive.stevenson.info/exhibitionsbs/muholi/text.htm (accessed 13 May 2021).
61 *Ibid.*
62 I. Bronner, 'Queering Portraits of "Maids" and "Madams" in Zanele Muholi's *"Massa" and Mina(h)*', *de arte*, 51 (2) 2016, 18.
63 *Ibid.*, 18.
64 *Ibid.*, 16.
65 Magona, *Living, Loving*, 39.
66 Bronner, 'Queering Portraits', 19.
67 *Ibid.*, 19.
68 Muholi, '"Eyes to See"'.
69 Valentine, 'Hail the Dark Lioness'.
70 Collins, *Black Feminist Thought*, 15–16 (emphasis added).

Bibliography

Berger, I. (2014) 'African Women's Movements in the Twentieth Century: A Hidden History', *African Studies Review*, 57 (3).
Boyce Davies, C. (2014) 'Pan-Africanism, Transnational Black Feminism and the Limits of Culturalist Analyses in African Gender Discourses', *Feminist Africa*, 19.
Bozzoli, B. (1983) 'Marxism, Feminism and South African studies', *Journal of Southern African Studies* 9 (2).
Brodie/Stevenson (2009) 'Zanele Muholi: Faces and Phases 9 July–8 August 2009', Stevenson gallery, www.archive.stevenson.info/exhibitions/muholi/index.html (accessed 1 Apr. 2021).
Bronner, I. (2016) 'Queering Portraits of "Maids" and "Madams" in Zanele Muholi's *"Massa" and Mina(h)*', *de arte*, 51 (2).
Burns, C. (1996) 'Louise Mvemve: A Woman's Advice to the Public on the Cure of Various Diseases', *Kronos*, 23.
Burton, A. (2003) *Dwelling in the Archive: Women Writing House, Home, and History in Late Colonial India*. Oxford: Oxford University Press.
Collins, P.H. (2000) *Black Feminist Thought: Knowledge, Consciousness, and the Politics of Empowerment*. New York: Routledge.
Council on Higher Education (CHE) (2018) 'History Departments at South African Universities', *Speaking CHE*, 4.
Crenshaw, K. (1989) 'Demarginalizing the Intersection of Race and Sex: A Black Feminist Critique of Antidiscrimination Doctrine, Feminist Theory and Antiracist Politics', *University of Chicago Legal Forum*, 1989, art. 8.
Davis, A. (1981) *Women, Race and Class*. New York: Random House.

De la Rey, C. (1997) 'South African Feminism, Race and Racism, *Agenda*, 13 (32).
Eboh, M.P. (1998) 'The Woman Question: African and Western Perspectives', in Eze, *African Philosophy*.
Essack, Z., and A. Strode (2012) '"I Feel Like Half a Woman All the Time": The Impacts of Coerced and Forced Sterilisations on HIV-Positive Women in South Africa', *Agenda*, 26 (2).
Eze, C. (ed.) (1998) *African Philosophy: An Anthology*. Oxford: Blackwell.
Gender Dynamix (2021) 'A Guide to LGBTQIA+ terms', drive.google.come/file/d/16e_mcYQsVVrikVRCRFYi9DxU0Td3iYvl/view (accessed 6 Oct. 2021).
Gevisser, M. (1995) 'A Different Fight for Freedom: A History of South African Lesbian and Gay Organisation from the 1950s to the 1990s', in M. Gevisser and E. Cameron (eds), *Defiant Desire: Gay and Lesbian Lives in South Africa*. New York: Routledge.
Hanretta, S. (1998) 'Women, Marginality and the Zulu State: Women's Institutions and Power in the Early Nineteenth Century', *Journal of African History*, 39 (3).
Harris, V. (2002) 'The Archival Silver: Power, Memory, and Archives in South Africa', *Archival Science*, 2.
Hassim, S. (2006) *Women's Organisations and Democracy in South Africa*. Madison: University of Wisconsin Press.
Healey-Clancy, M. (2017) 'The Family Politics of the Federation of South African Women: A History of Public Motherhood in Women's Antiracist Activism', *Signs: Journal of Women in Culture and Society*, 42 (4).
Hodes, R. (2013) 'The Medical History of Abortion in South Africa, c.1970–2000', *Journal of Southern African Studies*, 39 (3).
hooks, b. (1998) 'Black Women: Shaping Feminist Theory', in Eze, *African Philosophy*.
Jansen, E. (2019) *Like Family: Domestic Workers in South African History and Literature*. New York: New York University Press.
Klausen, S. (2015) *Abortion under Apartheid: Nationalism, Sexuality, and Women's Reproductive Rights in South Africa*. Oxford, Oxford University Press.
Loflin, C. (1996) 'White Women Can Learn Not to Call Us Girl? Linked Short Stories by a New South African Writer Sindiwe Magona', *Journal of Modern Literature*, 20 (1).
MacGregor, H., and E. Mills (2011) 'Framing Rights and Responsibilities: Accounts of Women with a History of AIDS Activism', *BMC International Health and Human Rights*, 11 (3).
Magona, S. (1990) *To My Children's Children*. Claremont: David Phillip.
Magona, S. (1991) *Living, Loving and Lying Awake at Night*. Claremont: David Phillip.
Magona, S. (2009) 'Please, Take Photographs', in *Please, Take Photographs*. Athlone: Modjaji Books.
Maunac, S., and M. Santos [c. 2012] 'Fragmentos de una nueva historia/Fragments of a New History', in *Zanele Muholi*, Fotógrafas Africanas/African Women Photographers no. 1. Las Palmas, Canary Islands: Casa África.
Mbali, M. (2013) *South African AIDS Activism and Global Health Politics*. New York: Palgrave Macmillan.

Mbali, M., and S. Mthembu (2012) 'Introduction: The Politics of Women's Health in South Africa', *Agenda*, 26 (2).
Meyerowitz, J. (2002) *How Sex Changed: A History of Transsexuality in the United States*. Cambridge, MA: Harvard University Press.
Morgan, R., and S. Wieringa (eds) (2013) *Tommy Boys, Lesbian Men and Ancestral Wives: Female Same-Sex Practices in Africa*. Sunnyside: Jacana.
Muholi, Z. (2009) 'So They Have "Eyes to See"', artist's statement, Stevenson gallery, http://archive.stevenson.info/exhibitionsbs/muholi/text.htm (accessed 13 May 2021).
Muholi, Z. [c. 2012] 'Ngibonile-Yo He Visto/Ngibonile – I Have Seen', in *Zanele Muholi*, Fotógrafas Africanas/African Women Photographers no. 1. Las Palmas, Canary Islands: Casa África.
Oyěwùmí, O. (1997) *The Invention of Women: Making an African Sense of Western Gender Discourses*. Minneapolis: University of Minnesota Press.
Rowbotham, S. (1973) *Hidden from History: 300 Years of Women's Oppression and the Fight against It*. London: Pluto Press.
Southern African Historical Society (2017) *Disputed Pasts, Fractured Futures and the Work of History*, SAHS 26th Biennial Conference Programme, held at the University of the Witwatersrand, 21–23 June 2017.
Stephens, R. (2013) *A History of African Motherhood: The Case of Uganda, 700–1900*. New York: Cambridge University Press.
Tate Modern (2020) 'Exhibition Guide: Zanele Muholi', tate.org.uk/whats-on/tate-modern/exhibition/zanele-muholi (accessed 6 Oct. 2021).
Thomas, K. (2010) 'Zanele Muholi's Intimate Archive: Photography and Post-apartheid Lesbian Lives', *Safundi*, 11 (4).
Valentine, V. (2019) 'Hail the Dark Lioness: Zanele Muholi's Exhibition of Striking Self-Portraits Opens at the Seattle Art Museum Tomorrow', *CultureType*, 9 July 2019, www.culturetype.com/2019/07/09/hail-the-dark-lioness-zanele-muholis-exhibition-of-striking-self-portraits-opens-at-the-seattle-art-museum-tomorrow/ (accessed 6 Oct. 2021).
Walker, C. (1995) 'Conceptualising Motherhood in Twentieth Century South Africa', *Journal of Southern African Studies*, 21 (3).
Xingwana, L. (2010) 'Statement by the Minister of Arts and Culture, Ms Lulu Xingwana, on Media Reports around the Innovative Art Exhibition', South African Government, 4 Mar. 2010, www.gov.za/statement-minister-arts-and-culture-ms-lulu-xingwana-media-reports-around-innovative-art-exhibition (accessed 1 Apr. 2022).

5

Vernacular traditions as counter-hegemonic archives in Eastern Cape historiography

Nomalanga Mkhize

There is a rich archive of African-language historical writing that was produced in South Africa in the late nineteenth and early to mid-twentieth century, but it has remained marginal to the debates that have shaped knowledge production about the country's past for nearly a century. By default or design, the discipline of history in South African universities has devoted ample attention and debate to works written in English and Afrikaans, largely by white historians, while works by African authors, especially in indigenous languages, have been engaged cursorily if at all. This indigenous archive includes not only classics such as Walter Rubusana's *Zemk'iinkomo Magwalandini* (1911) and Magema Fuze's *Abantu Abamnyama Lapa Bavela Ngakona* (1922) but also collections of praise poems, clan praises, oral traditions and folklore, all of which can be said to constitute an oeuvre of African historical authorship.[1] This oeuvre conveys not only historical narrative but also interpretation and debate regarding the past. One may call this broad collection of writings an 'African archive' in so far as it involves the preservation of African memory, by and for Africans.

The African archive

To define the body of black historical literature as an 'African archive' is neither to 'ethnicise' nor excise it from the broader archive of the nineteenth-century imperial age, but rather to position these works as intellectual products of the colonised and their attempts to write from their own position. It is at the same time *not* to jettison, diminish or relegate (to the status of 'archive' rather than 'history') whole swathes of accumulated historiography on account of past exclusionary practice.[2] Rather, calling this an African archive represents an aspiration to consider it collectively as a repository that can and must be employed in the task of developing a fuller historiography of South Africa. As Bhekizizwe Peterson argues:

Underlying the archive is the aim of ordering the past as inheritance. As we know, colonial and apartheid authorities consistently denied the existence of any legacy among Africans worth preserving, an attitude borne out in their insistence that Africans had no history. Alternatively, where robust forms of local knowledge could not be ignored or denied, colonial authorities sought to reshape and appropriate such 'archives' into the service of colonialism. The denial and active suppression of a native archive meant that its import, in the larger African nationalist project of transforming inheritance into deliverance, could be partially checked.[3]

On account of much early writing by Africans being printed and published by missionary presses, copies of many of these texts have been available for the past century and a half, and many survive today in archives and in print, especially those which formed part of black schools' curricula in the era of Bantu Education.[4] These early writings by Africans have, however, not generally been incorporated into the 'archive' of primary materials or into the canon of secondary literature that mainstream South African historiography has drawn on.

In this chapter, I will argue that the marginalisation of the African archive owes less to any paucity of material than to the marginality of black authors and writers among professional South African historians. It is still common, for example, for George McCall Theal to be considered the 'founder of South African historiography', without considering his contemporary, William Gqoba, who authored histories in Xhosa in the African press in the 1870s and 1880s. Yet Gqoba was so significant to the black tradition of publishing and disseminating history that the literary scholar A.C. Jordan has described him as 'the dominant literary figure of the earlier part of the 19th century' among black Christian writers.[5] For Jordan, Gqoba's writings 'constitute the earliest serious attempt' to compile a systematic account of Xhosa and Mfengu history in Xhosa.[6]

Jeff Opland, meanwhile, noted in his introduction to an anthology of Gqoba's histories and poetry that the concerned works had 'been celebrated as a significant Xhosa source of information [that] was concerned to confront and contradict the dominant interpretation found in English history textbooks'.[7] While other historians, such as Jeff Peires, Helen Bradford and Msokoli Qotole, have recognised the significance of these contributions, Gqoba is generally considered to be something of a nonentity in contemporary South African historiography.[8] It is to the impoverishment of the field that Gqoba and subsequent black writers, such as Samuel Mqhayi and Nontsizi Mgqwetho (who debated the nature of nationalism and the native question), have been ignored in the historiography rather than being placed in conversation with the likes of C.W. de Kiewiet and Eric Walker, who wrote on similar themes during the same period.[9]

The writings of Gqoba and other members of the African intelligentsia in the late nineteenth and early twentieth century formed part of what Ntongela Masilela has called 'the New African Movement'. The term denotes writings by Christian, mission-educated Africans who saw their task as being to both speak back to, and actively define themselves within, the broader South African imperial order.[10] It was precisely because these educated intellectuals considered themselves to be subjects that they used writing to advance their political causes and preserve their cultural histories in print, especially in newspapers.[11] These form part of the larger body of African-language historical works, written and oral, that I refer to in this chapter as the 'African archive'.

This is not to say that the African archive has been completely ignored. Black writing and oral traditions have been consulted as sources for empirical information in *some* accounts, which have sought to piece together 'African histories' from them. Early European travellers, and later missionaries and colonial administrators, for example, collected 'oral accounts' from African communities. Many of these sources would later filter into the mainstream of South African historiography. As Nomathamsanqa Tisani has noted in her account of Xhosa historiography, from the 1850s a range of historical texts on Africans in the Cape were produced 'mainly to inform, justify and legitimise colonial policy. The works were a combination of historical material and ethnographic data ... derived from Xhosa historical knowledge', and 'the writers must have relied on Xhosa informants'.[12]

Notable among the white scholars who appropriated these indigenous traditions is George Theal, the great settler historian. To paraphrase Alfred North Whitehead's famous dictum regarding the development of the Western philosophical tradition, the safest general characterisation of the evolution of South African historiography is that it consists of a series of footnotes to Theal. During his time at Lovedale mission school in the 1870s, Theal collected, transcribed and translated Xhosa folklore and oral traditions, and these appeared in his 1882 compendium *Kaffir Folklore*.[13] Sam Naidu has argued that these collected texts were 'hybrids', for 'containing at least three sets of authorial voices' – namely, the African oral sources consisting of 'ten or twelve individuals'; 'a circle of natives' who served as transcribers and revisors; and the colonial ethnographer, Theal himself.[14]

The 1990s and early 2000s also witnessed the emergence of orature studies, which gained traction in the History and Literature departments of the then University of Natal. Within this genre, attention focused on African traditions as sources of South African history writing. This interest in orature – particularly Zulu-language orature – was catalysed both by a longstanding interest in the historiography of the Zulu state, and particularly King Shaka, and by the extensive, longstanding engagement by Natal-based academics with the large collection of oral histories in the James Stuart Archive. Therefore, over time, historians of Zulu history have developed a template for handling oral and vernacular traditions. However, even this interest in Zulu historiography has tended to be structured in debates that consider the writings of A.T. Bryant to be foundational.

As far as Cape historiography is concerned, with the notable exception of Jeff Peires's work on Xhosa history, interest in the in-depth analysis of vernacular oratory and texts has been thin amongst scholars, with most of the engagement being located in literature and language departments. For example, Jeff Opland – who emerged as probably the foremost scholar in collecting, translating and publishing large volumes of Xhosa-language historical writing – was based in a literary studies department. This feature has had broader significance, given the centrality of the Cape in the South African historiographical canon. In most accounts of the Cape's development, texts by Africans have most often been used as sources to be mined for empirical data, while the black authors themselves have not been seen as important historians in their own right. A consideration of the works of Monica Wilson offers an illustration of my meaning. Her *Reaction to Conquest* (1936) and her chapters in the *Oxford History of South Africa* (1969) were considered pathbreaking, primarily for the insights and access that were accorded to her by her African informants, who included notable intellectuals such as Walter Rubusana.[15]

Yet Wilson's research process remained based on relations of knowledge production that relegated Africans to the status of informants and 'sources', while elevating white writers as 'scholars' and 'authors' whose works came to constitute the authentic historiographical 'canon'. This racialised bifurcation reinforced, even if it was not informed by, the Hegelian notion that Africans could not be producers of history. Black writing had to be 'written in' to South African historiography through white mediation. This applied even with the social historians of the 1970s and 1980s, who sought to rewrite the country's past from the ground up in ways that centred African voices. This presumption has informed an epistemic hierarchy within South African universities, whereby 'African texts' (whether published in manuscripts or packaged as folklore) remained the province of ethnography (or its heirs – namely, anthropology and '*volkekunde*') and/or literature studies, throughout the twentieth century.[16] The result was that South African historiography remained a largely white edifice, regardless of the colonial, liberal, Marxist or neo-Marxist hues that it assumed. Accordingly, historical inquiry – regardless of school – largely failed to grapple with the implications of the African-language archive for South African historiography.[17] This is unsurprising given that the experience of conquest meant that even the universities, and the knowledge they produced, were structurally skewed in favour of white-authored historiography, whatever the political stance adopted by the said institutions. This glaring and obvious structural problem in the formation of South African historical studies was consistently pointed out by the late Bernard Magubane, who argued during a conference on South African historiography, held in Uppsala in the early 2000s, that:

> What we study has a lot to do with relations of power. This at least to me is no better exemplified than in the so-called disputes between liberal historians and academic Marxists. When I read and reflected on these debates, I was always nagged by the question: Where is the black story of suffering? Why certain questions were never raised, or when raised, tended to be dealt with in a perfunctory manner? Indeed, why are African voices silenced in South African historiography?[18]

Between the 1960s and 1990s, at a time when the field of South African historiography was supposedly being revolutionised by the history wars between the liberals and the Marxists, Magubane's interventions went largely ignored. His account of a conversation he had with Shula Marks in the late 1960s about her work on the Bambatha Rebellion is revealing in this regard:

> I said to her: 'Have you read Vilakazi's poem on Bambatha, Amagcino kaZulu?' I cannot recall what she said. Getting more heated, I said: Bambatha holds a special place in the history of the defeat of Africans by the British and the imposition of passes. He is a great hero and one would have to have an emotional understanding of how Zulu people in the first place and Africans in general think about him to write meaningfully about him. Africans call him 'uBambata kaMancinza'. That is his Zulu praise name, which is mentioned reverentially. It is all those things that one would have to bring out in any study of the 1906 rebellion.[19]

Magubane and other black scholars of his generation such as Archie Mafeje had the double burden of demonstrating the deep shortcomings of mainstream scholarship while themselves bearing the brunt of marginalisation within South African university departments.[20] The missing contributions of black historians owed, not only to such consequences of white supremacy and apartheid as the realities of who had the right to exist within the hallowed halls of the academy, but also to scholarly practices that disregarded the canon of African knowledge that is central to the historical and intellectual practices of African-language speakers. Referring to this dismissal of African authors within the academy, John Wright pointed out that:

> The importance of this group [of early black writers] in South Africa's intellectual history took a long time to be recognised by the white academic establishment. This was largely because writing by African authors was not taken very seriously by the academics and managers who controlled the universities, the publishing houses, and most newspapers, but also because initially these authors wrote

much of their work in African languages, which very few white people could read or speak, and because much of their writing took the form of newspaper articles which soon became lost to sight.[21]

Wright's reflections raise the question: what are the intellectual underpinnings of South African academic historiography, if it has not sustained rigorous engagement with African vernacular oeuvres?

In 2001, Nomathamsanqa Tisani began the work of trying to fill in some of the conceptual and analytical lacunae in Eastern Cape historiography by making the first attempt to compare the writings of Xhosa writers on the colonial era with works produced by settler colonial historians such as Theal. In her dissertation 'Continuity and Change in Xhosa Historiography during the Nineteenth Century', Tisani provided an analysis of Eastern Cape historiography that integrated the works of colonists and colonised into one cohesive historiographical overview of the period. In so doing, she went beyond the entrenched practice of separating white writers such as a Theal from Africans such as Gqoba, and she paid particular attention to the latter's activities in recording Xhosa history in *Isigidimi samaXhosa* and *Imvo Zabantsundu*. In the process she pointed out that Gqoba and others were not isolated from the broader colonial public sphere, which meant that they both reacted to and prompted white colonial writers with their works.[22]

As noted, mainstream academic works on Eastern Cape history that have embraced the potential of clan genealogies in exploring precolonial history have been few. The most prominent exception has been Jeff Peires's *House of Phalo* (1982), which remains unrivalled for its incorporation of African perspectives of subjugation into its account of Eastern Cape history. Tisani acknowledged this significance, arguing:

> Peires' strength in his early Xhosa history comes from his wide use of *iimbali*. From the Sogas and Xhosa informants Peires was able to gather evidence that enabled him to break away from the Rharhabe-Ngqika focus, as stressed by [Heinrich] Lichtenstein, [Ludwig] Alberti and [Johannes] Van der Kemp, and provide the history of the line of Gcaleka and his descendants.[23]

Tisani argued, however, that Peires's work was limited by his overreliance on landmarks set by colonial-era writings dating from the 1700s, which made King Phalo central in Xhosa history simply because he was the first major king whom European travellers documented. The paradigm of Phalo as the royal house upon which Xhosa history was written shaped the broader historiography of the Cape, occupying much the same position as Zulu royal historiography in the story of KwaZulu-Natal, but having a much greater impact on the general historiography of South Africa, given the foundational nature of the Cape's history for the broader topic. As will be shown below, Tisani pointed to clan histories – as understood within the

Xhosa vernacular oral and written traditions – to provide narratives that competed with those proposed by Peires.

Clan genealogy as counter-hegemonic archive

One of the distinctive contributions made by the African writers was their recording of clan genealogies – *iziduko* and *izithakazelo* – which were often accompanied by clan praises and praise poetry. Nompumelelo Jafta has argued that 'the unique style of *izibongo* has no European parallel'.[24] Almost every black writer of Nguni vernacular histories who wrote between 1860 and 1940 concerned themselves with rendering African history through forms such as clan names and praises. At the most immediate level, *iziduko* and *izithakazelo* provided genealogies of patrilineal descent, listing key clan leaders. These names did not necessarily appear in *izithakazelo* in chronological order, and did not always refer to father and son, for regents were also mentioned. A further nuance is that splits and movements away from a particular house created new *izizwe* (clan-nations), which then developed their own genealogical clusters, which generally continued to pay homage to a shared great ancestor.

In the remainder of this chapter, I will explore the questions of the value of these genealogical forms for historians, and the implications that they carry for the epistemic organisation and framing of the past. I would argue these are key questions for two reasons. Firstly, clan genealogies are central for building the corpus of Eastern Cape precolonial history because they provide multiple perspectives of African social development that avoid having to start with European contact. This is necessary for steering the historiography beyond what is largely a story of 'contact and conquest', or what might, perhaps, a little derisively, be called 'apartheid studies' – that is, a historiography largely concerned with explaining the origins of the racial order, beginning with the establishment of the Cape Colony. The literature has never quite been able to transcend these limits. Secondly, clan genealogies are important for the living, because they impact people's sense of who they are and where they fit into a longer story of the region (and indeed the continent and the world) at large. *Iziduko* and *izithakazelo* form part of the lived cultural experiences of the majority of black South Africans, for through recitation and praise they form part of the ways in which children first come to grasp the idea that they are part of a larger family history.

David Hammond-Tooke levelled a critique in 1985 against the use of clan lineages in history, asking if there was indeed any historical utility at all to the concept of 'clan' in making sense of African political formations. He concluded that clans had little historical value, and could not tell us anything about the people who bore clan names in the present. In so doing, he was criticising the likes of Peires, Jeff Guy and John Wright, who delved into the clan lineages of living descendants. Hammond-Tocke's core contention was that:

> Clans are not today corporate groups, their members never come together as a group and their main function is to define marriage through the exogamy rules. There are no clan elders. It is important to realize that there are also no clan genealogies, and therefore no way in which relative status within a clan can be established. The reason for this is simple. Without the availability of written records it is just not possible to retain the memory of long extinct genealogical connection, particularly of collaterals ... [E]ffective genealogical memory peters out at about the level of grandfather or great-grandfather and this is the reason why genealogies of commoners tend to be four or five generations in depth.[25]

He further argued that clan identification in and of itself could not offer insights into the deep past:

> In the literature on the Nguni there has been a tendency to think of all the homestead heads whose names appear on the shared genealogy as forming a lineage. Yet the genealogy is no more than a construct that allows members of the agnatic clusters to define their relationship to one another and to other related clusters. For defining the groups, though, they use only a part of the genealogy – that dealing with their immediate kinsmen, descended from a common great grandfather. The point is that all those whose names appear on the five to six generation genealogy do not interact as, or even conceive themselves to be, a group in any sociological sense; only those who live close together and who in fact can collaborate do; in practice, these are descendants of a common great-grandfather.[26]

Finally, he argued that *izithakazelo* held more of a spiritual function (than offering a lineage record of kin formation), because:

> it is the clan ancestors who are primarily involved, through the calling of the name of the clan eponym, with his izithakazelo and praises. Thus the numerous little clan sections, scattered through-out the chiefdom territory, all worship the same pantheon of ancestral spirits – a 'community of (clan) saints'. Yet, and this is important, they do not do this as a collectivity, either as a clan or as a 'lineage', but merely as the small local group agnates.[27]

Hammond-Tooke's observations on the localised nature of agnatic kin clusters were likely correct at the time – that is, when observing colonised Africans. It is not a stretch to presume that colonisation ended the political and organisational function of clan naming. With the incorporation of Africans into the colonial and then capitalist industrial economy, the development of indigenous social formations and the power of clan identifications came to an end.

However, from a historiographical and indigenous archival perspective, *iziduko* and *izithakazelo* convey more than lineages of descent. This is because they form part of a genre of information that is directly tied to ritual and totemic practices, which in many clans serve a role in sustaining social relations in numerous ways, including providing a mythology of origins, offering social/political rank and status protocols, regulating social mores and duties, and more besides. In that sense, it is difficult to simply use the English term 'clan' as it does not quite convey the implied totemic meaning. Anne Kelk Mager and Phiko Velelo provide a useful description of the nature of genealogies:

> Genealogies are more than a list of names; they are short stories passed down through oral tradition, a mode of telling that people live by. Genealogies are a way of knowing. They set out historical time and identify who belongs to whom. They are deployed as a political tool. Chiefs name their ancestral line and make claims on authority and power, ordinary people repeat the citations to indicate their belonging. Genealogies do not operate in a vacuum – custom, personality and political context also play a part in determination of succession.[28]

Peires himself argued that while clan identities were not 'absolute', they were not wholly 'fluid' and flexible either, for they tended to endure down lineages. In his words:

> Clan identification is not absolute – clans have been known to split, clans have been known to incorporate outsiders – but it is far more durable than chiefly identification. Nevertheless, each clan has at least something of its history preserved in its clan-praises (iziduko) and different clans are therefore often linked with specific political entities. The lineage of SEK Mqhayi lived six generations among the amaRharhabe before the birth of the poet, but are still considered to be Thembu in origin because they belong to the amaZima, a Thembu clan. Similarly, the Poswayo family left Natal eight generations back and have been intimate councillors of the Qwathi chiefs for six generations but will always be recognised as Hlubi on account of their clan-name, which is Xaba.[29]

This means that even if present living people no longer forge political unity through clan names, these names are not acquired arbitrarily either, because as Tyatyeka (1995) argues:

> Enye enga ingacaca kukuba isiduko somntu sinye, izinqulo okanye izithutho zininzi.[30] (What needs to also be clarified is that a person can only have one clan name, but their praises can be many.)

As I have shown when discussing Mfecane historiography elsewhere, this failure to understand how a clan name is acquired and what it actually means as a ritual artefact with a social purpose led Julian Cobbing in 'Mfecane as Alibi' (1988) and Alan Webster in 'Emancipation of the Fingo' (1991) to make a basic error in their interpretation of the question of who amaMfengu were.[31] Had they understood idiomatically the ritual identification associated with *iziduko* clan naming, they would not have made the odd argument that the identity and origins story of amaMfengu was a colonial fabrication.[32] It would have been well-nigh impossible for colonists to invent and impose *isiduko* for an African in 1835. Surnames could be imposed by colonial assimilation, but *iziduko* are inherited totemic identities accorded by ancestral ritual. This critical element of indigenous naming systems was missed by many mainstream academic historians in the great debate about the Mfecane.

The question of who the amaMfengu were had already been answered in any case, by a Xhosa writer called Richard Kawa, whose book *Ibali lamaMfengu* was published in 1922 (reprinted in 2011) and detailed, for those who could read Xhosa, the very specific clan descent of Mfengu clans in the Eastern Cape, and why they distinguished their origins from the Xhosa. The fact that the gross error of interpretation by Cobbing and Webster was barely challenged by academic historians of Cape history until it was grappled with more recently by the likes of Nomalungisa Maxengana (2012, 2018) and Mkhize (2018) shows the crucial importance of understanding the meanings of these indigenous historical forms and the context in which they develop.[33]

A potentially helpful approach involves looking at what these categories and terms mean, by exploring them from within their own idioms. Larry Danielson uses the terms 'etic' and 'emic' to distinguish between knowledge as it is described from outside or within a culture. He argues: 'The terms "etic" and "emic" often appear in contemporary folklore studies. In informal academic usage "etic" has come to designate an outsider's point of view and system of classification, and "emic" the insider's conception of cultural categories.'[34] It is important to understand that from an insider's perspective, a clan is also a ritual artefact that inscribes children into the totemic and ritual practices of the clan. Clans are thus a critical element in ordinary people's histories and daily lives. Through the ritualisation of *iziduko*, an archive of history is imparted to the member of the clan.

Herbert Isaac Ernest Dhlomo and Archibald Campbell Jordan were amongst the first Africans to provide a major systematic conceptualisation of African-language literary forms that accorded them 'emic' analysis, and this at a time when white scholars argued that Africans had no literature. In *Towards an African Literature*, Jordan argued, for example, for the literary value of praise poetry, asserting that it constituted among the highest indigenous literary forms:

> To the Bantu-speaking Southern Africans, the praise-poem is their proudest artistic possession. It is in this genre that the greatest possibilities of a Bantu language as a medium of literary expression are to be found. The subject of a praise-poem may be a nation, a tribe, a clan, a person, an animal, or a lifeless object. The poem may be partly narrative, or partly or wholly descriptive. It abounds in epithets, very much like the Homeric ones, and the language in general is highly figurative. The bard, who was both composer and public reciter, was versed in tribal history and lore, as well as being witty. He held a position of honour in his community.[35]

Mbongiseni Buthelezi uses competing clan *izithakazelo* to make sense of suppressed regional histories, arguing that through 'rigorous engagement with Shaka's, Phungashe's and Zwide's *izibongo* (praises) and the *izithakazelo* (clan praises) of the Buthelezi and the Ndwandwe, this project calls into question the suppression of some significant histories and figures in the region'.[36]

Similarly, Tisani used *iziduko* to de-centre the dominance of Tshawe royal lineage in Xhosa historiography written by missionaries, which was later reproduced in academic historiography. For Tisani:

> Analysis of iziduko (clan praises and names) of amaCirha reveals remnants of the Cirha past, independent of the Tshawe narrative. The story of their lost royal status remained an important part of their past. Through iziduko amaCirha have kept the memory of their loss alive. One of their praises, 'Mhlomla-lidala kuba lineempondo' (Let us share because it [the eland] is big enough, it has horns) touches on the conflict of the 'brothers' Cirha and Jwarha with Tshawe over an eland.[37]

Rigorous engagement with *izithakazelo* requires the linguistic capability to deal with idiomatically embedded perspectives. Tisani again points out that the clan praises offer counter-hegemonic perspectives of Xhosa history, which de-centre Tshawe narratives:

> AmaQocwa are renowned as smiths among African communities in southern Africa. Their special knowledge of metals probably gave them a multiple identity, as they must have served and lived among different communities. It seems they were specially valued as makers of iron weaponry. Iziduko of amaQocwa do make reference to their skills: 'Zikhali mazembe, Xhwayimpi, Mkhont'ubomvu, Tsha'ng' elanga' (Axe weaponry, Stirrer of War, Red assegai that burns like the sun). If amaQocwa pre-date amaTshawe, as claimed in the text, that raises doubts about the claim that Tshawe returned with iron-working skills from his mother's people. The inclusion of amaQocwa in the list of izizwe may be seen as a statement by non-Tshawe that the Xhosa community before Tshawe was a vibrant society, with knowledge of metals.[38]

In other words, clan-based *iziduko* and *izithakazelo*, along with the associated clan praises, provide an archive of disputation and contestation, which underscores the inherently contested nature of indigenous historical praxis, for in no way are oral traditions accepted as sacrosanct or beyond dispute by Africans. In fact, the opposite is true – the recitation of *iziduko*, *izithakazelo* and *izibongo* invites heavy disputation and argumentation about the histories they convey. From an emic perspective, while *iziduko* are taken as 'artefacts of history', they are understood to be contestable narratives by whomever is using them.

Clan genealogy as vernacular classics

It is a function of colonial knowledge structures that African folklore is treated as ethnographic artefact while Greek folklore is considered a necessary philosophical oeuvre for understanding Greek history. In reality, of course, all historians have to grapple with mythology. Clan genealogies function in a similar vein. As Daniel Woolf has argued, the work of the historian has always been to put together various forms of orality in making sense of the past. By adopting this conception, we would see early African Christian historians doing the task of what Woolf called 'the modern antiquary [who] was not always so fortunate as to have tangible evidence close at hand'. He argued further:

> Yet the informal tales and folklore of early modern England do share with African traditions a sense of time alien to most western historians. Oral cultures have little sense of a relative past and either do not assign dates to events in their tradition or forget large parts of the past; the transmitters of such traditions thereby 'telescope' their own history and provide a chronology which, though it is comprehensible to the members of their group, will mislead outside observers conditioned to dealing in firm dates. What is true of the formal tribal narrative holds afortiori for rural early modern England, where the sense of the past was focused less on time than on space, less on dates than on locations.[39]

In his *Abantu Abamnyama*, Magema Fuze seemed aware that his work lived in part in the realm of mythology. He therefore urged:

> Do not be surprised that you are reading a book without horns (without effect) in that it treats events without dates, for you will see no year nor month nor day for the events which it treats ... but I am hoping that everybody will discover for themselves the dates of these events when they study the writings of the white people, if by chance they come upon them.[40]

South African historiography, it could be argued, lacks such foundational vernacular classics, and is accordingly impoverished conceptually and empirically. To further enrich historiography, far greater work needs to be done on vernacular writing and on the authors themselves. What they will challenge or support in existing interpretations within the historiography will not be known until they are studied. But more importantly, as a matter of intellectual and scholarly integrity, the work must be done lest the historiography perpetuate its own implicit myth – that black South Africans have had no significant contributions to make in the writing of their own history.

Notes

1 W.B. Rubusana, *Zemk'inkomo Magwalandini* (London: Butler and Tanner, 1911); M. Fuze, *The Black People and Whence they Came* (edited by A.T. Cope and translated by H.C. Lugg; Pietermaritzburg: University of Natal Press, 1979).
2 S.M. Ndlovu, *African Perspectives of King Dingane KaSenzangakhona: The Second Monarch of the Zulu Kingdom* (Cham: Springer International Publishing, 2017), 7.
3 B. Petersen, 'The Archives and the Political Imaginary', in C. Hamilton (ed.), *Refiguring the Archive* (Dordrecht: Kluwer Academic, 2002), 29.
4 For example, historical texts such as Rubusana's *Zemk'inkomo Magwalandini* were made available in abridged form in Xhosa-medium schools as part of the ethnolinguistic education policy of the apartheid regime.
5 A.C. Jordan, *Towards an African Literature: The Emergence of Literary Form in Xhosa* (Berkeley: University of California Press, 1974), 114.
6 W.W. Gqoba, *Isizwe Esinembali: Xhosa Histories and Poetry (1873–1888)*, Publications of the Opland Collection of Xhosa literature, vol. 1 (Pietermaritzburg: University of KwaZulu-Natal Press, 2015), 24.
7 J. Opland, 'Introduction', in *ibid.*, 27.
8 H. Bradford and M. Qotole, 'Ingxoxo Enkulu ngoNongqawuse (A great debate about Nongqawuse's era)', *Kronos*, 34 (1) Nov. 2008, 66–105.
9 A. Masola, 'The Politics of the 1920s Black Press: Charlotte Maxeke and Nontsizi Mgqwetho's Critique of Congress', *International Journal of African Renaissance Studies – Multi-, Inter- and Transdisciplinarity* 13 (2) 2018, 59–76.
10 N. Masilela, *An Outline of the New African Movement in South Africa* (Trenton, NJ: Africa World Press, [c. 2013]).
11 L. Switzer, 'The African Christian Community and Its Press in Victorian South Africa', *Cahiers d'études africaines*, 24 (96) 1984, 455–76; N. Tisani, 'Continuity and Change in Xhosa Historiography during the Nineteenth Century: An Exploration through Textual Analysis' (DPhil thesis, Rhodes University, 2000), 30; H. Mokoena, *Magema Fuze: The Making of a Kholwa Intellectual* (Scottsville: University of KwaZulu-Natal Press, 2011); A. Odendaal, *The Founders: The Origins of the ANC and the Struggle for Democracy in South Africa* (Johannesburg: Jacana, 2012), 56–66; P. Limb, 'The Empire Writes Back: African Challenges to the Brutish (South African) Empire in the Early 20th Century', *Journal of Southern African Studies*, 41 (3) 2015, 599–616.
12 Tisani, 'Continuity and Change', 38, 182.

13 *Ibid.*, 210.
14 S. Naidu, 'The Struggle for Authority in George McCall Theal's *Kaffir Folkore* (1882)', *Southern African Journal for Folklore Studies*, 24 (1) 2014, 81.
15 A. Bank, 'The "Intimate Politics" of Fieldwork: Monica Hunter and Her African Assistants, Pondoland and the Eastern Cape, 1931–1932', *Journal of Southern African Studies*, 34 (3) 2008, 557–74.
16 J. Sharp, 'The Roots and Development of Volkekunde in South Africa', *Journal of Southern African Studies*, 8 (1) 1981, 16–36.
17 B. Magubane, 'Whose Memory – Whose History? The Illusion of Liberal and Radical Historical Debates', in H.E. Stolten (ed.), *History Making and Present Day Politics: The Meaning of Collective Memory in South Africa* (Uppsala: Nordiska Afrikainstitutet, 2007), 251–79; N. Mkhize, 'Walter Rubusana's *Zemk'inkomo Magwalandini* and the Missing Idiom of African Historiography', in J. Bam, L. Ntsebeza and A. Zinn (eds), *Whose History Counts: Decolonising African Pre-colonial Historiography* (Stellenbosch: African Sun Media, 2018), 60–1.
18 Magubane, 'Whose History', 253.
19 B. Magubane, *My Life and Times* (Pietermaritzburg: University of Kwazulu-Natal Press, 2010), 251–2.
20 B. Nyoka, 'Bernard Magubane's *The Making of a Racist State* Revisited: 20 Years On', *Journal of Black Studies*, 47 (8) 2016, 903–27, and 'Archie Mafeje: An Intellectual Biography' (DPhil thesis, University of South Africa, 2017).
21 J. Wright, 'Thinking beyond "Tribal Traditions": Reflections on the Precolonial Archive', *South African Historical Journal*, 62 (2) 2010, 278.
22 Tisani, 'Continuity and Change'.
23 *Ibid.*, 61.
24 N.D. Jafta, 'The Impact and Development of Literature on the Xhosa People', Cory Library Pamphlet Box MS 16 599 (Box 9).
25 D. Hammond-Tooke, 'Descent Groups, Chiefdoms and South African Historiography', *Journal of Southern African Studies*, 11 (2) 1985, 314.
26 *Ibid.*, 316.
27 *Ibid.*, 317.
28 A. Mager and P. Velelo, *The House of Tshatshu: Power, Politics and Chiefs North-West of the Great Kei River, c.1818–2018* (Cape Town: University of Cape Town Press, 2018), 116.
29 J. Peires, '"He Wears Short Clothes!": Rethinking Rharhabe (c.1715–c.1782)', *Journal of Southern African Studies*, 38 (2) 2012, 350.
30 D.M. Tyatyeka, *Iziduko Nezibongo* (Pietermaritzburg: Shuter and Shooter, 1995), preface.
31 N. Mkhize, 'In Search of Native Dissidence: RT Kawa's Mfecane Historiography in *Ibali lamaMfengu* (1929)', *International Journal of African Renaissance Studies – Multi-, Inter- and Transdisciplinarity*, 13 (2) 2018, 92–111; N. Maxengana, 'The Impact of Missionary Activities and the Establishment of Victoria East, 1824–1860' (MA thesis, University of Fort Hare, 2012).
32 J. Cobbing, 'The Mfecane as Alibi: Thoughts on Dithakong and Mbolompo', *Journal of African History*, 29 (3) 1988, 487–519; A. Webster, 'Land Expropriation

and Labour Extraction under Cape Colonial Rule: The War of 1835 and the "Emancipation" of the Fingo' (MA thesis, Rhodes University, 1991).
33 Maxengana, 'Impact of Missionary Activities', 51; N. Maxengana, 'The History and Historiography of the Amamfengu of the Eastern Cape, 1820–1900' (PhD thesis, University of Fort Hare, 2018); Mkhize, 'Native Dissidence'.
34 L. Danielson, 'The Folklorist, the Oral Historian, and Local History', *Oral History Review*, 8, 1980, 63.
35 Jordan, *Towards an African Literature*, 101.
36 M. Buthelezi, '"*Kof'Abantu, Kosal'Izibongo?*": Contested Histories of Shaka, Phungashe and Zwide in *Izibongo* and *Izithakazelo*' (MA thesis, University of KwaZulu-Natal, 2004), 2.
37 Tisani, Continuity and Change', 143.
38 *Ibid.*, 143.
39 D. Woolf, 'The "Common Voice": History, Folklore and Oral Tradition in Early Modern England', *Past & Present*, 120, Aug. 1988, 27–8, 31.
40 Fuze, *Abantu Abamnyama*, vii.

Bibliography

Bank, A. (2008) 'The "Intimate Politics" of Fieldwork: Monica Hunter and Her African Assistants, Pondoland and the Eastern Cape, 1931–1932', *Journal of Southern African Studies*, 34 (3).

Bradford, H., and M. Qotole (2008) 'Ingxoxo Enkulu ngoNongqawuse (A great debate about Nongqawuse's era', *Kronos*, 34 (1).

Buthelezi, M. (2004) '"*Kof'Abantu, Kosal'Izibongo?*": Contested Histories of Shaka, Phungashe and Zwide in *Izibongo* and *Izithakazelo*'. MA thesis, University of KwaZulu-Natal.

Cobbing, J. (1988) 'The Mfecane as Alibi: Thoughts on Dithakong and Mbolompo', *Journal of African History*, 29 (3).

Danielson, L. (1980) 'The Folklorist, the Oral Historian, and Local History', *Oral History Review*, 8.

Fuze, M. (1979) *The Black People and Whence they Came*, edited by A.T. Cope, translated by H.C. Lugg. Pietermaritzburg: University of Natal Press.

Gqoba, W.W. (2015) *Isizwe Esinembali: Xhosa Histories and Poetry (1873–1888)*, Publications of the Opland Collection of Xhosa literature, vol. 1. Pietermaritzburg: University of KwaZulu-Natal Press.

Hammond-Tooke, D. (1985) 'Descent Groups, Chiefdoms and South African Historiography', *Journal of Southern African Studies*, 11 (2).

Jafta, N.D. (n.d.) 'The Impact and Development of Literature on the Xhosa People', Cory Library Pamphlet Box MS 16 599 (Box 9).

Jordan, A.C. (1974) *Towards an African Literature: The Emergence of Literary Form in Xhosa*. Berkeley: University of California Press.

Limb, P. (2015) 'The Empire Writes Back: African Challenges to the Brutish (South African) Empire in the Early 20th Century', *Journal of Southern African Studies*, 41 (3).

Mager, A., and P. Velelo (2018) *The House of Tshatshu: Power, Politics and Chiefs North-West of the Great Kei River, c.1818–2018*. Cape Town: University of Cape Town Press.

Magubane, B. (2007) 'Whose Memory – Whose History? The Illusion of Liberal and Radical Historical Debates', in H.E. Stolten (ed.), *History Making and Present Day Politics: The Meaning of Collective Memory in South Africa*. Uppsala: Nordiska Afrikainstitutet.

Magubane, B. (2010) *My Life and Times*. Pietermaritzburg: University of Kwazulu-Natal Press.

Masilela, N. [c. 2013] *An Outline of the New African Movement in South Africa*. Trenton, NJ: Africa World Press.

Masola, A. (2018) 'The Politics of the 1920s Black Press: Charlotte Maxeke and Nontsizi Mgqwetho's Critique of Congress', *International Journal of African Renaissance Studies – Multi-, Inter- and Transdisciplinarity*, 13 (2).

Maxengana, N. (2012) 'The Impact of Missionary Activities and the Establishment of Victoria East, 1824–1860'. MA thesis, University of Fort Hare.

Maxengana, N. (2018) 'The History and Historiography of the Amamfengu of the Eastern Cape, 1820–1900'. DPhil thesis, University of Fort Hare.

Mkhize, N. (2018) 'In Search of Native Dissidence: RT Kawa's Mfecane Historiography in *Ibali lamaMfengu* (1929)', *International Journal of African Renaissance Studies –Multi-, Inter- and Transdisciplinarity*, 13 (2).

Mkhize, N. (2018) 'Walter Rubusana's *Zemk'inkomo Magwalandini* and the Missing Idiom of African Historiography', in J. Bam, L. Ntsebeza and A. Zinn (eds), *Whose History Counts: Decolonising African Pre-colonial Historiography*. Stellenbosch: African Sun Media.

Mokoena, H. (2011) *Magema Fuze: The Making of a Kholwa Intellectual*. Scottsville: University of KwaZulu-Natal Press.

Naidu, S. (2012) 'Three Tales of Theal: Biography, History and Ethnography on the Eastern Frontier', *English in Africa*, 39 (1).

Naidu, S. (2014) 'The Struggle for Authority in George McCall Theal's *Kaffir Folklore* (1882)', *Southern African Journal for Folklore Studies*, 24 (1).

Ndlovu, S.M. (2017) *African Perspectives of King Dingane KaSenzangakhona: The Second Monarch of the Zulu Kingdom*. Cham: Springer International Publishing.

Nyoka, B. (2016) 'Bernard Magubane's *The Making of a Racist State* Revisited: 20 Years On', *Journal of Black Studies*, 47 (8).

Nyoka, B. (2017) 'Archie Mafeje: An Intellectual Biography'. DPhil thesis, University of South Africa.

Odendaal, A. (2012) *The Founders: The Origins of the ANC and the Struggle for Democracy in South Africa*. Johannesburg: Jacana.

Opland, J. (2015) 'Introduction', in Gqoba, *Isizwe Esinembali*.

Peires, J. (1982) *The House of Phalo: A History of the Xhosa People in the Days of Their Independence*. Berkeley: University of California Press.

Peires, J. (2012) '"He Wears Short Clothes!": Rethinking Rharhabe (c.1715–c.1782)', *Journal of Southern African Studies*, 38 (2).

Petersen, B. (2002) 'The Archives and the Political Imaginary', in C. Hamilton (ed.), *Refiguring the Archive*. Dordrecht: Kluwer Academic.

Rubusana, W.B. (1911) *Zemk'iinkomo Magwalandini*. London: Butler and Tanner.
Sharp, J. (1981) 'The Roots and Development of Volkekunde in South Africa', *Journal of Southern African Studies*, 8 (1).
Switzer, L. (1984) 'The African Christian Community and Its Press in Victorian South Africa', *Cahiers d'études africaines*, 24 (96).
Tisani, N. (2000) 'Continuity and Change in Xhosa Historiography during the Nineteenth Century: An Exploration through Textual Analysis'. DPhil thesis, Rhodes University.
Tyatyeka, D.M. (1995) *Iziduko Nezibongo*. Pietermaritzburg: Shuter and Shooter.
Webster, A. (1991) 'Land Expropriation and Labour Extraction under Cape Colonial Rule: The War of 1835 and the "Emancipation" of the Fingo'. MA thesis, Rhodes University.
Woolf, D. (1988) 'The "Common Voice": History, Folklore and Oral Tradition in Early Modern England', *Past & Present*, 120.
Wright, J. (2010) 'Thinking beyond "Tribal Traditions": Reflections on the Precolonial Archive', *South African Historical Journal*, 62 (2).

6

The revolution in South African historiography

Thula Simpson

The editors of the *Cambridge History of South Africa* (2010, 2012) stated of its two volumes that the first 'pulls together' while the second 'represents a culmination of' four decades of 'revisionist' scholarship.[1] The objective of offering a revisionist synthesis of the country's past was one shared by many of the general histories of South Africa that appeared during those forty years. One consequence of this is that the prefaces, introductions and forewords of those works offer a good summary of the revisionist position.

In *South Africa: A Modern History* (five editions: 1977–2000), Rodney Davenport wrote: 'The study of South African history, so dependent in the early part of the twentieth century on the work of George McCall Theal, has undergone two significant changes in this century and is now involved in a third.' The first followed W.M. Macmillan's turn against the 'presumption in favour of the "colonial" as against the "missionary" point of view in the inter-racial conflicts of the eighteenth and early nineteenth century', which was manifest in the works of Theal and others.[2] The second came with the two-volume *Oxford History of South Africa* (1969, 1971), of which Hermann Giliomee and Bernard Mbenga wrote in their *New History of South Africa* (2007) that 'for the first time extensive coverage was provided of the pre-colonial history of South Africa, with illuminating chapters by an archaeologist and an anthropologist'.[3] In *The Making of Modern South Africa* (2004), Nigel Worden pointed out that the *Oxford History* was itself challenged during the 1970s by 'a new group of young historians who were influenced by a neo-Marxist, or revisionist, paradigm. They explained apartheid not as the irrational racism of a pre-industrial colonial frontier, but as the direct product of South Africa's unique process of industrialization.' Worden added that 'acrimonious' though the early exchanges were, 'in the course of the past twenty years some of the dogmatism of the early revisionist writers has been tempered'.[4] The result, according to Leonard Thompson, was that 'liberals have been radicalized, radicals have been liberalized',[5] and William Beinart has stated: 'There is no longer one "school" of "revisionist" or radical history, but most authors have shared an opposition to apartheid and a commitment to discovering the history of black people.'[6]

Therefore, with some minor terminological differences (the 'neo-Marxists' termed 'radicals' by some are 'revisionists' to others, for example), there is general agreement on a 'historiographical revolution'[7] involving four broad stages: (1) the liberal revolt against Theal; (2) the *Oxford History*, with its pioneering use of interdisciplinary methodology to explore the precolonial past; (3) the neo-Marxist critique of liberal historiography; and (4) the revisionist synthesis, which combined points 1–3 into a common position that stood in basic opposition to the older, prosettler accounts.

This chapter revisits the historiographical revolution, and in the process challenges some of the abovementioned classifications, before discussing future directions of inquiry that such a reconsideration might open up. Before proceeding further, I must add the disclaimer that because the chapter engages principally with the literature on the historiographical revolution, it focuses on the histories considered canonical within that literature. The resulting omissions are not value judgements on any works thereby excluded. On the contrary, I believe that from the following revaluation of existing historiographical markers, an alternative landscape emerges that is both more inclusive of past scholarship and, hopefully, more generative of future growth.

The revolution that wasn't

By most accounts, the *Oxford History* is held to mark an important historiographical watershed. Most contemporary reviews of the first volume concurred with the view that its greatest contribution lay in how it managed to transcend the Eurocentrism of the existing literature.

In a review published in 1970, Shula Marks argued that 'South African history has continued to be the history of white settlement in the subcontinent, with little more than a cursory glance at the role of the black man except when his activities impinged on the consciousness or material welfare of his white rulers'.[8] Harrison Wright echoed this contention in 1975, claiming that it was only 'in the past decade' that 'historians of South Africa have, however belatedly, begun to emphasize the role of Africans in South African history'.[9] Many linked this shift to developments in the broader historiography of the African continent. Anthony Atmore argued that the first volume promised nothing less than to 'lift South African historiography into the main stream of African history',[10] while Ronald Hyam contended that 'the praise which some reviewers have given to the Oxford History (to volume

I rather than II) appears to stem largely from sheer amazement that any book should even attempt to bring South African history into line with that practised everywhere else in the African continent'.[1] Timothy Coghlan explained in closer detail what those broader historiographical trends had entailed: 'Modern historians have come to see African history as something dynamic rather than static, as extending long before the arrival of the European, and halted in its time period only by a lack of information', with contemporary scholars overcoming gaps in the knowledge of that past by embracing archaeological techniques.[12]

The *Oxford History*'s foregrounding of African agency was credited with having given it two distinctive features. One was its aforementioned engagement with the precolonial past, using sources beyond the written accounts usually favoured by historians. For Wyn Rees, this interdisciplinarity enabled the first volume to transcend the 'prejudices, distortions, and myths' of the existing literature, which 'to date has been the story of European achievement. It "starts" with the arrival of the Portuguese. Nonwhites appear as "problems".'[13] Lewis Hoskins argued that those myths, including 'the conventional claims of many South Africans that the whites found an empty subcontinent', had seeped into broader South African culture.[14] Shula Marks commented approvingly that 'in the Oxford History, it is only in chapter 5 that we arrive at "White Settlers and the Origin of a New Society, 1652–1778"'.[15]

The second distinctive feature was less an innovation than the extension of an older tradition, relating to how events following European settlement were characterised. As Leslie Duly noted, the *Oxford History*'s editors, Leonard Thompson and Monica Wilson, wrote in their preface that 'the central theme of South African history is interaction between peoples of diverse origins, languages, technologies, ideologies, and social systems, meeting on South African soil'.[16] For Merle Lipton, this declaration extended 'a clear message: that South African history is essentially about the interaction (in both conflict *and* co-operation) between many widely different societies and cultures, and is not the heroic story, beginning with the arrival of the Europeans in 1652, of the subjugation and civilisation of a barbaric land'.[17] Anthony Atmore argued that this focus on 'interaction' echoed a longer liberal interpretation, and he identified the *Oxford History* as 'the first serious attempt to survey the history of all the peoples of South Africa since the publication of C.W. de Kiewiet's *History of South Africa* in 1941'.[18]

In his historiographical survey, *The Making of the South African Past*, Chris Saunders cited these two features to support his contention that the *Oxford History* heralded the 'liberal Africanist' phase in the literature.[19]

Turning to the *Oxford History* itself, it is striking how closely these accounts accorded with the estimations that Thompson and Wilson themselves expressed of what they considered to be the most significant features of the volumes. Of the existing histories, they wrote:

> Nearly every one of them embodies the point of view of only one community ... They are primarily concerned with the achievements of white people in South Africa, and their relations with one another. The experiences of the other inhabitants of South Africa are not dealt with at any length: they are treated mainly as peoples who constituted 'Native', or 'Coloured', or 'Indian' problems for the whites.[20]

The second flaw was that the other works manifested 'a marked disciplinary focus, construing history in narrow terms'. Thompson and Wilson also identified De Kiewiet's *History* as a contribution that 'largely escapes these limitations'.[21]

What has perhaps been overlooked subsequently is how Thompson and Wilson felt compelled to almost immediately begin rowing back their critique when considering the earlier literature in closer detail. They devoted the greatest attention to the *Cambridge History of the British Empire* (*CHBE*, 1936, second edition 1963), the eighth volume of which focused on 'South Africa, Rhodesia and the Protectorates'. The *CHBE*'s editors, E.A. Benians and A.P. Newton, had written in their preface that the volume's two distinctive features were that 'our story begins long before the coming of the Portuguese', and that the perspective maintained throughout was that 'the history of South Africa differs from that of the other British Dominions by reason of the essential part played by the natives which appears in almost every part of our work'.[22]

In other words, they claimed to have foregrounded the two themes that the *Oxford History* is usually credited with having pioneered. But were they correct? Thompson and Wilson indicated that the claims possessed substantial truth, for they conceded that the *CHBE* 'includes a social anthropologist's summary of the condition of the inhabitants of South Africa before they mingled with people from Europe; an account of the early contacts of the East African coast with the outside world; and chapters which analyse the effects of contact upon the African peoples'. Thompson and Wilson acknowledged that this was 'pioneering work when these chapters were first written', but they added that 'our knowledge of African archaeology and anthropology has increased rapidly in recent years'.[23]

This was something quite different from the claim that the previous literature either overlooked non-Europeans, the precolonial period and the importance of 'interaction', or considered the past only in narrow disciplinary terms. The historiographical issue at stake was whether the *Oxford History* should be seen as a revolutionary or an evolutionary moment in these regards. Having essentially conceded the *latter* to be true, Thompson and

Wilson claimed 'the effect is additive rather than integrative, for the bulk of the work is concerned with white people and with politics'.[24] Yet we have seen that Benians and Newton would strongly contest even that qualified critique, for they insisted that the essential role of the indigenous population was emphasised in 'almost every part' of their volume (and they could have stated in support of their claim that it was only in chapter 5 of the *CHBE* that 'Foundation of the Cape Colony, 1652–1708' was reached).

If we consider the competing claims against the content of the respective Oxbridge volumes, a useful point of comparison would be the aspect that is often advanced as the *Oxford History*'s most important contribution – namely, its role in exploding what Shula Marks and Monica Wilson both termed the 'Empty Land' myth, referring to the process whereby historians from the 1960s onwards employed anthropological, archaeological and linguistic insights to overturn the conventional wisdom that when white people settled the Cape in the mid-seventeenth century, Bantu-language speakers had only recently crossed the Limpopo River in small numbers, and were settled in pockets of land that corresponded with the twentieth-century Bantustans.[25]

The famous chapters of the *Oxford History* that dealt with the question were authored by Monica Wilson and Ray Inskeep, who respectively estimated that by the time of white settlement, Bantu speakers had been in continuous settlement of wide areas of the north of (what became) South Africa since the eleventh century, and of the eastern seaboard up to the Umtata River by 1593, though Wilson added that some oral traditions claimed a much earlier arrival in the latter region.[26] As Newton and Benians pointed out, the *CHBE* also engaged the primacy of tenure question, and in the relevant chapter by Isaac Schapera, an archaeologist, the following chronology was offered: 'according to orthodox tradition, the earliest Bantu invaders reached South Africa about the eleventh or twelfth centuries A.D.', while Nguni speakers were present on the Natal coast by the end of the sixteenth century.[27]

There was therefore little if any difference between the two volumes on the land question, which supports the case for continuity rather than dramatic rupture in terms of their willingness to engage with the multidisciplinary scholarship on the topic.

But it is doubtful whether the conventional historiographical wisdom can even be applied to George Theal, the supposed father of 'settler' historiography (to borrow E.H. Brookes's term).[28] Thompson and Wilson did not mention Theal when they wrote 'we have profited from the work of our predecessors',[29] but Thompson was sole editor of *African Societies in Southern Africa*, another volume that appeared in 1969, where he noted in his introduction, titled 'The Forgotten Factor in Southern African History', that Theal's works were 'in one respect much more "modern" than many more recent writings on South African history: they say a great deal about Africans and much of what they say is based on oral traditions collected in the nineteenth century'.[30]

The contention that Theal considered Africans unworthy of attention except as problems for white people must reckon with passages such as the following in his *History and Ethnography of Africa South of the Zambezi* (1910):

> Before I entered the civil service of the Cape Colony in 1877 I had been engaged for many years in studying the traditions, habits, and power of thought of the Bantu tribes of the south-eastern coast ... I had already prepared a short History and Geography of South Africa, which was printed at the Lovedale missionary institution, and quickly passed through three editions. I had also collected among different Bantu tribes a number of folklore tales, some of which were published in magazines, and others at a later date in a small volume issued in London.[31]

Though Thompson argued that this interest separated Theal from other historians of South Africa, J. Michael Berning and Robert Shell have noted that George Cory (who succeeded Theal as South Africa's official historiographer, and is generally considered to be the second major settler historian)[32] also learned indigenous languages to enable him to interview Africans and 'Coloureds' about historical events. Berning and Shell drew a contrast with W.M. Macmillan in this regard, arguing that Cory should be considered the 'real methodological innovator and champion of African history'.[33]

Liberal historiography

An irony of South African historiography is that when George Theal died in 1919, he probably believed himself to have pioneered what would later be called Africanist scholarship. In his *History and Ethnography*, he requested his readers' forgiveness for beginning with the arrival of the Portuguese rather than the crossing of the Zambezi by the first 'Bantu invaders'. He attributed the omission to the Cape Government's abrupt withdrawal of support for his research, before offering the baton to his successors, stating: 'That must be done by some other hand more favoured by fortune than mine.'[34]

The charge directed at Theal, that he 'ignored' Africans, is not seriously defensible for the reasons outlined above, and the present section will instead consider the *Oxford History*'s second principal feature – namely, the manner in which it is said to have furthered liberal scholarship. The discussion will proceed by considering the characteristic features of the liberal tradition.

As noted, W.M. Macmillan is generally credited with having pioneered the liberal interpretation. He offered an early outline of his critique of the historiographical status quo in *The South African Agrarian Problem and Its Historical Development* (1919), where, having observed that 'it is perhaps unfortunate that South African history has been represented so much as an affair of governors and treaties', he contended that 'the South African history which is really significant is that which tells us about the everyday life of the people, how they lived, what they thought, and what they worked at, when they did think and work, what they produced and what and where they marketed, and the whole of their social organisation'. That history, he wrote, 'remains to be written'.[35]

Macmillan attempted to author that history in a famous trilogy that appeared towards the end of the following decade. The three books were *The Cape Colour Question: A Historical Survey* (1927), which used the papers of the missionary Doctor John Philip to revise Theal's and Cory's account of frontier conflict; *Bantu, Boer, and Briton: The Making of the South African Native Problem* (1929), which placed the struggle for land at the centre of the conflict between the three groups and identified African poverty as one of the lasting legacies of the contest; and *Complex South Africa: An Economic Foot-Note to History* (1930), which surveyed contemporary society and drew a connection between the poverty among the black and white populations.[36]

In his introduction to the *Cape Colour Question*, Macmillan expanded on his ideas regarding reconstruction in South African historiography. He wrote that 'in the learned world the equanimity of scientific historians has latterly been disturbed' in ways that undermined the previous situation, in which 'for a generation the critical investigation of sources has been the goal and end of all historical study'. In explaining the new approach, he cited Benedetto Croce's dictum that 'every true history is contemporary history', and argued that the statement both cautioned against the 'danger of too great aloofness from common life', while offering 'a warning that, without an effort to "think things together", the historian will inevitably fall into a snare'. It was in this regard that South African historians had fallen short for Macmillan, who argued that 'an inability to see the wood for the trees is a failing which particularly besets the writers of a young country like South Africa; incidents loom too large, distracting by reason of their family interest or local romance'. These scholarly shortcomings at once reflected and aggravated a broader societal failing in the country: South Africans had 'too little training and experience in hard political thinking', Macmillan claimed, and he specifically lamented the fact that 'for a whole generation the minds of the South African people have been absorbed in the abstract rivalries of Empire and Republic, to the neglect of pressing social and economic readjustments; and these problems have so largely been left to solve themselves, that they are now beyond mere legislative expedients'.[37]

As the quotes suggest, Macmillan was advocating a historiographical shift towards a focus on the origins of present-day social and economic problems. Yet in doing so, he was not arguing that the prevailing 'scientific' history lacked popular resonance. On the contrary, he was critiquing the malign effects of the prevailing public fixation on themes of mere 'family interest or local romance' – in faulting the past 'generation', he was accusing his peers.

It was a particularly bold challenge, given that, taken literally (considering the 1927 publication date), the reference to the past 'generation' would relegate events including the Second Anglo-Boer War, the unification of South Africa and the rise of Afrikaner nationalism (among others falling under the 'Empire and Republic' theme) to the status of historical abstractions. Macmillan soon made it clear that this was no slip, for he extended the argument beyond the previous generation and into the nineteenth century. Regarding the Great Trek, he wrote of the Cape Colony from which the Voortrekkers departed that 'men of two nations ... could hardly have had more in common than Dutch and British', and that it was only after the exodus that 'estrangement became antagonism', though he insisted that the hostility owed more to the hardships of the trek than any suffering encountered under British rule. Macmillan next considered subsequent relations between the Empire and the Voortrekker republics, and while conceding that 'occasions of sharp difference were not wanting, as in 1881' (presumably referring to the First Anglo-Boer War), he added 'it is generally conceded that in spite of everything, the promise of the early 'nineties was that Dutch and English in South Africa would settle down in peace and accord'.[38]

Though the decade ended with the two sides embroiled in the bloodiest conflict in South African history, we have seen this did nothing to shake his conviction about the illusoriness of conflict between Boer and Briton. The passages show Macmillan was *not* just arguing that the Empire versus Republic controversy was an abstraction from the social and economic challenges facing an industrialising South Africa in the 1920s; he was arguing that it was abstract from the challenges of the 1830s, 1880s, 1900s and, by clear implication, whenever and wherever else it might appear. It was *absolutely* abstract. At the same time, in offering the argument, he was not denying that past generations were as absorbed as his contemporaries in the controversies of Empire and Republic (given the levels of popular mobilisation involved – including mass migrations, cataclysmic wars, and the rise and fall of states – any such denial would have been untenable). This created the irony that while Macmillan's professed objective was to reconstruct South African historiography around the lives and thoughts of ordinary people, his reinterpretation of the country's past involved dismissing the testimony offered by those people – in both word and deed – regarding what they considered to be the most salient features of their experience.

Similar considerations apply when considering C.W. de Kiewiet, who was Macmillan's one-time pupil and is the historian usually held to have inherited his mantle as torchbearer of the liberal interpretation. The commonality in their outlook was illustrated in De Kiewiet's first couple of books. In *British Colonial Policy and the South African Republics* (1929), he warned readers that the work was not a 'complete history of South Africa', for completeness would require outlining how 'Europeans, natives and the Home Government are interlocked and inseparably intertwined',[39] and he pronounced himself on the nature of that intertwining in his *Imperial Factor in South Africa* (1937), where he declared that 'the most distinctive feature of the history of whites and natives is not race or colour, but a close economic association'.[40]

The focus in both works on imperial history, drawing on research conducted in London's Public Records Office, meant that this larger perspective was not fully developed in either book. Macmillan had also not been able to develop a general synthesis grounded in those principles. That task awaited De Kiewiet's *History of South Africa: Social and Economic* (1941). The essence of the argument that De Kiewiet advanced in his *History* was that while the 'Social and Economic' themes mentioned in the subtitle formed only part of the empirically observable content in South Africa's past, they explained the ever-closer association between different racial groups that was the key feature of the country's development.

The following are representative examples: De Kiewiet's account began with the arrival of white settlers, and he concluded of that process that the 'true history of South African colonization describes the growth, not of a settlement of Europeans, but of a totally new and unique society of different races and colours and cultural attainments'; then, of the country's subsequent development, he conceded the ubiquity of inter- and intraracial strife, but concluded that 'the greatest phenomenon of South African history most emphatically is not, in spite of all appearances, the rivalry between Boer and Briton. Nor is it, in spite of many and costly native wars, the antagonism of natives and colonists'; instead, 'the leading theme of South African history is the growth of a new society in which white and black are bound together in the closest dependence upon each other'. Turning to contemporary developments, De Kiewiet conceded that the 'language of public discussion and political debate freely uses terms such as "native question" and "segregation"' as if there were 'a real separation between two distinct communities', and he also freely acknowledged that 'the use of these terms can hardly be avoided' given 'great prejudices which race and colour engender', and a 'variety of things such as language, diet, legal and political status, education, and much more besides'. Yet he redoubled on his basic contention that these features 'must not be taken as an indication that the life and activity of white and black are really separate, or that each can be described within its own sphere without prejudice to the other.'[41]

The extracts show that Colin Bundy was surely correct in identifying Macmillan and De Kiewiet as 'South African representatives of a countercurrent within Western historiography generally, one challenging the primacy of political history in favor of socio-economic themes'.[42] Chris Saunders contended that the duo performed the following division of labour in accomplishing the shift: 'on the foundation laid by Macmillan, de Kiewiet was the first to build a general structure, in which such themes as the origins of migrant labour and the emergence of the colour bar in industry fell clearly into place in the overall history of the country'.[43]

Yet it is important to identify what was distinctive about the approach, for the liberal historians were not the first to foreground economic themes in South Africa's development. Macmillan and De Kiewiet would have been aware of this, having contributed alongside George Cory to the 1936 *CHBE*. In perhaps his last major work (he died prior to its publication), Cory's chapter focused on the 1820 British settlers, and he wrote that following initial hardships, from about 1823 there was a 'turn of the tide', with a critical role being played by the lucrative trade in ivory that was conducted with African hunters across the frontier. Cory wrote that while the British colonial authorities initially perpetuated the Dutch policy of suppressing the trade, they gradually shifted to regulating it as it grew in scale, and he contended that the commerce eventually fuelled the emergence of centres such as Port Elizabeth and Grahamstown.[44] The chapter only summarised material that was covered in much greater detail in Cory's multivolume *Rise of South Africa*, in which extensive attention was devoted to exploring economic themes, including a pioneering account of Cape slavery.[45]

Cory therefore neither ignored the importance of economics, nor overlooked the importance of interaction, for they were central to his account of the colonisation of the Eastern Province, which was the focus of his research career. The originality of the liberal interpretation lay not with the discovery of the existence or the importance of socioeconomic themes but with the assertion of their primacy, and the attempt to erect a general structure for all South African historiography on their foundation.

Yet in attempting to build that general structure, De Kiewiet faced the same difficulty that Macmillan encountered in laying the foundation. As noted in the extracts from De Kiewiet's *History* cited above, the liberal perspective hinged on the contention that the abundant evidence of conflict and division in South Africa's past should not be considered as a decisive indicator of what was significant in that history. Which raises the question: *why not*? This question can be put differently by referring back to the section where De Kiewiet argued of the impossibility of describing the lives and activities of the black and white populations as if they were 'really separate'. It bridged pages 179 and 180. But on page 178, he insisted: 'in the end South Africa is unique. It belongs to two societies, white and black, and stands upon two cultural levels'. The contradiction could not be resolved empirically, for the liberal interpretation involved taking different phases of South Africa's history, acknowledging the existence of elements of cooperation and conflict intermingled in each, before concluding that one was 'real' (or 'true') and the other only apparent. The interpretative problem was that, based on the empirical evidence alone, there was abundant support for both conclusions, raising the question of what reason there was to prefer one over the other.

Ultimately some reason had to be provided, for to keep repeating that one particular theme is 'real' or 'true' would be circular, in begging the question of what made it in any sense more real or true than any other feature of the historical landscape.

Radical and revisionist history

By most accounts, the radical critique developed in reaction to liberal scholarship. One consequence is that the ensuing debate between the two interpretations focused on how best to characterise the interaction between racial groups in the period following initial European settlement (for most liberal histories began with white settlement). One manifestation of this feature was the bifurcated response to the *Oxford History* that Ronald Hyam alluded to, whereby the generally positive reception of the first volume was not extended to the second, which considered events after the 1860s.

Anthony Atmore, for example, who had embraced the first volume, was more critical of the second, of which he observed that the contributors 'seem to have no appreciation that the South Africa of the 1960's might have been the result of a combination of apartheid *and* capitalism'.[46] He developed the argument in 'Liberal Dilemma: A Critique of the *Oxford History of South Africa*', a review article coauthored with Nancy Westlake, which advanced an alternative thesis of South Africa's development, in which the country's growth was 'dominated by its *colonial* character'. Atmore and Westlake defined colonialism as a process whereby 'the majority of the population [have] been and remain excluded from the centres of legal political power [by] immigrants from the metropolitan countries [and] their descendants'. This settler population in turn exploited its monopoly of power to induce 'politically unenfranchised Africans, on the basis of some form of coercion [to] operate the factories, mines, farms, kitchens, and nurseries of South Africa'. While the *'forms* of colonial domination ... changed over time in accordance with relatively specific economic and political developments' – and they mentioned shifts from a nonracial to a colour-bar franchise, from imperial to settler rule, and from agriculture to manufacturing as examples – they insisted that 'these specific changes of the form of domination occurred within, and did not alter, the colonial *content* of South African history'.[47]

This 'colonial' thesis was echoed by Martin Legassick, whose 'Dynamics of Modernization in South Africa' was another prominent review of the *Oxford History*. Legassick praised the *Oxford History*'s adoption of 'interaction' as its main theme, but he objected to how it was characterised. Rather than growing cooperation, he insisted the process was characterised by a 'system of forced labour' perpetuated by state coercion, while he contended that 'the slave, the "apprentice", the labour-tenant, the mining compound worker, the prison labourer ... represent a single social type, of whom the migrant labourer is the most contemporary form'.[48]

The dichotomy that Atmore and Westlake drew between South African history's 'form' and its 'content' was meanwhile reprised by Frederick Johnstone in an article on the 'New School' in South African historiography. Johnstone claimed that liberal historians 'tended to be highly empiricist: a little bit of this, a little bit of that, a little bit of constitutions, a little bit of laws, a little bit of politics', with the consequence that readers would 'as often as not, emerge from this labyrinth of "facts" with little clear understanding of *what it was all about*'. He added, apparently disbelievingly, that 'it did not seem to have dawned on anyone that perhaps the massive fact of South African history, the massive experience of the mass of the people in modern South Africa, was the super-exploitation of black labour by a racially structured capitalism, and that this, rather than ethnic groups, political parties, constitutions and so on, should be a starting point of analysis'.[49]

Grietjie Verhoef noted in her dissertation on radical historiography that many of its leading contributors objected to being considered a school, because this obscured important nuances between them (she identified 'Poulantzas-Althusser structuralists, Gramsci supporters, reasonably rigorous Marxists and neo-Marxists' as different shades of radical opinion). Yet she added, quoting Belinda Bozzoli approvingly, that a fundamental point on which the radicals agreed was their desire to oversee 'the great substitution of a "liberal" paradigm of analysis for a "Marxist" one'.[50]

This, however, renewed the question of criteria cited earlier, because, as with the liberals, the radicals made it clear that the rationale for favouring the Marxist paradigm was not an empirical one. Johnstone and Legassick both acknowledged that the liberals had devoted considerable attention to matters of class (such as inequality and exploitation) in their works. That was not the issue. Instead, according to Legassick, the problem was that 'the actual dynamics of South African society are obscured' in liberal accounts, while Johnstone protested that 'this was liberal political economy and not Marxist political economy. It was squarely situated, explicitly or implicitly, within the liberal paradigm.'[51]

In advancing the argument, Johnstone was reiterating his contention that racially structured capitalism ought to be the starting point of inquiry when considering the country's history. But again, *why*? In other words, we have seen that Macmillan conceded that if asked about what they considered to be the 'massive fact' in their experience, the majority of his contemporaries would likely have identified the clash of ethnic groups, the contest of political parties and the establishment of new constitutional dispensations as the key features. If Johnstone was to follow Macmillan in insisting that the people were mistaken in their judgement, it would need to be explained exactly *what* they had misunderstood. For him to counter that the error was that 'this was liberal political economy and not Marxist political economy' would be circular. And, again, some rationale was necessary, for without it there was not only no way of telling *which* paradigm was 'true', there was no reason to believe *any* of them to be true.

In introducing the second volume of the twenty-first century *Cambridge History*, Robert Ross, Anne Kelk Mager and Bill Nasson considered the process that led to the revisionist consensus: the 'temporary ascendancy of a heavily structuralist Marxism' was challenged by research that raised the 'basic empiricism of the historiography' and compelled 'even Marxist theorists to confront the challenging results of archival and other research'.[52]

In his article on the 'New School', Frederick Johnstone stated that of all the challenges posed by the emerging research, none generated as much interest as that of the potentially autonomous role of culture, subjectivity, ideology and psychology as causal factors.[53] In their reviews of the second volume of the *Cambridge History* (which dealt with events since 1885), David Gordon and Stephen Sparks listed Shula Marks, William Beinart, Patrick Harries and Peter Delius among those who helped to qualify the original structuralist position by emphasising the agency of African societies.[54] The result was that the relationship between 'structure' and 'agency' emerged as a key question in the literature. The course of the debate was also profoundly affected by contemporary political developments. South Africa's robust economic growth in the 1960s had influenced many early radical historians to posit a historical symbiosis between capitalism and racial discrimination, which led them to forecast that apartheid would not end absent a simultaneous reckoning with capitalism. The confounding of these predictions from the late 1970s onwards as the reform of apartheid gathered pace (with corporate South

Africa's enthusiastic support) contributed as much as any purely archival finding in qualifying the original structuralist position.[55]

Though the race versus class debate centred on the modern era, radical historians also conducted extensive research on the precolonial period, and that aspect of the work was also profoundly influenced by the insights of Marxist theory. This indebtedness was reflected in the structuring of the two volumes of the *Cambridge History*. Gordon Pirie noted in his review of the first volume that its eight chapters 'track the change from a homogeneous society ... of hunter gatherers to the emergence of a heterogeneous society living off agriculture, commerce, and industry', while Keith Breckenridge argued (without enthusiasm) of the second volume that its focus on 'documenting the machine of exploitation' by tracing the 'history of the mining industry and the making of the segregationist and Apartheid states' had the consequence that 'the story of the mines and their effects ... on the state's effort to mobilise labour appears in considerable detail in no less than six' of thirteen chapters, while Black Consciousness 'benefits from quite detailed discussions in five separate chapters'.[56]

There was nothing inevitable about this framing, which was informed by a distinct theoretical perspective. As Breckenridge and some other reviewers of the *Cambridge History* noted, the framing marginalised other themes – including scientific/technological, ecological, epidemiological and global/transnational histories – that had exercised no less profound an impact on the South African past.[57]

Conclusion

Although this chapter has largely emphasised continuities in the historiographical literature, it cannot be gainsaid that the twentieth century witnessed a huge transformation in terms of how historians of South Africa approached their subject. The ruptures touched on practically every aspect of history writing, including not only subject matter and interpretation but also basic aims and motives. Regarding the latter, Macmillan's call for social relevance compared with George Theal's statement in his *History of South Africa* that 'I have not tried to draw lessons from past events ... [W]hat I have kept constantly before me was to relate all events of importance, to arrange them generally in chronological order, to give dates for every occurrence,'[58] or George Cory's warning to readers of his *Rise of South Africa* to expect 'nothing of the nature of a philosophical disquisition on the springs of human conduct, or on the origin and growth of civil society, nor any views respecting the right principles to be adopted in the formation and government of Colonies', because only 'a straightforward, unbiassed account' would be provided.[59]

Much caution was required in treating such claims, because as Ken Smith noted in *The Changing Past*, his survey of South African historiography, 'much of the debate surrounding Theal is concerned with his claim to have written "without fear or favour"'.[60] An address delivered by Theal in Cape Town on 24 September 1909 on 'Questions in South African History Awaiting Solution' suggested that the scepticism was well founded. One question that Theal identified involved determining South Africa's first human inhabitants. In the process he warned against dismissing the issue as one of significance only for knowledge's sake, for he insisted that it touched on a question of great practical import – namely, dating the arrival of 'Bantu tribes' south of the Zambezi. He stressed the latter question's importance by referring to the contemporary regional situation, where a million whites ruled six to seven million black Africans, before cautioning that if the whites ever faced a united black population demanding equality or outright political power, they would find it difficult to resist. He suggested that history might be a useful aid in the struggle, *if* it could be invoked to prove that the black population possessed no greater ancestral right to southern Africa than the white.[61]

As noted earlier, Theal died having failed to resolve the issue, but his abiding interest in dating the arrival of the 'Bantu invaders' clearly had a practical context. It is also worth noting that in Theal's *History of South Africa*, just after stating he would simply narrate events as they occurred, he added that in presenting the facts he would be guided by what he felt his contemporaries would find interesting. He did not offer any reflection on how such considerations affected his historical representations, but contemporary influences were clearly critical in shaping both his selection of subject matter and his highly partial representation of events. Similarly, George's Cory's professed reluctance at deducing principles for colonial governance stood at odds with numerous other passages in his works, such as his discussion of the first encounter between white settlers and indigenous Africans in the Cape Peninsula, of which he concluded that 'conciliation was quite useless, as it ever has been; but is perhaps the only policy which can be adopted in a dependency where the mother country cannot or will not supply the means of enforcing obedience to her commands'.[62] As Cory's biographer Sandra Shell has noted, this lesson was reiterated throughout his *Rise of South Africa*, where 'the majority black population is represented as marauding, war-mongering thieves'.[63]

Though such explicit statements by Theal and Cory about motives were rare, the 'philosophical' underpinnings of their work were hardly subtle, and as Ken Smith indicated, few readers missed them. This raises a couple of points of broader historiographical significance: one is that Macmillan's claim about the impossibility of discerning the 'wood for the trees' in the works of his predecessors was surely unjust. In truth, most readers – including Macmillan himself – have found little trouble in disentangling the ideological agendas at play in the said works. Accordingly, any characterisation of the difference separating Theal, Cory and their successors as being between 'scientific' and 'philosophical' scholars – the former fixated on source criticism, the latter on extracting lessons for the present – is surely untenable. The difference centred on how (not if) to connect past and present.

The historiographical shift that Macmillan sought to engineer involved the explicit marshalling of history as a resource in addressing social and economic problems. This goal introduced new discourses into the literature, which are well illustrated by considering the case of Eric Walker. Ken Smith and Chris Saunders noted that it was Walker's *History of South Africa* (1928, reissued as the *History of Southern Africa* in 1965), rather than the works of Macmillan and De Kiewiet, that was most frequently prescribed as a textbook in English-medium South African universities between the 1930s and the 1960s. They credited Walker's greater success to the superior detail in his works, but they also faulted his *History* on those grounds. For Smith, Walker's *History* lacked 'any serious analysis of processes, of what South African history "was all about"', while Saunders argued that it 'tried to be comprehensive, and provided so much detail that the wood was lost for the trees'.[64]

But this was not for any want of trying on Walker's part. In the preface to his *History*, he claimed that his work was distinctive in having 'broken away from traditional methods' by making 'neither the struggle between British and Afrikaners nor the achievement of self-government or closer union the main theme', and instead seeking to 'trace the interplay' of all South Africa's peoples, which led him to identify the 'principals' of the country's history in the encounter between 'Western civilisation, tribal Africa and, to a less degree, theocratic Asia'.[65]

Walker therefore advanced a 'main theme' of interaction, which was consistent with modern approaches, but unlike Macmillan and De Kiewiet he defined it in ethnic rather than socioeconomic terms, thereby invoking traditional explanations in the literature. The hybrid of new and old in Walker marked him as a transitional figure, and it has also coloured the reception of his work. His midcentury ascendancy showed that many of his contemporaries remained wedded to the established frames, but as the subsequent criticisms by Smith and Saunders indicated, an important conceptual shift was underway among professional historians. By the 1960s a critical mass was reached that ended the hegemony of the older interpretative frames in the English-language (though not Afrikaans-language) historiography.

In the context of this broader shift, Macmillan and De Kiewiet's significance was that they could be identified as having anticipated the correct approach (involving the identification of a main theme, and understanding that it would be economic in nature), but to have mischaracterised its dynamics. The liberal–radical controversy dug into the details of this issue, but for all the rancour of the dispute, it was conducted within a framework of shared assumptions. At the same time, in a field in which 'structure' and 'agency' emerged as the dominant analytical categories, the fate of Walker's *History* provided a cautionary tale to those who continued to interpret through frames such as 'Western civilisation', 'tribal Africa' and 'theocratic Asia'. It was not that Walker had failed to offer an analysis of what it 'was all about', rather the problem was that by the mid-1960s such categories were no longer taken seriously.

The revisionist consensus that emerged from the liberal–radical controversy incorporated findings from each interpretation into a new synthesis of South African history. That resolution has significance for the issue of what we might take to be the 'Questions in South African History Awaiting Solution' in the twenty-first century. This is because, in fusing formerly distinct positions, the synthesis ultimately fudged the original question ('What is the main theme of South African history?') that had animated the liberal–radical controversy. The synthesis raised the question of what objection there could be to integrating perspectives from elsewhere in the literature (Walker's 'principals', for example?). But that would require abandoning rather than continuing to try to answer the question around which the controversy had been structured.

The historiographical tradition, however, suggests a further way of reading the various intellectual turns that have marked its course. Having invoked the principle that 'every true history is contemporary history', Macmillan almost immediately set about tethering it to an untenable theory of truth that required the disastrous step of divorcing empirical evidence from reality. By contrast, taking the terms of Croce's dictum in their ordinary sense would untie a number of the knots into which subsequent debates (those centred on nature of the dichotomy between 'form' and 'content', and the supposed distinction between 'appearance' and 'reality') have become entangled. It would, *inter alia*, offer reasons as to why South Africa's rapid industrialisation in Macmillan's own time was accompanied by a growing concern with social and economic themes, or why African decolonisation a generation later occasioned renewed interest in uncovering the past achievements of the continent's indigenous peoples. It would also help to explain why the long period bridging the Russian Revolution and the fall of the

Berlin Wall witnessed such strong engagement among historians with the issue of identifying a single principle capable of accounting for all recorded history – and why subsequent historians, reared in very different times, might not feel the same urgency about performing such tasks as defining what the entirety of South African history 'is'.

Such a pragmatic reading would free future historians to interpret the past for the present, without being bound by the restrictions of the problematic that has driven the formation of schools in their discipline for at least a couple of generations.

Notes

1   C. Hamilton, B.K. Mbenga and R. Ross (eds), *The Cambridge History of South Africa*, vol. 1, *From Early Times to 1885* (Cambridge: Cambridge University Press, 2010), i; R. Ross, A.K. Mager and B. Nasson (eds), *The Cambridge History of South Africa*, vol. 2, *1885–1994* (Cambridge: Cambridge University Press, 2012), 1.
2   T.R.H. Davenport, *South Africa: A Modern History* (London: Macmillan, 1977), xiii; R. Davenport and C. Saunders, *South Africa: A Modern History* (Basingstoke: Palgrave Macmillan, 2000), xxiii.
3   H. Giliomee and B. Mbenga (eds), *New History of South Africa* (Cape Town: Tafelberg, 2007), viii (quote), ix–x.
4   N. Worden, *The Making of Modern South Africa* (Oxford: Blackwell, 2004), 2–3.
5   L. Thompson, *A History of South Africa* (New Haven, CT: Yale Nota Bene, 2001), xvi.
6   W. Beinart, *Twentieth-Century South Africa* (Oxford: Oxford University Press, 1994), v.
7   B.A. Le Cordeur, 'The Reconstruction of South African History', *South African Historical Journal*, 17 (1) 1985, 6; I.R. Smith, 'The Revolution in South African Historiography', *History Today*, 38 (2) Feb. 1988, www.historytoday.com/archive/revolution-south-african-historiography (accessed 31 Mar. 2020); Worden, *Making of Modern South Africa*, 2.
8   S. Marks, 'African and Afrikaner History', *Journal of African History*, 11 (3) 1970, 435.
9   H.M. Wright, review of *The Rise of African Nationalism in South Africa* and *The Oxford History of South Africa*, vol. 2, *American Historical Review*, 80 (2) Apr. 1975, 456.
10 A. Atmore, review of *The Oxford History of South Africa*, vol. 1, *Bulletin of the School of Oriental and African Studies*, 33 (2) 1970, 435.
11 R. Hyam, 'Are We Any Nearer an African History of South Africa?' *Historical Journal*, 16 (3) Sept. 1973, 620.

12 T. Coghlan, review of *The Oxford History of South Africa*, *Geographical Journal*, 135 (4) Dec. 1969, 605.
13 W. Rees, review of *The Oxford History of South Africa*, vol. 1, *American Historical Review*, 75 (3) Feb. 1970, 899.
14 L.M. Hoskins, review of *The Oxford History of South Africa*, vol. 1, *Annals of the American Academy of Political and Social Science*, 386, Nov. 1969, 214.
15 Marks, 'African and Afrikaner History', 435.
16 L.C. Duly, review of *The Oxford History of South Africa*, vol. 1, *African Historical Studies*, 3 (1) 1970, 206.
17 M. Lipton, review of *The Oxford History of South Africa*, vol. 1, *International Affairs (Royal Institute of International Affairs 1944–)*, 49 (1) Jan. 1973, 140–1.
18 Atmore, review of *The Oxford History of South Africa*, vol. 1, 435.
19 C. Saunders, *The Making of the South African Past: Major Historians on Race and Class* (Cape Town: David Philip, 1988), 143–61.
20 M. Wilson and L. Thompson, 'Preface', in *Oxford History*, vol. 1, *South Africa to 1870*, v.
21 *Ibid*., vi, vii.
22 A.P. Newton and E.A. Benians, 'Preface', in A.P. Newton and E.A. Benians (eds), *The Cambridge History of the British Empire*, vol. 8 (Cambridge: Cambridge University Press, 1936), v–vi.
23 Wilson and Thompson, 'Preface', vi.
24 *Ibid*.
25 S. Marks, 'South Africa: "The Myth of the Empty Land"', *History Today*, 30 (1) Jan. 1980, www.historytoday.com/shula-marks/south-africa-myth-empty-land (accessed 21 Mar. 2022); *Rand Daily Mail*, 12 Sept. 1975.
26 R.R. Inskeep, 'The Archaeological Background', and M. Wilson, 'The Nguni People', in Wilson and Thompson, *Oxford History*, vol. 1, *South Africa to 1870*, 39, 87.
27 I. Schapera, 'The Native Inhabitants', in Newton and Benians, *Cambridge History of the British Empire*, 36–8.
28 *Rand Daily Mail*, 18 May 1929 and 29 Apr. 1935.
29 Wilson and Thompson, 'Preface', vi.
30 L. Thompson, 'The Forgotten Factor in Southern African History', in L. Thompson (ed.), *African Societies in Southern Africa* (London: Heinemann, 1969), 4.
31 G.M. Theal, *History and Ethnography of Africa South of the Zambesi*, vol. 1 (London: Swan Sonnenschein, 1910), iii–iv.
32 *Rand Daily Mail*, 18 May 1929 and 29 Apr. 1935.
33 J.M. Berning and R. Shell, 'The Machine Gun and the Feather: Aspects of South African Nation-Building Historiography, 1903–1919', unpublished paper, 3, 4, 35 (quote).
34 Theal, *History and Ethnography*, vi–vii.
35 W.M. Macmillan, *The South African Agrarian Problem and Its Historical Development* (Johannesburg: Central News Agency, 1919), 23.
36 W.M. Macmillan, *The Cape Colour Question: A Historical Survey* (London: Faber and Faber, 1927); *Bantu, Boer and Briton: The Making of the South*

African Native Problem (London: Faber and Gwyer, 1929); and *Complex South Africa: An Economic Foot-Note to History* (London: Faber and Faber, 1930).
37 Macmillan, *Cape Colour Question*, 3–4.
38 *Ibid.*, 8–9.
39 C.W. de Kiewiet, *British Colonial Policy and the South African Republics, 1848–1872* (London: Longmans, Green, 1929), 3.
40 C.W. de Kiewiet, *The Imperial Factor in South Africa: A Study in Politics and Economics* (Cambridge: Cambridge University Press, 1937), 1.
41 C.W. de Kiewiet, *A History of South Africa: Social and Economic* (Oxford: Oxford University Press, 1978), 19, 79, 179–80.
42 C. Bundy, 'An Image of Its Own Past? Towards a Comparison of American and South African Historiography', in J. Brown, P. Manning, K. Shapiro, J. Wiener, B. Bozzoli and P. Delius (eds), *History from South Africa: Alternative Visions and Practices* (Philadelphia, PA: Temple University Press, 1991), 89.
43 Saunders, *South African Past*, 94.
44 G. Cory, 'The British Settlers of 1820', in Benians, Walker and Mansergh, *Cambridge History of the British Empire*, 238–43.
45 See G. Cory, *The Rise of South Africa*, vol. 2 (Cape Town: Struik, 1965), chapters 1–5; the discussion of slavery is in vol. 3, chapter 1.
46 A. Atmore, review of *The Oxford History of South Africa*, vol. 2, *Bulletin of the School of Oriental and African Studies*, 35 (3) 1972, 679.
47 A. Atmore and N. Westlake, 'A Liberal Dilemma: A Critique of the *Oxford History of South Africa*', *Race and Class*, 14 (2) Oct. 1972, 126–31 (quotes, in order, at 129, 131, 131, 130, 130).
48 M. Legassick, 'The Dynamics of Modernization in South Africa', *Journal of African History*, 13 (1) Jan. 1972, 147.
49 F. Johnstone, '"Most Painful to Our Hearts": South Africa through the Eyes of the New School', *Canadian Journal of African Studies/Revue canadienne des études africaines*, 16 (1) 1982, 6, 7.
50 G. Verhoef, 'Die Radikale Geskiedskrywing oor Suid-Afrika: 'n Historiografiese Studie' (MA thesis, Rand Afrikaans University, 1982), 44, 46.
51 Legassick, 'Dynamics of Modernization', 146; Johnstone, '"Most Painful to Our Hearts"', 9.
52 R. Ross, A.K. Mager and B. Nasson, 'Introduction', in *Cambridge History of South Africa*, vol. 2, 12.
53 Johnstone, '"Most Painful to Our Hearts"', 22–3.
54 D.M. Gordon, review of *The Cambridge History of South Africa*, vvol. 2, *International Journal of African Historical Studies*, 45 (3) 2012, 463; S. Sparks, 'New Turks and Old Turks: The Historiographical Legacies of South African Social History', *Historia* 58 (1) May 2013, 219–20.
55 For more on these debates, see M. Lipton, *Liberals, Marxists, and Nationalists: Competing Interpretations of South African History* (New York: Palgrave Macmillan, 2007), chapters 2–5 and the appendices.
56 G. Pirie, review of *The Cambridge History of South Africa*, vol. 1, *African Affairs*, 110 (438), 137; K. Breckenridge, review of *The Cambridge History of South Africa*, vol. 2, *South African Historical Journal*, 66 (4) 2014, 722–3.

57 *Ibid.*, 723.
58 G.M. Theal, *History of South Africa under the Administration of the Dutch East India Company [1652 to 1795]*, vol. 1 (London: Swan, Sonnenschein, 1897), xv–xvi.
59 Cory, *Rise of South Africa*, vol. 1, v.
60 K. Smith, *The Changing Past: Trends in South African Historical Writing* (Johannesburg: Southern, 1988), 36.
61 *Rand Daily Mail*, 28 Sept. 1909.
62 Cory, *Rise of South Africa*, vol. 1, 7.
63 S.R. Shell, *Protean Paradox: George Edward Cory (1862–1935): Navigating Life and South African History* (Grahamstown: Rhodes University, 2017), 241.
64 K. Smith, *Changing Past*, 113; Saunders, *South African Past*, 91, 129.
65 E.A. Walker, *A History of South Africa* (London: Longmans, Green, 1928), vi.

Bibliography

Atmore, A. (1970) Review of *The Oxford History of South Africa*, vol. 1, *Bulletin of the School of Oriental and African Studies*, 33 (2).
Atmore, A. (1972) Review of *The Oxford History of South Africa*, vol. 2, *Bulletin of the School of Oriental and African Studies*, 35 (3).
Atmore, A., and N. Westlake (1972) 'A Liberal Dilemma: A Critique of the *Oxford History of South Africa*', *Race and Class*, 14 (2).
Beinart, W. (1994) *Twentieth-Century South Africa*. Oxford: Oxford University Press.
Benians, E.A., E.A. Walker and N. Mansergh (eds) (1963) *The Cambridge History of the British Empire*, vol. 8. Cambridge: Cambridge University Press.
Berning, J.M., and R. Shell (n.d.) 'The Machine Gun and the Feather: Aspects of South African Nation-Building Historiography, 1903–1919'. Unpublished paper.
Breckenridge, K. (2014) Review of *The Cambridge History of South Africa*, vol. 2, *South African Historical Journal*, 66 (4).
Bundy, C. (1991) 'An Image of Its Own Past? Towards a Comparison of American and South African Historiography', in J. Brown, P. Manning, K. Shapiro, J. Wiener, B. Bozzoli and P. Delius (eds), *History from South Africa: Alternative Visions and Practices*. Philadelphia, PA: Temple University Press.
Coghlan, T. (1969) Review of *The Oxford History of South Africa*, *Geographical Journal*, 135 (4).
Cory, G. (1963) 'The British Settlers of 1820', in Benians, Walker and Mansergh, *Cambridge History of the British Empire*.
Cory, G. (1965) *The Rise of South Africa*, 5 vols. Cape Town: Struik.
Davenport, R. and C. Saunders (2000) *South Africa: A Modern History*. Basingstoke: Palgrave Macmillan.
Davenport, T.R.H. (1977) *South Africa: A Modern History*. London: Macmillan.
De Kiewiet, C.W. (1929) *British Colonial Policy and the South African Republics, 1848–1872*. London: Longmans, Green.

De Kiewiet, C.W. (1937) *The Imperial Factor in South Africa: A Study in Politics and Economics*. Cambridge: Cambridge University Press.

De Kiewiet, C.W. (1978) *A History of South Africa: Social and Economic*. Oxford: Oxford University Press.

Duly, L.C. (1970) Review of *The Oxford History of South Africa*, vol. 1, *African Historical Studies*, 3 (1).

Giliomee, H., and B. Mbenga (eds) (2007) *New History of South Africa*. Cape Town: Tafelberg.

Gordon, D.M. (2012) Review of *The Cambridge History of South Africa*, vol. 2, *International Journal of African Historical Studies*, 45 (3).

Hamilton, C., B.K. Mbenga and R. Ross (eds) (2010) *The Cambridge History of South Africa*, vol. 1, *From Early Times to 1885*. Cambridge: Cambridge University Press.

Hoskins, L.M. (1969) Review of *The Oxford History of South Africa*, vol. 1, *Annals of the American Academy of Political and Social Science*, 386.

Hyam, R. (1973) 'Are We Any Nearer an African History of South Africa?' *Historical Journal*, 16 (3).

Inskeep, R.R. (1969) 'The Archaeological Background', in Wilson and Thompson, *Oxford History*, vol. 1, *South Africa to 1870*.

Johnstone, F. (1982) '"Most Painful to Our Hearts": South Africa through the Eyes of the New School', *Canadian Journal of African Studies/Revue canadienne des études africaines*, 16 (1).

Le Cordeur, B.A. (1985) 'The Reconstruction of South African History', *South African Historical Journal*, 17 (1).

Legassick, M. (1972) 'The Dynamics of Modernization in South Africa', *Journal of African History*, 13 (1).

Lipton, M. (1973) Review of *The Oxford History of South Africa*, vol. 1, *International Affairs (Royal Institute of International Affairs 1944–)*, 49 (1).

Lipton, M. (2007) *Liberals, Marxists, and Nationalists: Competing Interpretations of South African History*. New York: Palgrave Macmillan.

Macmillan, W.M. (1919) *The South African Agrarian Problem and Its Historical Development*. Johannesburg: Central News Agency.

Macmillan, W.M. (1927) *The Cape Colour Question: A Historical Survey*. London: Faber and Faber.

Macmillan, W.M. (1929) *Bantu, Boer and Briton: The Making of the South African Native Problem*. London: Faber and Gwyer.

Macmillan, W.M. (1930) *Complex South Africa: An Economic Foot-Note to History*. London: Faber and Faber.

Marks, S. (1970) 'African and Afrikaner History', *Journal of African History*, 11 (3).

Marks, S. (1980) 'South Africa: "The Myth of the Empty Land"', *History Today*, 30 (1), www.historytoday.com/shula-marks/south-africa-myth-empty-land (accessed 21 Mar. 2022).

Newton, A.P., and E.A. Benians (eds) (1936) *The Cambridge History of the British Empire*, vol. 8. Cambridge: Cambridge University Press.

Newton, A.P., and E.A. Benians (1936) 'Preface', in *Cambridge History of the British Empire*.

Pirie, G. (2011) Review of *The Cambridge History of South Africa*, vol. 1, *African Affairs*, 110 (438).
Rees, W. (1970) Review of *The Oxford History of South Africa*, vol. 1, *American Historical Review*, 75 (3).
Ross, R., A.K. Mager and B. Nasson (eds) (2012) *The Cambridge History of South Africa*, vol. 2, *1885–1994*. Cambridge: Cambridge University Press.
Ross, R., A.K. Mager and B. Nasson, (2012) 'Introduction', in *Cambridge History of South Africa*.
Saunders, C. (1988) *The Making of the South African Past: Major Historians on Race and Class*. Cape Town: David Philip.
Schapera, I. (1936) 'The Native Inhabitants', in Newton and Benians, *Cambridge History of the British Empire*.
Shell, S.R. (2017) *Protean Paradox: George Edward Cory (1862–1935): Navigating Life and South African History*. Grahamstown: Rhodes University.
Smith, I.R. (1988) 'The Revolution in South African Historiography', *History Today*, 38 (2), www.historytoday.com/archive/revolution-south-african-historiography (accessed 31 Mar. 2020).
Smith, K. (1988) *The Changing Past: Trends in South African Historical Writing*. Johannesburg: Southern.
Sparks, S. (2013) 'New Turks and Old Turks: The Historiographical Legacies of South African Social History', *Historia*, 58 (1).
Theal, G.M. (1897) *History of South Africa under the Administration of the Dutch East India Company [1652 to 1795]*, vol. 1. London: Swan, Sonnenschein.
Theal, G.M. (1910) *History and Ethnography of Africa South of the Zambesi*, vol. 1. London: Swan Sonnenschein.
Thompson, L. (1969) 'The Forgotten Factor in Southern African History', in L. Thompson (ed.), *African Societies in Southern Africa*. London: Heinemann.
Thompson, L. (2001) *A History of South Africa*. New Haven, CT: Yale Nota Bene.
Verhoef, G. (1982) 'Die Radikale Geskiedskrywing oor Suid-Afrika: 'n Historiografiese Studie'. MA thesis, Rand Afrikaans University.
Walker, E.A. (1928) *A History of South Africa*. London: Longmans, Green.
Wilson. M. (1969) 'The Nguni People', in Wilson and Thompson, *Oxford History*, vol. 1, *South Africa to 1870*.
Wilson, M., and L. Thompson (1969, 1971), *The Oxford History of South Africa*, 2 vols. Oxford: Clarendon Press.
Wilson. M., and L. Thompson (1969) 'Preface', in *Oxford History*, vol. 1, *South Africa to 1870*.
Worden, N. (2004) *The Making of Modern South Africa*. Oxford: Blackwell.
Wright, H.W. (1975) Review of *The Rise of African Nationalism in South Africa* and *The Oxford History of South Africa*, vol. 2, *American Historical Review*, 80 (2).

7

From grand narratives to complicated subjects: biography in the postapartheid era

Lindie Koorts

Historiography, by its nature, focuses its lens on the historian. The same goes for biography, where it is widely acknowledged that biographical works are infused with the autobiographical. This much I have to acknowledge in my own work, and in the reflections offered in this chapter. I wrote a biography of D.F. Malan, the first apartheid prime minister, and it was the first comprehensive biography of an apartheid leader after 1994.[1] I stumbled across Malan, almost by accident, during the course of my postgraduate studies. As an Afrikaner who came of age in the midst of South Africa's transition to democracy, studying Malan appealed to my deep-rooted need to unravel Afrikaner thought, and writing his biography allowed me to engage with my dual sense of alienation from and complicity with Afrikaner history.

This sense of duality is key to the pursuit of biography itself. To ring true, biography demands both scholarly and personal immersion. Instead of the much-vaunted critical distance, the biographer enters into a critical relationship with the subject – the biographer's 'dialectical dance'.[2] There are pitfalls when the biographer has a deep-seated admiration for the subject, as the work can easily descend into hagiography. In that sense, a 'perpetrator biography', such as that which I wrote of Malan, seemed, to me at least, to be a safer space, as I was forced to navigate between simultaneous impulses of empathy, abhorrence, familiarity and discomfort.

The 'safety' of my scholarly discomfort stood in contrast to my very real fears about my choice of subject in relation to the world around me. In the initial stages of my project, I was almost paralysed by the fear of being labelled a nationalist myself. Only by shutting myself off from the immediate public discourse, and immersing myself in the biography for its own sake, was I able to write it.

Distancing myself from public debate did not diminish my deep-seated drive to challenge the nationalist narrative by demythologising Malan and the Nationalists, and in its place, to unravel, to understand, and to explain

– but never to hide or to justify – through the powerful medium of an almost literary narrative. This approach was not, however, an option once the book was published. It appeared in 2014, to favourable reviews. Yet I encountered an underlying frustration: readers and reviewers felt uncomfortable with the duality underpinning the book, and especially my humanisation of Malan. The newspaper editor Mondli Makhanya pointed to this when opening his review: 'What I hated most about DF Malan and the Rise of Afrikaner Nationalism was that the author drills so effectively into her subject that you end up identifying with apartheid's founding father. It's like that guilty feeling you get while watching a movie and the villain's character has been so well scripted and brilliantly acted that you are drawn to them.'[3]

Makhanya understood that this did not imply a favourable or sympathetic picture of Malan, but others challenged me to take a more definite position and to condemn Malan outright. That would have made it easier for them. There was a need to make sense of the biographer, as if positioning me would allow them to position the book and their response to it. I encountered several pointed references to my age (young – at least at the time), and my being a woman (as opposed to my very male subject). The obvious binaries, wherein I differed from my subject, seemed puzzling to others. Strangely enough, my 'defining' qualities, at least in relation to the book, of being an Afrikaner and a historian with questions, hardly came into play.

This very public engagement with my book carried over into 2015, when it was shortlisted for notable nonfiction prizes – at the same time that the student protests of that year burst onto the scene. These events, which had been building up for quite some time, could not help but send me into a new round of reflection – on the nature of biography, the tension between scholarly work and public consumption, and, in particular, its place in South Africa's shifting political narratives and discourse. This contribution is therefore something of a participant-observer's reflection on these themes.

On biography and the contestations of the archive

The South African biographical landscape is varied and diffuse. It does not help that here, as elsewhere, the term 'biography' is bandied about with the utmost ease, and is easily fused into the equally popular term 'life-writing', which includes memoirs, autobiography, creative nonfiction, and even biographical and autobiographical fiction. In the popular mind, there is often little distinction between a biography and an autobiography, and in the public imagination (as well as in the publishing industry) they are often accorded the same weight.

Furthermore, biography is not the exclusive domain of scholars. Instead, professional researchers share shelf space with popular nonfiction writers who churn out money-spinners on athletes and entertainers, all meant for quick and edible consumption. It is little wonder that biography has been labelled the stepchild of history, as there is often little distinction between popular biography and critical, scholarly biography. In recent years, biography has won greater appeal and acceptance among scholars, but even then it is often a case of the term being appropriated for works that are in reality far removed from the genre. Social historians, for example, who use the tales of individuals to illuminate their narratives, do not hesitate to call their work 'biographical' – even though this practice is vastly different from the meticulous excavation of a single life.

However, a rigid definition of 'biography' in the South African context runs the risk of too narrow a view, thereby excluding the extent to which biography is shaped by the country's wider, vibrant culture of life-writing; how works that may not stand up to academic scrutiny are nevertheless important drivers of ideas; and the realities of the archival landscape in shaping whose biographies are written, and how they are approached.

Biography (like history) is a matter of sources, for the ideal is to excavate private letters and diaries that offer insight into the subject's inner world and help to explain their motives and decisions. It is therefore no small wonder that, globally, there are so many biographies of artists, writers and intellectuals who documented their own lives through their letters and diaries, and politicians whose every act was scrutinised and recorded, and who were powerful and important enough to warrant private archival collections. Of course, there are many lives that have been documented without such intimate materials, but even then biographers may still have access to alternative sources, scattered as they may be, which provide a multi-angled view of the subject.

However, in countries where power relations are skewed, such as South Africa, well-documented and well-preserved lives are essentially elite lives and, by implication, mostly white lives, and this reality has elicited significant pushback since the 1970s, as left-leaning historians sought to elevate the lives of workers, women and the marginalised, in defiance of so-called 'Great Man' history. The Wits History Workshop consciously set out to defy Great Man history by writing hitherto neglected histories. Deeply influenced by a Marxist analytical framework, it also eschewed a focus on individuals, and instead favoured wider analysis, in particular the role of class.[4] This approach instilled an academic culture which still remains prevalent among South African historians today and determines perceptions of what research priorities ought to be.

The reality of South African archives is that the majority of materials collected before the fall of apartheid in 1994 reflected the preoccupations of a white elite. Post-1994, initial attempts to broaden the archives were quickly supplanted by neglect, underfunding, corruption and a renewed secrecy.[5] Even university archives, which are the custodians of many private collections, face crippling budget constraints. The devastating wildfire that wreaked havoc on the University of Cape Town's African Studies Collection in April 2021 is a testament to the precariousness of the archive.[6] Consequently, South African biographers and historians work under increasingly challenging conditions. In addition to the limits presented by the archives, there is the somewhat more contentious question of the limits presented by written sources, as South Africa's transition from an oral culture to the written word is fairly recent.[7]

In sub-Saharan Africa, precolonial and early colonial Africans were often recorded in the papers of European travellers, administrators and missionaries. This changed as literacy spread, but until the twentieth century the papers of literate Africans were, essentially, papers of a small, Westernised elite.[8] Their preservation, given the priorities of a white, colonial state, was uneven and precarious. As a result, there is a relatively small but growing body of 'conventional', scholarly biographies of Africans who lived in the late nineteenth and early twentieth centuries. Most prominent among them are the founding members of the African National Congress (ANC), such as Sol Plaatje, John Dube and Pixley ka Isaka Seme.[9]

Hlonipha Mokoena's biography of the early African intellectual Magema Fuze (1840–1922) is a key example of this dilemma. Mokoena wrote that Fuze was 'a classic example of how first-generation converts made the transition from oral to literate cultures, the homestead to the mission and from being "native informants" to being *kholwa* intellectuals ... caught ... between the promise of full and equal incorporation into colonial society and the ties that bound them to traditional society and culture.'[10]

In some instances, scholars sought to challenge the limits of written sources by drawing on oral history to fill the gaps in the colonial archive. While oral history is an accepted research methodology the world over, in South Africa it was imbued with political meaning in that it sought to give a voice to the marginalised, and address the archive's skewed power relations. Tim Couzens sought to supplement the written record, and to create context for his biographical subject through oral interviews,[11] while Charles van Onselen used oral history to create a record where none existed in *The Seed Is Mine*, his magisterial, 535-page biography of the sharecropper Kas Maine, who had left only a single documentary trace of his existence in the state archives – a fine for not being in possession of a dog licence. Oral history defied the limitations of the archive by proving that 'in an industrialising society characterised by a high level of illiteracy, history lives on in the minds of its people far more powerfully than the cracked parchment of officialdom might know'.[12] The work aimed, in Van Onselen's words, to 'set right a historic wrong, to recreate the life of a man who deserves to be remembered for far more than his failure to produce a dog license ... Kas Maine, the members of his family, and thousands like them were central to the building, feeding and shaping of this tortured country as it struggled to brush aside the racial goblins that guarded entry to the modern world.'[13] However, for Van Onselen it was not merely a matter of elevating an otherwise unknown life. Kas Maine offered a lens to understanding wider processes of rural dispossession in twentieth-century South Africa. Similarly, Mokoena used Fuze's life to understand the transition of the first generation of African intellectuals from an oral to a written culture. These lives were representative of a wider South African tale.

More recently, this tale has been extended, as biographers such as Jonathan Hyslop, Carel van der Merwe and, again, Charles van Onselen have followed important international historiographical trends in expanding their scope beyond the national borders (and archives) by tracing late nineteenth- and early twentieth-century transnational lives that integrate South Africa into global history.[14] What unites these works is their scholarly rigour. Though they were not devoid of activist intentions (in that they sought to defy African subjugation and marginalisation), they stand in contrast to the explosion of more popular struggle biographies and memoirs which flooded the market after 1994.

While sources may determine biographers' ability to write critical and comprehensive biographies, a country's political narrative also determines whose lives are deemed worthy of recollection. While South African scholars and activists have made a strong case for elevating the marginalised over the 'Great Men', in a country where politics has been driven by various forms of nationalism for over a century it is inevitable that most biographies have been devoted to political leaders.

The pre-1994 era was dominated by biographies of Afrikaner nationalist heroes – from Voortrekker leaders and presidents of the former Boer republics, to apartheid's architects. A number of these biographies were written by respected scholars and were meticulously researched. Yet, the biographers' unquestioned acceptance of Afrikaner nationalism doomed their work to be dismissed as hagiography once apartheid ended.[15]

Post-1994, the new South African state was concerned with a nation-building project, and compromises were made to include both black and white in the country's national symbols. The national anthem became a hybrid, sung in five of the country's eleven official languages, combining the Xhosa hymn *Nkosi Sikelel' iAfrika* with *Die Stem*, the former national anthem. Former nationalist monuments remained in place, and new monuments were erected, in some cases, alongside them – visitors to Pretoria, for example, would encounter the silhouette of the Voortrekker Monument, the most triumphalist of Afrikaner nationalist monuments to the west, and on a neighbouring eastern hill, the illuminated reeds of Freedom Park, a heritage site that memorialises martyrs of South Africa's liberation struggle.

These initial attempts could not, however, withstand the ascendance of a much larger, triumphalist metanarrative. As Colin Bundy wrote, wryly: 'the need for forgiveness and reconciliation, and the oneness of the rainbow nation ... did not survive [Nelson Mandela's] presidency'.[16] The new ruling party, the ANC, centralised history in public commemorations that followed, and the liberation struggle quickly consumed South Africa's literary landscape. There was an insatiable appetite for stories about the fight against apartheid, and a plethora of memoirs and biographies flooded the market.[17]

The book that contributed most to set the trend was Nelson Mandela's *Long Walk to Freedom*. Published in 1994, it has never gone out of print, and it sparked a veritable Mandela industry. Publications ranged from an authorised biography and scholarly critiques to the memoirs of Mandela's personal assistant, his prison warder and his chef.[18] Soon, as one commentator noted, everyone wanted their own *Long Walk to Freedom* – but the results were uneven.[19] This could be seen in the veritable boom in biographies, autobiographies and memoirs, many of which focused on members and icons of the liberation-struggle aristocracy, such as Albert Luthuli, Oliver Tambo, Walter and Albertina Sisulu, Steve Biko and Mac Maharaj.[20] Some were meticulously researched, others were more concerned with eulogising their subjects.

Since most of the post-1994 publications dealt with more recent events, at the time of their writing many of their subjects were still alive. Some of the individuals in question wanted to control the narrative by writing their own memoirs (or having them ghostwritten). In a sense, memoirs, like newspapers, became the first draft of South Africa's postliberation history – a history that was being recollected much faster than it could be recorded. Some of the memoirs were nevertheless recognised for their literary quality, and awarded important nonfiction prizes.[21] While biographers might bristle at the idea of being placed in the same category as memoirists and life-writers, in South Africa, where the boundaries of memory and history are blurred, it was inevitable that the literary community generally accorded them the same weight.

What this first round of biographies, autobiographies and memoirs generally had in common was that they established a heroic narrative in which the great white men of yesteryear were replaced by their adversaries from within the liberation struggle. Tales of heroic women were not entirely absent, but they belonged to a much smaller subset, and were often presented as partners in political power couples, such as Albertina Sisulu and Ruth First, who became the subjects of joint biographies. In Winnie Madikizela-Mandela's case, as will be discussed later, feminist scholars made a concerted effort to study her in her own right, and 'not just [as] Nelson's wife'.[22] However, for the most part, memoir and autobiography (rather than biography) remained the genres in which women documented their part in the struggle, with the accounts of Ellen Kuzwayo, Emma Mashinini and Fatima Meer forming part of a small, but notable canon.[23] Overall, masculine heroics dominated the field.[24]

In search of 'acceptable' white men

The turn towards struggle biographies also had a profound influence on Afrikaner biography. Its turn away from a nationalist-dominated narrative was already discernible by the late 1980s, as the apartheid edifice began to crumble.

In 1987, the founders of the newly established Institute for a Democratic Alternative in South Africa, Frederik van Zyl Slabbert and Alex Boraine, as well as Slabbert's close friend the poet Breyten Breytenbach, led sixty-one South African intellectuals – half of them Afrikaners – to Dakar, Senegal, to meet directly with the exiled ANC, much to the chagrin of the National Party government.[25] Among the Afrikaner delegates was the historian Hermann Giliomee, who participated in a television debate while in Dakar, with the future state president Thabo Mbeki. During the discussion, Mbeki insisted that the postapartheid government would appoint a committee to decide on South Africa's historical heroes, and it would also commission the rewriting of the country's history. He did, however, offer an assurance that the new rendering would include white Afrikaner heroes, and particularly antiapartheid figures such as Bram Fischer and Beyers Naudé.[26]

Fischer was the grandson of Abraham Fischer, the former president of the Orange River Colony, as the Orange Free State was known directly after the Anglo-Boer War. He was considered Afrikaner political royalty and, with his glittering legal career, was poised to become a prominent member of the Afrikaner political elite. Yet he turned to communism and led Nelson Mandela and his coaccused's defence at the Rivonia Treason Trial. Fischer was subsequently persecuted by the apartheid government for his underground activities, and finally served a life sentence.[27] Beyers Naudé came from an equally impressive family of theologians. A talented clergyman, he defied the Dutch Reformed Church's slavish support for the National

Party and its attempts at providing a theological justification for apartheid. He left the Church, but continued to campaign against apartheid.[28]

Within three years of the Dakar meeting, apartheid collapsed. The liberation struggle became the foundational myth of the new state, and as Mbeki had suggested, there was a discernible shift towards the stories of Afrikaners who had resisted apartheid. By far the most notable was Fischer, followed closely by Naudé, who both had streets and buildings named after them.

The collapse of Afrikaner nationalism had enormous implications for Afrikaner historiography. By the early 1990s, new trends were discernible. One was a concerted move away from formal political history: after years of isolation and academic boycotts (which were compounded by living under the political and intellectual siege of a repressive state) Afrikaner historians joined in wider, international trends in historical research. Gendered histories flourished: work on the much idealised *Volksmoeder* (mother of the nation) challenged nationalist stereotypes, while also excavating Afrikaner working-class pasts.[29] This was accompanied by a new interest in social and cultural themes, which deconstructed nationalist symbols.[30] Histories of Afrikaner protest music and consumption meanwhile formed part of a wider drive to tell the stories of antiestablishment and impoverished Afrikaners.[31]

Upon the centennial of the Second Anglo-Boer War (1899–1902), which now became the South African War, historians emphasised the role of black participants in that conflict and explored the deprivations of black concentration camps, which had been ignored by nationalist historians.[32] Other key events in the nationalist narrative, such as the 1914 Rebellion, were demythologised, and its heroes – most notably Koos de la Rey – became not only fallible human beings, but also to some extent questionable characters.[33]

In the sphere of public commemoration, Afrikaner (and white English) milestones disappeared entirely from the state-sanctioned narrative. The 350-year anniversary of Jan van Riebeeck's landing, the centennial of South Africa's unification and the bicentennial of the landing of the 1820 British settlers all came and went without commemoration in the early twenty-first century. By the time of the fifty-year anniversary of the Republic in 2021, the Afrikaans newspapers published some historical reflections,[34] but there were no calls for celebration. This muted response belied the Afrikaner community's underlying sense of alienation and exclusion during these years.

Afrikaner historians, for their part, seemed liberated from the confines of nationalism.[35] Yet, with some notable exceptions, very little of their work transcended academic circles. A growing divide was discernible between the insights garnered by original academic research and the popular consumption of Afrikaner history, shaped by decades of Christian National Education.[36] The antiquarian market, particularly in relation to the South African War, continued to thrive. Memoirs and biographies of the war were considered (somewhat naively) to be untainted by apartheid, with many early twentieth-century diaries, memoirs and histories that had gone out of print being republished. Among the new works written for this market, very little was based on fresh research or new interpretation, and scant heed was taken of the new, more racially inclusive approach to the South African War. The works instead tapped into a popular and nostalgic market, and had little influence on the field of academic history.[37] Coupled with this was the rise of memoirs and histories of South Africa's Border War (1966–89), which found a ready market in the ex-soldiers who, decades later, sought to make sense of their experiences.[38]

That most accessible of genres, biography – and in particular political biography – was, however, notably absent from the initial, post-1994 corpus of work. This was not surprising, as Afrikaner politics were so thoroughly tainted. Publishers gave it a wide berth. As Alex Mouton noted, there was a common sentiment that 'Afrikaners [had] no desire to read about conservative and racist pre-1990 politicians whose lives have the potential of being a source of embarrassment and discomfort in the new South Africa.'[39]

The most significant biography of an Afrikaner to emerge during this time was written not by an Afrikaner but by an author who described himself as an outsider: an English-speaking South African of Jewish extraction.[40] Steven Clingman's 1998 biography *Bram Fischer: Afrikaner Revolutionary* was an artfully crafted and deeply researched work, which shared the Alan Paton Prize with Antjie Krog's memoir of the Truth and Reconciliation Commission (TRC), *Country of My Skull*.[41] The biography placed Fischer firmly among the pantheon of liberation leaders, in an apparent vindication of Thabo Mbeki's hopes.

Yet the other party to that television debate in Dakar bucked this trend. In 2003, Giliomee published *The Afrikaners: Biography of a People*, which had been more than ten years in the making.[42] The book was arguably the most influential contribution to post-1994 Afrikaner historiography, and also reflected a key aspect of post-1994 Afrikaner biography. In tracing the history of the Afrikaners, it highlighted a number of prominent individuals who represented the many dimensions of this group. The selection of these individuals was significant. It did not latch on to the new regime's choice of Afrikaner heroes, but instead reflected the American political theorist Michael Walzer's model of the connected critic – that is, an individual bound to their community, who nonetheless remained close enough to its periphery to be critical of its excesses.[43] 'Criticism', Walzer had argued, 'is most properly the work of "insiders", men and women mindful of and committed to the society whose policies and practices they call into question – who *care about* what happens to it'. Walzer considered Breyten Breytenbach an example of such a connected critic, and devoted a chapter of his book *The Company of Critics* to the Afrikaner poet.[44]

The politicians among Giliomee's group of connected critics were few and far between. Instead, the intellectual and poet N.P. van Wyk Louw, the journalist and author Maria Elizabeth Rothman, and the newspaper editors Piet Cillié and Schalk Pienaar – all individuals who were loyal Afrikaners, but critical of nationalist excesses – came to represent the Afrikaners' conscience.[45] The one notable politician in this new pantheon was Frederik van Zyl Slabbert, who, like Bram Fischer, was a golden boy: academic, handsome, charismatic and a talented player of that most holy of Afrikaner sports – rugby. Slabbert could have become the crown prince of the Nationalist establishment if he had wanted, but chose to defy it and joined the liberal opposition in 1974, becoming its leader by 1979. However, he resigned from politics in 1986, calling the institution of parliament irrelevant, and instead entered civil society by forming the Institute for a Democratic Alternative in South Africa. While it was a blow to the Nationalist government to be opposed by one of its own, Slabbert never wandered as far left as Fischer, thus being more of a connected critic than an Afrikaner revolutionary, and in spite of his ambitions, he was never fully integrated into the new, post-1994 ruling elite.[46]

What emerged were two sets of Afrikaners: the Fischers, who fitted neatly into the struggle narrative, and the connected critics, who remained ensconced in their community, as its conscience. This new pantheon of Afrikaner critics was also recognised by the new regime. The ANC government bestowed its national order for achievement in arts and journalism, the Order of Ikhamanga, on, among others, the poets N.P. van Wyk Louw and Ingrid Jonker, the novelists André Brink, Elsa Joubert and Marlene van Niekerk, the philosopher Johan Degenaar, and Schalk Pienaar: all intellectuals who had criticised nationalism and apartheid from within.[47]

These individuals and their associates became the focus of post-1994 Afrikaner biography. Since they were novelists, poets and editors, it meant that the proverbial pantheon of Afrikaner leaders – and, by implication, Afrikaner biography – shifted from politicians to intellectuals. The field was dominated by two biographers: literary scholars John Kannemeyer and Jaap Steyn. Kannemeyer wrote, among others, biographies of Jan Rabie and Etienne Leroux, who, like André Brink and Ingrid Jonker, formed part of the *Sestigers* (the Sixties Movement), a group of novelists and poets who challenged Afrikaner nationalism and apartheid. Jaap Steyn wrote biographies of Van Wyk Louw, Rothman and Cillié.[48] Alex Mouton joined this movement by writing a biography of Schalk Pienaar.[49] These biographies, which ranged from the concise (Mouton) to the encyclopaedic (Kannemeyer and Steyn), tended towards description rather than narration, bearing methodological traces of twentieth-century 'objective scientific' Afrikaner historiography. It was their choice of subject that differentiated them from the biographies of a bygone era.

This new cast of characters represented a safer and more acceptable narrative for Afrikaners, one that could establish Afrikaners as a people with a conscience and a place in a new dispensation. It was also critically important in defying the narrowness of the nationalist narrative, by widening the Afrikaner experience and highlighting a multiplicity of voices and the heterogeneity of a community that had been subject to simplistic and stereotypical portrayals – not least by its 'own' historians. Instead of apartheid denialism or a sanitisation of Afrikaner history, it reflected Afrikaners' own discomfort with apartheid. Yet, the attempts at creating new heroes, be they black or white, came under severe pressure early in 2015.

Everything must fall

Clouds soon appeared on the horizon of Nelson Mandela and Desmond Tutu's 'Rainbow Nation'.[50] In 1998, Mandela's deputy president, Thabo Mbeki, delivered his famed speech that South Africa consisted of two nations – one white and relatively wealthy, the other poor and black.[51] After he ascended to the presidency a year later, the government's focus on racial inequality grew. By the time he was ejected from office in 2008, his populist successor, Jacob Zuma, and Zuma's young battering ram, Julius Malema, had built their base among the disaffected black poor.

The rainbow quickly faded into nostalgia, revived only periodically around significant sporting events. In this regard, popular sporting biographies and autobiographies became reliable sources of revenue for struggling publishers. As Jonathan Ball, the famed South African publisher, remarked drily, 'the way to stay afloat was to make sure you had a biography of (or memoir by) one prominent Jew [sic] and one prominent sportsman on your list every year'.[52]

The heroics of the liberation struggle, for their part, were blatantly appropriated for political legitimacy to offset Zuma's scandal-clad record. In 2005, Zuma was dismissed as deputy president following a corruption scandal in which his financial advisor, Schabir Shaik, was jailed for soliciting bribes on his behalf.[53] Zuma, however, successfully thwarted the justice system through endless delays on technicalities, and by claiming a political conspiracy against him, which led to the charges being dropped shortly before his election as national president in 2009 (the charges were reinstated shortly after his removal from office in 2018).[54]

A year after the initial corruption charges, Zuma was tried for rape in 2006. There was a time when such charges would have sunk a political career, but Zuma's fightback displayed a brazenness that soon became commonplace among populist leaders the world over. In his supporters' eyes, he could do no wrong. They toyi-toyied outside the courthouse and jubilantly celebrated him as a '100% Zuluboy', referring to Zuma's assertion of both his masculine and tribal identity.[55] Shortly after the trial, the house of the rape accuser, Fezekile Kuzwayo, was burned down.[56] The rape charges, like the corruption charges, were framed as a political plot. Zuma was acquitted after Kuzwayo, who had been raped three times as a child, was painted by the defence as a promiscuous woman with a habit of accusing men of rape.[57] Following the trial, she fled the country. In the years that followed, Zuma and his associates plundered the state coffers and, with the help of the now-defunct British public relations firm Bell Pottinger, deflected any criticism by blaming the country's growing inequality on 'White Monopoly Capital'.[58]

During those years, the generation born after 1994 – the 'Born Frees' – came of age. By 2014, the new generation was making its dissent clear. While the majority of the youth were crippled by debilitating poverty, those lucky enough to escape its clutches by accessing formerly white schools and universities found themselves forced to conform to institutionalised cultures that had, in many respects, remained unchanged. The resulting alienation found expression in 2014 in a book by the then twenty-two-year-old Malaika wa Azania, *Memoirs of a Born Free: Reflections on the Rainbow Nation*, which argued that the postapartheid generation that had gained access to formerly white institutions still had to fight for its psychological liberation.[59]

This festering sore burst open in early 2015, when students at the University of Cape Town demanded that a statue of Cecil John Rhodes be removed. The #RhodesMustFall movement inspired activists at university campuses nationwide.[60] By the year's end, the hitherto-fragmented protests had morphed into #FeesMustFall, which demanded free university education at all South African institutions. The 'Fallists' pushed not only for the removal of colonial-era statues and university fees, but also for the 'decolonisation' of the entire university system.[61] This fed into global debates around critical race theory, and offered striking parallels with the Black Lives Matter movement in the United States.

In the context of 'State Capture' (the term given to a series of corruption scandals implicating senior ANC politicians), the renewed focus on race and the accompanying disillusionment with South Africa's negotiated settlement, a new turn was discernible in the literary landscape. Publishers became activists in their own right, with book-length exposes of political corruption quickly becoming a staple in South African bookstores.[62] This development was also manifest among biographies, as new works were published that challenged the rainbow nation narrative.

My biography of D.F. Malan was launched in this new environment, in March 2014. A few months later, another significant perpetrator biography appeared: Jacob Dlamini's *Askari*,[63] which was the result of rigorous documentary research, interviews and sophisticated theoretical analysis. The book focused on Glory Sedibe, an ANC cadre who was captured by the apartheid security police, tortured and turned. He became a notorious *askari* (i.e., an apartheid collaborator who betrayed his erstwhile comrades). Dlamini's book evoked anger among the ANC establishment: given the tradition of heroic biographies in South Africa, there was an immediate assumption that to write about Sedibe was to eulogise him. I made this observation while attending one of Dlamini's book launches, where a number of ANC stalwarts expressed anger at Sedibe's betrayal, and the fact that he had become the subject of a book. Yet what Dlamini was doing was complicating the triumphalist narrative by overturning assumed white/black, perpetrator/victim categories and challenging simplistic 'fictions of racial solidarity'. The book also highlighted the afterlife of secrets in postapartheid South Africa. Dlamini diverged from 'conventional biography' in that he did not offer a chronological narrative of Sedibe's life. He instead opted for a patchwork of themes, interspersed with autobiographical accounts in which he ruminated on his own everyday complicity while growing up under apartheid. In doing so – as the historian Danelle van Zyl-Hermann noted in her review of the book – Dlamini put himself on trial along with his subject, forcing his readers 'to acknowledge their own moral ambiguity in the past and present'. In this sense, Dlamini was concerned with using the life of an individual as 'a lens onto the phenomenon of collaboration'.[64]

The discomfort that biography evoked could be visceral at times, as Anemari Jansen's biography of Eugene de Kock demonstrated. During the 1980s, De Kock, widely known as 'Prime Evil', commanded a covert police unit named Vlakplaas, which was tasked with 'removing' black activists from society. Politicians later hid behind this euphemism, claiming they never gave any commands for assassinations to be carried out. To De Kock and his operatives, the phrase was anything but ambiguous. His unit tortured and killed hundreds of activists, and turned a number of Umkhonto we Sizwe (the ANC's military wing) operatives into askaris. Testifying before the TRC, De Kock was brutally honest and did not flinch from naming names, thereby forcing many other operatives to come into the open and apply for amnesty. What set him apart in the eyes of some observers was the fact that he expressed unqualified remorse, which contrasted with many other perpetrators, and even other significant historical figures internationally, such as Adolf Eichmann, who refused to see any wrong in his deeds.[65] While De Kock received amnesty for a number of the atrocities he committed, some of his deeds were deemed criminal (rather than politically motivated), and as such, he was sentenced to 212 years in prison. He was one of only three white men jailed for apartheid-era atrocities.[66]

The public maintained a grim fascination with De Kock, and he became the subject of more than one book. One of the most significant was authored by Pumla Gobodo-Madikizela, a highly respected clinical psychologist and academic, and one of the TRC's commissioners. Her *A Human Being Died That Night* was published in 2003 and won the Alan Paton Prize. The book grappled with the concept of evil and the dilemma of feeling a certain empathy for a perpetrator.[67] In De Kock's quest for forgiveness, Gobodo-Madikizela heard 'the voice of an outcast begging to rejoin the world of the living'.[68]

In the years following his imprisonment, De Kock assisted the National Prosecuting Authority's Missing Persons Task Team to locate the remains of victims, and he also met with several victims' families.[69] While many were cynical about his displays of contrition, this was not the case for Gobodo-Madikizela or for a number of the families of his victims.[70] As De Kock repeatedly applied for parole, they and other prominent voices joined in supporting him. These included Jacob Dlamini, Max du Preez and Antjie Krog.[71] Gobodo-Madikizela and Dlamini in particular argued that De Kock's reentry into society would force many to reexamine their own complicity, instead of placing a safe distance between themselves and him.

This was a matter that surfaced repeatedly in debates around De Kock's release. As noted, he was disowned by his superiors and by the community in whose name his killing sprees had been perpetrated. This context was what made Anemari Jansen's biography so significant. It was published early in 2015, coinciding with De Kock's release and the heated debates about race and reconciliation that were sparked by the Fallist movement's rise.[72]

Jansen has a postgraduate degree in literature, yet she framed herself as an apolitical mother of three, whose life was dictated by constant relocations due to her husband's work as a civil engineer, while she stressed her identity as a child of apartheid who had benefited from De Kock's atrocities. A chance encounter with a friend of De Kock's led to her meeting him in prison. The experience left her shaken and aghast at his background. As she put it:

> Had I been asleep in the 1980s and the early 1990s? Born in 1964, I had grown up in apartheid's zenith. Thinking back to my youth, I am surprised and shocked at how uninformed and naïve I was. Did I not want to know why our country was burning, or was I just blind?[73]

Jansen's biography was published in both English and Afrikaans, with its reception being split accordingly: while the English media lauded her for humanising De Kock and complicating the postapartheid narrative,[74] no Afrikaans newspaper (they form a tightly woven network that is owned by the same company) reviewed the book. Instead, the leading Afrikaans Sunday newspaper selected descriptions of her meetings with De Kock to imply, in loaded terms, that Jansen had been 'captivated' by his physical presence. It went on to make pointed references to her husband and her debut novel, published the year before, which had as its seemingly autobiographical subject the relationship between a woman and her troubled engineer-husband.[75] Gobodo-Madikizela faced similar insinuations while conducting her research. 'Are you in love with him?'; 'He must be a very good-looking man', she recalled being asked. She responded: 'Casting my professional interest in de Kock in terms of a romantic motive ("in love with him") or as something mysterious ("She's so fascinated by him!") makes it too easy for my listeners to distance themselves from the reality of interacting with the man ... It allows them to dismiss my work as something unnatural, something kinky.'[76]

These experiences resonated with mine. I could not be accused of a romantic fascination with a living subject, but, as mentioned earlier, my being a young woman was often an issue. There were even some insinuations about my physical appearance, as opposed to Malan's notoriously dour façade, and questions, seemingly in jest, as to how I could have been interested in studying such an old, unattractive man. Perhaps male authors have to navigate such innuendos. Perhaps not. I concur with Gobodo-Madikizela: it is a way of avoiding the discomfort that a perpetrator biography evokes.

Jansen's book made it to the local bestseller lists, a *Sunday Times* reviewer listed it as one of the must-read books of 2015,[77] and it was long-listed for the Alan Paton Prize.[78] She was invited to participate in the prestigious Franschhoek Literary Festival, where the Alan Paton Prize shortlist would be announced, yet the event showed that support for her book and for De Kock's release were severely qualified. She had invited De Kock to attend various launches of her book, but his parole conditions made it impossible.[79] However, by the time of the Franschhoek Literary Festival, those restrictions had been lifted. When De Kock appeared in the audience while the biography was being discussed, and then later accompanied Jansen to the shortlist party, shockwaves reverberated through the town and indeed nationwide. At the party, authors banded together and, led by the dystopian novelist Lauren Beukes, asked him to leave. De Kock did not protest. Instead, he thanked Beukes and left.[80]

The incident evoked a flurry of opinion pieces. Many expressed shock at Jansen's insensitivity for inviting him, and De Kock's supposed callousness for showing up. A publisher later related, 'I never imagined I would run into the man. In my head he would go find a farm and live as far as possible from people ... [W]hy does he think he can just socialise?"⁸¹ The journalist Rebecca Davis, who was also present, mused similarly:

> I am left pondering the psychology of a man who would turn up to hear his own terrible history dissected in public. In Jacob Dlamini's superb account of apartheid's collaborators, *Askari*, he mentions several intriguing facts about De Kock: that he was 'unhinged' by his pre-Vlakplaas experiences in the notorious Koevoet military unit; that he took anti-anxiety medication. These facts, while interesting, don't help me ... [S]hould I be speculating about his motives, when that places the focus on the perpetrator rather than his many victims?⁸²

One of the most moving pieces was, however, written by the publisher Palesa Morudu, whose brother had been strangled by the security police, his body tied to a pole and blown up with explosives, so that his bones could never be found.⁸³ Her mother, desperate to know what had happened to her son, had visited De Kock in prison. Without knowing it, De Kock sat down next to Morudu during the discussion of Jansen's book. Both victim and perpetrator cried softly and privately during the discussion. Afterwards they spoke. De Kock remembered the encounter with her mother. 'I'm glad I could help,' he said. 'I am completely conflicted,' Morudu wrote.

> While De Kock walks the earth, I hope that if he does nothing else, he helps many more families who are yet to find closure. There are many who would like to know where they can find the bones of their loved ones, if only in a symbolic sense. De Kock is a free man. His presence at Franschhoek caused some to elicit moral outrage. I have a different take. If you walk, talk and drink in the same space as Neil [*sic*] Barnard, FW de Klerk, Pik Botha and their ilk, add Eugene de Kock to your list. He was their foot soldier. He took the proverbial bullet. Apartheid was prime evil; De Kock was simply its loyal servant. You can't be morally outraged by De Kock and not be morally outraged by De Klerk, or the devastation apartheid brought to black South Africans. So as Shakespeare might have said, screw your courage to the sticking place. And again, I ask, who was it who truly screwed South Africa? A brutal apartheid cop, or those who gave the orders?⁸⁴

Two women for the moment

While Dlamini's and Jansen's books forced confrontation with the question of complicity, other works registered a significant impact on the public discourse and the turn against Zuma.

In August 2016, as Jacob Zuma was announcing the results of the country's municipal elections (in which the ANC had suffered a significant setback), four young women dressed in black walked quietly into the hall and, backs turned to the president, held up five placards to the audience and television cameras, which read: 'I am 1 in 3,' '#', '10 years later', 'Khanga' and 'Remember Khwezi.' (Khanga referred to the traditional garment, similar to a sarong, that Jacob Zuma's rape accuser wore on that fateful night, and which he notoriously regarded as an invitation to his sexual advances; Khwezi was the pseudonym Fezekile Kuzwayo assumed to protect her identity in the face of public vilification and threats against her life; and '1 in 3' referred to the estimated number of women who experience sexual abuse in their lifetime.)[85] The protest elicited a storm, and it was in the wake of this public outburst that Redi Thlabi's *Khwezi: The Remarkable Story of Fezekile Ntsukela Kuzwayo* was published in October 2016.[86]

Thlabi is a well-known public figure in South Africa. A radio presenter and broadcast journalist, she made a name for herself as an author when her memoir, *Endings and Beginnings: A Story of Healing*, won the Alan Paton Prize.[87] She has also distinguished herself as a feminist activist, and it is through this lens that she and Khwezi, who had since returned to South Africa, set out to record her story. Thlabi's book restored Kuzwayo's name, and the two women dreamed of a triumphal launch where this restoration would happen. However, Kuzwayo, who had been HIV positive for years, died before the book was completed. Instead of being a coauthor and ghostwriter, Thlabi suddenly found herself thrust into the role of biographer.

Kuzwayo's story, which was constructed through countless interviews with her and her family and friends, was told through Thlabi's eyes. It was a powerful and compelling story. However, the power of the book lay in the moments where Thlabi shifted the lens beyond Kuzwayo to the wider tale she represented: the sexual abuse of women and children through the course of the liberation struggle, which had hitherto remained unacknowledged. Even the TRC failed to have a category for gender violence against women, and its investigators refused to investigate countless tales of rape. Apart from rape perpetrated by apartheid-era police, Thlabi wrote:

> The rape of some women and children in exile debunks the heroic narrative of the struggle. The ruling party has, largely, been in denial about this, choosing instead a narrative that speaks only of the heroism and sacrifices of so many gallant comrades – a narrative that is true, but incomplete. The war against apartheid was fought on and across women's and children's bodies.[88]

The book offered a challenge to South Africa's intensely patriarchal society and the heroic struggle narrative that glossed over the abuse of women and children perpetrated during its prosecution. Kuzwayo, who was an activist in her life, now had a biography that became an activist work in her afterlife.

By 2018, the country's attention had turned to another feminist icon: Winnie Madikizela-Mandela, who after apartheid had become the rallying symbol for an angry younger generation who rejected the historic compromises of the negotiated settlement. Madikizela-Mandela also became a source of fascination for feminist scholars and activists, who were determined to view her in her own right, and not merely as the former wife of an international icon. Portrayals of her had veered between depictions of a righteous warrior and a Lady Macbeth – she was both 'damnable and heroic', as Sisonke Msimang, one of her biographers, put it. Madikizela-Mandela's complicated character and her turn to violence was contrasted with Nelson Mandela's sainted appeal for reconciliation. In a postapartheid South Africa, 'both of them became icons in their distinct ways. Madiba [Nelson Mandela] came to be seen as a figurehead for peace, while Winnie was seen as a symbol of defiance.'[89]

It was Madikizela-Mandela who spoke to the mood of the country following the student protests of 2015 and 2016, and she became a mentor to a new political movement of young, disaffected black activists and politicians. Her death in April 2018 evoked more raw emotion in South Africa than Nelson Mandela's in 2013. Commentators, used to easy binaries of heroes and villains, battled to make sense of her legacy.[90] Six months after her death, in October and November 2018, two polar opposite biographical works were published.

Fred Bridgland's *Truth, Lies and Alibis: A Winnie Mandela Story* appeared first.[91] Bridgland is a Scottish-born foreign correspondent who had spent more than three decades covering Southern Africa.[92] *Truth, Lies and Alibis* was more exposé than biography, and it delved into the murders of anti-apartheid activists – one of whom, Stompie Seipei, was a child of fourteen – allegedly at the hands of Madikizela-Mandela and her associates during apartheid's dying days. The publication caused an outcry, not so much for its content, but for the publisher Tafelberg's decision to use quotations from prominent black commentators (these were taken from newspaper articles, and all were clearly referenced) that conveyed Madikizela-Mandela's complex legacy. The commentators reacted with anger at being quoted without their explicit consent. In the ensuing war of words, in which the author was accused of being an apartheid apologist, the publisher recalled the printed copies in order for them to be rejacketed, without the quotations.[93]

The cited commentators had included Thlabi and Msimang, who had publicly reflected on Madikizela-Mandela's complicated legacy, but had done so from a standpoint of underlying sympathy. For Bridgland, as he made clear in the book's dedication, there was also a story to be told and justice to be sought for 'those "little" and "unimportant" people who suffered, and … died, at the hands of the Mandela United Football Club' – the name given to the coterie of young men who surrounded Madikizela-Mandela in the 1980s.[94]

The book sank like a stone. There were a number of reviews, in which there was a consensus that Bridgland had demonstrated that Madkizela-Mandela had gotten away with murder.[95] Yet emotions ran too high for this to be able to spark a debate about her newly resurrected heroism. It indicated that while the heroic struggle narrative might have been dented by Dlamini and Thlabi, in its place stood a new one, fostered by the Fallist movement, in which Madikizela-Mandela was a leading protagonist.

Sisonke Msimang's *The Resurrection of Winnie Mandela: A Biography of Survival*, published in November 2018, stood in stark contrast to Bridgland's book. An activist and columnist, Msimang was raised in exile by her ANC-activist parents. On returning to South Africa, members of her family took up prominent positions in the new ANC government. Her memoir, *Always Another Country: A Memoir of Exile and Home*, was shortlisted for the Alan Paton Prize. A superficial read of *The Resurrection of Winnie Mandela* might give the impression of a hagiographic enterprise. For example, in her introduction, Msimang proclaimed – using the respectful, yet familiar, form of address for an African elder: 'I am interested in redeeming Ma Winnie.'[96] Yet, that is not what she did. Instead, she pointed to the double standards whereby male and female freedom fighters were judged:

> In the 1980s, South Africa was burning. There were army trucks swarming through the townships and a 'people's war' had been declared by liberation-movement structures within and outside the country. Winnie was not the only African National Congress (ANC) leader who traded in recklessness and fiery rhetoric. But she was the only *woman* who was visibly doing so. ANC activist Harry Gwala, who was implicated in countless assassinations and political crimes in the 1990s, was depicted as the Lion of the Midlands. He was not tarnished in the same way as Ma Winnie, even though she was operating in the conventions of her political party at the time … The hypocrisy is obvious: the party leaders urged others to undertake these acts but did not wish to get their own hands dirty. Worse, they were ashamed when Winnie adopted the violent tactics they advocated. She was a woman and a wife, so her actions were deemed to be repugnant.[97]

Instead of trying to navigate Winnie Mandela's contradictions, Msimang embraced them as a more realistic reflection of postapartheid South Africa's messiness, one in which 'all of us were both victims and perpetrators', rather than 'the orgy of sentimentality that gripped this country in the 1990s'.[98]

The book's biographical merits can be questioned. Its introduction and conclusion offer searing commentaries on gender, feminism and the anger of a new generation, but its narrative, written as a paean to Madikizela-Mandela, is jarring.[99] The book is an attempt at interpreting Winnie Mandela within the context of a Fallist South Africa and through a feminist lens. As was the case with so many of the other South African biographies, Msimang's rendering of Madikizela-Mandela's life reflected the psyche of a nation at a contested moment in history.

Conclusion

South African biography reflects the wider political and intellectual landscape, both in its subjects and its approach. It is a genre easily beholden to grand political narratives: it once elevated great white men, only to replace them with great black men when the political tide turned. It answers to the continual urge to elevate heroes – and less frequently heroines – who reflect the values of the moment. This could be seen in Afrikaner biographers' search for new, acceptable heroes after apartheid, and even the Fallist movement, despite its rejection of the political compromises of the negotiated settlement, was quick to turn to new individuals who could represent its emerging narrative. In such instances, biography becomes a symbol that often obscures the individual's complexity.

This is not to say that there cannot be critical biographies of revered figures. There are key examples of meticulously researched academic biographies of figures such as Nelson Mandela, Sol Plaatje and John Dube.[100] South African biography is embedded in its scholarly landscape, however tenuously, and as a consequence the genre has been shaped by broader historiographical trends, which can be seen in its use as a tool to defy the limits of the archive in excavating marginalised lives. In exploring the discomforts of complicity by humanising apartheid perpetrators, and challenging the heroic struggle narrative by highlighting its darker side, biography can demythologise grand narratives and add nuance to our understanding of the past. In doing so, it becomes a disruptive voice in the wider public discourse.

Biography offers a messy space where scholars and activists rub shoulders, with the consequence that the field sways between meticulously researched tomes and hastily written polemic. Yet, in both instances, it is underpinned by the deeper need to understand and answer to the contestations that mark postapartheid South Africa. This is not to accord the same scholarly weight to each. There is much to be said for the methodology of critical, scholarly biography. However, in their reception and impact, it is necessary to understand how the various forms of biography coexist and interact, and how they shape public discourse, commemoration and grand narratives. Critical biography is a scholarly pursuit and an ideal, but in its reception it roams far beyond the confines of the ivory tower.

Notes

1. L. Koorts, *DF Malan and the Rise of Afrikaner Nationalism* (Cape Town: Tafelberg, 2014).
2. Biographer Heather Hughes has made fruitful use of this concept, coined by Eric Hobsbawm, in her exploration of John Dube. See H. Hughes, 'Dialectical Dances: Exploring John Dube's Public Life', *South African Historical Journal*, 64 (3) Sept. 2012, 418–33.
3. M. Makhanya, 'Book Review – Insight into a Champion of Afrikaner Nationalism', *City Press*, 27 Apr. 2014, www.news24.com/Archives/City-Press/Book-review-Insight-into-a-champion-of-Afrikaner-nationalism-20150430 (accessed 23 June 2021).
4. K. Smith, *The Changing Past: Trends in South African Historical Writing* (Johannesburg: Southern Book Publishers, 1988), 165–7.
5. See the Archival Platform, 'State of the Archives: An Analysis of South Africa's National Archival System, 2014', Archive and Public Culture Research Initiative, www.apc.uct.ac.za/apc/projects/state-of-the-archives-report (accessed 11 June 2021).
6. S. Morreira, 'Significant Archives Are under Threat in Cape Town's Fire. Why They Matter So Much', *The Conversation*, 19 Apr. 2021, https://theconversation.com/significant-archives-are-under-threat-in-cape-towns-fire-why-they-matter-so-much-159299 (accessed 21 June 2021).
7. H. Mokoena, 'The Making of a *Kholwa* Intellectual: A Discursive Biography of Magema Magwaza Fuze' (DPhil thesis, University of Cape Town, 2005), 5.
8. Ibid., 5.
9. See B. Willan, *Sol Plaatje: A Life of Solomon Tshekisho Plaatje, 1876–1932* (Johannesburg: Jacana, 2018); H. Hughes, *The First President: A Life of John L. Dube, Founding President of the ANC* (Johannesburg: Jacana, 2011); H. Mokoena, *Magema Fuze: The Making of a Kholwa Intellectual* (Pietermaritzburg: UKZN Press, 2011); B. Ngqulanga, *The Man Who Founded the ANC: A Biography of Pixley ka Isaka Seme* (Cape Town: Penguin, 2017); C. Higgs, *The Ghost of Equality: The Public Lives of D.D.T. Jabavu of South Africa, 1885–1959* (Athens: Ohio University Press, 1997); T. Couzens, *The New African: A Study of the Life and Work of HIE Dhlomo* (Johannesburg: Raven Press, 1986).
10. H. Mokoena, homepage of the book *Magema Fuze*, University of Kwa-Zulu-Natal Press, n.d., www.ukznpress.co.za/?class=bb_ukzn_sample_chapters&method=view_sample&global[fields][_id]=356 (accessed 31 Mar. 2022).
11. Couzens, *New African*; see also the review by Isabel Hofmeyr, 'Review: *The New African: A Study of the Life and Work of H. I. E. Dhlomo* by Tim Couzens, H. I. E. Dhlomo; *H. I. E. Dhlomo: Collected Works* by Tim Couzens, Nick Visser, H. I. E. Dhlomo', *English in Africa* 13 (1) May 1986, 93–8.
12. C. van Onselen, *The Seed Is Mine: The Life of Kas Maine, a South African Sharecropper, 1894–1985* (New York: Hill and Wang, 1997), 10.

13 *Ibid.*, 11.
14 See J. Hyslop, *The Notorious Syndicalist: J.T. Bain – A Scottish Rebel in Colonial South Africa* (Johannesburg: Jacana, 2004); C. van Onselen, *The Fox and the Flies: The World of Joseph Silver, Racketeer and Psychopath* (London: Jonathan Cape, 2007); C. van Onselen, *Showdown at the Red Lion: The Life and Times of Jack McLoughlin, 1859–1910* (Johannesburg: Jonathan Ball, 2015); C. van Onselen, *The Cowboy Capitalist: John Hays Hammond, the American West and the Jameson Raid* (Johannesburg: Jonathan Ball, 2017); C. van der Merwe, *Donker Stroom: Eugène Marais en die Anglo-Boereoorlog* (Cape Town: Tafelberg, 2015); C. van der Merwe, *Kansvatter: Die Rustelose Lewe van Ben Viljoen* (Pretoria: Protea Boekhuis, 2019).
15 For example, B. Booyens, *Die Lewe van D.F. Malan: Die Eerste Veertig Jaar* (Cape Town: Tafelberg, 1969); H.B. Thom, *D.F. Malan* (Cape Town: Tafelberg, 1980).
16 C. Bundy, *Nelson Mandela: A Jacana Pocket Biography* (Johannesburg: Jacana, 2015), 139.
17 Nancy Jacobs and Andrew Bank crunched the numbers. According to their survey, between 1990 and 2017, there appeared 225 English-language political biographies and around 200 political autobiographies. See N. Jacobs and A. Bank, 'Biography in Post-apartheid South Africa: A Call for Awkwardness', *African Studies*, 78 (2), 2019, 165–82.
18 See, as examples, Bundy, *Nelson Mandela*; A. Sampson, *Mandela: The Authorised Biography* (New York: Harper Collins, 1999); T. Lodge, *Mandela: A Critical Life* (Oxford: Oxford University Press, 2007); C. Brand and B. Jones, *Doing Life with Mandela* (Johannesburg: Jonathan Ball, 2014); Z. la Grange, *Good Morning, Mr Mandela* (London: Penguin, 2015); B. Ladds, *The Madiba Appreciation Club: A Chef's Story* (Johannesburg: Jonathan Ball, 2018).
19 S. de Waal, 'Pearls in an Oyster of Ferment', *Mail & Guardian*, 23 Apr. 2015, http://mg.co.za/article/2015-04-23-pearls-in-an-oyster-of-ferment (accessed 31 Mar. 2022).
20 See E. Sisulu, *Walter & Albertina Sisulu: In Our Lifetime* (Claremont: David Phillip, 2002); L. Callinnicos, *Oliver Tambo: Beyond the Engeli Mountains* (Claremont: David Phillip, 2004); P. O'Malley, *Shades of Difference: Mac Maharaj and the Struggle for South Africa* (New York: Viking, 2007); S. Couper, *Albert Luthuli: Bound by Faith* (Scottsville: UKZN Press, 2010); X. Mangcu, *Biko: A Biography* (Cape Town: Tafelberg, 2012).
21 H. Lewin, *Stones against the Mirror: Friendship in the Time of the South African Struggle* (Cape Town: Umuzi, 2011).
22 See S. Hassim, 'Not Just Nelson's Wife: Winnie Madikizela-Mandela, Violence and Radicalism in South Africa', *Journal of Southern African Studies*, 44 (5) 2018, 895–912.
23 See, for example, Sisulu, *Walter & Albertina Sisulu*, and A. Wieder, *Ruth First and Joe Slovo in the War against Apartheid* (New York: Monthly Review Press, 2013); A.M. du Preez Bezdrob, *Winnie Mandela: A Life* (Cape Town: Zebra Press, 2003); W. Mandela, *Part of My Soul Went with Him*, adapted by

Mary Benson (London: Penguin, 1985); W. Madikizela-Mandela, *491 Days: Prisoner Number 1323/69* (Athens: Ohio University Press, 2013). There are important examples of women's memoirs and autobiography which predate the fall of apartheid, but which did not translate into full biographies after apartheid. Instead, they were republished. Examples include E. Kuzwayo, *Call Me Woman* (Johannesburg: Picador Africa, 2018); E. Mashinini, *Strikes Have Followed Me All My Life: A South African Autobiography* (Johannesburg: Picador Africa, 2012); F. Meer, *Memories of Love and Struggle* (Cape Town: Kwela Books, 2017).

24 Here, it is useful to look at Jacobs and Bank's numbers again. Only fifteen authors chose women as the subject of book-long biographies. In the twenty-eight years covered by their survey, they were able to identify only nine biographies that were of women who were not also activists' wives. See Jacobs and Bank, 'Biography in Post-apartheid South Africa', 168.

25 H. Giliomee, '*True Confessions, End Papers* and the Dakar Conference: A Review of Political Arguments', *Tydskrif vir Letterkunde*, 46 (2), 2009, 32–3.

26 H. Giliomee, 'Rediscovering and Re-imagining the Afrikaners in a New South Africa: Autobiographical Notes on Writing an Uncommon Biography', *Itinerario* 27 (3–4), 2003, 9–48.

27 S. Clingman, *Bram Fischer: Afrikaner Revolutionary* (Claremont: David Phillip, 1998).

28 B. Naudé, *My Land van Hoop: Die Lewe van Beyers Naudé* (Cape Town: Tafelberg, 1995).

29 E. Brink, '"Maar net 'n Klomp Factory Meide": Afrikaner Family and Community on the Witwatersrand', in B. Bozzoli (ed.), *Class, Community and Conflict: South African Perspectives* (Johannesburg: Ravan, 1987); L. Vincent, 'The Power behind the Scenes: The Afrikaner Nationalist Women's Parties, 1915 to 1931', *South African Historical Journal*, 40, 1999, 51–73; M. du Toit, 'The Domesticity of Afrikaner Nationalism: Volksmoeders and the ACVV, 1904–1929', *Journal of Southern African Studies*, 29 (1) 2003, 155–76.

30 A. Grundlingh and H. Sapire, 'From Feverish Festival to Repetitive Ritual? The Changing Fortunes of Great Trek Mythology in an Industrialising South Africa, 1938–1988', *South African Historical Journal*, 21 (1) 1989, 19–38.

31 See, for example, R. Morrel (ed.), *White but Poor: Essays on the History of Poor Whites in Southern Africa* (Pretoria: University of South Africa Press, 1992); A. Grundlingh and S. Huigen (eds), *Van Volksmoeder tot Fokofpolisiekar: Kritiese Opstelle oor Afrikaanse Herinneringsplekke* (Stellenbosch: Sun Press, 2008); A. Grundlingh, '"Rocking the Boat in South Africa?" Voëlvry Music and Afrikaans Anti-apartheid Social Protest in the 1980s', *International Journal of African Historical Studies*, 37 (3) 2004, 483–514; A. Grundlingh, '"Are We Afrikaners Getting Too Rich?" Cornucopia and Change in Afrikanerdom in the 1960s', *Journal of Historical Sociology*, 21 (2–3) 2008, 143–65.

32 G. Cuthbertson, A. Grundlingh and M.L. Suttie (eds), *Writing a Wider War: Rethinking Gender, Race and Identity in the South African War, 1899–1902* (Cape Town: David Phillip, 2002).
33 A. Grundlingh and S. Swart, *Radelose Rebellie? Dinamika van die 1914–1915 Afrikanerrebellie* (Pretoria: Protea Boekhuis, 2009).
34 See, for example, R. Warwick, 'Triomf, vrees op 31 Mei', *Netwerk24*, 29 May 2021, www.netwerk24.com/Stemme/Aktueel/triomf-vrees-op-31-mei-20210528 (accessed 31 Mar. 2022).
35 A. Grundlingh, 'Herhistorisering en Herposisionering: Perspektiewe op Aspekte van Geskiedsbeoefening in Hedendaagse Suid-Afrika', *Historia* 46 (2) 2001, 320.
36 I can personally attest to this. I write a monthly column in the Afrikaans press, and am regularly trolled whenever I offer a version of history that differs from, or is critical of, the old nationalist narrative. There has been a growing hardening of attitudes, which reflects international trends.
37 In this regard, the Afrikaans publisher Protea Boekhuis leads the field. It publishes a curious mix of antiquarian works and notable scholarly histories and biographies, especially those overlooked by larger trade publishers. This can be seen in their catalogue at https://proteabooks.com/index.php/protea/biographies.html?p=1 (accessed 31 Mar. 2022).
38 This new trend was set off in 2000 when the journalist Chris Louw (who later committed suicide) wrote an open letter entitled 'Boetman Is die Bliksem In', which roughly translates as 'Boetman is beyond p*ssed off.' Boetman is a common, somewhat paternalistic, term of endearment for young boys. The letter articulated the anger and disillusionment of an ex-conscript, which struck a deep chord and set off the so-called Boetman debate. For an English translation, see C. Louw, 'Boetman Is die Bliksem In,' *News24*, 28 July 2014, www.news24.com/news24/MyNews24/Boetman-is-die-bliksem-in-20140728 (accessed 31 Mar. 2022).
39 A. Mouton, 'The Good, the Bad and the Ugly: Professional Historians and Political Biography of South African Parliamentary Politics, 1910–1990', *Journal for Contemporary History*, 36 (1) 2011, 66.
40 Clingman, *Bram Fischer*, xi.
41 A. Krog, *Country of My Skull* (London: Vintage, 1999).
42 H. Giliomee, *The Afrikaners: Biography of a People* (Cape Town: Tafelberg, 2003).
43 Giliomee, 'Rediscovering and Re-imagining', 22.
44 M. Walzer, *The Company of Critics: Social Criticism and Political Commitment in the Twentieth Century* (New York: Basic Books, 2002), xi.
45 See Giliomee, *Afrikaners*, 547–50.
46 *Ibid.*. Slabbert has also become the subject of a biography. See A. Grundlingh, *Slabbert: Man on a Mission* (Johannesburg: Jonathan Ball, 2021).
47 The Order of Ikhamanga is one of the South African government's National Orders, and is awarded to South African citizens for exceptional achievement in the fields of arts, culture, literature, music, journalism or sport. The Presidency,

Republic of South Africa, 'The Order of Ikhamanga', www.thepresidency.gov.za/national-orders/order-ikhamanga-0#:~:text=The%20Order%20of%20Ikhamanga%20is,Order%20is%20awarded%20in%20gold. (accessed 16 Apr. 2022).
48 J.C. Kannemeyer, *Jan Rabie: Prosapionier en Politieke Wegwyser* (Cape Town: Tafelberg, 2004); J.C. Kannemeyer, *Leroux: 'n Lewe* (Pretoria: Protea Boekhuis, 2008); J.C. Steyn, *Van Wyk Louw: 'n Lewensverhaal* (Cape Town: Tafelberg, 1998); J.C. Steyn, *Penvegter: Piet Cillié van 'Die Burger'* (Cape Town: Tafelberg, 2002); J.C. Steyn, *Die 100 Jaar van MER* (Cape Town: Tafelberg, 2004).
49 A. Mouton, *Voorloper: Die Lewe van Schalk Pienaar* (Cape Town: Tafelberg, 2002).
50 The heading of this section is borrowed from the film by Rehad Desai, which traced the student protests in the latter half of 2015. See the film's website, R. Desai, 'Everything Must Fall', http://everythingmustfall.co.za/ (accessed 31 Mar. 2022).
51 Thabo Mbeki, 'Statement of Deputy President Thabo Mbeki at the Opening of the Debate in the National Assembly, on "Reconciliation and Nation Building", National Assembly Cape Town, 29 May 1998', Department of International Relations and Cooperation, www.dirco.gov.za/docs/speeches/1998/mbek0529.htm (accessed 31 Mar. 2022).
52 M. Gevisser, 'Jonathan Ball: A Very Human Being', *Daily Maverick*, 7 Apr. 2021, www.dailymaverick.co.za/article/2021-04-07-jonathan-ball-a-very-human-being/ (accessed 22 June 2021).
53 *Mail & Guardian*, 14 Jun. 2005.
54 *Irish Times*, 23 May 2019; G. Nicholson, 'Court Lashes Jacob Zuma's Language and Finds No Merits in His Appeal Argument', *Daily Maverick*, 29 Nov. 2019, www.dailymaverick.co.za/article/2019-11-29-court-lashes-jacob-zumas-language-and-finds-no-merits-in-his-appeal-argument/ (accessed 31 Mar. 2022); S. Mavuso, 'Jacob Zuma Pleads Not Guilty to 18 Corruption Charges', *IOL*, 26 May 2021, www.iol.co.za/news/politics/jacob-zuma-pleads-not-guilty-to-18-corruption-charges-e5d7fe94-9e4a-4883-ab7f-e6625ab48556 (accessed 22 June 2021).
55 F.N. Moya, '100% Zuluboy', *Mail & Guardian*, 6 Apr. 2006, https://mg.co.za/article/2006-04-06-100-zuluboy/ (accessed 31 Mar. 2022).
56 M. Thamm, '#RememberKhwezi: Zuma's Rape Accuser Dies, Never Having Known Freedom', *Daily Maverick*, 9 Oct. 2019, www.dailymaverick.co.za/article/2016-10-09-rememberkhwezi-zumas-rape-accuser-dies-never-having-known-freedom/ (accessed 31 Mar. 2022).
57 *The Guardian* (London), 8 May 2006.
58 D. Segal, 'How Bell Pottinger, P.R. Firm for Despots and Rogues, Met Its End in South Africa', *New York Times*, 4 Feb. 2018, www.nytimes.com/2018/02/04/business/bell-pottinger-guptas-zuma-south-africa.html (accessed 31 Mar. 2022).
59 See, for example, M. wa Azania, *Memoirs of a Born Free: Reflections on the Rainbow Nation* (Johannesburg: Jacana, 2014).
60 D. Foster, 'After Rhodes Fell: The New Movement to Africanize South Africa', *The Atlantic*, 25 Apr. 2015, www.theatlantic.com/international/archive/2015/04/after-rhodes-fell-south-africa-statue/391457/ (accessed 31 Mar. 2022).

61 R. Desai, '#FeesMustFall: How Student Movements Shaped a New South Africa', *Al Jazeera*, 10 May 2019, www.aljazeera.com/blogs/africa/2019/05/feesmustfall-student-movements-shaped-south-africa-190507073038858.html (accessed 17 Dec. 2019).
62 A. Olivier, 'Om die Internasionale Taal van Boeke te Praat', *Netwerk24*, 25 Nov. 2019, www.netwerk24.com/netwerk24/Stemme/Menings/om-die-internasionale-taal-van-boeke-te-praat-20191122 (accessed 31 Mar. 2022); J. van Loggerenberg and A. Lackay, *Rogue: The Inside Story of SARS's Crime-Busting Unit* (Johannesburg: Jonathan Ball, 2016); J. Pauw, *The President's Keepers: Those Keeping Zuma in Power and out of Prison* (Cape Town: Tafelberg, 2017); C. Olver, *How to Steal a City: The Battle for Nelson Mandela Bay* (Johannesburg: Jonathan Ball, 2017); P. Myburgh, *The Republic of Gupta: A Story of State Capture* (Johannesburg: Penguin Random House, 2017) and *Gangster State: Unravelling Ace Magashule's Web of Capture* (Johannesburg: Penguin Random House, 2019); J.B. Styan and P. Vecchiatto, *The Bosasa Billions: How the ANC Sold its Soul for Braaipacks, Booze and Bags of Cash* (Pretoria: Lapa, 2019).
63 J. Dlamini, *Askari: A Story of Collaboration and Betrayal in die Anti-apartheid Struggle* (Johannesburg: Jacana, 2014).
64 D. van Zyl-Hermann, 'History Made Human: Confronting the Unpalatable Past through Biographical Writing in Post-apartheid South Africa', *African Historical Review*, 47 (2) 2015, 115–31.
65 P. Gobodo-Madikizela, *A Human Being Died That Night* (Cape Town: David Phillip, 2003), 6, 14–15, 22–3, 67–9; A. Jansen, *Eugene de Kock: Assassin for the State* (Cape Town: Tafelberg, 2015), 241–4.
66 J. van der Leun, 'The Odd Couple: Why an Apartheid Activist Joined Forces with a Murderer', *The Guardian* (London), 6 June 2015, www.theguardian.com/global/2015/jun/06/odd-couple-apartheid-activist-madeleine-fullard-convicted-policeman-eugene-de-kock (accessed 25 Aug. 2017).
67 Gobodo-Madikizela, *A Human Being*, 117–19, 130–2.
68 *Ibid.*, 115.
69 Van der Leun, 'Odd Couple'.
70 Gobodo-Madikizela, *A Human Being*, 14–15, 138–9; Jansen, *Eugene de Kock*, 245–6.
71 P. Gobodo-Madikizela, 'Towards an Anatomy of Violence', *Mail & Guardian*, 15 Jan. 2010, https://mg.co.za/article/2010-01-15-towards-an-anatomy-of-violence (accessed 25 Aug. 2017); J. Dlamini, 'De Kock Can Help State Bring Apartheid Criminals to Justice', *Business Day*, 7 Feb. 2014, www.pressreader.com/south-africa/business-day/20140207/281509339073773 (accessed 25 Aug. 2017); A. Krog, 'Can an Evil Man Change? The Repentance of Eugene de Kock', *New York Times*, 13 Mar. 2015, www.nytimes.com/2015/03/14/opinion/sunday/the-repentance-of-eugene-de-kock-apartheid-assassin.html?mcubz=0 (accessed 25 Aug. 2017).
72 Full disclosure: at the time of writing, I have never met or interacted with Anemari Jansen, but we do share the same publisher and editor.
73 Jansen, *Eugene de Kock*, 1–9.

74 M. Thamm, 'One Woman's Extraordinary Journey: Je Suis Eugene de Kock', *Daily Maverick*, 4 May 2015, www.dailymaverick.co.za/article/2015-05-04-one-womans-extraordinary-journey-je-suis-eugene-de-kock/#.Waaq68gjHIU (accessed 30 Aug. 2017); *Business Day*, 24 July 2015.

75 H. Scholtz, 'Eugene se Stem het Haar Bekoor', *Netwerk24*, 22 Mar. 2015, www.netwerk24.com/Nuus/Misdaad/Eugene-se-stem-het-haar-bekoor-20150322# (accessed 31 Mar. 2022).

76 Gobodo-Madikizela, *A Human Being*, 122–3.

77 'The Best Books of 2015: Sunday Times Book Reviewers Choose Their Top Reads of the Year, *Books Live*, 7 Dec. 2015, http://bookslive.co.za/blog/2015/12/07/the-best-books-of-2015-sunday-times-book-reviewers-choose-their-top-reads-of-the-year/ (accessed 31 Mar. 2022).

78 'The 2016 Sunday Times Alan Paton Award Longlist', *Books Live*, 4 Apr. 2016, http://bookslive..za/blog/2016/04/04/the-2016-sunday-times-alan-paton-award-longlist/ (accessed 31 Mar. 2022).

79 'SA Is Baie Vreemd vir De Kock, Sê Skrywer', *Netwerk24*, 30 Aug. 2015, www.netwerk24.com/Nuus/Misdaad/SA-is-baie-vreemd-vir-De-Kock-se-skrywer-20150830 (accessed 31 Mar. 2022).

80 'Not Welcome: Thabiso Mahlape and Lauren Beukes on Eugene de Kock's Presence at the Sunday Times Literary Awards Shortlist Event', *Books Live*, 15 May 2016, http://bookslive.co.za/blog/2016/05/15/not-welcome-thabiso-mahlape-and-lauren-beukes-on-eugene-de-kocks-presence-at-the-sunday-times-literary-awards-shortlist-event/ (accessed 31 Mar. 2022).

81 *Ibid.*

82 R. Davis, 'Least Stealthy Assassin Ever: Why Was Eugene de Kock at the Franschoek Literary Festival?', *Mail & Guardian*, 20 May 2016, https://mg.co.za/article/2016-05-20-00-why-did-de-kock-put-in-an-appearance-at-the-franschhoek-literary-festival (accessed 31 Mar. 2022).

83 P. Morudu, 'Remember the Past and Question the Present', *Business Day*, 29 Oct. 2013, www.businesslive.co.za/bd/opinion/columnists/2013-10-29-remember-the-past-and-question-the-present/ (accessed 31 Mar. 2022).

84 P. Morudu, 'Eugene de Kock at the Franschoek Literary Festival: Of Screwed Courage and a Screwed Country', *Daily Maverick*, 16 May 2016, www.dailymaverick.co.za/article/2016-05-16-eugene-de-kock-at-the-franschhoek-literary-festival-of-screwed-courage-and-a-screwed-country/#.WabLkcgjHIU (accessed 31 Mar. 2022).

85 R. Pather, 'Four Women, the President and the Protest That Shook the Results Ceremony', *Mail & Guardian*, 6 Aug. 2016, https://mg.co.za/article/2016-08-06-four-women-the-president-and-the-protest-that-shoock-the-election-results-ceremony/ (accessed 31 Mar. 2022).

86 R. Thlabi, *Khwezi: The Remarkable Story of Fezekile Ntsukela Kuzwayo* (Johannesburg: Jonathan Ball, 2017).

87 R. Thlabi, *Endings and Beginnings: A Story of Healing* (Johannesburg: Jacana, 2013).

88 Thlabi, *Khwezi*, 41–3.

89 S. Msimang, *The Resurrection of Winnie Mandela* (Johannesburg: Jonathan Ball, 2018), 148.
90 See, for example, R. Pather, 'Even in Death, Mam' Winnie Can't Catch a Break', *Mail & Guardian*, 3 Apr. 2018, https://mg.co.za/article/2018-04-03-in-death-mam-winnie-has-rallied-her-mourners/ (accessed 31 Mar. 2022); A. Hirsch, 'Winnie Mandela Was a Hero. If She'd Been White, There Would Be No Debate', *The Guardian* (London), 3 Apr. 2018, www.theguardian.com/commentisfree/2018/apr/03/winnie-mandela-hero-white-protest-apartheid (accessed 31 Mar. 2022); N. Mabasa, 'Youth Inspired Anew by AN Icon They Barely Knew', *Daily Maverick*, 12 Apr. 2018, www.dailymaverick.co.za/article/2018-04-12-remembering-winnie-youth-inspired-anew-by-an-icon-they-barely-knew/ (accessed 31 Mar. 2022); S. Jacobs, 'How Do We Write about Winnie's Life Sympathetically?', *Mail & Guardian*, 13 Apr. 2018, https://mg.co.za/article/2018-04-12-how-do-we-write-about-winnies-life-sympathetically/ (accessed 31 Mar. 2022).
91 F. Bridgland, *Truth, Lies and Alibis: A Winnie Mandela Story* (Cape Town: Tafelberg, 2018).
92 See Bridgland's author page, NB Publishers, www.nb.co.za/en/authors (accessed 2 Sept. 2022).
93 J. Levitt, 'Anger over New Winnie Mandela Book, Accusations of Fake Shout-Outs', *TimesLive*, 30 Oct. 2018, www.timeslive.co.za/news/south-africa/2018-10-30-anger-over-new-winnie-mandela-book-accusations-of-fake-shout-outs/ (accessed 31 Mar. 2022); I. Mahlangu, 'Outcry over Cover of New Winnie Book', *SowetanLive*, 31 Oct. 2018, www.sowetanlive.co.za/news/south-africa/2018-10-31-outcry-over-cover-of-new-winnie-book/ (accessed 31 Mar. 2022); J. Levitt, 'I'm No Apartheid Apologist, Says Author of Controversial Winnie Mandela Book', *TimesLive*, 31 Oct. 2018, www.timeslive.co.za/news/south-africa/2018-10-31-im-no-apartheid-apologist-says-author-of-controversial-winnie-mandela-book/ (accessed 31 Mar. 2022).
94 See the dedication page, Bridgland, *Truth, Lies and Alibis*.
95 P. Trewhela, 'Winnie Mandela – An Issue for Christians?', *Daily Maverick*, 18 Oct. 2018, www.dailymaverick.co.za/opinionista/2018-10-18-winnie-mandela-an-issue-for-christians/ (accessed 31 Mar. 2022); E. Naki, 'Book Review: *Truth, Lies and Alibis – A Winnie Mandela Story*', *Citizen*, 14 Feb. 2019, www.citizen.co.za/entertainment/2083397/book-review-truth-lies-and-alibis-a-winnie-mandela-story/ (accessed 31 Mar. 2022); 'How ANC Shielded Winnie', *City Press*, 7 Oct. 2018, www.news24.com/citypress/news/how-anc-shielded-winnie-20181007 (accessed 31 Mar. 2022).
96 S. Msimang, *Always Another Country: A Memoir of Exile and Home* (Johannesburg: Jonathan Ball, 2017), 19.
97 Msimang, *Resurrection of Winnie Mandela*, 14.
98 Ibid., 153, 156.
99 Hassim, 'Not Just Nelson's Wife'; S. Hassim, 'The Impossible Contract: The Political and Private Marriage of Nelson and Winnie Mandela', *Journal of Southern African Studies*, 45 (6) 2019, 1151–71.

100 See for example Willan, *Sol Plaatje*; Hughes, *First President*; and Sampson, *Mandela*.

Bibliography

'The 2016 Sunday Times Alan Paton Award Longlist' (2016) *Books Live*, 4 Apr., http://bookslive..za/blog/2016/04/04/the-2016-sunday-times-alan-paton-award-longlist/ (accessed 31 Mar. 2022).

The Archival Platform (2014) 'State of the Archives: An Analysis of South Africa's National Archival System, 2014', Archive and Public Culture Research Initiative, www.apc.uct.ac.za/apc/projects/state-of-the-archives-report (accessed 23 June 2021).

'The Best Books of 2015: Sunday Times Book Reviewers Choose Their Top Reads of the Year' (2015) *Books Live*, 7 Dec., http://bookslive.co.za/blog/2015/12/07/the-best-books-of-2015-sunday-times-book-reviewers-choose-their-top-reads-of-the-year/ (accessed 31 Mar. 2022).

Booyens, B. (1969) *Die Lewe van D.F. Malan: Die Eerste Veertig Jaar*. Cape Town: Tafelberg.

Brand, C., and B. Jones (2014) *Doing Life with Mandela*. Johannesburg: Jonathan Ball.

Bridgland, F. (2018) *Truth, Lies and Alibis: A Winnie Mandela Story*. Cape Town: Tafelberg.

Brink, E. (1987) '"Maar net 'n Klomp Factory Meide": Afrikaner Family and Community on the Witwatersrand', in B. Bozzoli (ed.), *Class, Community and Conflict: South African Perspectives*. Johannesburg: Ravan.

Bundy, C. (2015) *Nelson Mandela: A Jacana Pocket Biography*. Johannesburg: Jacana.

Callinicos, L. (2004) *Oliver Tambo: Beyond the Engeli Mountains*. Claremont: David Phillip.

Clingman, S. (1998) *Bram Fischer: Afrikaner Revolutionary*. Claremont: David Phillip.

Couper, S. (2010) *Albert Luthuli: Bound by Faith*. Scottsville: UKZN Press.

Couzens, T. (1986) *The New African: A Study of the Life and Work of HIE Dhlomo*. Johannesburg: Ravan.

Cuthbertson, G., A. Grundlingh and M.L. Suttie (eds) (2002) *Writing a Wider War: Rethinking Gender, Race and Identity in the South African War, 1899–1902*. Cape Town: David Phillip.

Davis, R. (2016) 'Least Stealthy Assassin Ever: Why Was Eugene de Kock at the Franschoek Literary Festival?', *Mail & Guardian*, 20 May, https://mg.co.za/article/2016-05-20-00-why-did-de-kock-put-in-an-appearance-at-the-franschhoek-literary-festival (accessed 31 Mar. 2022).

Desai, R. (2018) 'Everything Must Fall', http://everythingmustfall.co.za/ (accessed 31 Mar. 2022).

Desai, R. (2019) '#FeesMustFall: How Student Movements Shaped a New South Africa', *Al Jazeera*, 10 May, www.aljazeera.com/blogs/africa/2019/05/feesmustfall-student-movements-shaped-south-africa-190507073038858.html (accessed 17 Dec. 2019).

De Waal, S. (2015) 'Pearls in an Oyster of Ferment', *Mail & Guardian*, 23 Apr., http://mg.co.za/article/2015-04-23-pearls-in-an-oyster-of-ferment (accessed 31 Mar. 2022).
Dlamini, J. (2014) *Askari: A Story of Collaboration and Betrayal in die Anti-apartheid Struggle*. Johannesburg: Jacana.
Dlamini, J. (2014) 'De Kock Can Help State Bring Apartheid Criminals to Justice', *Business Day*, 7 Feb., www.pressreader.com/south-africa/business-day/20140207/281509339073773 (accessed 25 Aug. 2017).
Du Preez Bezdrob, A.M. (2003) *Winnie Mandela: A Life*. Cape Town: Zebra Press.
Du Toit, M. (2003) 'The Domesticity of Afrikaner Nationalism: Volksmoeders and the ACVV, 1904–1929', *Journal of Southern African Studies*, 29 (1).
Foster, D. (2015) 'After Rhodes Fell: The New Movement to Africanize South Africa', *The Atlantic*, 25 Apr., www.theatlantic.com/international/archive/2015/04/after-rhodes-fell-south-africa-statue/391457/ (accessed 31 Mar. 2022).
Gevisser, M. (2021) 'Jonathan Ball: A Very Human Being', *Daily Maverick*, 7 Apr., www.dailymaverick.co.za/article/2021-04-07-jonathan-ball-a-very-human-being/ (accessed 22 June 2021).
Giliomee, H. (2003) *The Afrikaners: Biography of a People*. Cape Town: Tafelberg.
Giliomee, H. (2003) 'Rediscovering and Re-imagining the Afrikaners in a New South Africa: Autobiographical Notes on Writing an Uncommon Biography', *Itinerario* 27 (3–4).
Giliomee, H. (2009) '*True Confessions, End Papers* and the Dakar Conference: A Review of Political Arguments', *Tydskrif vir Letterkunde*, 46 (2).
Gobodo-Madikizela, P. (2003) *A Human Being Died That Night*. Cape Town: David Phillip.
Gobodo-Madikizela, P. (2010) 'Towards an Anatomy of Violence', *Mail & Guardian*, 15 Jan., https://mg.co.za/article/2010-01-15-towards-an-anatomy-of-violence (accessed 25 Aug. 2017).
Grundlingh, A. (2001) 'Herhistorisering en Herposisionering: Perspektiewe op Aspekte van Geskiedsbeoefening in Hedendaagse Suid-Afrika', *Historia* 46 (2).
Grundlingh, A. (2004) '"Rocking the Boat in South Africa?" Voëlvry Music and Afrikaans Anti-apartheid Social Protest in the 1980s', *International Journal of African Historical Studies*, 37 (3).
Grundlingh, A. (2008) '"Are We Afrikaners Getting Too Rich?" Cornucopia and Change in Afrikanerdom in the 1960s', *Journal of Historical Sociology*, 21 (2–3).
Grundlingh, A. (2021) *Slabbert: Man on a Mission*. Johannesburg: Jonathan Ball.
Grundlingh, A., and S. Huigen (eds) (2008) *Van Volksmoeder tot Fokofpolisiekar: Kritiese Opstelle oor Afrikaanse Herinneringsplekke*. Stellenbosch: Sun Press.
Grundlingh, A., and H. Sapire (1989) 'From Feverish Festival to Repetitive Ritual? The Changing Fortunes of Great Trek Mythology in an Industrialising South Africa, 1938–1988', *South African Historical Journal*, 21 (1).
Grundlingh, A., and S. Swart (2009) *Radelose Rebellie? Dinamika van die 1914–1915 Afrikanerrebellie*. Pretoria: Protea Boekhuis.
Hassim, S. (2018) 'Not Just Nelson's Wife: Winnie Madikizela-Mandela, Violence and Radicalism in South Africa', *Journal of Southern African Studies*, 44 (5).

Hassim, S. (2019) 'The Impossible Contract: The Political and Private Marriage of Nelson and Winnie Mandela', *Journal of Southern African Studies*, 45 (6).

Higgs, C. (1997) *The Ghost of Equality: The Public Lives of D.D.T. Jabavu of South Africa, 1885–1959*. Athens: Ohio University Press.

Hirsch, A. (2018) 'Winnie Mandela Was a Hero. If She'd Been White, There Would Be No Debate', *The Guardian* (London), 3 Apr., www.theguardian.com/commentisfree/2018/apr/03/winnie-mandela-hero-white-protest-apartheid (accessed 31 Mar. 2022).

Hofmeyr, I. (1986) 'Review: *The New African: A Study of the Life and Work of H. I. E. Dhlomo* by Tim Couzens, H. I. E. Dhlomo; *H. I. E. Dhlomo: Collected Works* by Tim Couzens, Nick Visser, H. I. E. Dhlomo', *English in Africa* 13 (1).

'How ANC Shielded Winnie' (2018) *City Press*, 7 Oct., www.news24.com/citypress/news/how-anc-shielded-winnie-20181007 (accessed 31 Mar. 2022).

Hughes, H. (2011) *The First President: A Life of John L. Dube, Founding President of the ANC*. Johannesburg: Jacana.

Hughes, H. (2012) 'Dialectical Dances: Exploring John Dube's Public Life', *South African Historical Journal*, 64 (3).

Hyslop, J. (2004) *The Notorious Syndicalist: J.T. Bain – A Scottish Rebel in Colonial South Africa*. Johannesburg: Jacana.

Jacobs, N., and A. Bank (2019) 'Biography in Post-apartheid South Africa: A Call for Awkwardness', *African Studies*, 78 (2).

Jacobs, S. (2018) 'How Do We Write about Winnie's Life Sympathetically?', *Mail & Guardian*, 13 Apr., https://mg.co.za/article/2018–04–12-how-do-we-write-about-winnies-life-sympathetically/ (accessed 31 Mar. 2022).

Jansen, A. (2015) *Eugene de Kock: Assassin for the State*. Cape Town: Tafelberg.

Kannemeyer, J. (2004) *Jan Rabie: Prosapionier en Politieke Wegwyser*. Cape Town: Tafelberg.

Kannemyer, J. (2008) *Leroux: 'n Lewe*. Pretoria: Protea Boekhuis.

Koorts, L. (2014) *DF Malan and the Rise of Afrikaner Nationalism*. Cape Town: Tafelberg.

Krog, A. (1999) *Country of My Skull*. London: Vintage.

Krog, A. (2015) 'Can an Evil Man Change? The Repentance of Eugene de Kock', *New York Times*, 13 Mar., www.nytimes.com/2015/03/14/opinion/sunday/the-repentance-of-eugene-de-kock-apartheid-assassin.html?mcubz=0 (accessed 25 Aug. 2017).

Kuzwayo, E. (2018) *Call Me Woman*. Johannesburg: Picador Africa.

Ladds, B. (2018) *The Madiba Appreciation Club: A Chef's Story*. Johannesburg: Jonathan Ball.

La Grange, Z. (2015) *Good Morning, Mr Mandela*. London: Penguin.

Levitt, J. (2018) 'Anger over New Winnie Mandela Book, Accusations of Fake Shout-Outs', *TimesLive*, 30 Oct., www.timeslive.co.za/news/south-africa/2018–10–30-anger-over-new-winnie-mandela-book-accusations-of-fake-shout-outs/ (accessed 31 Mar. 2022).

Levitt, J. (2018) 'I'm No Apartheid Apologist, Says Author of Controversial Winnie Mandela Book', *TimesLive*, 31 Oct., www.timeslive.co.za/news/south-africa/

2018-10-31-im-no-apartheid-apologist-says-author-of-controversial-winnie-mandela-book/ (accessed 31 Mar. 2022).
Lewin, H. (2011) *Stones against the Mirror: Friendship in the Time of the South African Struggle*. Cape Town: Umuzi.
Lodge, T. (2007) *Mandela: A Critical Life*. Oxford: Oxford University Press.
Louw, C. (2014), 'Boetman Is die Bliksem In', *News24*, 28 July, www.news24.com/news24/MyNews24/Boetman-is-die-bliksem-in-20140728 (accessed 31 Mar. 2022).
Mabasa, N. (2018) 'Youth Inspired Anew by an Icon They Barely Knew', *Daily Maverick*, 12 Apr., www.dailymaverick.co.za/article/2018-04-12-remembering-winnie-youth-inspired-anew-by-an-icon-they-barely-knew/ (accessed 31 Mar. 2022).
Madikizela-Mandela, W. (2013) *491 Days: Prisoner Number 1323/69*. Athens: Ohio University Press.
Mahlangu, I. (2018) 'Outcry over Cover of New Winnie Book', *SowetanLive*, 31 Oct., www.sowetanlive.co.za/news/south-africa/2018-10-31-outcry-over-cover-of-new-winnie-book/ (accessed 31 Mar. 2022).
Makhanya, M. (2014) 'Book Review – Insight into a Champion of Afrikaner Nationalism', *City Press*, 27 Apr., www.news24.com/Archives/City-Press/Book-review-Insight-into-a-champion-of-Afrikaner-nationalism-20150430 (accessed 23 June 2021).
Mandela, W. (1985) *Part of My Soul Went with Him*, adapted by Mary Benson. London: Penguin.
Mangcu, X. (2012) *Biko: A Biography*. Cape Town: Tafelberg.
Mashinini, E. (2012) *Strikes Have Followed Me All My Life: A South African Autobiography*. Johannesburg: Picador Africa.
Mavuso, S. (2021) 'Jacob Zuma Pleads Not Guilty to 18 Corruption Charges', *IOL*. 26 May, www.iol.co.za/news/politics/jacob-zuma-pleads-not-guilty-to-18-corruption-charges-e5d7fe94-9e4a-4883-ab7f-e6625ab48556 (accessed 22 June 2021).
Mbeki, T. (1998) 'Statement of Deputy President Thabo Mbeki at the Opening of the Debate in the National Assembly, on "Reconciliation and Nation Building", National Assembly Cape Town, 29 May 1998', Department of International Relations and Cooperation, www.dirco.gov.za/docs/speeches/1998/mbek0529.htm (accessed 31 Mar. 2022).
Meer, F. (2017) *Memories of Love and Struggle*. Cape Town: Kwela Books.
Mokoena, H. (n.d.) Homepage of the book *Magema Fuze*, University of Kwa-Zulu-Natal Press, www.uknpress.co.za/?class=bb_ukzn_sample_chapters&method=view_sample&global[fields][_id]=356 (accessed 31 Mar. 2022).
Mokoena, H. (2005) 'The Making of a *Kholwa* Intellectual: A Discursive Biography of Magema Magwaza Fuze'. DPhil thesis, University of Cape Town.
Mokoena, H. (2011) *Magema Fuze: The Making of a Kholwa Intellectual*. Pietermaritzburg: UKZN Press.
Morreira, S. (2021) 'Significant Archives Are under Threat in Cape Town's Fire. Why They Matter So Much', *The Conversation*, 19 Apr., https://theconversation.com/significant-archives-are-under-threat-in-cape-towns-fire-why-they-matter-so-much-159299 (accessed 21 June 2021).

Morrel, R. (ed.) (1992) *White but Poor: Essays on the History of Poor Whites in Southern Africa*. Pretoria: University of South Africa Press.

Morudu, P. (2013) 'Remember the Past and Question the Present', *Business Day*, 29 Oct., www.businesslive.co.za/bd/opinion/columnists/2013-10-29-remember-the-past-and-question-the-present/ (accessed 31 Mar. 2022).

Morudu, P. (2016) 'Eugene de Kock at the Franschoek Literary Festival: Of Screwed Courage and a Screwed Country', *Daily Maverick*, 16 May, www.dailymaverick.co.za/article/2016-05-16-eugene-de-kock-at-the-franschoek-literary-festival-of-screwed-courage-and-a-screwed-country/#.WabLkcgjHIU (accessed 31 Mar. 2022).

Mouton, A. (2002) *Voorloper: Die lewe van Schalk Pienaar*. Cape Town: Tafelberg.

Mouton, A. (2011) 'The Good, the Bad and the Ugly: Professional Historians and Political Biography of South African Parliamentary Politics, 1910–1990', *Journal for Contemporary History*, 36 (1).

Moya, F.N. (2006) '100% Zuluboy', *Mail & Guardian*, 6 Apr., https://mg.co.za/article/2006-04-06-100-zuluboy/ (accessed 31 Mar. 2022).

Msimang, S. (2017) *Always Another Country: A Memoir of Exile and Home*. Johannesburg: Jonathan Ball.

Msimang, S. (2018) *The Resurrection of Winnie Mandela*. Johannesburg: Jonathan Ball.

Myburgh, P. (2017) *The Republic of Gupta: A Story of State Capture*. Johannesburg: Penguin Random House.

Myburgh, P. (2019) *Gangster State: Unravelling Ace Magashule's Web of Capture*. Johannesburg: Penguin Random House.

Naki, E. (2019) 'Book Review: Truth, Lies and Alibis – A Winnie Mandela Story', *Citizen*, 14 Feb., www.citizen.co.za/entertainment/2083397/book-review-truth-lies-and-alibis-a-winnie-mandela-story/ (accessed 31 Mar. 2022).

Naudé, B. (1995) *My Land van Hoop: Die Lewe van Beyers Naudé*. Cape Town: Tafelberg.

Ngqulanga, B. (2017) *The Man Who Founded the ANC: A Biography of Pixley ka Isaka Seme*. Cape Town: Penguin.

Nicholson, G. (2019) 'Court Lashes Jacob Zuma's Language and Finds No Merits in His Appeal Argument', *Daily Maverick*, 29 Nov., www.dailymaverick.co.za/article/2019-11-29-court-lashes-jacob-zumas-language-and-finds-no-merits-in-his-appeal-argument/ (accessed 31 Mar. 2022).

'Not Welcome: Thabiso Mahlape and Lauren Beukes on Eugene de Kock's Presence at the Sunday Times Literary Awards Shortlist Event' (2016) *Books Live*, 15 May, http://bookslive.co.za/blog/2016/05/15/not-welcome-thabiso-mahlape-and-lauren-beukes-on-eugene-de-kocks-presence-at-the-sunday-times-literary-awards-shortlist-event/ (accessed 31 Mar. 2022).

Olivier, A. (2019) 'Om die Internasionale Taal van Boeke te Praat', *Netwerk24*, 25 Nov., www.netwerk24.com/netwerk24/Stemme/Menings/om-die-internasionale-taal-van-boeke-te-praat-20191122 (accessed 31 Mar. 2022).

Olver, C. (2017) *How to Steal a City: The Battle for Nelson Mandela Bay*. Johannesburg: Jonathan Ball.

O'Malley, P. (2007) *Shades of Difference: Mac Maharaj and the Struggle for South Africa*. New York: Viking.

Pather, R. (2016) 'Four Women, the President and the Protest That Shook the Results Ceremony', *Mail & Guardian*, 6 Aug., https://mg.co.za/article/2016-08-06-four-women-the-president-and-the-protest-that-shoock-the-election-results-ceremony/ (accessed 31 Mar. 2022).

Pather, R. (2018) 'Even in Death, Mam' Winnie Can't Catch a Break', *Mail & Guardian*, 3 Apr., https://mg.co.za/article/2018-04-03-in-death-mam-winnie-has-rallied-her-mourners/ (accessed 31 Mar. 2022).

Pauw, J. (2017) *The President's Keepers: Those Keeping Zuma in Power and out of Prison*. Cape Town: Tafelberg.

The Presidency, Republic of South Africa (n.d.) 'The Order of Ikhamanga', www.thepresidency.gov.za/national-orders/order-ikhamanga-0#:~:text=The%20Order%20of%20Ikhamanga%20is,Order%20is%20awarded%20in%20gold (accessed 16 Apr. 2022).

'SA Is Baie Vreemd vir De Kock, Sê Skrywer' (2015) *Netwerk24*, 30 Aug., www.netwerk24.com/Nuus/Misdaad/SA-is-baie-vreemd-vir-De-Kock-se-skrywer-20150830 (accessed 31 Mar. 2022).

Sampson, A. (1999) *Mandela: The Authorised Biography*. New York: Harper Collins.

Scholtz, H. (2015) 'Eugene se Stem het Haar Bekoor', *Netwerk24*, 22 Mar., www.netwerk24.com/Nuus/Misdaad/Eugene-se-stem-het-haar-bekoor-20150322# (accessed 31 Mar. 2022).

Segal, D. (2018) 'How Bell Pottinger, P.R. Firm for Despots and Rogues, Met Its End in South Africa', *New York Times*, 4 Feb., www.nytimes.com/2018/02/04/business/bell-pottinger-guptas-zuma-south-africa.html (accessed 31 Mar. 2022).

Sisulu, E. (2002) *Walter & Albertina Sisulu: In Our Lifetime*. Claremont: David Phillip.

Smith, K. (1988) *The Changing Past: Trends in South African Historical Writing*. Johannesburg: Southern Book Publishers.

Steyn, J. (1998) *Van Wyk Louw: 'n Lewensverhaal*. Cape Town: Tafelberg.

Steyn, J. (2002) *Penvegter: Piet Cillié van 'Die Burger'*. Cape Town: Tafelberg.

Steyn, J. (2004) *Die 100 Jaar van MER*. Cape Town: Tafelberg.

Styan, J.B., and P. Vecchiatto (2019) *The Bosasa Billions: How the ANC Sold Its Soul for Braaipacks, Booze and Bags of Cash*. Pretoria: Lapa.

Thamm, M. (2015) 'One Woman's Extraordinary Journey: Je Suis Eugene de Kock', *Daily Maverick*, 4 May, www.dailymaverick.co.za/article/2015-05-04-one-womans-extraordinary-journey-je-suis-eugene-de-kock/#.Waaq68gjHIU (accessed 30 Aug. 2017).

Thamm, M. (2019) '#RememberKhwezi: Zuma's Rape Accuser Dies, Never Having Known Freedom', *Daily Maverick*, 9 Oct., www.dailymaverick.co.za/article/2016-10-09-rememberkhwezi-zumas-rape-accuser-dies-never-having-known-freedom/ (accessed 31 Mar. 2022).

Thlabi, R. (2013) *Endings and Beginnings: A Story of Healing*. Johannesburg: Jacana.

Thlabi, R. (2017) *Khwezi: The Remarkable Story of Fezekile Ntsukela Kuzwayo*. Johannesburg: Jonathan Ball.

Thom, H.B. (1980) *D.F. Malan*. Cape Town: Tafelberg.

Trewhela, P. (2018) 'Winnie Mandela – An Issue for Christians?', *Daily Maverick*, 18 Oct., www.dailymaverick.co.za/opinionista/2018–10–18-winnie-mandela-an-issue-for-christians/ (accessed 31 Mar. 2022).

Van der Leun, J. (2015) 'The Odd Couple: Why an Apartheid Activist Joined Forces with a Murderer', *The Guardian* (London), 6 June, www.theguardian.com/global/2015/jun/06/odd-couple-apartheid-activist-madeleine-fullard-convicted-policeman-eugene-de-kock (accessed 25 Aug. 2017).

Van der Merwe, C. (2015) *Donker Stroom: Eugène Marais en die Anglo-Boereoorlog*. Cape Town: Tafelberg.

Van der Merwe, C. (2019) *Kansvatter: Die Rustelose Lewe van Ben Viljoen*. Pretoria: Protea Boekhuis.

Van Loggerenberg, J., and A. Lackay (2016) *Rogue: The Inside Story of SARS's Crime-Busting Unit*. Johannesburg: Jonathan Ball.

Van Onselen, C. (1997) *The Seed Is Mine: The Life of Kas Maine, a South African Sharecropper, 1894–1985*. New York: Hill and Wang.

Van Onselen, C. (2007) *The Fox and the Flies: The World of Joseph Silver, Racketeer and Psychopath*. London: Jonathan Cape.

Van Onselen, C. (2015) *Showdown at the Red Lion: The Life and Times of Jack McLoughlin, 1859–1910*. Johannesburg: Jonathan Ball.

Van Onselen, C. (2017) *The Cowboy Capitalist: John Hays Hammond, the American West and the Jameson Raid*. Johannesburg: Jonathan Ball.

Van Zyl-Hermann, D. (2015) 'History Made Human: Confronting the Unpalatable Past through Biographical Writing in Post-apartheid South Africa', *African Historical Review*, 47 (2).

Vincent, L. (1999) 'The Power behind the Scenes: The Afrikaner Nationalist Women's Parties, 1915 to 1931', *South African Historical Journal*, 40.

Wa Azania, M. (2014) *Memoirs of a Born Free: Reflections on the Rainbow Nation*. Johannesburg: Jacana.

Walzer, M. (2002) *The Company of Critics: Social Criticism and Political Commitment in the Twentieth Century*. New York: Basic Books.

Warwick, R. (2021) 'Triomf, vrees op 31 Mei', *Netwerk24*, 29 May, www.netwerk24.com/Stemme/Aktueel/triomf-vrees-op-31-mei-20210528 (accessed 31 Mar. 2022).

Wieder, A. (2013) *Ruth First and Joe Slovo in the War against Apartheid*. New York: Monthly Review Press.

Willan, B. (2018) *Sol Plaatje: A Life of Solomon Tshekisho Plaatje, 1876–1932*. Johannesburg: Jacana.

8

Whiteness must fall: whiteness, whites and insurgent history writing

Neil Roos

The problem of the twentieth century would be that of the colour line, W.E.B. Du Bois famously predicted in the early 1900s. His prediction proved correct, for notwithstanding more than a century of global politics grounded in anticolonialism, antiracism and human rights, the colour line was never erased. Questions associated with whiteness, its resilience, the privilege it sustains and the violence which regularly accompanies it – physical and epistemic – have resurfaced in many parts of the world in the twenty-first century as potent political, ethical and social issues.

In France, the questions have welled up in the continuing marginalisation and exclusion of black citizens from the mainstream of the republic's public life, and the official alarm that the resulting seething discontent might offer a reservoir for jihadist Islamic movements to draw recruits. In the USA the questions are manifest by outrage in Ferguson, Baltimore, New York, Minneapolis and elsewhere at police brutality, all too often lethal, against black men. And of course, the emergence of the Alt-Right, the political mobilisation of lower-middle-class whites and the rise of Trump. In South Africa they are vividly seen in mass student-led protests around the stifling symbols of continuing white supremacy and the barrenness of postapartheid economic and social transformation. Also, in widespread denialism among whites of any association with apartheid's injustices, with this being accompanied, among younger ones – the 'born frees' – by a general reluctance to countenance any suggestion that they too are beneficiaries of class, social and racial relations established under apartheid and earlier.

Despite whiteness encroaching upon global society in so many diverse yet similar ways, the very idea of whiteness as a legitimate field of study is often met with suspicion, cynicism or downright outrage within the academy. In African studies circles and, closer to home, the more progressive reaches of South African history writing, the presumption that studies of whites represent an injudicious avenue of enquiry is not new. To Frederick Cooper's generation of Africanists, educated in American universities during the late

1960s and steeped in the 'Ibadan school', precolonial history or resistance to colonialism constituted genuine African history, while a focus on the colonial state or society suggested a 'throwback to imperial history'.[1] Terence Ranger made a similar point in 1978, expressing uneasiness that studies of whites might mark a return to 'historiographic colonialism'.[2]

In South Africa, history writing has carried heavy political freight, and for much of the twentieth century it served the interests of white supremacy. Not surprisingly, it concentrated on white male elites, whether liberals, Afrikaner nationalists or 'South Africanists' like Jan Smuts. By the 1970s, a highly articulate and influential minority of historians, who associated themselves politically and intellectually with the struggle against apartheid, had begun to emerge. Yet with some notable exceptions, discussed below, they demonstrated the same sense of tepidity and disquiet towards histories of white people as Cooper and Ranger. While they undertook fine-grained enquiry into the lives and experiences of black South Africans, there was no equivalent attention to whites.

Fast-forward nearly half a century later, and the winds of decolonial change blast through South African universities. The movement represents a loose alignment of diverse, sometimes intersecting currents, but most activist-intellectuals who supported demands for decolonising research, teaching and the very structures of knowledge production at South African universities would agree that central to the project is the overthrow of those intellectual traditions which privilege Western (white) knowledge and place Europeans at the centre of inquiry. These positions straddle various poles of historiography and politics, but they share an emphasis that whites cannot and should not be privileged in tellings of the past. According to this argument, focusing on whites reaffirms the kinds of knowledge, the kinds of history, that were so important for sustaining colonialism, imperialism and apartheid.

Thus, on the one hand, ideologies, policies, language, groups and individuals acting – implicitly or explicitly – in the interests of whiteness continue to pose dangers to freedom, to life, to the possibility of the kind of deep and comprehensive decolonisation envisaged by Fanon and others.[3] But on the other hand, fragments that are far apart not only in time but in the sort of institutional milieu from which they emerge, all indicate that among those opposed to colonialism, apartheid and their present-day legacies, there is little appetite to write histories of whites. In fact, sentiments that studies of whites represent something of a bogus field are widespread.

In this chapter, I attempt to take on these contradictions and address them from within South African historiography: can we write histories of white people that are narratives against whiteness – antiracist histories, so to speak? Histories that take whites as their subject, yet contribute to a decolonial turn? Much of my writing as a professional historian has focused on precisely these unfashionable questions. Initially, I wrote about whites who opposed segregation and apartheid, including communists, members of the Springbok Legion and the Congress of Democrats. Realising that these men and women, along with the kinds of resistance they undertook, were something of an anomaly in apartheid society, I then became more interested in the majority of whites, who not only accepted but were deeply invested in sustaining the racialised class structure of mid-twentieth-century South Africa. Although never in its inner circles, I have identified with the Marxist-oriented South African social history movement for more than three decades and, with many social historians, globally and in South Africa, I share a sense of sadness at its declining influence since the 1990s. Its authority within the broader discipline was eroded as new approaches, most notably the so-called 'cultural turn', gained currency.[4] These new approaches collectively emphasised the analytic dead-ends which a historiography shaped by certain kinds of Marxism supposedly ran into. Critiques developed by a new vanguard steeped in postcolonial theory and, often, the methodologies of literary criticism meanwhile also side-lined the political and pedagogic work that was so central to the project of social history – a point to which I shall return. But, most critically, a version of social history moored in a particular conceptual scaffolding was not able to predict, mobilise or build coalitions around the kinds of political battles that emerged in the new millennium. As I survey how whites have featured in some contemporary South African historiographies, I ponder whether and how these histories might be brought into closer conversation with some of the political questions of the day – antiracism and decolonisation above all. I hope also to comment on some of the ways in which social histories of race may be written in ways that transcend national boundaries. In undertaking these explorations, I hope also to grapple with some of the directions of South African social history at a time when its legacies seem consigned more to the realm of nostalgia than that of analysis, pedagogy and action.

This essay consists of three parts: it begins with the emergence of the South African social history movement in the 1980s, a period of accelerating mass struggle against apartheid. In that first section, I describe the political and intellectual contexts out of which Marxist South African social history emerged. I discuss the focus of this historiography, the topics that predominated, and how whites featured. In the next section, I address the decline that Marxist-inspired history encountered globally from the 1990s. Recognising some of the post-structuralist successors to Marxism that claimed to address elements of historical process, social organisation and change (or, for that matter, the absence of change), I concentrate on the culturally oriented 'whiteness studies' that emerged in South Africa during the first decade of the new millennium. In the third section, I propose a new social history of race – in this case, of whites. I suggest that such a history, conceived carefully in a spirt of historiographic eclecticism, and with due consideration to ongoing developments in the discipline and in the wider society, may help not only to revitalise South African social history but also to connect it to wider worlds of activism and even insurgency.

Possibility

In the early 1970s a wave of historians inspired by Marxist theory began to expand their influence within the South African academy. Influenced by major currents within Western European Marxism, especially the writing of Louis Althusser and Nicos Poulantzas, their approach was highly structural and concentrated on accounting for the alliances or 'fractions' of capital which dominated the South African state at particular stages of its historical development. By the 1980s, structuralist approaches had lost ground to Marxist-inclined social history inspired by British and North American Marxists like E.P. Thompson, Eric Hobsbawm and Eugene Genovese, which was in turn underpinned by the theoretical and political work of Antonio Gramsci. The South African social historians were clustered around the History Workshop at the University of the Witwatersrand, and they sought to excavate the 'hidden histories' of ordinary people and communities traditionally excluded from mainstream historical narratives of the South African past. Many of the social historians were committed to the overthrow of apartheid, and in the popular struggles of the 1980s, they championed history as a mobilising tool. Accordingly, the social historians tended to write histories of black urban life and the making of the black working class. Their allegiance to a self-consciously insurgent historiography, which could conscientise and energise people in the struggle against apartheid, meant that they tended to disregard the histories of whites, who seemed irreclaimable.

Although not the first to do so, the social historians presented a model of historical scholarship that, by uncovering hidden episodes of people's agency and ability to organise and resist in the face of daunting odds, rested on a strong activist and pedagogic foundation. This is a significant consideration that any new historiography of the social must reckon with, and build on. Unlike earlier historians who considered racism, segregation and apartheid to be a matter of backward prejudice, this collective connected modern state-sanctioned racism in South Africa to the development of capitalism. However, much like the British Marxist social historians of the day, they demonstrated some irritation towards High Theory.[5] This disposition contributed to the empirical richness of their work, but it ultimately made their approaches and the categories they employed ('community' being a favoured one) quite inflexible and also rendered them vulnerable to the theoretical critiques and changing political circumstances that emerged in the 1990s.

Some scholarship within this tradition explored the complexity of white society, including Charles van Onselen's essays on the struggles of the white poor against mine owners and Johannesburg planning authorities, and Tim Clynick's doctoral thesis on relations between diamond prospectors and *meneeren*, rural notables, in the western Transvaal. From outside the History Workshop group, Albert Grundlingh wrote on the social history of '*hendsoppers*' and 'joiners' among the republican armies during the Anglo-Boer/ South African War, on poor white woodcutters and later on rugby, and no discussion of the social history of whites would be complete without acknowledging the contributions made by the volume on poor whites edited by Robert Morrell.[6]

In his book on the 1922 Rand Revolt, Jeremy Krikler directed attention to silences and the unsaid, two themes that would assume greater historiographic significance from the 1990s onwards.[7] Striking mineworkers, he pointed out, did not have to raise the question of the imperial connection in their demands. Although of great significance to white workers' conditions and the political dispensation they sought, protagonists on both sides of that deadly conflict knew how this matter had been resolved elsewhere and they understood how linkages with Britain would feature after the strike. By the 1990s, some historians had begun to problematise whiteness, or the idea of generalised racial supremacy. These historians were influenced by David Roediger's seminal *The Wages of Whiteness: Race and the Making of the American Working Class*, published in 1991.[8] Deborah Posel also wrote about the histories of white civil servants, concentrating on the Public Servants' Association.[9] I worked on the social histories of white war veterans, focusing on the identities they took on after the war and how they negotiated their way through the early years of apartheid society. They were indeed white men, but in a relationship of mutual suspicion with the National Party regime in the late 1940s and early 1950s.[10] Quite rare among South African social historians was Jonathan Hyslop's adoption of an international perspective that linked class formation and the presumption of white privilege to the development of a self-consciously white imperial working class.[11]

These historians all addressed Roediger's observation that being white represented a significant social and psychological wage. While few would contest the assertion that white racial privilege constituted a 'wage', it was not in the South African case the salient feature that distinguished white workers from black workers. In South Africa, histories of racialised class struggle gave white workers a colour bar and a very real monied wage and class advantage over black workers. This difference represents a warning against 'traveling theory' and applying hypotheses developed elsewhere too easily in the South African case.

Dismay

In 2001, the History Workshop organised a conference on 'Whiteness and Blackness in Modern South Africa'. There were neither many papers presented nor any big conceptual or historiographic advances in those that were, yet the conference nonetheless marked the emergence of whiteness studies – in this instance, popular race making among whites – as a field of engagement among some historians in South Africa. It was, however, a field that never really took off. Firstly, it was adrift from any clear political project. And secondly, these studies fell within the theoretical and methodological ambit of social history, which was itself on the back foot globally as well as locally. The local variant seemed particularly unable to muster the theoretical and historiographic arsenal necessary to defend and renew itself in the face of multiple challenges to Marxist-inclined history writing.

South Africa's cultural turn, including 'whiteness studies', thus proved controversial from the outset. Alistair Bonnett points out that globally, there were two strands in the latter field: one concentrating on whiteness as a factor in historical process, and one more interested in how whiteness shapes 'lived experience'.[12] If earlier studies of whiteness in South Africa (those undertaken by Posel, Hyslop and myself, for instance) were aligned with the historical strand, then those that emerged from around the millennium were more concerned with the latter category of the sociology of contemporary society and the language and aesthetics of identity.

In 2013, the University of Johannesburg's Visual Identities in Art and Design Research Centre hosted a conference called Whitewash, which was the first South African event catering specifically for scholars with an interest in whiteness. Most participants were themselves white, and Melissa Steyn, undoubtedly the doyenne of the strand of South African scholarship most interested in the sociologies of whiteness and white identity, was a keynote speaker.[13] She reminded her audience of the core premises of whiteness studies – namely, that whiteness is primarily about power, and is remarkably resilient, largely because of its capacity to simultaneously 'transform' while remaining 'invisible'. One cannot, of course, dispute this. But what power? How does it work? What accounts for its resilience? Are there different racisms? And above all, what exactly is 'whiteness'? The statement of the fairly obvious, along with an absence of engagement with issues of historical context, social relations or capital, was emblematic of this iteration of whiteness studies. Inevitably, one must ask what it adds to our specific understanding of race, whiteness and racism, in specific circumstances.

Whitewash represented the high tide of sociological and sociolinguistically inclined whiteness studies in South Africa. Their dominant reference point seemed to be identity politics, and the tendency was towards insularity. The journalist Ferial Haffajee was another keynote speaker, and she used her address to express irritation and impatience with the orientation of whiteness studies as stated by the majority of presenters. She railed against the esoteric nature of most of the presentations and how they went about 'navel-gazing on minor issues ... Why not just share your swimming pool, sponsor a kid's school fees or give half your wealth away as businessman Patrice Motsepe did? This is a better salve than self-obsession.'[14]

For me – a social historian whose interest in whites was closer to the historical strand identified by Bonnett – Haffajee's taunt about the self-obsession, the dullness and, ultimately, the banality of whiteness studies hit home. It brought into stark relief the fog of self-indulgence which permeated dominant South African approaches to the subject. It forced me to reflect on how historians, and especially social historians, were almost completely marginalised. They were left unable (or unwilling) to intervene in debates about whiteness, to point to the analytic and political problems that come from thinking about whiteness outside of history, or to anchor discussions of whites to larger discussions about race. My dismay at how I understood the developments in South African whiteness studies was deepened by a more generalised drift away from an intellectual culture that not only had politics at its very heart but was also deeply pedagogical. Speaking in a different context, but voicing sentiments highly relevant for how studies of whites and whiteness shifted from history to cultural studies, Ileana Rodriguez, a member of the Latin American Subaltern Studies Group, noted that these approaches privileged a sort of theoretical calisthenics that put their adherents at an advantage in the northern academy. This, at the expense of scholarship that would perform the interconnected political and pedagogic tasks of exposing and teaching against oppression.[15]

Challenge

The politics of the times have shaped how whites have featured in South African historiography. Could the political moods of the second decade of the twenty-first century prompt us to think differently about histories of whites, and specifically to consider delivering histories that might have whites as their subject but which concentrate on larger questions about race, and are connected to contemporary, radical political projects, or that might re-energise the subfield by encouraging social historians to think carefully about the theoretical, historiographic and methodological underpinnings of their craft, and its insurgent and pedagogical possibilities?

Since about 2016, one of the strongest currents in local intellectual and activist circles, ranging from the university-based #FeesMustFall protesters to social movements like *Abahlali*, has been the demand for a Fanonian type of decolonisation. University-based advocates of decolonisation are particularly concerned about the kind of knowledge generated in tertiary institutions. They are scathing in what they see as the uncritical transmission of 'Western' knowledge with its accompanying hierarchies, categories and assumptions. They are also united in their cynicism and outrage at how, in postapartheid society, race flourishes. Racial exclusion thrives in the academy and in society more generally, and access to resources still coincides closely with the apartheid race divide. Certain types of knowledge are privileged, and some voices are taken more seriously than others.

While the decolonisation movement is rich, eclectic and anything but ideologically absolutist, its adherents generally agree that until racial hierarchies and whiteness are dismantled, postapartheid society will remain a bitter well of disappointment, despite the formal abolition of racial discrimination. They are also sensitive to how white supremacy transforms itself, and a common demand is to unmask and then demolish whiteness as an invented idea of racial supremacy.[16] In parts of the decolonial movement there is a deeply humanist strand. Noting that colonialism, segregation and apartheid dehumanised both whites and blacks, they ask how we may write histories which challenge the binaries of race that have organised modern South African society, the ways its history is told, and how this hollows out the humanity of all those subject to its classifications. Some – to be sure a minority – recognise that white people were robbed of something owing to their position and participation in a racist society. This represents a genealogy stretching back to Du Bois, who famously commented on the cost of whiteness to white workers:

> It was bad enough to have the consequences of [racist] thought fall upon colored people the world over, but in the end it was even worse when one considers what this attitude did to the [white] worker. His aim and ideal was distorted ... He began to want, not comfort for all men, but power over other men ... He did not love humanity and he hated n***rs.[17]

This was picked up in South Africa during the 1970s by Steve Biko and Richard Turner, who both pointed out the important conscientising work that needed to be done among whites to bring them to 'love humanity'.[18]

This brings us to an important historical and political crossroads. It is an exciting moment and poses a challenge to historians of whites who align themselves with the broad intellectual and political goals of the decolonisation movement. In particular, the concerns of the decolonial movement invite them to show how racial categories like whiteness emerge and how race operates. In so doing it will help them face an 'elephant in the room' identified by anthropologist Francis Nyamnjoh in his critique of postapartheid South African anthropology.[19] He points out that since white anthropologists seldom do fieldwork 'at home' among people much like themselves, whites in South Africa are all too often left 'beyond ethnographic contemplation'. Unambiguously taking on the history of these subjects – respectable middle-class ones (and not only the criminal, the deviant, the semi-indigent and other whites on the margins of society) – will help to address the blind spot identified by Nyamnjoh.

That being said, a history of white people cast in this mould is not meant to be a feel-good, add-a-human-face-to-apartheid project. It must be an uncompromisingly antiracist history, one that derives its *raison d'etre* from its insurgent capacity to challenge the very idea of stable racial categories, of race as something natural, something overdetermined in the past and already determined in the present and future. In short, something very different from the wave of whiteness studies on show at Whitewash.

And these studies should be grounded in Marxism. In South Africa, race is central to class formation and class exploitation. Once we lose the capacity offered by class analysis to develop an immanent critique of how race operates across a range of settings shaped by contemporary capitalism, we succumb to self-absorption and ultimately political conservativism of the kind demonstrated by South African iterations of whiteness identity studies. Marxism is, of course, a hydra-headed framework of analysis. Even among Marxist historians of South Africa, for instance, there were vast differences in approach – for example, between followers of Althusser and Poulantzas on the one hand, and Gramsci on the other. One of the more recent public controversies among stalwarts of left-wing social history has been the debate between the historians of India Vivek Chibber and Partha Chatterjee concerning 'Marxism and the legacy of Subaltern Studies'.[20]

While esoteric, this debate points to the kind of Marxism that could most fruitfully be deployed in the service of a social history of race in South Africa – and elsewhere too, perhaps. Chatterjee and a number of historians associated with the Subaltern Studies Group refused to be bound by the primacy of class as a category for social analysis.[21] They argued that society was simultaneously constituted around other fault lines, and according to other categories. In Indian historiography, caste was an obvious one, as was gender. Chibber attacked Chatterjee for breaking the left into 'isolated cabals', as he and others replaced class, that traditional tool of Marxist analysis, with all manner of other categories.

Faced with this choice of theoretical tools for a social history of race, I would opt for those used by Chatterjee. The move by him and others away from the universalism – or at least the centrality – of class, by acknowledging 'actually existing' categories, does not necessarily erode the foundations of class analysis. With respect to writing social histories of white people, this position invites one to think ethnographically and empirically about relations of domination and subordination, much in the style of E.P. Thompson.[22] It prompts us to mark and observe smaller, lower level units of analysis beyond class: the dissident, the drunkard, the family man, the asylum inmate, the public servant, the anonymous individual in a crowd. All of these individuals might (or might not) be members of a working class, broadly defined, but they are bound into apartheid by other relations. And this is where we may find shards of humanity, contrariness or alternate racial identities, all central to any radical history.

Following Geoff Eley, no history writing can change the world, but a radical historiography committed to social change should at least probe misleadingly familiar ideas and assumptions, clarify the present and provide foundations for the future: 'Depending on how the story is told the past provides potential sites for opposition. It allows us to say, "it didn't have to happen like this. And in future it could be different."'[23] And these are directions of enquiry that may contribute to a broad agenda of decolonisation by their capacity to expose the historically contingent, ambiguous, morally bankrupt and occasionally contested nature of racial categories and racial belonging.

In light of these entry points, what topics, what angles of investigation would feature in a new social history of race that takes whites as its focus? As the sociologist Deborah Posel points out, histories of below can no longer be considered simply as histories from below.[24] Put differently, social worlds are made both top-down and bottom-up. And given the apartheid state's centrality in shaping the lives of blacks and whites, its history is a logical starting point.

It could begin by asking how elites, including the National Party (NP), state bureaucrats and Afrikaner nationalist intellectuals, along with a few non-Afrikaner fellow travellers, sought to 'make' whites racialised citizens within an evolving set of class relations. It could consider how the legislative and administrative apparatus of the apartheid state shaped, organised and controlled the lives of white people. Such questions have been widely posed of the black experience, but are generally absent in the historiography of white South Africans. Among the apartheid government's earliest pieces of legislation after the NP assumed power in 1948 were laws to reestablish work colonies for white men, and prohibit them from having sexual or marital relations with people of other races. The fact that in its first months in office, the NP – despite holding only a fragile parliamentary majority – concentrated its legislative energies as much, if not more, on whites than blacks, makes this question significant.[25]

In addition to ideology, legislation and methods of governance, science and the role of intellectuals should feature prominently in questions on how apartheid elites sought to constitute whiteness – meaning, in this case, white racial identities. This could extend to how ideology was 'made real' for ordinary whites. This stratum of 'ordinary' whites was made up of people from the working class, whites who broke their way into the 'middle class', the destitute and those separated from the mainstream of '*ordentlike*' (respectable) white society. It encompassed Afrikaans speakers, who formed a substantial component of the NP's constituency, as well as English speakers (including immigrants, who were sometimes nominal English speakers).

In the early years of apartheid, social science became increasingly influential in Afrikaner nationalist thinking and apartheid public policy. Anthropology (*volkekunde*) assumed a significant role in shaping state policy towards blacks. Sociology played a similar role with respect to whites. Intellectuals from Afrikaans-speaking universities, like the University of Pretoria sociologist and technocrat Geoffrey Cronje, exercised considerable influence within the state as members of boards, ministerial advisors and appointees to senior public service jobs. Their published work has received attention from Saul Dubow and Aletta Norval.[26] If, however, we hope to examine how the ideas developed by Cronje and others impacted on the everyday life of whites, we need to venture beyond the parameters of conventional intellectual history. We need to explore how they in fact penetrated the taken-for-granted wisdoms and routines of ordinary white daily life.

A tale from the archive illustrates the point. Based simultaneously on a concern that idle, degenerate, lazy white men posed a threat to white society and that these men could be 'reformed', Cronje was able to parlay his prestige as a 'Hollander' – one of those men who had studied in the Netherlands and who had gravitated to the very heart of Afrikaner intellectual culture – to drive the development of apartheid-era work colonies. These labour camps in remote places were designed to punish and rehabilitate drunkards, homosexuals, those involved in mixed-race unions and those who in the opinion of social workers failed to care properly for their families. These unfortunates were detained in work colonies for three years – significantly, not by judicial conviction but by the order of a social worker. On admission, and again before release, detainees were given a threefold exam, with medical, psychological and sociological components. Cronje designed the sociological section, which included questions about topics as cryptic as church attendance and masturbation. By the early 1960s, white women considered to be excessive drinkers were being interned in 'alcohol retreats', which had an ambience more medical than penal – the women were described as 'patients' rather than detainees. Once again, Cronje was the major driving force in the establishment of these institutions.

Questions of this order, from the top down, can and should be included in a history of whites that responds to the challenges posed by the decolonial agenda. These historiographic vectors all tell us how particular styles of being white were made and transgressors were monitored, punished or 'rehabilitated'. Concerns such as these, around ideology and representation, surveillance and the ambition to reform, began to feature prominently in global historiographies through the first two decades of the present millennium. It is, however, problematic both historiographically and politically to ask only these kinds of questions.

The social historian of India Sumit Sarkar wrote that heavy concentration on how subaltern (or 'ordinary') people are represented raises the intellectually and politically debilitating prospect of 'reifying' the subaltern.[27] This 'reified subaltern' trudges through history wearing a constricting cloak of hagiography, unable to express agency, energy, contrariness or will. In approaching histories of whites, the sort of top-down approach that Sarkar warned of reifies not only the subaltern but also the notion of an essentialised whiteness. Moreover, failure to centrally address questions of agency leaves the way open for ultimately cynical and bad faith assertions of ignorance about the crimes of apartheid, of claims that 'I didn't know.'

Social historians of South Africa have, of course, explored questions of consciousness and agency for years, with the aim of highlighting the resilience of black people in resisting segregation and apartheid. But resistance, long a major trope of Marxist-inspired social history in this country and elsewhere, is not appropriate for studying white everyday life, culture and society under apartheid. For that demographic, accommodation, complicity, collusion and co-optation are more fitting themes.

A social history of race featuring white people should show how particular versions of whiteness emerged, and the role of ordinary people in shaping these trajectories. It should also show the historical grounds for accommodation, and instances of transgression. It could pose questions about the material, ideological and cultural grounds for accommodation, taking care to identify gender, ethnic or class differences, and how these were deployed in particular times. Certainly, the expansion of the apartheid public service, which by the late 1950s employed around 30 per cent of all working whites (making it the largest single employer of whites in South Africa), represented a very real *quid pro quo* for accommodation.[28] It might also ask how, and if so to what extent, whites transgressed the always-evolving codes of whiteness? Remembering crucially that such transgression seldom represented resistance to white supremacy itself.

Instances of transgression and indocility are hard to find, and do not feature much in the secondary historical or anthropological literature. A wonderful exception is Katie Mooney's study of ducktails in the 1950s.[29] And the men detailed in the work colonies represent another example.[30] These men defied the discipline that came with committal to the work colony: they ran away, they smoked *dagga* (cannabis) and, according to one work colony superintendent, 'carried on with native women'. I have, however, found no instances of any of them repudiating the privileges of whiteness. And we find evidence of whites (public servants at that) seeking alternate cosmologies – not Protestant, not Calvinistic and not even Christian. These bureaucrats were instead seeking Eastern insight and healing from a character from Langlaagte, Johannesburg, known as *Die Wit Yogi* (the white yogi). Even at the moment when the spiritual primacy of the Church was challenged, however, *Die Wit Yogi* and his public service clients retained their fidelity to apartheid respectability: he was not just any yogi, but a white one!

Apartheid was violent; violence was coded into its very DNA.[31] But beyond the fairly well-documented instances of state brutality, there were also occasions of popular violence, instigated by ordinary white people. These latter iterations are important for a social history of race, as they shine a light from the bottom up on the nature of the state. In particular, they raise questions about how ordinary white people, undertaking acts of racist violence, upset the matrix of class relations and the form of racial domination that underlay apartheid statecraft. They also remind us that apartheid society may have included many different, perhaps competing, variants of racism and white supremacy.

Another example, again from the state archive, illustrates this point. In 1957, one G.O. Opperman, a white man who worked as a clerk in the Department of Labour, was riding his bicycle in the corridor of an office 'when his progress was impeded by a native who was walking through the doorway'. It appeared that this obstruction annoyed Opperman, who 'thereupon assaulted the native'. Opperman found himself dishonourably discharged from the public service, charged by the police and sentenced to three months imprisonment. Of the African, nothing is heard, not even a name. Despite the localised, if brutal, scale of this conflict, it generated volumes of correspondence, reminding us that racial violence under apartheid had diverse starting points in white society and understanding them is of some use in comprehending how a category as menacing as whiteness functioned historically.[32] And it suggests that the kind of violence displayed by Opperman upset the 'order' imagined under apartheid, where violence was bureaucratic and the prerogative of the state, even as it was often murderous.

The American historian Nell Irvin Painter points out that in the American South, most historians followed (and continue to follow) segregation's decree and write about the South as though people of different races occupied entirely different spheres. She writes that, first of all, white historians 'made up a lily-white southern history' that included few blacks except those who loved serving whites. After the civil rights movement, black historians and their allies sought to address this imbalance by publishing the history of blacks as though whites existed only as 'faceless oppressors'.[33] Similarly, in South African historiography there is very little scholarship on Painter's 'histories across the color line' – or, more particularly, histories of collaboration, cooperation, friendship and alliance across lines of colour. Notably, there have been few attempts to search for and understand these kinds of relationships in the realm of the everyday.[34] Yet these histories are important and valuable to the extent that they sometimes reveal acts of defiance against the prevailing cultural, ideological and legal codes. They also touch on questions raised not only by advocates of decolonisation but also, lest we forget, by the likes of Du Bois and Biko, of how a racist society dehumanised not only blacks but also whites.

My mother Sheila may be used to illustrate the point. I grew up during the late 1960s and early 1970s in a working-class Durban neighbourhood, close to the racial borders defined by the 1950 Group Areas Act. My mother had a great interest: horse racing. For her it wasn't about the glamour of the track, but rather figuring out small wages to place with the bookie or the off-course totalisator. Horse races took place on Wednesdays and Saturdays, so she would spend Tuesday and Friday evenings in her living room with her friends Mrs G_____ and Mrs N_____. They would drink tea, smoke and debate form. Under South Africa's race laws, neither Mrs G_____ nor Mrs N_____ was classified as white. Nonetheless, these three friends met to figure out how to beat the odds. Under the emerging apartheid social order, it also represented a little act of defiance, and a humble, mostly unnoticed, enactment of history across the colour line. This shard of history also points to the affective shifts necessary as Sheila moved from crossing the colour line on Tuesday and Friday nights, participating in a shared humanity, and then stepping back into the racial laagers of apartheid South Africa.

Not only do histories like these rupture – or, at least, complicate – older Afrikaner nationalist narratives about the homogeneity and coherence of white society, but also more recent black nationalist histories that posit whiteness as immutable. Despite the dehumanising effects of whiteness as an ideology of supremacy, exclusion and power, the friendship that my mother shared with these women gave the opportunity to reclaim something of her own humanity through acts of solidarity founded on a shared interest in horse racing, milky tea and far too many cigarettes. As such, histories across the colour line, if they exist, are small but important building blocks for a radical history of whites.

From whiteness to writing new histories of whites

All the questions that I have suggested challenge the idea of whiteness as a generic category, an ahistorical entity. They problematise the historical production of racial categories and point to some degrees of humanity that had to be surrendered in return for the privilege of being white. They also throw into relief the historical basis of moral questions including accommodation and complicity, as well as defiance and its limits. As such, these histories lay open whiteness as a historically constructed invention – with associated, corollary potential for historical challenge and dismantling.

But the intellectual and historiographic project of writing a new history of whites must do more. Just like the acceleration of the antiapartheid struggle did for an earlier generation of South African social historians in the 1980s, the moment of decolonisation demands action. Just as this social history should be shaped by some of the concerns raised by the decolonial movement, social historians of race should actively listen to and interact with its organic intellectuals and activists. They are deeply engaged with facing race and the politics of antiracism, even as they approach these matters from a slightly different set of assumptions and foundations than those that I – for instance – have sketched. But as David Roediger reminds us, working across disagreement is a 'hopeful place regarding the theorizing of race and class'.[35] It also emphasises the value of solidarity in building antiracist (and, conceivably, anticapitalist) political and teaching coalitions. Closer to home, the greater the distance between those social historians of race investigating the histories of whites and those at the coalface of decolonisation struggles, the greater the risk of these histories succumbing to the debilitating self-indulgence characteristic of whiteness studies.

A final point: it cannot remain the case that social histories which take whites as their subject are written exclusively – or even largely – by whites. As Roediger observes, some of the most compelling insights into the 'souls of white folk' in America come from African Americans like James Baldwin, W.E.B. Du Bois and bell hooks, whose 'secret' knowledge of whites comes from 'seeing without being observed'.[36] The same applies in South Africa, yet I seldom see historians of whites citing, say, Solomon Plaatje or Steve Biko on the white condition. Based on their experience of the other side of the colour line, black writers are well positioned to comment on how whiteness works in routine, everyday ways. In his autobiography, *Long Walk to Freedom*, Nelson Mandela shows, for instance, how Christo Brand, a white prison warder on Robben Island, exhibited at the same time *baasskap* (white supremacy) and considerable compassion to Mandela and other black political prisoners gaoled on the Island.[37] And black students should be encouraged to take on these unfashionable subjects – perhaps they are more fundamentally histories of race than histories of whites.

In a recent conversation about the future of social history, Dipesh Chakrabarty proclaimed the end of what he called 'old left wing history based on class', at which point I politely disagreed with my old friend. And in this essay I have argued for a new social history of race, focusing, in this instance, on whites, which could draw on some of the abiding strengths of Marxist social history – notably, its attention to class and relations of production, but also its empirical richness and theoretical iconoclasm. Moreover, it should be built on a self-conscious ethic of insurgency.

Indeed, Chibber's most fundamental critique of Chatterjee is a forceful blast as he insists that our understanding of social phenomena – including, in our case, white supremacy, white identity and expressions of white racism – must be situated within an exposition of both the logic of capital and the historical development of capitalism. Within such parameters, this historiography ranges around studies of power, ideology, representation and linguistics, as well as the archive, drawing on theories and methodologies that were not widely available in the late twentieth-century heyday of South African social history. As such, it approximates Roediger's 'open Marxism' or Eley's new 'history of society', marked by disciplinary, theoretical and methodological eclecticism.[38]

While acknowledging a strong Marxist core to this history, I do not advocate a return to Marxism's Grand Narrative. It might, however, be possible to connect the social history that I advocate in this essay to smaller-scale emancipatory ends, themselves tied to a critique of capital and the categories and divisions it both produces and sustains. This means, for instance, ruthlessly shattering the idea of whiteness as a stable, homogeneous category. It means writing with understanding but never apologia. And such foci coincide with a decolonial intellectual agenda.

A historiography of the sort that I have tried to map does not claim to be a regional iteration of theory (or history) from the South. Nor does it claim to be a South African version of history developed elsewhere – even as I acknowledge a debt to scholars and activists like Du Bois and Roediger. It is, rather, a history of below founded on the genealogy of particular intellectual and political developments. And it is cast in a specific historical moment. Hopefully it will disturb (or even energise) histories of race and, more specifically, of whites, and help us to rethink the values, possibilities and limitations of social history within the broader discipline.

Notes

1. F. Cooper, 'Conflict and Connection: Rethinking Colonial African History', *American Historical Review*, 99 (5) Dec. 1994, 1522; see also J. Ki-Zerbo, 'General Introduction', in J. Ki-Zerbo (ed.), *General History of Africa*, vol. 1, *Methodology and African Prehistory* (London: Unesco, 1989), 1–23.
2. T. Ranger, 'White Presence and Power in Africa', *Journal of African History*, 20 (4) 1979, 463–9.
3. F. Fanon, *The Wretched of the Earth* (New York: Grove Weidenfeld, 1963), 97–141.
4. See F. Jameson, *The Cultural Turn: Selected Writings in the Postmodern, 1983–1998* (New York: Verso, 1998); C. Barnett, 'A Critique of the Cultural Turn', in J. Duncan, N. Johnson and R. Schein (eds), *A Companion to Cultural Geography* (Oxford: Blackwell, 2004), 38–48.
5. A position best exemplified in E.P. Thompson, *The Poverty of Theory; or, An Orrery of Errors* (New York: Monthly Review Press, 1978).
6. C. van Onselen, *New Babylon, New Nineveh: Everyday Life on the Witwatersrand, 1886–1914* (Johannesburg: Ravan, 2001); T. Clynick, 'Afrikaner Political Mobilization in the Western Transvaal: Popular Consciousness and the State, 1920–1930' (DPhil thesis, Queen's University, 1996); A. Grundlingh, *Die Hendsoppers en Joiners: Die Rasioneel en Verskynsel van Verraad* (Pretoria: Protea Boekhuis, 2000), and '"God het Ons Arme Mense die Houtjies Gegee": Poor White Woodcutters in the Southern Cape Forest Area, c. 1900–1939', in R. Morrell (ed.), *White but Poor: Essays on the History of Poor Whites in Southern Africa, 1880–1940* (Pretoria: Unisa Press, 1992). 'Hendsoppers' derives from the phrase 'hand-uppers', and it emerged in the context of the South African War (1899–1902) . It was a derogatory term used by those who preferred war to be waged to the 'bitter end' ('bittereinders') to describe those Boer combatants who laid down their arms after the occupation of the Boer capitals Bloemfontein (February 1900) and Pretoria (June 1900).
7. J. Krikler, *The Rand Revolt: The 1922 Insurrection and Racial Killing in South Africa* (Johannesburg: Jonathan Ball, 2005).
8. D.R. Roediger, *The Wages of Whiteness: Race and the Making of the American Working Class* (New York: Verso, 1991).
9. D. Posel, 'Whiteness and Power in the South African Civil Service: Paradoxes of the Apartheid State', *Journal of Southern African Studies*, 25 (1) Mar. 1999.
10. N. Roos, *Ordinary Springboks: Ordinary Servicemen and Social Justice in South Africa, 1939–1961* (Aldershot: Ashgate, 2005).
11. J. Hyslop, 'The Imperial Working Class Makes Itself White: White Laborism in Britain, Australia and South Africa', *Journal of Historical Sociology*, 12 (4) Dec. 1999, 398.

12 A. Bonnett, 'White Studies Revisited', *Ethnic and Racial Studies*, 33 (1) Jan. 2008, 185–96.
13 M. Steyn, *Whiteness Just Isn't What It Used to Be* (Albany, NY: SUNY Press, 2001).
14 *City Press*, 31 Mar. 2013.
15 I. Rodriguez, 'A New Debate on Subaltern Studies', *LASA Forum, Latin American Studies Association*, XXXIII, 2002, 14–15.
16 D.T. Goldberg, *The Racist State* (Malden, MA: Blackwell, 2002).
17 W.E.B. Du Bois, *The World and Africa: An Inquiry into the Part Which Africa Has Played in World History* (New York: International Publishers, 1965), 21.
18 A. Stubbs (ed.), *I Write What I Like: Steve Biko, a Selection of His Writings* (Johannesburg: Picador Africa, 2004); R. Turner, *The Eye of the Needle: Towards Participatory Democracy in South Africa* (Johannesburg: Ravan, 1980).
19 F.B. Nyamnjoh, 'Blinded by Sight: Divining the Future of Anthropology in Africa', *Afrika Spectrum*, 47 (2/3) 2012, 63–92.
20 V. Chibber, *Postcolonial Theory and the Specter of Capital* (London: Verso, 2013); see also 'Debate: Marxism & the Legacy of Subaltern Studies – Historical Materialism NY 2013', YouTube, 6 May 2013, www.youtube.com/watch?v=xbM8HJrxSJ4 (accessed 27 Mar. 2022); and 'Subaltern Studies Revisited: Vivek Chibber's Response to Partha Chatterjee', Verso blog, 25 Feb. 2014, www.versobooks.com/blogs/1529-subaltern-studies-revisited-vivek-chibber-s-response-to-partha-chatterjee (accessed 27 Mar. 2022).
21 D. Ludden (ed.), *Reading Subaltern Studies: Critical History, Contested Meaning and the Globalisation of South Asia* (Delhi: Permanent Black, 2001).
22 B. Dubbeld, 'Translating E.P. Thompson's Marxian Critique: Contesting "Context" in South African Studies', *Social Dynamics*, 46 (1) 2020, 67–85.
23 G. Eley, *A Crooked Line: From Cultural History to the History of Society* (Ann Arbor: University of Michigan Press, 2005), 9–10; see also 190.
24 D. Posel, 'Social History and the Wits History Workshop', *African Studies*, 69 (1) Apr. 2010.
25 The NP in alliance with the Afrikaner Party held seventy-nine seats. Ranged against this bloc, the United Party and the Labour Party mustered a combined total of seventy-four seats.
26 S. Dubow, *Science and Society in Southern Africa* (Manchester: Manchester University Press, 2001) and *A Commonwealth of Knowledge: Science, Sensibility and White South Africa, 1820–2000* (Oxford: Oxford University Press, 2006); A.J. Norval, *Deconstructing Apartheid Discourse* (London: Verso, 1996).
27 S. Sarkar, 'The Decline of the Subaltern in Subaltern Studies', in Ludden, *Reading Subaltern Studies*, 400–29.
28 University of the Free State, Archive for Contemporary Affairs, C.D. Taylor Papers, 1/11/4/9/1/10/1, Notes on Public Service.
29 K. Mooney, '"Ducktails, Flickknives and Pugnacity": Subcultural and Hegemonic Masculinities in South Africa, 1848–1960', *Journal of Southern African Studies*, 24 (4) Dec. 1998, and 'Identities in the Ducktail Youth Subculture in Post-World-War-Two South Africa', *Journal of Youth Studies*, 8 (1) 2005.

30 N. Roos 'Work Colonies for White Men and the Historiography of Apartheid', *Social History*, 36 (1) Feb. 2011, 54–76.
31 J. Higginson, *Collective Violence and the Agrarian Origins of South African Apartheid, 1900–1948* (New York: Cambridge University Press, 2015).
32 National Archives of South Africa, Central Archives Repository (Pretoria), ARB 907 1000/21/1/1/10, vol. 6, 25 Jan. 1957 to 27 May 1957.
33 N. Painter, *Southern History across the Color Line* (Chapel Hill: University of North Carolina Press, 2002), 2.
34 A.L. Stoler, *Carnal Knowledge and Imperial Power: Race and the Intimate in Colonial Rule* (Berkeley: University of California Press, 2002); C. Hall, 'Review of *Carnal Knowledge and Imperial Power: Race and the Intimate in Colonial Rule* by Ann Laura Stoler', *Social History*, 29 (4) 2004, 532–4.
35 D. Roediger, *Class, Race and Marxism* (London: Verso, 2017), 1–7, quote at 3.
36 b. hooks, 'Representations of Whiteness in the Black Imagination', in D. Roediger, *Black on White: Black Writers on What It Means to Be White* (New York: Schocken, 1999), 38–53; J. Baldwin, 'On Being "White" ... and Other Lies', in Roediger, *Black on White*, 177–80; W.E.B. Du Bois, 'The Souls of White Folk', in Roediger, *Black on White*, 184–203; Roediger, *Black on White*, 4–5 (idea of 'seeing without being observed'); see also D. Roediger, 'Critical Studies of Whiteness, USA: Origins and Arguments', *Theoria*, 98, Dec. 2001, 72–98.
37 N. Mandela, *Long Walk to Freedom: The Autobiography of Nelson Mandela* (London: Little, Brown, 1995).
38 S. Virdee, 'Race, Class and Roediger's Open Marxism', *Salvage*, 27 Oct. 2017, http://eprints.gla.ac.uk/150702/1/150702.pdf (accessed 27 Mar. 2022); Eley, *Crooked Line*, 193–200.

Bibliography

Baldwin, J. (1999) 'On Being "White" ... and Other Lies', in Roediger, *Black on White*.
Barnett, C. (2004) 'A Critique of the Cultural Turn', in J. Duncan, N.C. Johnson and R.H. Schein (eds), *A Companion to Cultural Geography*. Oxford: Blackwell.
Bonnett, A. (2008) 'White Studies Revisited', *Ethnic and Racial Studies*, 33 (1).
Chibber, V. (2013) *Postcolonial Theory and the Specter of Capital*. London: Verso.
Clynick, T. (1996) 'Afrikaner Political Mobilization in the Western Transvaal: Popular Consciousness and the State, 1920–1930'. DPhil thesis, Queen's University.
Cooper, F. (1994) 'Conflict and Connection: Rethinking Colonial African History', *American Historical Review*, 99 (5).
'Debate: Marxism & the Legacy of Subaltern Studies – Historical Materialism NY 2013' (2013) YouTube, 6 May, www.youtube.com/watch?v=xbM8HJrxSJ4 (accessed 27 Mar. 2022).
Dubbeld, B. (2020) 'Translating E.P. Thompson's Marxian Critique: Contesting "Context" in South African Studies', *Social Dynamics*, 46 (1).

Du Bois, W.E.B. (1965) *The World and Africa: An Inquiry into the Part Which Africa Has Played in World History*. New York: International Publishers.

Du Bois, W.E.B. (1999) 'The Souls of White Folk', in Roediger, *Black on White*.

Dubow, S. (2001) *Science and Society in Southern Africa*. Manchester: Manchester University Press.

Dubow, S. (2006) *A Commonwealth of Knowledge: Science, Sensibility and White South Africa, 1820–2000*. Oxford: Oxford University Press.

Eley, G. (2005) *A Crooked Line: From Cultural History to the History of Society*. Ann Arbor: University of Michigan Press.

Fanon, F. (1963) *The Wretched of the Earth*. New York: Grove Weidenfeld.

Hall, C. (2004) 'Review of *Carnal Knowledge and Imperial Power: Race and the Intimate in Colonial Rule* by Ann Laura Stoler', *Social History*, 29 (4).

hooks, b. (1999) 'Representations of Whiteness in the Black Imagination', in Roediger, *Black on White*.

Hyslop, J. (1999) 'The Imperial Working Class Makes Itself White: White Laborism in Britain, Australia and South Africa', *Journal of Historical Sociology*, 12 (4).

Goldberg, D.T. (2002) *The Racist State*. Malden, MA: Blackwell.

Grundlingh, A. (1992) '"God het Ons Arme Mense die Houtjies Gegee": Poor White Woodcutters in the Southern Cape Forest Area, c. 1900–1939', in Morrell (ed.), *White but Poor*.

Grundlingh, A. (2000) *Die Hendsoppers en Joiners: Die Rasioneel en Verskynsel van Verraad*. Pretoria: Protea Boekhuis.

Higginson, J. (2015) *Collective Violence and the Agrarian Origins of South African Apartheid, 1900–1948*. New York: Cambridge University Press.

Jameson, F. (1998) *The Cultural Turn: Selected Writings in the Postmodern, 1983–1998*. New York: Verso.

Ki-Zerbo, J. (1989) 'General Introduction', in J. Ki-Zerbo (ed.), *General History of Africa*, vol. 1, *Methodology and African Prehistory*. London: Unesco.

Krikler, J. (2005) *The Rand Revolt: The 1922 Insurrection and Racial Killing in South Africa*. Johannesburg: Jonathan Ball.

Ludden, D. (ed.) (2001) *Reading Subaltern Studies: Critical History, Contested Meaning and the Globalisation of South Asia*. Delhi: Permanent Black.

Mandela, N. (1995) *Long Walk to Freedom: The Autobiography of Nelson Mandela*. London: Little, Brown.

Mooney, K. (1998) '"Ducktails, Flickknives and Pugnacity": Subcultural and Hegemonic Masculinities in South Africa, 1848–1960', *Journal of Southern African Studies*, 24 (4).

Mooney, K. (2005) 'Identities in the Ducktail Youth Subculture in Post-World-War-Two South Africa', *Journal of Youth Studies*, 8 (1).

Morrell, R. (ed.) (1992) *White but Poor: Essays on the History of Poor Whites in Southern Africa, 1880–1940*. Pretoria: Unisa Press.

National Archives of South Africa, Central Archives Repository (Pretoria), ARB 907 1000/21/1/1/10, vol. 6, 25 Jan. 1957 to 27 May 1957.

Norval, A.J. (1996) *Deconstructing Apartheid Discourse*. London: Verso.

Nyamnjoh, F. (2012) 'Blinded by Sight: Divining the Future of Anthropology in Africa', *Afrika Spectrum*, 47 (2/3).

Painter, N. (2002) *Southern History across the Color Line*. Chapel Hill: University of North Carolina Press.
Posel, D. (1999) 'Whiteness and Power in the South African Civil Service: Paradoxes of the Apartheid State', *Journal of Southern African Studies*, 25 (1).
Posel, D. (2010) 'Social History and the Wits History Workshop', *African Studies*, 69 (1).
Ranger, T. (1979) 'White Presence and Power in Africa', *Journal of African History*, 20 (4).
Rodriguez, I. (2002) 'A New Debate on Subaltern Studies', *LASA Forum, Latin American Studies Association*, XXXIII.
Roediger, D. (1991) *The Wages of Whiteness: Race and the Making of the American Working Class*. New York: Verso.
Roediger, D. (ed.) (1999) *Black on White: Black Writers on What It Means to Be White*. New York: Schocken.
Roediger, D. (2001) 'Critical Studies of Whiteness, USA: Origins and Arguments', *Theoria*, 98.
Roediger, D. (2017) *Class, Race and Marxism*. London: Verso.
Roos, N. (2005) *Ordinary Springboks: Ordinary Servicemen and Social Justice in South Africa, 1939–1961*. Aldershot: Ashgate.
Roos, N. (2011) 'Work Colonies for White Men and the Historiography of Apartheid', *Social History*, 36 (1).
Sarkar, S. (2001) 'The Decline of the Subaltern in Subaltern Studies', in Ludden, *Reading Subaltern Studies*.
Steyn, M. (2001) *Whiteness Just Isn't What It Used to Be*. Albany, NY: SUNY Press.
Stoler, A. (2002) *Carnal Knowledge and Imperial Power: Race and the Intimate in Colonial Rule*. Berkeley: University of California Press.
Stubbs, A. (ed.) (2004) *I Write What I Like: Steve Biko, a Selection of His Writings*. Johannesburg: Picador Africa.
'Subaltern Studies Revisited: Vivek Chibber's Response to Partha Chatterjee' (2014) Verso blog, 25 Feb., www.versobooks.com/blogs/1529-subaltern-studies-revisited-vivek-chibber-s-response-to-partha-chatterjee (accessed 27 Mar. 2022).
Thompson, E.P. (1978) *The Poverty of Theory; or, An Orrery of Errors*. New York: Monthly Review Press.
Turner, R. (1980) *The Eye of the Needle: Towards Participatory Democracy in South Africa*. Johannesburg: Ravan.
University of the Free State, Archive for Contemporary Affairs, C.D. Taylor Papers, 1/11/4/9/1/10/1, Notes on Public Service.
Van Onselen, C. (2001) *New Babylon, New Nineveh: Everyday Life on the Witwatersrand, 1886–1914*. Johannesburg: Ravan.
Virdee, S. (2017) 'Race, Class and Roediger's Open Marxism', *Salvage*, 27 Oct., http://eprints.gla.ac.uk/150702/1/150702.pdf (accessed 27 Mar. 2022).

9

Bringing white workers back in: new histories of race and class in South Africa

Danelle van Zyl-Hermann

Race and class have been intertwined for much of South Africa's modern history. Apartheid explicitly sought to entrench patterns of black subjugation, dispossession and exploitation that were established during earlier eras of slavery and segregation. As Deborah Posel has shown, the apartheid state's racial classifications were deeply enmeshed with lived hierarchies of class. In time, institutional categorisations and subjective experiences functioned in a mutually reinforcing fashion to fix race as class, and vice versa.[1]

Since the end of apartheid and the establishment of majority rule, this familiar entanglement has begun to unravel. The rapid post-1994 expansion of the black middle class and elite – the so-called 'black diamonds' – demonstrates that the racial divide between black and white no longer neatly maps onto divisions of poverty and wealth.[2] Indeed, within a decade of the end of apartheid, some scholars argued that class was overtaking race as the main determinant of social inequality amid the deepening of intraracial inequality. Nevertheless, the vast majority of South Africans living in poverty were black, while many white South Africans continued to enjoy relative wealth, security, access to education and employment opportunities.[3] Even as the race–class entanglement is unravelling in some sections of society, it is becoming more entrenched elsewhere.

These realities play a central role in shaping contemporary South African politics. The legitimacy and electoral support of the ruling African National Congress (ANC) has long been based on its historical credentials as leader of the struggle against white minority rule. The political liberation of the black majority was famously achieved by an alliance between the ANC, black labour and the broader left. This coalition has taken institutional form in the Tripartite Alliance, which brings together the ANC, the Congress of South African Trade Unions and the South African Communist Party. This governing alliance is, however, by no means united on how to address issues of social inequality, poverty and unemployment. Meanwhile, its failure to match political liberation with economic liberation – reflected in the deepening of unemployment and inequality since 1994 – has seen its political hegemony challenged, particularly by the likes of the left-populist Economic Freedom Fighters, which routinely casts South African politics as a battle between the black proletariat and white capital. On the other side of the political aisle, the Democratic Alliance's efforts at liberal nonracialism have continuously come up against the reality of persisting race-based inequality. With many in the Democratic Alliance claiming that race should not matter – either in internal party politics or national policy – the main opposition party has been unable to formulate a meaningful response to the country's challenges.

Present-day South African politics therefore remains deeply rooted in and yet confounded by race and class. The (dis)entanglement of race and class in its various permutations also poses analytical challenges for scholars. Should we try to think of race and class separately, or not? What are the implications of taking this intersection seriously throughout South Africa's modern history, and why has this approach sometimes been neglected? What are the limitations of existing historical analyses of this nexus, and how might we move beyond them? What new insights might doing so offer into local, national and global realities, and contemporary debates on identity and inequality?

These questions themselves draw on a rich body of scholarship on South African labour and social history. It is not the intention of this chapter to critique this scholarship, but rather to argue for an extension of its conceptual and analytical insights for the purpose of reexamining existing interpretations and uncovering new perspectives. As such, this chapter effectively suggests the deployment of an old subject matter in a new context.

The field of white labour history has long been a wellspring of new historiographical approaches and debates surrounding race and class, stimulating the production of important and innovative scholarship. Yet the temporal focus of this scholarship – and hence the insights it has been able to offer – has been restricted to South Africa's initial industrialisation in the late nineteenth and early twentieth century. The neglect of white workers as a historical subject in the second half of the twentieth century reflects popular perceptions and scholarly understandings of the effects of National Party (NP) rule on the material position of whites. The consensus has been that the deepening of racial discrimination after 1948 facilitated rapid upward mobility and the disappearance of white workers as a social class. Yet, while the evidence is fragmented, it is clear that the actual material advantage of the NP's pro-white policies was spread very unevenly, that a significant section of the working white population remained in blue-collar employment throughout the apartheid period and that white embourgeoisement was often quite shallow. Nevertheless, histories of especially late- and postapartheid South Africa tend to treat the white population as largely homogeneous – uniformly wealthy and skilled. In a country in which one cannot speak about race without speaking about class, historians have effectively ceased to do so when it comes to the white population.

This chapter advocates studying the history of white working-class lives, politics and organisation in the apartheid and postapartheid periods. The chapter opens with a survey of the vibrant and wide-ranging historical insights which scholarship on white labour in early industrial and pre-World War Two South Africa has produced. Next, it explains the scholarly neglect of white workers as historical subjects after 1948. After pointing to structural and cultural evidence attesting to the continued reality of class cleavages in white society, the chapter calls attention to new research avenues that are bringing white workers into analyses of South Africa's recent past, and shows how this serves to rectify analytical blind spots and distorted interpretations. It does so by demonstrating how attention to white workers in the decades following 1948 facilitates new perspectives on the apartheid state, its relations with and regulation of white society, and the limitations of race-based ideology, experience and identity during this period. Then it shows how a focus on white working-class politics and experience in the late-apartheid period permits the revision of existing understandings of class formation and reveals alternative chronologies of change in South Africa that are embedded in broader global processes. This is further demonstrated in the final section, on the postapartheid present. Here, it is contended that bringing class back into studies of ethnic politics and social relationships through a focus on white working-class lives reveals the emergence of new social strategies, political tactics and subjectivities that have a continuing, transnational resonance.

A robust scholarship: white workers in South African historiography

The last half-century of South African history writing has been characterised by intense theoretical debate and methodological innovation. This intellectual engagement has been closely tied to the country's shifting political fortunes. White workers have featured as a key historical subject throughout, with successive historiographical 'turns' demonstrating the empirical richness and analytical value obtainable from close scrutiny of this social group.

White workers first surfaced as a testing ground for new historical interpretations from the late 1960s, amid the emergence of the so-called race–class debate. Arguably South African historiography's most heated scholarly altercation, this debate witnessed a new generation of politically engaged and Marxist-inspired historians challenging the intellectual dominance of liberal interpretations of South African history and society. Liberal historians had argued that the twin developments of economic integration and political segregation – which had long characterised South African society, but had accelerated dramatically with the advent of the mineral revolution – were fundamentally antithetical. This scholarship – most famously associated with *The Oxford History of South Africa* – was characterised by the centrality of racial groups, the identification of ideology and prejudice as the main driving forces in the making of the country, and the conviction that race-based policies stymied capitalist development.[4] From this view it followed that freeing market forces from racist regulations would facilitate the establishment of an inclusive, multiracial order.

However, reflecting on the rapid economic growth of the 1960s, as well as the apartheid regime's ever-harsher suppression of the black majority, a new generation of historians rejected the liberal view of racism as an irrational deviation from capitalist imperatives. They argued that racism was in fact complementary to capitalist development, and that class and material interests were the main drivers of South African history. For these scholars, a united labour movement was key to achieving the overthrow of capitalism and the establishment of an egalitarian order. Writing in the 1970s, they saw this conviction borne out by increased black worker militancy in opposition to the exploitation and repression of apartheid.[5]

It was within this materialist framework that white labour attracted special attention, particularly in terms of its apparent support for the racist order. A number of revisionist historians therefore placed white workers at the centre of their analyses. They concentrated specifically on the country's early industrial development, marked by dramatic industrial conflicts, to understand white labour's relationship with capital and the state, and its role in the making of racial capitalism. Frederick Johnstone used a case study of the gold-mining industry between 1910 and 1926 to argue that it was white workers' class position of extreme structural insecurity, born of the perpetual threat of displacement by a large and exploitable black labour reserve, that motivated their early twentieth-century militancy and demand for job colour bars.[6] Robert Davies took a broader view of the South African political economy as a whole between 1900 and 1960, and he highlighted the state's accommodation of white workers' demands during those years as evidence of the state's role as an instrument of capitalist interests. He argued that the institutionalisation of race-based labour hierarchies and an industrial conciliation machinery, following the most dramatic instance of white working-class militancy in 1922, facilitated the division of the working class along racial lines, thereby defusing potential challenges during the process of capital accumulation. This effectively rendered white workers subservient, disempowered and isolated from the black majority workforce, in exchange for which they received limited race-based privileges.[7]

Dan O'Meara sought to account for ethnic identifications within the racial capitalist order by offering a materialist analysis of the rise of Afrikaner nationalism between 1934 and 1948. This ideological construction, he argued, was formulated by specific petty bourgeois class forces as a vehicle for mobilising white Afrikaans speakers in an Afrikaner class alliance which would capture economic and later political power, thereby securing the basis for larger capital accumulation.[8] The Nationalists' triple mythology of the black, Anglo and Communist threat disciplined white and particularly Afrikaner workers 'into adopting an ideology that neatly justified their exploitation and replaced class consciousness with race anxieties.'[9] According to some scholars, race-based privileges that accrued to white labour on account of its alliance with capital rendered it a 'labour aristocracy' rather than an authentic part of the working class.[10] Others went further, arguing that the very existence of a white working class in South Africa was 'mythical', given that white workers performed mainly supervisory work and themselves benefitted from the exploitation of black labour.[11] Rather than a 'labour aristocracy' they should more accurately be regarded as a 'new middle class'.[12]

Parallel to the revisionist school, a related, though distinct, strand of scholarship emerged which broadened the thematic and methodological approaches taken to white workers as historical actors. This 'social history' also adopted a broadly materialist approach, but in contrast to the often theory-laden and abstract structuralist analyses of the revisionists, social historians investigated issues of class formation, conflict and consciousness through close attention to human agency and everyday life as they were shaped and limited by oppressive structural forces. Inspired by the scholarship of British social historian E.P. Thompson, these scholars developed an understanding of class which was more relational in nature and offered space to start taking issues of ideology and identity as seriously as structure. Like revisionist scholars, social history writing was inspired by the crescendo of worker militancy in the 1970s and 1980s, yet social historians focused less on working-class organisation and more on everyday experiences and politically relevant aspects of cultural and social life. Alongside documentary sources, wherever possible they also employed oral history methodologies to capture the voices of ordinary people. White working-class people, communities and households provided rich subject matter for them. This social history 'from below' often stood in stark contrast to the determinism and abstract emphasis on the collective to the neglect of working-class agency which often marked revisionist analyses. Charles van Onselen's *New Babylon New Nineveh*, Belinda Bozzoli's *Class, Community and Conflict*, and various contributions in Robert Morrell's *White but Poor* examined the experiences and struggles of lower-class whites, including brickmakers, prostitutes, factory workers, railway men and woodcutters.[13] The 1980s and 1990s saw feminist scholars adopt the social history approach to critique existing scholarship for having neglected women's agency. Their critique, which highlighted the gender oppression alongside that of class and race, produced a number of studies examining the role of white working-class women in Afrikaner nationalist politics and society, and nonracial trade unionism during the 1930s and 1940s.[14]

By the late twentieth century, the importance of class and the value of a political economy approach to history writing was firmly established. Yet in the context of labour and social reforms, and big business's criticism of the constraints apartheid policies placed on economic growth, it was clear that racism could in fact be dysfunctional to capitalist development. Clearly, analyses focused on class alone suffered analytical limitations similar to those that concentrated exclusively on race. A more nuanced approach, recognising the fluidity, coconstitution and historical contingency of these categories was needed.[15] Contrary to Davies's revisionist interpretation, Merle Lipton argued that there was no evidence that white capital deliberately imposed apartheid to divide the working class. Rather, white workers actively sought racially discriminatory legislation, with their racial prejudice reinforced by their structural interests.[16] David Yudelman in turn suggested that both liberal and revisionist scholars failed to see the state as an autonomous social actor with distinct interests of its own. He demonstrated how between 1902 and 1939 the state increasingly intervened in the protracted struggle for industrial dominance between labour and capital in the gold-mining industry, thus expanding its power and role in the process.[17] Eddie Webster, meanwhile, criticised Marxist-inspired analyses for taking inadequate account of worker agency. While continuing to work within a materialist framework, Webster used the metal industry as a case study to demonstrate white and black workers' resistance to capital's efforts to gain control over their labour.[18]

By the 1990s, such arguments alongside the innovative scholarship flowing from social history writing had established an understanding of race and class as being deeply intertwined. With the end of the global Cold War, and the concomitant rise of ideas suggesting the 'End of History', the triumph of capitalism or the 'Clash of Civilizations',[19] structuralist analyses increasingly seemed obsolete. Scholarly interest shifted from class to culture and identity. This acted in synergy with political developments in South Africa, where the advent of majority rule also saw the central race–class debate on the relationship between capitalism and racist oppression dissipate. New scholarship reflected a turn towards analyses of discourse and power, drawing on insights from literary studies, and postcolonial and postmodern theory.

White working-class lives continued to provide fruitful material for analysis, forming the subject matter of some of the most exciting and innovate new studies, which were authored by the likes of Jeremy Krikler, Neil Roos and Jonathan Hyslop, who offered original analyses emphasising how race and class evolved in the discourses and subjectivities of South Africa's early twentieth-century white working class.[20]

These scholars drew inspiration from histories of 'whiteness' – historical analyses of white power, privilege and ideologies of superiority in the vein of critical race studies – as articulated by American labour historians like David Roediger.[21] These studies offered valuable insight into how class shaped the construction of white racial identities and subjectivities during South Africa's early industrial development, in ways that built on the heritage of white supremacy established in earlier eras. Hyslop in particular placed such analyses of white working-class subjectivities in a broader transnational context, arguing that in the era before World War One, the unprecedented global mobility of capital and labour meant that white workers in South Africa belonged to an imperial working class that was bound together by a 'common ideology of White Labourism'. Hyslop showed how class consciousness and racism were inextricably entangled in this ideology.[22] The transnational turn offered a fresh historiographical approach, as historians sought to move beyond national frames of analysis to highlight processes of integration and difference on a global scale.[23]

Historiographical developments since the 1960s therefore produced a body of scholarship on white workers that is diverse in terms of its content, method and interpretation.[24] From this has emerged a broad convergence which sees the study of white labour revolve around the investigation of how class – relational, constructed, and intimately bound up with other categories of analysis and experience such as race, gender and ethnicity – was made in different historical contexts.

The end of white working-class history: embourgeoisement and its limitations

As historical subjects, white workers therefore continue to be at the forefront of historiographical debates and innovation. This scholarship, however, is strongly concentrated on the first decades of the 1900s, with only a handful of studies stretching beyond the advent of apartheid in 1948.[25]

This historiographical blind spot may be attributed to prevalent understandings of the beneficial effects which apartheid policies had on the material position of white South Africans. To be sure, after coming to power in 1948, the NP extended racially discriminatory legislation that privileged the position of whites in the labour market, in education and in the provision of social security.[26] These policies, fuelled by strong postwar economic growth, are understood to have facilitated dramatic upward mobility for whites, leading to the disappearance of white workers as a social class. This narrative of embourgeoisement sees the story of South Africa's white workers – which is so vividly portrayed by historians for the first half of the century – fall silent. Instead, scholars have focused on the high politics of the NP, the construction of the apartheid state, and, conversely, antiapartheid resistance and the escalation of the liberation struggle. Scholarship on South Africa's working class during this period focuses on African (and to a lesser extent, Indian and coloured) workers,[27] and mentions of white proletarians become incidental, typically accompanied by assumptions of their support for conservative or right-wing political parties.[28] Thus, in a country in which it is essentially impossible to discuss race without discussing class, historians effectively stopped doing so for the white population – echoing, by implication, nationalist ideology's foregrounding of racial and ethnic identity and representation of Afrikaners as a 'classless volk'.[29]

This scholarly consensus results in a homogenising view of white society which distorts our understanding of both the apartheid and postapartheid eras. Since the end of minority rule, there has been a proliferation of sociological and social anthropological research examining how the white population and Afrikaners in particular have sought to negotiate their loss of political power and navigate the realities of majority rule. This work takes a keen interest in identity (re)construction and shifting subjectivities among postapartheid whites, yet displays little sensitivity to issues of class and the history of class formation in South Africa. Instead, 'whites' or 'Afrikaners' are typically treated as self-evidently homogeneous groups. To be sure, a number of studies identify a scope of reactions within these groups to the collapse of the racial state and their loss of political power.[30] On the basis of these various reactions and efforts, scholars pronounce the fracturing of white society or ethnic identity. Such conclusions reveal understandings of pre-1994 white society as having been monolithic, thus perpetuating the impression that experience must run along racial and ethnic lines. Arguably, the sources and methodologies employed in these studies – analyses of letters to the editors of mainstream newspapers, participant observation at cultural festivals, interviews with whites residing in gated communities, statistics on emigration – are themselves biased towards middle-class or elite participants and settings. This both reflects and perpetuates the orthodoxy of wholescale white embourgeoisement under apartheid.

However fragmented, the available evidence clearly shows that white workers remained a significant part of the white population throughout the apartheid period. Although there is no comprehensive economic analysis of the class structure of the white population, some scholars have pointed to the uneven impact of the NP's pro-white policies and the shallow nature of Afrikaner embourgeoisement. O'Meara argued that an emerging class of urban Afrikaner financial, industrial and commercial capitalists were the major beneficiaries of the NP's discriminatory policies. Nevertheless, throughout the 1960s blue-collar workers in artisan and production work formed the *largest* occupational category of Afrikaans-speaking white males and *one of the lowest earning*, relative to other racial groups.[31] Occupational data offered by Sadie shows that a substantial part of the Afrikaner population remained in blue-collar positions throughout the late apartheid period, with 31.5 per cent of Afrikaners in blue-collar jobs in 1980, and 29.1 per cent in 1991.[32] Crankshaw's quantitative study of labour patterns between 1965 and 1990 similarly showed that substantial numbers of whites were employed in routine, white-collar, frontline supervisory, skilled and semiskilled occupational categories throughout this period. In terms of labour organisation, some four hundred thousand white workers, or 29 per cent of the economically active white population, were organised in trade unions in the 1970s.[33] Although they certainly formed a minority of the labour force in primary and secondary industry, these white workers represented a crucial part of the workforce, holding the majority of supervisory and skilled jobs, and a significant proportion of semiskilled positions. In terms of earnings, Terreblanche noted that the poorest 40 per cent of white, 'mainly Afrikaner' households experienced a significant decline in income in the second half of the apartheid period. He suggested that this trend could be explained 'in terms of the rapid (perhaps too rapid) embourgeoisement of Afrikaners in the third quarter of the [twentieth] century, and the inability of many ... to maintain their income levels when economic conditions deteriorated'. He added that it would 'be a mistake to underestimate the traumatic experiences of many Afrikaners who had progressed from relative poverty in the first half of the twentieth century to substantial wealth during the third quarter, and then regressed to substantially lower standards of living in the last quarter'.[34]

This structural data is complemented by evidence from the cultural realm. White working-class life and culture has been a vibrant and often quite lucrative field in pre- and post-1994 popular culture and literature. In the midst of the turbulent final decade of apartheid, the most popular Afrikaans sitcom on public television was *Orkney Snork Nie!* which followed the exploits of the Van Tonder family in the mining town of Orkney, southwest of Johannesburg. The series, which ran for four seasons, was lauded for its authentic portrayal of 'typical people',[35] such as the chauvinist father figure (and miner) Hendrik; the nagging housewife, Maggie; their dull-witted mechanic son, Ouboet; and his gaudy part-time hairdresser wife,

Jolanda, amongst others. Alongside these employment markers, the humour functioned on the basis of the characters' working-class tastes, language and concerns. The popularity of the series led to the production of two movies, which were highly successful at the box office. In 2006, *Orkney* was rebroadcast on an Afrikaans pay-television channel, demonstrating its continued appeal.[36] Jeanne Goosen's 2002 novel *'n Pawpaw vir My Darling* similarly highlighted white working-class life, this time in the form of the Beeslaer family in the fictional Damnville – a play on the working-class suburb of Danville in Pretoria's industrial western suburbs.[37] The book describes the fortunes of the Beeslaers and their community – whose financial concerns, health problems and family intrigues were routinely ameliorated by cheap brandy – and combines humour and pathos in its depiction of postapartheid white working-class life. Its subsequent adaptation to film in 2016 erred on the side of comedy, presenting class tensions between down-and-out Damnville and wealthy Afrikaners from Pretoria East as being much more enduring than the petty squabbles between the white Beeslaers and their black neighbours, or the tensions produced by their son's interracial relationship.[38] Featuring a number of top names in Afrikaans acting, *Pawpaw* produced another box office hit, earning R1.1 million in its first five days on circuit.[39]

Much less palatable to the South African public was Marlene van Niekerk's *Triomf*, published in 1994, a novel revolving around poverty, incest and sexual violence in a white Afrikaans family. Set on the eve of South Africa's first democratic elections, Van Niekerk presented a graphic indictment, not simply of apartheid's failure to affect the material or moral upliftment of its intended beneficiaries, but of the grotesque consequences of its policies of racial exclusivity. Crucially, the novel grounds the family's fortunes in the historical experiences of white urbanisation and proletarianisation earlier in the century. In addition to a number of literary prizes and its translation into English, Dutch and French, the novel – with its Freudian, feminist and postcolonial motifs – continues to attract scholarly attention.[40] On the musical front too, recent years have seen the appearance of white working-class imagery and themes, most notably with the particular fusion of rap, hip-hop and punk associated with Jack Parow and Die Antwoord respectively. These artists' subject matter often revolves around the authenticity of their caricatured lower-class, or 'zef', personas, supported by visuals ranging from gaudy working-class domesticity to sexual transgression, deformity and violence. Despite a growing scholarship on these artists, particularly in terms of issues of Afrikaner identity reconstruction, racialisation and cultural appropriation, little attention has been given to the class markers on which their work turns.[41]

The preceding discussion of the existing scholarship on white workers before 1948, of structural evidence of their presence post-1948, and of popular representations of white working-class lives and culture suggests that there is much to be gained from bringing white workers back into analyses of apartheid and postapartheid South Africa. Clearly, this is not simply a matter of gaining insight into the experiences and struggles of a particular, hitherto-overlooked social group – valuable as that might be in its own right. Rather, existing scholarship on the period of South Africa's early industrial development has shown that white workers represent a productive lens on to key historical processes that have local, national and global significance. This is, arguably, even more true for the apartheid and postapartheid periods – contexts firmly associated with wide-ranging white power and privilege, in which lower-class whites seem so anomalous. The following section seeks to spotlight a number of potential and emerging avenues of inquiry in this regard.

Bringing white workers back in

The orthodoxy of white embourgeoisement insists that whites under NP rule became uniformly wealthy, a largely homogeneous group firmly established in and incorporated into the dominant political, economic and social structures of the racist state. What cleavages are acknowledged are those of ethnicity – often in the form of tensions between an Afrikaner-controlled state and English-run business, or ostensibly conservative Afrikaner versus more liberal, English-speaking white society. However, even these divisions are understood to have faded with time, particularly in the face of overwhelming racial demographic changes and rising opposition to minority rule. Thus, beyond initial apprehensions about the Afrikaner nationalist government, and, later, growing electoral support for the NP, we know little about whites' relationship with the state or, indeed, how the state viewed the white populace.

Taking class seriously reveals that the apartheid state was very much concerned with the lives of working-class whites, often regarding them as objects requiring discipline and surveillance. This has been broached in work by the late Bill Freund on urban planning in the towns of Vanderbijlpark and Sasolburg, which were established to serve the state-run steel and oil-from-coal industries respectively. Freund showed how housing schemes for white workers in these 'company towns' were designed to create quiescent working-class populations which conformed to the racial and class order of the apartheid state. Towns were designed not only to minimise contact between white and black but also to separate whites into different neighbourhoods according to their social status. In addition to this spatial enforcement of class differences, white workers were also subject to regulations enforcing notions of suburban respectability – state efforts, in Freund's words, to 'civilise the paler skinned natives'.[42]

Clearly, white workers were expected to know their place in the apartheid town and state. These insights by Freund formed part of a larger project by him focused on the South African developmental state.[43] A more concentrated challenge to ideas of apartheid-era white homogeneity and state benevolence has been mounted by Neil Roos in an important and growing body of work (see also his chapter in this volume). Roos demonstrates how apartheid bureaucrats perceived lower-class elements of white society as potentially subversive or dangerous, and traces state efforts to subject them to discipline and social engineering. This included work colonies designed to confine and resocialise white men 'pushed to the margins of white society through poverty, idleness or miscreancy'.[44] Roos has argued that such efforts at imposing order on the white citizenry provided insight into how white society was imagined and reproduced, the anxieties and ideologies driving state interventions, and the production, exercise and evolution of colonial power. This also extended into the private sphere, as demonstrated by Annika Teppo's historical ethnography of a housing scheme set up in the 1930s by a company based in Cape Town. Throughout the apartheid period, the scheme sought to provide housing for lower-class whites deemed in need of 'rehabilitation' because of their struggles with, for instance, debt, alcohol or marital difficulties.[45] Both Roos and Freund have shown how such regimentation from above 'bred rebelliousness' from below, offering evidence of working-class defiance.[46] Teppo, in turn, paid close attention to the subjectivities and strategies which efforts at social control produced among beneficiaries of the housing scheme, including their efforts to perform respectability as 'good whites' in order to access resources and prestige. Teppo argues that such 'social games' became ever-harder to maintain as social differentiation among the residents increased during apartheid.

These studies begin to show the extent to which intrawhite class cleavages remained a reality throughout the apartheid era. Class position shaped relations with the state – for lower-class whites, this involved the paternalist, disciplining and rehabilitative gaze of the state, and the disparaging and disdainful attention of middle-class whites. These findings demand the revision of existing understandings of white homogeneity and state benevolence towards whites. Crucially, they force us to rethink the character, role and activities of the state in the maintenance of white minority rule and racial capitalism, for they subjected the black and white populations alike to social engineering. To be sure, this recognition does not diminish the devastation and violence wrought on black lives by such measures as forced removals or the pass laws. Rather, it seeks to provide a fuller understanding of the shaping of South African society during the second half of the twentieth century.

Attention to lower-class whites also demonstrates that race did not unproblematically supersede class after 1948, but that racial status, identity and subjectivities continued to be deeply coloured by class position throughout the period. White workers' class position clearly rendered them less secure in the imaginary of the apartheid state, in which class attributes – from income and employment to behaviour, character and culture – were understood in racial terms. Social histories of white working-class communities and lives during the apartheid period may shed more light on how these were connected to wider concerns in apartheid society. Freund's and Teppo's work demonstrates the rich potential of urban history in this regard – a point already well established by social historians interested in the everyday lives of the black population under apartheid. This suggests potential avenues for comparison and intersection.

Attention to white working-class organisation and subjectivities can also provide important insights into South Africa's political transition of the early 1990s, as well as the trajectories of class formation which pervaded the decades leading up to that point. Existing scholarship connects the changing class base and related subjectivities of white, particularly Afrikaans-speaking South Africans with the NP's moves towards first reform and then negotiations. By the 1970s, according to this reading, the NP's core constituency was white middle-class suburbanites and corporate Afrikanerdom, strengthened by postwar economic growth and state privilege. Ever less reliant on the support and capital derived from industrial working-class and agricultural support bases, both the party and business community moved away from a commitment to strict apartheid. Particularly after the departure of the more conservative elements in its ranks in 1982, the NP increasingly represented itself as a bourgeois party and whites as a modernising and adaptive elite.[47] Newly bourgeois Afrikanerdom had become more concerned with material prosperity and comfort than with the racist nationalism which had facilitated its empowerment during the early apartheid period. This, Hyslop argues, was due not only to improved material conditions but also the impact of modernising cultural influences such as globalised consumerism: traditional 'subjectivities, which were to a large extent organised around a modernist and racist project of state building, were replaced by a more self-regarding, individualist consumerist identity.'[48]

Yet, recent research on the late-apartheid era suggests a different reality for working-class segments of white society. By the mid-1970s, global economic crisis, restrictions produced by apartheid legislation, and increasingly vocal black resistance came together to seriously undermine economic growth and political stability. The NP, reflecting its new priorities, set its sights on labour reform. A Commission of Inquiry was appointed to investigate and make recommendations for the reform of South Africa's industrial dispensation. In 1979, the Wiehahn Commission – as it became known (after its chairman, Nic Wiehahn) – recommended the removal of race-based labour legislation and incorporation of African workers in the labour relations system. Wessel Visser's work on the all-white Mineworkers' Union (MWU) chronicles its efforts to mobilise political support and labour power to block these reforms.[49] The MWU, founded in 1902, represented white production workers at the lowest end of the mining skills and supervisory hierarchy. These miners often worked directly alongside African workers. The MWU had been at the forefront of the industrial struggles of the early twentieth century, and its members were direct beneficiaries of the subsequent institutionalisation of the colour bar and the establishment of South Africa's race-based industrial conciliation machinery – the very co-optation into capitalist interests through state mechanisms described by revisionist historians. By the late 1970s, the over eighteen thousand workers represented by the MWU remained dependent on legislative measures to protect them against black competition in the workplace. Their privileged access to jobs and high wages was supported by the state, while many of the job-related housing, healthcare and leisure benefits they and their families enjoyed were similarly contingent on their position in the racialised labour hierarchy. My own research on testimony brought by white unions before the Wiehahn Commission shows workers insisted that the colour bar remained necessary to protect them against the threats of capitalist exploitation and displacement by black labour. Key testimonies reveal white poverty not only as a prominent feature of the historical consciousness of white workers, but as a present-day anxiety in the face of the prospect of labour reform. In the context of the racial state, white workers demanded protective legislation as their political right, arguing that its removal would amount to a denial of their citizenship.[50]

This evidence prompts a revision of existing understandings of twentieth-century class formation. For many whites, their privileged lifestyle did not reflect actual shifts in their class position. Material comfort did not necessarily translate into bourgeois subjectivities, interests and politics. Rather, the evidence suggests the continuation of both working-class consciousness and dependence on race-based legislation, highlighting just how fragile class position rendered racial privilege in the late-apartheid era. Existing scholarship overestimates the extent and solidity of upward white social mobility under apartheid.

White working-class perceptions and experiences of labour reform also demand the revision of existing narratives of the transition. The granting of industrial rights to Africans called the established convergence between race and rights into question, reversing the full citizenship white workers had secured in the 1920s. The inclusion of Africans in industrial conciliation processes and the removal of race-based job reservation from 1979 effectively represented the withdrawal of state support for white working-class privilege and status, amounting to workers' exclusion from the racial state at a time when white minority rule was still firmly entrenched. This not only alerts us to the class conflicts produced within white society by the political challenges and shifting capitalist imperatives of this period, but also suggests an alternative chronology for the transition. To be sure, late-apartheid reforms are rightly understood in terms of the apartheid government's failure to grant Africans full citizenship. But because the existing historiography overwhelmingly views the reforms of the late 1970s in conservative terms, it overlooks the implications and consequences for this section of the white population. Existing scholarship presents 1994 as the key moment of white loss and dislocation. Yet for white workers, the withdrawal of power and privilege occurred more than a decade before. Oral history interviews with reform-era MWU members confirm this as a key turning point in white working-class experience.[51] This opens up new perspectives on the transition from a labour point of view, and suggests a chronology which aligns more broadly with global trends regarding the disciplining of labour and ascent of neoliberal policies.

Contemporary politics and global intersections

This brings us, finally, to the recent history of capitalism and contemporary political developments in South Africa. Revisionist and social historians used white workers as a focal point for understanding the making of the political economy and for examining everyday agency and strategies in response to particular structural and social forces in early industrial South Africa. The current historical juncture, too, necessitates inquiry into these issues, and white workers as historical subjects have much to offer. A scattering of scholarship, displaying the strong focus on urban space noted earlier, starts to provide evidence in this regard.

The historical context of Irma du Plessis's examination of everyday lives in a lower-class white Johannesburg suburb chimes strongly with Teppo's.[52] Du Plessis studies Jan Hofmeyr, a council housing scheme originally established in the 1930s to provide subsidised housing for indigent whites. Her analysis, however, is placed firmly in the context of postapartheid processes of desegregation, state retreat and the privatisation of state housing. Du Plessis shows how this confronts residents with new challenges and opportunities, and they are forced to reimagine the future of their neighbourhood and community. Thus Du Plessis provides a fascinating case study of the making of race, class and space in the postcolonial city amid the retreating state. Works by Johan Smuts, and by John Sharp and Stephan van Wyk, examine the impact of deindustrialisation and the changing priorities of the postapartheid state by also focusing on white working-class lives in the postapartheid city. These authors all ground these processes in the neoliberal turn taken by the NP from the 1980s and continued by the ANC after 1994. The studies are all located in the deindustrialising suburbs of Pretoria West – the same area invoked by the fictional Damnville of *'n Pawpaw vir My Darling*. Smuts examines the evolving relationship between class and gender amid the decline of heavy industry, rising male unemployment and the feminisation of the labour market. His analysis uncovers everyday strategies and reformulated subjectivities for coping with challenges to masculine identity, domestic security and patriarchal structures brought on by these structural shifts.[53] Sharp and Van Wyk also investigate white cost-of-living struggles in Pretoria that were born of recent processes of labour rationalisation and deindustrialisation. Focusing on unemployed individuals' efforts to adapt to these new circumstances, the authors uncover evidence of remarkable economic and social pragmatism, including openness to cross-racial campaigning and intimacy.[54]

As part of their study, Sharp and Van Wyk identify charitable initiatives driven by white Pretorians with apparently racially exclusive nationalist agendas as one form of recourse for unemployed whites.[55] Here their research intersects with my own work, pointing to further questions raised when one pays attention to white workers. Earlier scholarship on the role of white workers in the making of racial capitalism, their relationship to the state and their political strategies were developed in a context in which white labour formed an important political constituency. The shifts in NP policies and priorities described earlier clearly show the diminishing political importance of this class vis-à-vis other white interests in the course of the 1970s and 1980s. By contrast, since the end of minority rule, whites are generally not considered a significant political force. Yet attention to white workers in the postapartheid context can offer insight into political dynamics unfolding since 1994 which demand a return to earlier questions about the nature of capitalism, relations with the state and political strategies.

The charity efforts identified by Sharp and Van Wyk are part of a much broader range of initiatives taken in recent years by Solidarity, a self-assertive Afrikaner social movement which has rapidly gained public prominence since the early 2000s. Solidarity is in fact the successor organisation of the MWU, mentioned earlier. The expansion of the union's membership beyond the mining industry was an immediate response to labour reforms after the Wiehahn Commission, as it set out to create a 'super white union' representing blue-collar workers across industries. Its reinvention as a social movement formulated in ethnic terms dovetailed with this expansion from the mid-1990s as a new generation of middle-class leaders entered the union alongside its mineworking old guard.[56]

Today, Solidarity defines itself as the voice of South Africa's white Afrikaans-speaking minority.[57] Presenting minorities in general and Afrikaners in particular as marginalised and excluded by black majority rule, it has a track record of legal action against government policies and state action which it regards as discriminatory in cultural or racial terms. In recent years, the movement has launched a number of initiatives to provide Afrikaners with the support, protection and services which, in black-majority-ruled South Africa, they are ostensibly being denied. This includes collective and individual labour representation; investment in Afrikaans-medium education and training in the form of a private Afrikaans university, technical training institute and school support programmes; service delivery projects in local municipalities; an online media and news platform; a nationally active civil rights organisation, with a youth division active on university campuses; a lobby group for business interests; a think tank; and a range of financial services. Throughout, these initiatives are presented as 'do[ing] the things the government is not doing for Afrikaners'.[58] Solidarity therefore vocally asserts itself as an actor on the South African political stage, and through its various initiatives, the movement's narratives, support and reach expand into various social spheres.

While Solidarity can no longer be seen as an exclusively blue-collar organisation, it retains a substantial white working-class base, and trade unionism remains one of its core activities. I have argued elsewhere that its initiatives may be seen as efforts to secure Afrikaner power and privilege by creating community-based, institutional and even virtual spaces of autonomy through civil society rather than formal political processes.[59] This suggests a new role for white workers and their organisation as political agents under majority rule. Even more provocatively, it points to the emergence of strategies of extraparliamentary political action taken in the context of lost political hegemony.

The Solidarity Movement demonstrates the necessity of bringing class back into studies of ethnic politics and relationships, and offers an avenue for investigating the formulation of class interests in cultural terms. These are questions which resonate far beyond the local politics of postapartheid South Africa, because the consequences of globalising neoliberalism and austerity policies in the wake of the 2008 global financial crisis – alongside growing alienation between citizens and political elites as evidenced in disquieting trends towards populist nationalism and xenophobia – have trained attention on the intersection of identity politics with structurally induced vulnerabilities. In particular, the related phenomena of Brexit and Trumpism have wrenched white industrial workers and communities into the spotlight as once-powerful groups who have been politically and economically 'left behind' by the acceleration of globalised neoliberalism and multicultural politics since the 1970s.[60] This both suggests powerful intersections and reveals disjunctures between white workers internationally and within South Africa. These touchpoints start to demonstrate the continued transnational potential of white South African workers as historical subject matter.

Extricating white workers from the historiographical oblivion into which they have been cast in most histories of late- and postapartheid South Africa would serve to reinsert class into a scholarship that is at present largely dominated by racial frames of understanding. This chapter has argued that, in addition to uncovering rich new aspects of historical experience and history from below, this approach also offers the opportunity to reexamine older certainties and uncover new perspectives on such matters as the history of capitalism, class formation and the state in South Africa, and the extent and limits of ethnic and racial identification, while it would also facilitate the critical reexamination of existing historical explanations and narratives surrounding apartheid society, the transition and the postapartheid denouement.

Notes

1 D. Posel, 'Race as Common Sense: Racial Classification in Twentieth-Century South Africa', *African Studies Review*, 44 (2) 2001, 87–113.
2 R. Southall, *The New Black Middle Class in South Africa* (Auckland Park: Jacana, 2016).
3 S. Terreblanche, *A History of Inequality in South Africa: 1652–2002* (Pietermaritzburg: University of Kwa-Zulu-Natal Press, 2003); J. Seekings and N. Nattrass, *Class, Race, and Inequality in South Africa* (New Haven, CT: Yale University Press, 2005). For recent statistics on the intersection of race and wealth, see S. Mbewe and I. Woolard, *Cross-Sectional Features of Wealth Inequality in South Africa: Evidence from The National Income Dynamics Study*, SALDRU Working Papers (Cape Town: SALDRU, 2016).
4 M. Wilson and L. Thompson (eds), *The Oxford History of South Africa*, vol. 1, *South Africa to 1870* (Oxford: Oxford University Press, 1969), and vol. 2, *South Africa 1870–1966* (Oxford: Oxford University Press, 1971).
5 For more on the race–class debate, see C. Saunders, *The Making of the South African Past: Major Historians on Race and Class* (Cape Town: David Philip, 1988); R. Ross, A.K. Mager and B. Nasson, 'Introduction', in R. Ross, A.K. Mager and B. Nasson (eds), *The Cambridge History of South Africa*, vol. 2, *1885–1994* (Cambridge: Cambridge University Press, 2011), 1–16; N. Worden, *The*

Making of Modern South Africa: Conquest, Apartheid, Democracy (Chichester: Wiley-Blackwell, 2012), 1–8.
6 F.A. Johnstone, *Class, Race and Gold: A Study of Class Relations and Racial Discrimination in South Africa* (London: Routledge and Kegan Paul, 1976).
7 R.H. Davies, *Capital, State and White Labour in South Africa 1900–1960: A Historical Materialist Analysis of Class Formation and Class Relations*, Harvester Studies in African Political Economy (Atlantic Highlands, NJ: Humanities Press, 1979).
8 D. O'Meara, *Volkskapitalisme: Class, Capital and Ideology in the Development of Afrikaner Nationalism* (Johannesburg: Ravan, 1983).
9 C. van der Westhuizen, *White Power and the Rise and Fall of the National Party* (Cape Town: Zebra Press, 2007), 31–2. Van der Westhuizen draws heavily on O'Meara's arguments.
10 E.N. Katz, *A Trade Union Aristocracy: A History of White Workers in the Transvaal and the General Strike of 1913* (Johannesburg: African Studies Institute, University of the Witwatersrand, 1976); R. Davies, 'Mining Capital, the State and Unskilled White Workers in South Africa, 1901–1913', *Journal of Southern African Studies*, 3 (1) 1976, 41–69. For critiques of the undifferentiated use of the term 'labour aristocracy', see J. Lewis, *Industrialisation and Trade Union Organisation in South Africa, 1924–1955: The Rise and Fall of the South African Trades and Labour Council* (Cambridge: Cambridge University Press, 1984), 17–18; S.B. Greenberg, *Race and State in Capitalist Development: South Africa in Comparative Perspective* (Johannesburg: Ravan, 1980), 276–7.
11 H. Simson, 'The Myth of the White Working Class in South Africa', *African Affairs*, 4 (2) 1974, 189–203.
12 H. Wolpe, 'The "White Working Class" in South Africa', *Economy and Society*, 5 (2) 1976, 197–240.
13 C. van Onselen, *Studies in the Social and Economic History of the Witwatersrand, 1886–1914: New Nineveh* (Harlow: Longman, 1982); E. Brink, 'Maar 'n Klomp "Factory" Meide': Afrikaner Family and Community on the Witwatersrand during the 1920s', in B. Bozzoli (ed.), *Class, Community and Conflict: South African Perspectives* (Johannesburg: Ravan), 177–208; M. Nicol, '"Joh'burg Hotheads" and the "Gullible Children of Cape Town": The Transvaal Garment Workers' Union's Assault on Low Wages in the Cape Town Clothing Industry, 1930–1931', in Bozzoli, *Class, Community and Conflict*, 209–34; L. Witz, 'A Case of Schizophrenia: The Rise and Fall of the Independent Labour Party', in Bozzoli, *Class, Community and Conflict*, 261–91; A. Grundlingh, '"God het Ons Arme Mense die Houtjies Gegee": Poor White Woodcutters in the Southern Cape Forest Area, ca. 1900–1939', in R. Morrell (ed.), *White but Poor: Essays on the History of Poor Whites in Southern Africa, 1880–1940* (Pretoria: University of South Africa, 1992), 40–56; G. Pirie, 'White Railway Labour in South Africa, 1873–1924', in Morrell, *White but Poor*, 101–14. Also see L. Lange, *White, Poor and Angry: White Working Class Families in Johannesburg* (Aldershot: Ashgate, 2003).

14 E. Brink, 'Man-Made Women: Gender, Class and the Ideology of the Volksmoeder', in C. Walker (ed.), *Women and Gender in Southern Africa to 1945* (London: James Currey, 1990), 273–92; M. du Toit, 'The Domesticity of Afrikaner Nationalism: Volksmoeders and the ACVV, 1904–1929', *Journal of Southern African Studies*, 29 (1) 2003, 155–76; J. Hyslop, 'White Working-Class Women and the Invention of Apartheid: "Purified" Afrikaner Nationalist Agitation against "Mixed" Marriages, 1934–1939', *Journal of African History*, 36 (1) 1995, 57–81; L. Vincent, 'Bread and Honour: White Working Class Women and Afrikaner Nationalism in the 1930s', *Journal of Southern African Studies*, 26 (1) 2000, 61–78; J. Mawbey, 'Afrikaner Women of the Garment Union during the Thirties and Forties', in E. Webster (ed.), *Essays in Southern African Labour History* (Johannesburg: Ravan, 1978), 192–208; I. Berger, 'Solidarity Fragmented: Garment Workers of the Transvaal, 1930–1960', in S. Marks and S. Trapido (eds), *The Politics of Race, Class and Nationalism in Twentieth Century South Africa* (London: Longman, 1987), 124–55; I. Berger, *Threads of Solidarity: Women in South African Industry, 1900–1980* (Bloomington: Indiana University Press, 1992).

15 D. Posel, 'Rethinking the "Race-Class Debate" in South African Historiography', *Social Dynamics: A Journal of African Studies*, 9 (1) 1983, 50–66.

16 M. Lipton, *Capitalism and Apartheid: South Africa, 1910–1984* (Aldershot: Gower, 1985).

17 D. Yudelman, *The Emergence of Modern South Africa: State, Capital, and the Incorporation of Organized Labor on the South African Goldfields, 1902–1939* (London: Greenwood, 1983).

18 E. Webster, *Cast in a Racial Mould: Labour Process and Trade Unionism in the Foundries* (Johannesburg: Ravan, 1985).

19 F. Fukuyama, *The End of History and the Last Man* (New York: Free Press, 1992); S.P. Huntington, *The Clash of Civilizations and the Remaking of the World Order* (New York: Simon and Schuster, 1996).

20 J. Krikler, *The Rand Revolt: The 1922 Insurrection and Racial Killings in South Africa* (Johannesburg: Jonathan Ball, 2005); N. Roos, 'The Springbok and the Skunk: War Veterans and the Politics of Whiteness in South Africa during the 1940s and 1950s', *Journal of Southern African Studies*, 35 (3) 2009, 643–61.

21 D. Roediger, *The Wages of Whiteness: Race and the Making of the American Working Class* (London: Verso, 1991). Krikler and Roediger were later involved in a collaboration addressing the entanglement of race and class in a variety of contexts: W.D. Hund, J. Krikler and D.R. Roediger (eds), *Wages of Whiteness and Racist Symbolic Capital* (Berlin: Lit Verlag, 2010); see also J. Krikler, 'Review Article: Lessons from America: The Writings of David Roediger', *Journal of Southern African Studies*, 20 (4) 1994, 663–9.

22 On 'White Labourism', see J. Hyslop, 'The Imperial Working Class Makes Itself "White": White Labourism in Britain, Australia, and South Africa before the First World War', *Journal of Historical Sociology*, 12 (4) 1999, 399; see also J. Hyslop, 'Scottish Labour, Race, and Southern African Empire c. 1880–1922: A Reply to Kenefick', *International Review of Social History*, 55 (1) 2010, 63–81.

23 See the following, all by J. Hyslop: *The Notorious Syndicalist J.T. Bain: A Scottish Rebel in Colonial South Africa* (Johannesburg: Jacana, 2004); 'The World Voyage of James Keir Hardie: Indian Nationalism, Zulu Insurgency and the British Labour Diaspora, 1907–1908', *Journal of Global History*, 1 (3) 2006, 343–62; '"Undesirable Inhabitant of the Union … Supplying Liquor to Natives": D.F. Malan and the Deportation of South Africa's British and Irish Lumpen Proletarians, 1924–1933', *Kronos*, 40, 2014, 178–97; 'The Strange Death of Liberal England and the Strange Birth of Illiberal South Africa: British Trade Unionists, Indian Labourers and Afrikaner Rebels, 1910–1914', *Labour History Review* 79 (1) 2014, 95–118; 'The Politics of Disembarkation: Empire, Shipping and Labor in the Port of Durban, 1897–1947', *International Labor and Working-Class History*, 93, 2018, 176–200. In addition to Hyslop, see also L. van der Walt, 'The First Globalisation and Transnational Labour Activism in Southern Africa: White Labourism, the IWW and the ICU, 1904–1934', *African Studies*, 66 (2–3) 2007, 223–51; J. Higginson, 'Privileging the Machines: American Engineers, Indentured Chinese and White Workers in South Africa's Deep-Level Gold Mines, 1902–1907', *International Review of Social History*, 52 (1) 2007, 1–34; M. Lake and H. Reynolds, *Drawing the Global Colour Line: White Men's Countries and the International Challenge of Racial Equality* (Cambridge: Cambridge University Press, 2008).

24 Naturally, it also produced a wealth of scholarship on other historical subjects beyond the focus of this chapter, including African workers. For overviews, see Ross *et al.*, 'Introduction', 1–16; B. Freund, 'Labour Studies and Labour History in South Africa: Perspectives from the Apartheid Era and After', *International Review of Social History*, 58 (3) 2013, 493–519.

25 See Davies, Webster and Berger mentioned above.

26 D. O'Meara, *Forty Lost Years: The Apartheid State and the Politics of the National Party, 1948–1994* (Randburg: Ravan, 1996), 74–80; C. Bundy, *Poverty in South Africa: Past and Present* (Auckland Park: Jacana, 2016), 40–53.

27 For an overview, see T. Lodge, 'Resistance and Reform, 1973–1994,' in Ross *et al.*, *Cambridge History of South Africa*, 409–91.

28 H. Giliomee, *The Afrikaners: Biography of a People* (Cape Town: Tafelberg, 2011), 549, 606–8; Van der Westhuizen, *White Power*, 117–18; O'Meara, *Forty Lost Years*, 295–312; Terreblanche, *History of Inequality*, 355.

29 O'Meara, *Forty Lost Years*, 164–6.

30 See, for instance, M. Vestergaard, 'Who's Got the Map? The Negotiation of Afrikaner Identities in Post-Apartheid South Africa', *Daedalus*, 130 (1) 2001, 19–44; M. Steyn, 'Rehabilitating a Whiteness Disgraced: Afrikaner White Talk in Post-apartheid South Africa', *Communication Quarterly*, 52 (2) 2004, 143–69; R. Ballard, 'Assimilation, Emigration, Semigration, and Integration: "White" People's Strategies for Finding a Comfort Zone in Post-apartheid South Africa', in N. Distiller and M. Steyn (eds), *Under Construction: 'Race' and Identity in South Africa Today* (Sandton: Heineman, 2004), 51–66; M. Steyn and D. Foster, 'Repertoires for Talking White: Resistant Whiteness in Post-apartheid

South Africa', *Ethnic and Racial Studies*, 31 (1) 2008, 25–51; C. Verwey and M. Quayle, 'Whiteness, Racism and Afrikaner Identity in Post-apartheid South Africa', *African Affairs*, 111 (445) 2012, 551–75.
31 O'Meara, *Forty Lost Years*, 136–40.
32 J.L. Sadie, *The Fall and Rise of the Afrikaner in the South African Economy* (Stellenbosch: University of Stellenbosch Annale, 2002), 54.
33 South African Institute of Race Relations, *A Survey of Race Relations in South Africa 1970* (Johannesburg: SAIRR, 1971), 81, 126.
34 Terreblanche, *History of inequality*, 391.
35 S. Bouwer, '*Orkney Snork Nie!*: Onderweg na 'n Lesing', *Communicare: Journal for Communication Sciences in Southern Africa*, 10 (2) 1991, 19. Indeed, Bouwer notes the imperative for both the SABC (South African Broadcasting Corporation) and the series producer (albeit for divergent ideological reasons) to depict an 'ordinary' Afrikaans family.
36 Wikipedia contributors, 'Orkney Snork Nie', *Wikipedia, The Free Encyclopedia*, https://en.wikipedia.org/wiki/Orkney_Snork_Nie (accessed 17 Jan. 2020).
37 J. Goosen, *'n Pawpaw vir My Darling* (Cape Town: Kwela Boeke, 2002).
38 L. van Nierop, *Daar Doer in die Fliek: 'n Persoonlike Blik op die Geskiedenis van die Afrikaanse Rolprent* (Pretoria: Protea Boekhuis, 2016), 376–83.
39 '*'n Pawpaw vir My Darling* Earns More than a Million at the Box Office', Media Update, 13 Jan. 2016, www.mediaupdate.co.za/media/91849/n-pawpaw-vir-my-darling-earns-more-than-a-million-at-the-box-office (accessed 17 Jan. 2020).
40 See, for instance, L. Viljoen, 'Postcolonialism and Recent Women's Writing in Afrikaans', *World Literature Today*, 70 (1) 1996, 63–72; M. Heyns, 'The Whole Country's Truth: Confession and Narrative in Recent White South African Writing', *Modern Fiction Studies*, 46, 2000, 407–54; M. Brophy, 'Shadowing Afrikaner Nationalism: Jungian Archetypes, Incest, and the Uncanny in Marlene van Niekerk's *Triomf*', *Journal of Literary Studies*, 22 (1–2) 2006, 96–112; K. Barris, 'The Afrikaner Grotesque: Mediating between Colonial Self and Colonised Other in Three Post-apartheid South African Novels', *English in Africa*, 41 (1) 2014, 91–107.
41 See, for instance, M. Lewis, *Performing Whitely in the Postcolony: Afrikaners in South African Theatrical and Public Life* (Iowa City: University of Iowa Press, 2016); H. Marx and V.C. Milton, 'Bastardised Whiteness: "Zef"-Culture, Die Antwoord and the Reconfiguration of Contemporary Afrikaans Identities', *Social Identities*, 17 (6) 2011, 723–45; Roundtable on Die Antwoord, *Safundi*, 13 (3–4) 2012, 393–423.
42 B. Freund, 'White People Fit for a New South Africa? State Planning, Policy and Social Response in the Parastatal Cities of the Vaal, 1940–1990', in D. Money and D. van Zyl-Hermann (eds), *Rethinking White Societies in Southern Africa, 1930s–1990s* (Abingdon: Routledge, 2020), 88.
43 B. Freund, *Twentieth Century South Africa: A Developmental History* (Cambridge: Cambridge University Press, 2019).
44 N. Roos, 'Work Colonies and South African Historiography', *Social History*, 36 (1) 2011, 74.

45 A. Teppo, *The Making of a Good White: Historical Ethnography of the Rehabilitation of Poor Whites in a Suburb of Cape Town* (Helsinki: University of Helsinki, 2004).
46 Freund, 'White People', 90; N. Roos, 'Alcohol Panic, Social Engineering, and Some Reflections on the Management of Whites in Early Apartheid Society, 1948–1960', *Historical Journal*, 58 (4) 2015, 1167–89.
47 O'Meara, *Forty Lost Years*, 78–9, 120, 139–40; S. Terreblanche, *Lost in Transformation? South Africa's Search for a New Future since 1986* (Johannesburg: KMM Review Publishing, 2012), 54; A. Grundlingh, '"Are We Afrikaners Getting Too Rich?" Cornucopia and Change in Afrikanerdom in the 1960s', *Journal of Historical Sociology*, 21 (2–3) 2008, 159.
48 J. Hyslop, 'Why Did Apartheid's Supporters Capitulate? "Whiteness", Class and Consumption in Urban South Africa, 1985–1995', *Society in Transition*, 31 (1) 2000, 36. See also Van der Westhuizen, *White Power*, 110–8.
49 W. Visser, *Van MWU tot Solidariteit: Geskiedenis van die Mynwerkersunie 1902–2002* (Centurion: Solidariteit, 2008).
50 D. van Zyl-Hermann, 'White Workers and the Unravelling of Racial Citizenship in Late Apartheid South Africa', in Money and Van Zyl-Hermann, *Rethinking White Societies*, 194–214.
51 These arguments are presented in D. van Zyl-Hermann, *Privileged Precariat: White Workers and South Africa's Long Transition to Majority Rule* (Cambridge: Cambridge University Press, 2021).
52 I. du Plessis, 'Living in "Jan Bom": Making and Imagining Lives after Apartheid in a Council Housing Scheme in Johannesburg', *Current Sociology*, 52 (5) 2004, 879–908.
53 J. Smuts, 'Male Trouble: Independent Women and Male Dependency in a White Working-Class Suburb of Pretoria', *Agenda*, 20 (68) 2006, 80–7.
54 J. Sharp, 'Market, Race and Nation: History of the White Working Class in Pretoria', in K. Hart and J. Sharp (eds), *People, Money and Power in Economic Crisis: Perspectives from the Global South* (New York: Berghahn Books, 2015), 82–105; J. Sharp and S. van Wyk, 'Beyond the Market: White Workers in Pretoria', in K. Hart (ed.), *Economy for and against Democracy* (New York: Berghahn Books, 2015), 120–36.
55 Sharp and Van Wyk, 'Beyond the Market'.
56 See Van Zyl-Hermann, *Privileged Precariat*.
57 Quoted in D. van Zyl-Hermann, 'Make Afrikaners Great Again! National Populism, Democracy and the New White Minority Politics in Post-apartheid South Africa', *Ethnic and Racial Studies*, 41 (15) 2018, 2677.
58 In 2015, Solidarity claimed over 320,000 members. In interviews, movement executives would casually extend this figure to claim that, if one included the households of official members, Solidarity represented some 1 million Afrikaners – a powerful claim off an overall national population of some 2.7 million white, Afrikaans-speaking South Africans.
59 Van Zyl-Hermann, 'Make Afrikaners Great Again!'
60 For an overview and critique of emerging arguments around the political role of the white working class, see G.K. Bhambra, 'Brexit, Trump, and "Methodological

Whiteness": On the Misrecognition of Race and Class', *British Journal of Sociology*, 68 (S1) 2017, 214–32.

Bibliography

Ballard, R. (2004) 'Assimilation, Emigration, Semigration, and Integration: "White" People's Strategies for Finding a Comfort Zone in Post-apartheid South Africa', in N. Distiller and M.E. Steyn (eds), *Under Construction: 'Race' and Identity in South Africa Today*. Sandton: Heinemann.

Barris, K. (2014) 'The Afrikaner Grotesque: Mediating between Colonial Self and Colonised Other in Three Post-apartheid South African Novels', *English in Africa*, 41 (1).

Berger, I. (1987) 'Solidarity Fragmented: Garment Workers of the Transvaal, 1930–1960', in S. Marks and S. Trapido (eds) *The Politics of Race, Class and Nationalism in Twentieth Century South Africa*. London: Longman.

Berger, I. (1992) *Threads of Solidarity: Women in South African Industry, 1900–1980*. Bloomington: Indiana University Press.

Bhambra, G.K. (2017) 'Brexit, Trump, and "Methodological Whiteness": On the Misrecognition of Race and Class', *British Journal of Sociology*, 68 (S1).

Bouwer, S. (1991) '*Orkney Snork Nie!*: Onderweg na 'n Lesing', *Communicare: Journal for Communication Sciences in Southern Africa*, 10 (2).

Bozzoli, B. (ed.) (1987) *Class, Community and Conflict: South African Perspectives*. Johannesburg: Ravan.

Brink, E. (1987) 'Maar'n Klomp "Factory" Meide: Afrikaner Family and Community on the Witwatersrand during the 1920s', in Bozzoli, *Class, Community and Conflict*.

Brink, E. (1990) 'Man-Made Women: Gender, Class and the Ideology of the Volksmoeder', in C. Walker (ed.), *Women and Gender in Southern Africa to 1945*. London: James Currey.

Brophy, M. (2006) 'Shadowing Afrikaner Nationalism: Jungian Archetypes, Incest, and the Uncanny in Marlene van Niekerk's *Triomf*', *Journal of Literary Studies*, 22 (1–2).

Bundy, C. (2016) *Poverty in South Africa: Past and Present*. Auckland Park: Jacana.

Davies, R. (1976) 'Mining Capital, the State and Unskilled White Workers in South Africa, 1901–1913', *Journal of Southern African Studies*, 3 (1).

Davies, R. (1979) *Capital, State and White Labour in South Africa 1900–1960: A Historical Materialist Analysis of Class Formation and Class Relations*, Harvester Studies in African Political Economy. Atlantic Highlands, NJ: Humanities Press.

Du Plessis, I. (2004) 'Living in "Jan Bom": Making and Imagining Lives after Apartheid in a Council Housing Scheme in Johannesburg', *Current Sociology*, 52 (5).

Du Toit, M. (2003) 'The Domesticity of Afrikaner Nationalism: Volksmoeders and the ACVV, 1904–1929', *Journal of Southern African Studies*, 29 (1).

Freund, B. (2013) 'Labour Studies and Labour History in South Africa: Perspectives from the Apartheid Era and After', *International Review of Social History*, 58 (3).

Freund, B. (2019) *Twentieth-Century South Africa: A Developmental History.* Cambridge: Cambridge University Press.

Freund, B. (2020) 'White People Fit for a New South Africa? State Planning, Policy and Social Response in the Parastatal Cities of the Vaal, 1940–1990', in Money and Van Zyl-Hermann, *Rethinking White Societies.*

Fukuyama, F. (1992) *The End of History and the Last Man.* New York: Free Press.

Giliomee, H. (2011) *The Afrikaners: Biography of a People.* Cape Town: Tafelberg.

Goosen, J. (2002) *'n Pawpaw vir My Darling.* Cape Town: Kwela Boeke.

Greenberg, S.B. (1980) *Race and State in Capitalist Development: South Africa in Comparative Perspective.* Johannesburg: Ravan.

Grundlingh, A. (1992) '"God het Ons Arme Mense die Houtjies Gegee": Poor White Woodcutters in the Southern Cape Forest Area, ca. 1900–1939', in Morrell, *White but Poor.*

Grundlingh, A. (2008) '"Are We Afrikaners Getting Too Rich?" Cornucopia and Change in Afrikanerdom in the 1960s', *Journal of Historical Sociology,* 21 (2–3).

Heyns, M. (2000) 'The Whole Country's Truth: Confession and Narrative in Recent White South African Writing', *Modern Fiction Studies,* 46.

Higginson, J. (2007) 'Privileging the Machines: American Engineers, Indentured Chinese and White Workers in South Africa's Deep-Level Gold Mines, 1902–1907', *International Review of Social History,* 52 (1).

Hund, W.D., J. Krikler and D.R. Roediger (eds) (2010) *Wages of Whiteness and Racist Symbolic Capital.* Berlin: Lit Verlag.

Huntington, S.P. (1996) *The Clash of Civilizations and the Remaking of World Order.* New York: Simon and Schuster.

Hyslop, J. (1995) 'White Working-Class Women and the Invention of Apartheid: "Purified" Afrikaner Nationalist Agitation for Legislation against "Mixed" Marriages, 1934–1939', *Journal of African History,* 36 (1).

Hyslop, J. (1999) 'The Imperial Working Class Makes Itself "White": White Labourism in Britain, Australia, and South Africa before the First World War', *Journal of Historical Sociology,* 12 (4).

Hyslop, J. (2000) 'Why Did Apartheid's Supporters Capitulate? "Whiteness", Class and Consumption in Urban South Africa, 1985–1995', *Society in Transition,* 31 (1).

Hyslop, J. (2004) *The Notorious Syndicalist J.T. Bain: A Scottish Rebel in Colonial South Africa.* Johannesburg: Jacana.

Hyslop, J. (2006) 'The World Voyage of James Keir Hardie: Indian Nationalism, Zulu Insurgency and the British Labour Diaspora 1907–1908', *Journal of Global History,* 1 (3).

Hyslop, J. (2010) 'Scottish Labour, Race, and Southern African Empire, c.1880–1922: A Reply to Kenefick', *International Review of Social History,* 55 (1).

Hyslop, J. (2014) 'The Strange Death of Liberal England and the Strange Birth of Illiberal South Africa: British Trade Unionists, Indian Labourers and Afrikaner Rebels, 1910–1914', *Labour History Review,* 79 (1).

Hyslop, J. (2014) '"Undesirable Inhabitant of the Union … Supplying Liquor to Natives": D. F. Malan and the Deportation of South Africa's British and Irish Lumpen Proletarians, 1924–1933', *Kronos,* 40.

Hyslop, J. (2018) 'The Politics of Disembarkation: Empire, Shipping and Labor in the Port of Durban, 1897–1947', *International Labor and Working-Class History*, 93.

Johnstone, F.A. (1976) *Class, Race and Gold: A Study of Class Relations and Racial Discrimination in South Africa*. London: Routledge and Kegan Paul.

Katz, E.N. (1976) *A Trade Union Aristocracy: A History of White Workers in the Transvaal and the General Strike of 1913*. Johannesburg: African Studies Institute, University of the Witwatersrand.

Krikler, J. (1994) 'Review Article: Lessons from America: The Writings of David Roediger', *Journal of Southern African Studies*, 20 (4).

Krikler, J. (2005) *The Rand Revolt: The 1922 Insurrection and Racial Killings in South Africa*. Johannesburg: Jonathan Ball.

Lake, M., and H. Reynolds (2008) *Drawing the Global Colour Line: White Men's Countries and the International Challenge of Racial Equality*. Cambridge: Cambridge University Press.

Lange, L. (2003) *White, Poor and Angry: White Working Class Families in Johannesburg*. Aldershot: Ashgate.

Lewis, J. (1984) *Industrialisation and Trade Union Organization in South Africa, 1924–1955: The Rise and Fall of the South African Trades and Labour Council*. Cambridge: Cambridge University Press.

Lewis, M. (2016) *Performing Whitely in the Postcolony: Afrikaners in South African Theatrical and Public Life*. Iowa City: University of Iowa Press.

Lipton, M. (1985) *Capitalism and Apartheid: South Africa, 1910–1984*. Aldershot: Gower.

Lodge, T. (2011) 'Resistance and Reform, 1973–1994', in Ross, Mager and Nasson, *Cambridge History of South Africa*.

Marx, H., and V.C. Milton (2011) 'Bastardised Whiteness: 'Zef'-Culture, *Die Antwoord* and the Reconfiguration of Contemporary Afrikaans Identities', *Social Identities*, 17 (6).

Mawbey, J. (1978) 'Afrikaner Women of the Garment Union during the Thirties and Forties', in E. Webster (ed.), *Essays in Southern African Labour History*. Johannesburg: Ravan.

Mbewe, S., and I. Woolard (2016) *Cross-Sectional Features of Wealth Inequality in South Africa: Evidence from the National Income Dynamics Study*. SALDRU Working Papers. Cape Town: SALDRU.

Money, D., and D. van Zyl-Hermann (eds) (2020) *Rethinking White Societies in Southern Africa: 1930s–1990s*. Abingdon: Routledge.

Morrell, R. (ed.) (1992) *White but Poor: Essays on the History of Poor Whites in Southern Africa, 1880–1940*. Pretoria: University of South Africa.

Nicol, M. (1987) '"Joh'burg Hotheads" and the "Gullible Children of Cape Town": The Transvaal Garment Workers' Union's Assault on Low Wages in the Cape Town Clothing Industry, 1930–1931', in Bozzoli, *Class, Community and Conflict*.

''n Pawpaw vir My Darling Earns More than a Million at the Box Office' (2016) Media Update, 13 Jan., www.mediaupdate.co.za/media/91849/n-pawpaw-vir-my-darling-earns-more-than-a-million-at-the-box-office (accessed 17 Jan. 2020).

O'Meara, D. (1983) *Volkskapitalisme: Class, Capital and Ideology in the Development of Afrikaner Nationalism, 1934–1948*. Johannesburg: Ravan.

O'Meara, D. (1996) *Forty Lost Years: The Apartheid State and the Politics of the National Party, 1948–1994*. Randburg: Ravan.

Pirie, G. (1992) 'White Railway Labour in South Africa, 1873–1924', in Morrell, *White but Poor*.

Posel, D. (1983) 'Rethinking the "Race-Class Debate" in South African Historiography', *Social Dynamics: A Journal of African Studies*, 9 (1).

Posel, D. (2001) 'Race as Common Sense: Racial Classification in Twentieth-Century South Africa', *African Studies Review*, 44 (2).

Roediger, D.R. (1991) *The Wages of Whiteness: Race and the Making of the American Working Class*. London: Verso.

Roos, N. (2009) 'The Springbok and the Skunk: War Veterans and the Politics of Whiteness in South Africa during the 1940s and 1950s', *Journal of Southern African Studies*, 35 (3).

Roos, N. (2011) 'Work Colonies and South African Historiography', *Social History*, 36 (1).

Roos, N. (2015) 'Alcohol Panic, Social Engineering, and Some Reflections on the Management of Whites in Early Apartheid Society, 1948–1960' *Historical Journal*, 58 (4).

Ross, R., A.K. Mager and B. Nasson (eds) (2011) *The Cambridge History of South Africa*, vol. 2, *1885–1994*. Cambridge: Cambridge University Press.

Ross, R., A.K. Mager and B. Nasson (2011) 'Introduction', in *Cambridge History of South Africa*.

'Roundtable on *Die Antwoord*' (2012) *Safundi*, 13 (3–4).

Sadie, J.L. (2002) *The Fall and Rise of the Afrikaner in the South African Economy*. Stellenbosch: University of Stellenbosch Annale.

Saunders, C. (1988) *The Making of the South African Past: Major Historians on Race and Class*. Cape Town: David Philip.

Seekings, J., and N. Nattrass (2005) *Class, Race, and Inequality in South Africa*. New Haven, CT: Yale University Press.

Sharp, J. (2015) 'Market, Race and Nation: History of the White Working Class in Pretoria', in K. Hart and J. Sharp (eds), *People, Money, and Power in the Economic Crisis: Perspectives from the Global South*. New York: Berghahn Books.

Sharp, J., and S. van Wyk (2015) 'Beyond the Market: White Workers in Pretoria', in K. Hart (ed.), *Economy for and against Democracy*. New York: Berghahn Books.

Simson, H. (1974) 'The Myth of the White Working Class in South Africa', *African Affairs*, 4 (2).

Smuts, J. (2006) 'Male Trouble: Independent Women and Male Dependency in a White Working-Class Suburb of Pretoria', *Agenda*, 20 (68).

South African Institute of Race Relations (1971) *A Survey of Race Relations in South Africa 1970*. Johannesburg: SAIRR.

Southall, R. (2016) *The New Black Middle Class in South Africa*. Auckland Park: Jacana.

Steyn, M. (2004) 'Rehabilitating a Whiteness Disgraced: Afrikaner White Talk in Post-apartheid South Africa', *Communication Quarterly*, 52 (2).

Steyn, M., and D. Foster (2008) 'Repertoires for Talking White: Resistant Whiteness in Post-apartheid South Africa', *Ethnic and Racial Studies*, 31 (1).
Teppo, A. (2004) *The Making of a Good White: A Historical Ethnography of the Rehabilitation of Poor Whites in a Suburb of Cape Town*. Helsinki: University of Helsinki.
Terreblanche, S. (2003) *A History of Inequality in South Africa, 1652–2002*. Pietermaritzburg: University of KwaZulu-Natal Press.
Terreblanche, S. (2012) *Lost in Transformation: South Africa's Search for a New Future since 1986*. Johannesburg: KMM Review Publishing.
Van der Walt, L. (2007) 'The First Globalisation and Transnational Labour Activism in Southern Africa: White Labourism, the IWW, and the ICU, 1904–1934', *African Studies*, 66 (2–3).
Van der Westhuizen, C. (2007) *White Power and the Rise and Fall of the National Party*. Cape Town: Zebra Press.
Van Nierop, L. (2016) *Daar Doer in die Fliek: 'n Persoonlike Blik op die Geskiedenis van die Afrikaanse Rolprent*. Pretoria: Protea Boekhuis.
Van Onselen, C. (1982) *Studies in the Social and Economic History of the Witwatersrand 1886–1914: New Nineveh*. Harlow: Longman.
Van Zyl-Hermann, D. (2018) 'Make Afrikaners Great Again! National Populism, Democracy and the New White Minority Politics in Post-apartheid South Africa', *Ethnic and Racial Studies*, 41 (15).
Van Zyl-Hermann, D. (2020) 'White Workers and the Unravelling of Racial Citizenship in Late Apartheid South Africa', in Money and Van Zyl-Hermann, *Rethinking White Societies*.
Van Zyl-Hermann, D. (2021) *Privileged Precariat: White Workers and South Africa's Long Transition to Majority Rule*. Cambridge: Cambridge University Press.
Verwey, C., and M. Quayle (2012) 'Whiteness, Racism, and Afrikaner Identity in Post-apartheid South Africa', *African Affairs*, 111 (445).
Vestergaard, M. (2001) 'Who's Got the Map? The Negotiation of Afrikaner Identities in Post-apartheid South Africa', *Daedalus*, 130 (1).
Viljoen, L. (1996) 'Postcolonialism and Recent Women's Writing in Afrikaans', *World Literature Today*, 70 (1).
Vincent, L. (2000) 'Bread and Honour: White Working Class Women and Afrikaner Nationalism in the 1930s', *Journal of Southern African Studies*, 26 (1).
Visser, W. (2008) *Van MWU tot Solidariteit: Geskiedenis van die Mynwerkersunie, 1902–2002*. Centurion: Solidariteit.
Webster, E. (1985) *Cast in a Racial Mould: Labour Process and Trade Unionism in the Foundries*. Johannesburg: Ravan.
Wikipedia contributors, 'Orkney Snork Nie', *Wikipedia, The Free Encyclopedia*, https://en.wikipedia.org/wiki/Orkney_Snork_Nie (accessed 17 Jan. 2020).
Wilson, M., and L. Thompson (eds) (1969) *The Oxford History of South Africa*, vol. 1, *South Africa to 1870*. Oxford: Oxford University Press.
Wilson, M., and L. Thompson (eds) (1971) *The Oxford History of South Africa*, vol. 2, *South Africa 1870–1966*. Oxford: Oxford University Press.
Witz, L. (1987) 'A Case of Schizophrenia: The Rise and Fall of the Independent Labour Party', in Bozzoli, *Class, Community and Conflict*.

Wolpe, H. (1976) 'The "White Working Class" in South Africa', *Economy and Society*, 5 (2).
Worden, N. (2012) *The Making of Modern South Africa: Conquest, Apartheid, Democracy*. Chichester: Wiley-Blackwell.
Yudelman, D. (1983) *The Emergence of Modern South Africa: State, Capital, and the Incorporation of Organized Labor on the South African Gold Fields, 1902–1939*. London: Greenwood.

10

The transnational nation: South African history beyond and across borders

Rob Skinner

National histories do not exist in a vacuum, but emerge out of interactions between local, regional and global processes.[1] As such, South African historical experiences have, over the past century, been shaped by developments that might be regarded as universal in their impact. The consolidation, weakening and collapse of European empires, the emergence of a world order shaped by codependence between nation states, the increasing density and complexity of transnational networks, can be presented as essential ingredients of South African history that accentuate the connections and continuities between the national and the global. Even though a 'myth of South African exceptionalism' has been a filter in some accounts of historical change and present-day experiences, such accounts tend to call upon international and global comparisons rather than disavow them.[2]

And yet, in recent years, sceptical and contrary views of globalisation and 'globalism' have become a feature of debates within the field of global history, fuelled at least in part by the inequalities that have been heightened and amplified in an interconnected world. Jeremy Adelman's 2017 essay in *Aeon* magazine set out the field's trajectory as a rapidly rising hegemonic force, lauded by some as providing the intellectual basis for a new form of global identity, just as the nation-centred histories of the nineteenth and twentieth centuries served the rise of the nation state. Adelman, ultimately, did not reject global history but called instead for approaches that paid attention to disjunctures and particularisms beyond the Anglocentric orientation of the field.[3] Similarly, although more provocatively, David Bell's review of *A World Connecting* suggested that global history had simply run its course and historians needed to return to 'small spaces'.[4] Prompted by these trenchant interventions, Richard Drayton and David Motadel launched their own defence of global history as being not in decline but rather 'dynamic' and 'of pressing importance'.[5] Perhaps the strongest critique of global history has been that it has often reproduced rather than challenged the unequal relations of intellectual power between the academies of the Global North and the peripheral voices of scholars based in Africa, Asia and Latin America.[6]

While many are now wary of narratives that seem to rehearse the 'Rise of the West', global historical approaches too often marginalise those who occupy spaces on the edges of the 'world system'. Global histories of slavery, for example, have tended to centre on transoceanic exchanges, with the African continent placed on the margins.[7]

Nonetheless, I would argue that global history has much to offer historians of South Africa. South Africa has never been a 'small space', but a broad territory of disparate historical experiences, whose political geography has been defined by the interactions between both internal and external centres of power and influence. Political borders are arbitrary, and perhaps none more so than those established to serve colonial interests. In the nineteenth and twentieth centuries, epistemological practices of mapping, forms of governmentality designed to serve the material interests of distant powers and the contingencies of freelance imperialism created political territories whose borders became reified as a fixed and meaningful definition of the boundaries of 'the nation'. Statues may fall, but the legacy of Rhodes remains hardwired into the existence of South Africa, traced along its northern boundary.[8] Transnational history thus reveals the essential fantasy of 'border thinking', but also, arguably, it forms the necessary precondition for the decolonisation of South African history.[9]

Furthermore, the 'stuff' – tangible and intangible – that crosses these borders has had significant impact on the development of social, political and cultural life. Structures of belief and systems of knowledge are shaped and reshaped by ideas, information and values that travel with the movement of people and also, increasingly, by digital communication. These packets of knowledge have, moreover, been crucial to the development of localised narratives about the past and visions of the future, offering a major stimulus to the crafting, via 'imagined communities', of national pasts.[10] The elements of a national history have emerged through a process of mediation between local experiences and others of diverse and dispersed origins. Racial and ethnic identity, practices of colonial administration, discourses of state power, symbols of modern cultural meaning and the practices of everyday life are informed by interactions between the proximate and the distant, between 'here' and 'there'. Global and transnational histories seek to make these interactions manifest in historical interpretation. In short, ideas, beliefs and practices permeate national boundaries, and interactions between 'global' and 'local' are constitutive of national histories.

South Africa in imperial and global history

Empires have occupied a significant place in recent histories of globalisation, just as processes of connection and exchange have helped to reframe accounts of imperialism.[11] In particular, South Africa features prominently in John Darwin's detailed account of the construction of a British imperial 'world-system'. Darwin's study positions empire as a foundational structure of globalisation and thus global history, within which South African history is framed with reference to imperial wars, ideas of Dominion and Commonwealth, and the role of empire in twentieth-century world conflicts. South Africa was, in Darwin's assessment, the 'weakest link' in British settler colonialism, for the presence of both a significant non-British white population and a resilient indigenous majority meant that imperial policies were stretched between models of self-governance (for settler communities) and direct control (over African polities).[12] In short, South Africa was an imperial anomaly. In this account, the narrative of South African history from a world perspective is one shaped by metropole and settler; Briton and Boer; convention, treaty and dominion. This is not to argue that the 'imperial factor' should be minimised in global histories, but the task of mapping the power and influence of imperial networks does not necessarily imply that world history is synonymous with imperial history. It is possible to view British imperialism as foundational to the development of globalisation *and* interrogate imperial history from multiple vantage points. As Antoinette Burton notes, we are able to consider the South African War as 'a global war whose center was not self-evidently the British empire' and consider, for example, how the war was perceived from the perspective of China.[13] For the Chinese journalist (and later politician) Liang Qichao, the South African War exemplified the systematic destruction of indigenous economies and political structures undertaken by Western imperialism at the turn of the twentieth century. The pattern of conquest through both territorial conquest and the procurement of concessionary rights evoked comparisons between the war in the Transvaal, the Philippine-American conflict and the suppression of the Boxer Rebellion in China.[14]

Global and imperial histories overlap, but do not coincide. South African historical experiences have nevertheless tended to be offered as exemplars of the globality of British imperialism. In his magisterial account of the multicentred origins of modernity, *The Birth of the Modern World*, Christopher Bayly sought to decentre a rise-of-the-West narrative, while acknowledging the dominant dynamics of Western economic and political power. Within this framework, familiar themes in South African history are foregrounded, but recontextualised, as part of a global process of political transformation. The South African War, again, becomes a cardinal illustration of the process by which the world of nation states emerged in the late nineteenth century. Bayly also locates southern African settler colonialism within a larger 'white deluge' and the interconnected processes of marginalisation and destruction of indigenous societies across the world the nineteenth century.[15] Similarly, James Belich presents South African examples as part of a global narrative of violent dispossession, incomplete assimilationist endeavours and emerging scientific discourses of difference.[16] The concept of a 'white deluge' as descriptive of a global synthesis of settler expansionism and the creation of 'native peoples' in the nineteenth century is persuasive, but tends to obscure significant local characteristics: if global histories simply remind us of the ways in which white settlers conquered indigenous populations and developed systems of knowledge that 'explained' these processes, they run the risk of reproducing colonial relations of power.

A similar approach is evident in Jurgen Osterhammel's weighty analysis of the global transformations of the nineteenth century *The Transformation of the World*. South African history is encountered in the work in a comparative analysis of 'frontier processes' (that is, the expansion of settler control through warfare and conquest of indigenous peoples) in the Americas. In Osterhammel's account, while America's 'Indian Wars' and the establishment of settler control over the South African interior were largely completed by the 1880s, the agricultural economy of African societies, and the conjuncture of conquest and the rapid development of mineral-based industrialisation, meant that the experiences of the conquered in South Africa diverged significantly from their Native American counterparts.[17] As a comparative account of colonial conquest, *The Transformation of the World* does much to position South African experiences within a broader historical framework, even where Osterhammel's primary points of reference configure settler communities as the principal agents of change. Moreover, while Osterhammel concedes that the concept of the frontier 'is only intermittently applicable to South Africa', he argues that, after 1948, the 'political and cultural values of the Boer frontier took hold of the entire state', passing over decades of scholarship exploring the relationships between capitalism, modernity, segregation and apartheid.[18]

Other recent works have highlighted the overlapping, but distinct, conceptual frameworks employed by imperial and global histories. Moreover, imperial history might be considered a valuable enterprise in its own right, rather than being subsumed within global history. Like global history, imperial histories can emphasise connectedness, but the interactions they reveal are often 'less than global' in important ways. These include that they circumnavigated the globe but were not globally all-encompassing, and, moreover, individuals operating within webs of empire did not conceive of themselves as acting globally, but as subjects of empire and nation.[19] Yet as Potter and Saha suggest, recent histories of empire have demonstrated the value of transnational approaches and global frameworks. This has helped to reveal new dimensions of South African history.

During the 1990s and early 2000s, imperial historians responded to Ann Stoler and Frederick Cooper's plea that histories of colonialism should combine imperial metropolis and colonial periphery in a 'single analytical field'.[20] Their work challenged approaches that treated national and imperial histories as discrete fields, or imagined a diffusion of political power, ideas and culture from an imperial centre. In the context of South African history, one of the first works to examine colonialism as a series of interconnected fields of exchange was Alan Lester's *Imperial Networks* (2001), which reframed nineteenth-century missionary histories as narratives of the transnational construction of new forms of governmentality.[21] His work demonstrated the entanglements of politics in London and the Cape in the first half of the nineteenth century. Like Catherine Hall and other proponents of the 'new' imperial history, Lester showed that activists in the Cape and their metropolitan supporters and sponsors mutually shaped a discourse of humanitarianism.[22]

For Lester, these developments were cast not within a unitary and static single field but in a dynamic network of individuals and organisations that mediated the exchange of ideas across Britain's imperial territories. In subsequent work, notably in collaboration with David Lambert, he explored the ways in which colonial philanthropists and their metropolitan correspondents (these networks often centred on key figures in the powerful antislavery movement) established a web of knowledge that connected London, the Caribbean, the Cape, Australia and New Zealand.[23]

During the first half of the nineteenth century, this network seemed able to translate local indigenous grievances into a humanitarian discourse; it also operated in tension with settler discourses and projects in which the extensive reach of colonial philanthropic networks represented a significant threat. These accounts, cast more as historical geography rather than global history, nonetheless helped to locate South African histories of humanitarianism not only in the context of local colonial endeavours, geared towards establishing relations of power and domination, but within a multiplicity of forms of global colonial power. Comparative accounts of nineteenth-century humanitarian endeavours demonstrate, for example, that the settlement at Kat River in the Cape, and other nineteenth-century sites of humanitarian intervention like Frere Town in Kenya, evoke parallels with contemporary provisions for displaced peoples in Africa and the 'persistence of certain visions of engagement with Africa'.[24] Imperial histories of missionary encounters thus became global and transnational histories of humanitarian discourses.

These histories of humanitarian encounters demonstrated the ways in which South African historical experiences could be located within broader accounts of the processes by which categories of colonial 'others' were constituted. Moreover, they highlighted the multidirectional cultural and social impact of missionary endeavours. Notwithstanding the real inequalities of power inherent in colonial society, South African evangelical Christianity was formed and transformed in mutual exchanges of belief and practice.[25]

In her pioneering account of the transnational cultural journeys of John Bunyan's *Pilgrim's Progress*, Isabel Hofmeyr elaborated an approach to the study of cultural 'diffusion' that sought to confront the assumptions that had underpinned histories of supposedly parochial texts.[26] Hofmeyr's research addressed the seemingly paradoxical process by which the narrowly nationalist writings of Bunyan became 'internationalised'. In parallel with global historians' efforts to interpret interactions between the universal and the local, Hofmeyr's transnational cultural history sought to understand not why Bunyan's text became 'universal', but what the process of its diffusion tells us about the ways that cultural expressions are formed and reformed as they spread internationally. Readers in southern Africa encountered *Pilgrim's Progress* in numerous forms: abridged, extracted and translated. These additions in turn made sense of the text in ways that called into question the notion that an unchanging core meaning of the text had migrated globally from seventeenth-century England. Moreover, Hofmeyr argued that the export and translation of Bunyan's text in a sense made it 'English', suggesting that we should consider such English texts as colonial products. Thus, while historical geographies of imperial networks suggested that colonial policies and ideologies were enmeshed in a wider imperial web, Hofmeyr's work illuminated the ways that these webs created and reinterpreted the meanings of the ideas, values and prescriptions for action, rather than merely communicating them.

In somewhat different ways, similar concerns around the global communication and transnational circulation of ideas across borders were paralleled in international studies of twentieth-century South African politics. In the mid-1990s, social and political scientists began to examine interlinked networks of activism and their role in defining new global norms that shaped relations between state and extra-state actors. Seminal works such as Keck and Sikkink's *Activists beyond Borders* drew on the example of global antiapartheid as a case study in the development of transnational forms of activism, which, the authors argued, became a significant dimension of nonstate political organisation after 1945.[27] Similarly, Audie Klotz examined the formative role of debates around sanctions against apartheid as part of the development of a global norm of antiracism, which, she argued, came to be a determining element in international relations.[28] As Bayly suggested, the Sharpeville shootings 'seemed to point to an international struggle against racial discrimination', and apartheid ultimately met its demise because it was 'a system abhorrent to peoples and governments'.[29] The idea of 'apartheid South Africa' that has been mobilised as an empirical illustration of broader global models, and in political science, just as in everyday political campaigns, apartheid served as a marker of the South African exceptionalism that warranted its inclusion in global debate.

More recently, historians have begun to pay attention to the international intellectual histories of these same norms, and the broader conceptual frameworks within which they were located. Ideas of an 'international civil society' and discourses of human rights and humanitarian responsibility underpinned reactions to and engagement with the questions of race, sovereignty and citizenship that were starkly foregrounded in debates around racial injustice in South Africa. Works by Susan Pedersen on the concepts of international society that were defined around the League of Nations, as well as Mark Mazower's examination of the League's transition to the United Nations (especially concerning the conceptualisation of minority rights), established a body of scholarship that sought to lay out the intellectual foundations of the post-1945 international order.[30] Samuel Moyn has subsequently undertaken a significant revision of the history of human rights, suggesting that rather than being a set of ideas rooted in the Enlightenment or in the founding principles of the United Nations, the concept of human rights (at least in the form most widely understood today) emerged most forcefully in the late 1970s as a way of framing the distinctions between liberal freedom and communist control.[31] South Africa has been a key reference point in these and other works, but often as an illustration of the complexity and contingencies that offer caution against overgeneralised visions of global norms.[32]

Global and transnational histories of South Africa have contributed to the ongoing reconceptualisation of colonialism, illuminating the ways in which local experiences of colonial power were woven into a global web of ideas and practices that sought to sustain and challenge various forms of colonialism. Moreover, transnational histories have shown how local, national and global encounters with texts and ideas were entangled, and how actors in various forms mediated and transformed the meanings of South African experiences for international audiences. These examples suggest that what was often at stake was the conceptualisation of 'universal' human experience. Statements and positions which centre on universal frames of reference – from Christian narratives of redemption to notions of human rights or humanitarian discourses of needs – tend to be normative, serving to bolster claims to global legitimacy. Global and transnational histories can illuminate the ways in which local experiences intersect with global discourses, but also how those experiences can be reframed in order to enact forms of international solidarity that align with local political cultures around the world.

Global thinking about apartheid and antiapartheid

Global and transnational approaches have been particularly prominent in historical accounts of the contested politics of race in twentieth-century South Africa, and especially in attempts to historicise the activists, organisations and movements that have engaged with debates around race, segregation and apartheid. In his sequel to the *Making of the Modern World*, Bayly also pays close attention to the global significance of the African National Congress (ANC) and the postwar mobilisation that it led against apartheid – developments that might be set alongside the civil rights movement in the USA, and other nationalist movements inspired by Gandhian principles of nonviolent protest. In this reading, the crisis that followed the Sharpeville shootings of 1960 was one element of an 'international struggle against racial discrimination'.[33] South African liberation movements' turn to armed struggle in the early 1960s was meanwhile paralleled by similar processes in French- and Portuguese-ruled Africa. These wars of liberation meanwhile prefigured a shift to militant and revolutionary violence on the part of both black activists in the USA and radical political groups in Europe by the end of the decade.

This section will focus on recent scholarship on the antiapartheid movement, which has sought to examine histories of international solidarity as connected to (but also distinct from) the standard narratives of liberation struggle. These studies generally envision antiapartheid as transnational, of course, and constituted by an interconnected network of global, local and South African movements. Histories of antiapartheid have themselves drawn on a body of scholarship that has, since the late 1990s, sought to elaborate an international history of various national struggles for racial justice. The interest shown by African American campaigners in foreign affairs has been a primary of focus such works, as well as the entanglement of the civil rights, anticolonialism and anti-nuclear-weapons movements in the 1950s and 1960s.[34] Similarly, recent world histories have explicitly highlighted international influences on the development of the ANC as a major force in South African popular politics from the 1940s, from the Atlantic Charter to pan-Africanism, Gandhism and civil rights, and the post-Sharpeville radicalisation and turn towards communism and revolutionary violence.[35]

Many causes energised popular activism in the twentieth century, but as contemporary observers of the landmark South African elections in 1994 noted, few 'had the strength to galvanise a movement of such moral conviction as the worldwide movement against apartheid'.[36] Fewer still could associate themselves with a historical achievement as major as sweeping away 'three centuries of white racist rule'.[37] But histories of international solidarity and transnational antiapartheid activism have echoed a broader interest in processes of political globalisation and the potential development of a 'global civil society'. Since the turn of the twentieth century, an increased interest in *movements* has paralleled and been reinforced by interest in the global dimensions of South African history. Again, imperial history provided a starting point: histories of the development of an 'imperial working class' and global white labourism have focused attention on the years immediately before World War One as a nexus of transnational political activism. Jonathan Hyslop focused attention on the place of working-class migration in the development of South African labour movements, whose combined radical vision and ideology of white labourism chimed with an 'internationally constructed synthesis of militant labour and racist visions' shared by workers' movements across the British Empire.[38] As Hyslop suggests, the oft-cited slogan of the 1922 Rand Revolt – 'Workers of the World Unite for a White South Africa' – represented not parochialism but alignment with sentiments that pervaded imperial labour politics in the early part of the twentieth century.

Undermining the recent contention that interest in global history has ignored small-scale historical experiences, Hyslop developed his account of white labourism with a microhistory of the life of Scottish trade union activist and syndicalist J.T. Bain, who embodied the combination of radical anticapitalism and white labourism that Hyslop identified as a general tendency of the imperial working class in the years preceding World War One. In a further development of his analysis of white labourism, Hyslop argued that the transnational ideologies of the imperial working class had to be set alongside the concurrent rise in anticolonial nationalism, specifically in India. In an examination of British Labour Party founder Keir Hardie's world tour in 1907–8, Hyslop shows how Hardie's support for Indian claims for the rights of imperial citizenship set him at odds with the tenets of white labourism in both Australia and South Africa, and presented the British Labour Party with a choice between alignment with the narrow interests of a white working class and 'the egalitarian, humanist imperatives of his own ethical socialism'.[39]

The value of global historical approaches to histories of work was underlined in a 2007 special issue of *African Studies* focused on locating South African labour within global 'worlds of labour'. Alongside the emphasis on considering labour movements beyond the national frame, the issue's editors emphasised the value of oceanic 'worlds' as an important unit of comparison.[40] They noted the need to expand the focus from Transatlantic to Indian Ocean spheres, paralleling work by Hofmeyr on Gandhi and the transoceanic print cultures of Indian nationalism.[41] The *African Studies* collection also highlighted the ways that transnational histories have shown that the global movement of capital and labour is characterised by 'hops' rather than 'flows', shifting the focus to cities and localities. They added, using the case of the late nineteenth-century diaspora of Cornish miners, that the travels of labour migrants should be regarded as 'oscillating' rather than unilinear.[42] In their examination of activist and revisionist scholarship the editors again critiqued the tendency to frame the history of working-class politics as national.[43] In this context, it is worth noting that several significant texts of South African radical scholarship, including the Simonses' *Class and Colour in South Africa* and Govan Mbeki's *South Africa: The Peasants Revolt*, were published or republished in London as part of the Penguin Africa Library, a series edited by South African exile Ronald Segal, which was influenced by the radical agenda of the publisher's general editor, Tony Godwin.[44] In one sense, then, these histories were themselves transnational, products of the burgeoning diaspora of South African political exiles. Mbeki's book, for example, travelled with its editor Ruth First into exile in London in 1964, and was steered by Segal into publication in July, shortly after the author began his twenty-four-year imprisonment on Robben Island.[45]

Despite embodying the diasporic and exile experience of South African radicals in the 1960s, the works of the Penguin African Series maintained the long-held assumption that the nation state was the fundamental unit of South African history. This presumption has been echoed by subsequent accounts of international solidarity, which have also tended to be national in character. Works by Donald Culverson on the USA, Roger Fieldhouse on Britain and Christine Jennet on Australia have looked at local campaigns focused on South African issues, but they have considered them in isolation rather than as elements of a transnational movement.[46] A similar approach is found in the structure of the third volume of the South African Democracy Education Trust's *Road to Democracy* series, which brings together twenty national accounts of solidarity with the struggle against apartheid.[47]

Many of these studies employed methodologies developed by a wider scholarship on social movements, which has centred on the perceived transformation of nongovernmental organisations, political lobby groups and more loosely organised forms of social protest since the 1960s. Researchers have variously focused on the ways in which movements have been shaped by their capacity to mobilise resources (including financial capital and mass manpower), to exploit communications technologies and the media, and to co-opt specific local systems and institutions of power. Culverson's study of antiapartheid in the United States, for example, paid close attention to the ability of antiapartheid campaigners to lobby politicians inside the Beltway during the 1980s.[48] More recently, following the lead of Håkan Thörn's *Anti-apartheid and the Emergence of a Global Civil Society* (2004), histories of antiapartheid and international solidarity have drawn on the

1970s concept of 'new social movements', which concerns itself with the formation of movement identities and the use of media to communicate specific sets of values, alongside (or instead of) more traditional forms of political engagement.[49]

In Thörn's account of antiapartheid activism in Britain and Scandinavia, he sketched what he defined as a transnational social movement whose character was shaped in part by its emergence at the conjuncture of decolonisation and the beginning of the Cold War. From the start of the second decade of the twenty-first century, histories of antiapartheid have increasingly emphasised the transnational connections of the movement – for example, in its formative years before 1964, in the form of relations between antiapartheid movements and the ANC in exile, and the complicated relations between transnational movements and supranational and national authorities within the European Community.[50] During the 1960s, antiapartheid campaigns became truly transnational in character as they took shape through networks and institutions that connected national bodies and international organisations such as the United Nations (UN). The World Campaign for the Release of South African Political Prisoners, for example, was launched by the British Anti-Apartheid Movement in 1963, but worked closely with the UN Commission on Human Rights in developing a body of international human rights law, while South African activists participated in meetings such as the UN Human Rights Seminar held in Brasilia in 1966.[51]

More recently, the first efforts have been made to present a global history of the movement.[52] Although yet to be fully formed, such a global history would certainly include microhistories of those international institutions, including UN bodies such as the Human Rights Commission, that sustained and shaped antiapartheid activism on the world stage. These connections bear close examination, as they reveal that the salience of apartheid in debates around 'universal' human rights was often determined by concerns of specific interest to South African liberation movements, such as the discussion of the rights of armed fighters at the Tehran UN International Conference on Human Rights in 1968.[53] At the same time, however, the global appeal of the antiapartheid message was often framed in terms of humanitarian urgency. Speaking at the World Conference against Apartheid in Lagos in August 1977, Canon John Collins, the head of the fundraising organisation International Defence and Aid, spoke of human suffering in South Africa and 'the inescapable duty of the world community to do all in its power to render humanitarian assistance'.[54] But the language of humanitarian responsibility also had the capacity to reproduce the global hierarchies of power that the antiapartheid movement rejected. By incorporating a broad array of voices and institutions, a global history of antiapartheid might begin to overcome the anglophone and Eurocentric tendencies that critics have highlighted.[55] Through work such as this, histories of antiapartheid will broaden the range of transnational connections and global comparisons that have shaped South African history.

There remains much work before the hallmarks of a 'global history' of antiapartheid can be defined. A key issue, identified by Saul Dubow, is whether antiapartheid should be regarded as a global movement or an array of connected, but nonetheless distinct, local ones.[56] The task of resolving this question raises another: can historical experiences be segmented into distinct 'scales' of analysis? As the examples discussed above suggest, the languages of humanitarianism and human rights offer partial, but by no means complete, understanding of the 'universal' appeal of antiapartheid. Focusing on the spaces in which the globalisation of antiapartheid took place – the conference halls and seminar rooms that played host to networks of activists and officials – might help to identify the broad contours of 'grounded' global history. But they would also reveal some of its limits. The World Conference for Action against Apartheid in 1977, jointly organised by the UN, the Organisation of African Unity and the Nigerian government, was one such space. It aimed to assess conditions in South Africa a year after the Soweto Uprising, to audit international government action against apartheid, to identify 'practical aid' that might be offered to South African people and to consider a draft declaration that could be adopted by the UN.[57] It provided an opportunity for interactions among representatives of South African movements, African states and Western diplomats, but for all the authentic expressions of solidarity at the conference, it was a discussion restricted to a narrow elite of state officials, international diplomats and exiled leaders of South African opposition movements.

Global histories of antiapartheid might do much more, then, to incorporate responses to apartheid on the African continent within histories of solidarity. There are compelling reasons to suggest that African engagement with the apartheid state was significantly different from that of other parts of the globe: the proximity of African states to South Africa and the realities of the economic and military power of the apartheid state engendered international relations significantly and materially different from Pretoria's relations with European, North American and Asian nations.[58] At the same time, apartheid was a reference point in African political discourse; in the 1960s, it was an oft-cited example (alongside Algeria) of the threat of neocolonialism, and was employed by postcolonial African states as a primary focus of ultimately unsuccessful efforts to develop an effective lobby at the UN.[59] One exception to this overall pattern has been the collection edited by Hilary Sapire and Chris Saunders, which explicitly set out to trace the transnational 'linkages and connections' between regional movements and international supporters.[60]

In his own work, Saunders has offered timely reminders that transnational histories of international solidarity should not restrict their focus to South African movements. He argues that they should incorporate considerations of Namibian and other southern African national liberation struggles. These should, he argues, be integrated into wider histories of global antiapartheid but also understood on their own terms and in the light of local contingencies and agendas.[61]

Work on the regional dimensions of the South African experience, moreover, has raised important new questions around the nature of nationalism itself. Recent work on military camps, for example, has begun to sketch the ways in which activists created new forms of transnational experiences beyond the framework of 'national struggle'.[62] As the articles collected by Luise White and Miles Larmer in 2014 demonstrate, the life stories of fighters across southern Africa were forged in an 'un-national' context, in which struggles for national liberation were experienced in spaces unconnected to the nation itself.[63] More recently still, Jocelyn Alexander, JoAnn McGregor and Blessing-Miles Tendi have edited a collection that further examines the connections of southern African liberation movements, drawing on recent interest in the 'global Cold War', an examination of diplomatic networks, and the transnational connections within both insurgent and counterinsurgent groups, reflecting 'African appropriations, adaptations and rejections of global ideologies'.[64]

These new approaches have helped to lay new foundations for transnational histories of regional struggles against settler colonialism, setting apartheid and antiapartheid in a nexus of distinct local conditions. A transnational history of antiapartheid can thus provide a case study in both the possibilities and challenges inherent in global historical approaches. Furthermore, antiapartheid is by no means the only frame in which global political struggles have intersected with South African history – for example, the ongoing work on antifascism by Jonathan Hyslop and Kaspar Braskén, and Peter Cole's recently published transnational history of dockworkers in the United States and South Africa.[65] And, despite the expanding list of works examining the histories of international antiapartheid and other forms of radical international solidarity, work has also begun to set the foreign relations of the apartheid regime itself within the framework of international history.[66] Similarly, further work might be undertaken to assess apartheid itself not as an exceptional form of nationalism but as a variant of ethnic nationalism that was comparable to contemporaneous developments in Israel and also, as Faisal Devji has suggested, in the 'Muslim Zion' of Pakistan.[67]

Histories of apartheid and antiapartheid might benefit from a starting point that acknowledges the intertwined and coconstructed nature of global and local experiences and processes.[68] Rather than seeing connectedness and heterogeneity diametrically opposed, Bayly has suggested that uniformity and disjuncture are codependent constituents of globalisation; that what global histories must engage with is the 'ambivalent relationship between the global and the local'.[69] In the case of the histories of global antiapartheid and southern African national liberation movements, this ambivalence is evident: rather than resolving the contradictions between global and local experiences, current research has shown that tensions between perspectives can foster new approaches to, and categories of, historical analysis.

Future directions and ongoing challenges

The discussion in the preceding section suggests global historians should acknowledge that the ambivalence and contradictions they struggle with *are* the main focus of their subject, not problems that might guide us on our way towards a 'global' synthesis. Global histories look outwards from the grounded histories of localities, but also look inwards, at multiple 'small spaces', and seek to interpret the historical significance that emerges from a translocal perspective. Such a perspective has much to offer historians of South Africa in indicating directions for future research. Global antiapartheid will continue to provide a foundation for transnational histories that incorporate South African historical narratives into global trajectories and conjunctures, albeit one that might reach further beyond the narrative of the liberation struggle. The existing literature has, moreover, focused somewhat narrowly on organisational histories that often centre the actions and agency of elites and leaders.

Notwithstanding the distinctions between local liberation struggles and global 'antiapartheid', for example, we might consider the value of a comparative analysis of grassroots activists and the everyday life of resistance and opposition to apartheid across different localities. The value of these approaches is illustrated by recent work on the history of decolonisation, which has also begun to emphasise global contexts and transnational connections. Global histories of the Cold War and transnational histories of Afro-Asian solidarity have begun to unshackle decolonisation from narrowly nationalist narratives and 'a singular story of triumph or tragedy'.[70]

The methodological distinctions between transnational histories and histories of transnational movements should not be underestimated, however. A transnational history of antiapartheid would place greater emphasis on comparison and local particularities, perhaps, but this might preclude the development of valuable insights when considering the same histories at a global scale. In practical terms, this would necessitate multiarchival research undertaken by highly mobile researchers, which in turn raises critical questions around power and resources. If transnational and global histories necessitate internationalising research practices, how can we guard against replicating global inequalities within the academy? Moreover, global histories tend to be communicated in English, a form of monolingualism that renders the task of combining diverse narratives harder and undermines efforts to overcome Eurocentrism.[71] The need for multilingual research in South African history is of perennial concern: while global perspectives on much-discussed events such as the Mfecane might open up fertile new avenues for historical understanding, the question remains whether this can be achieved without a deep understanding of African languages, as Nomalanga Mkhize's chapter in this collection indicates. This is not to suggest that historians as individuals must be multilingual (although this is a worthy ambition), but that multi-perspective histories might be best achieved through collaboration and partnership alongside individual research. Global and transnational history might thus benefit by adopting practices of listening and coproduction.

A fundamental concern in global and transnational histories has involved tracing physical movements and circulations: of people (and nonhuman entities such as commodities, capital and other material stuff). The movement of ideas and cultural forms is invariably facilitated by the movement of objects that embody epistemological, aesthetic and conceptual value and meaning. It is perhaps no coincidence that the *Journal of Global History*, launched in 2003, emerged from an intellectual network of economic historians concerned with the connective ties of trade and exchange,[72] historians whose work was rooted in the political economy of empire, and new questions about the nature of modernity and how Europe's central role in the development of industrial capitalism accelerated the growth of 'global' history during the early twenty-first century. Movement, connection, circulation and comparisons across widely dispersed geographical locations are thus the central concerns of contemporary global history.

And beyond histories of radical political activism and labour movements, global perspectives on South African history might be discerned through the lens of global financial capital. The ideological dominance of free-market discourse has been explored in Quinn Slobodian's recent intellectual history of neoliberalism, which emphasises the role of 'race thinking' and of the apartheid state in the development of 'globalist' ideas in the 1970s and 1980s.[73] The sociological implications of the relationship between apartheid and neoliberalism have, moreover, begun to be explored by Deborah Posel in her recent studies of market research and the African consumer.[74] In short, while the spectre of capitalism has loomed large in modern South African historiography, a history of South African capitalism that incorporates both national and global perspectives is only now emerging.

While global and transnational histories broaden the scope of South African history, they also have the capacity to provoke a reassessment of accepted chronologies of the country's past. The field of global history is fraught with debate around the chronologies of globalisation – we can talk about 'ancient', 'early modern' or 'imperial' globalisation, or, alternatively, suggest that the process began only in the 1970s. Already, significant work has begun to investigate the two-thousand-year history of the integration of southern Africa within broader networks of trade and cultural and knowledge exchange. Much of the focus of this work has been on trade routes (e.g., of copper from Central Africa to the Atlantic and Indian Ocean worlds), which constitute 'conduits for the exchange of ideas as well as goods across oceans and continents'.[75] Environmental and animal histories, in particular, engender an approach that often seeks to foreground more-than-human frameworks of experience that redefine, cut across or erase entirely the categories of human social, political and cultural history. Global perspectives can therefore stretch the chronologies of South African history beyond usual definitions that often remain tied to structures of empire and settler colonialism. But they might also encourage a reconsideration of the standard narratives of modern and contemporary South African history, articulated around key moments (for example, debates around when we might identify the 'turning point' that ended apartheid). Histories that address the nature and impact of global historical phenomena – including post-1970s neoliberalism, the politics and discourses of human rights, and the everyday economic histories of consumption – do not easily fit chronological frameworks determined by liberation struggles and may perhaps allow space for new histories of South African 'transition'.

The international relations of postapartheid South Africa might also give pointers towards new directions. Notwithstanding the very real dominance of North–South relations and circulations in imperial and Cold War contexts, 'South–South' histories could contextualise and deepen historical understanding of connections embodied in groupings such as BRICS (Brazil, Russia, India, China and South Africa). Aside from accounts of relations between South African liberation movements and the Soviet Union at the level of organised politics, recent work to map networks of Afro-Asian solidarity in the period after 1945 have identified, but not yet fully assessed, the place of southern African political movements and activists in this network. Moreover, historians of China have begun to sketch the history of the globalisation of Chinese migrant labour in the late nineteenth and early twentieth centuries, offering new insight into the dynamics of migrant labour in southern Africa; itself a topic that has yet to fully engage with the transnational dimensions and border crossings involved in the recruitment and transport of workers across the wider southern African region.

Transatlantic connections, meanwhile, have tended to focus on links to North America. Even here, efforts to conceptualise South African history within the African diaspora have focused on drawing parallels with the Black Power movement, and offering comparative histories of racial thought and white supremacy. Much less work has been undertaken on connections between southern Africa and Latin America.[76] Here, we might consider transnational histories of the apartheid state, developing the work undertaken by Jamie Miller, but also South Africa's place in the history of what might be described as a 'global moment' of truth and reconciliation in the 1990s. Similarly, while antiapartheid activists invested significant time in measuring and monitoring apartheid South Africa's global financial and trade connections, little recent work has been undertaken to examine the country's economic history from a global and transnational perspective.[77] Again, such an endeavour might need to dissolve the chronological boundaries between apartheid and postapartheid.

As Duncan Brown has argued, studies of the South African past have grappled with longstanding tensions between 'global' and 'nationalist' visions, but as we have seen, these tensions have been perceived as more pressing in recent years.[78] Critics have suggested that global and transnational histories might infer a 'globalist' vision of historical development and that they primarily serve an ideological purpose. Global history can thus be rendered as a history of globalisation that seems complicit in the same processes it purports to critique. But it nevertheless remains important to consider what might happen to global and transnational histories in the face of 'deglobalisation', the burgeoning power of the nation state and political trajectory towards strong borders and walls. I have suggested several reasons why global connections will continue to be a legitimate concern for historians, but I would also add the comment made by Richard Drayton and David Motadel in their defence of global history – that we are no more likely to sideline global historical approaches than we are to return to the general assumption that the primary unit of historical analysis is elite white men.[79]

Similarly, Pierre-Yves Saunier has noted that we should consider *who* the audiences are for transnational histories. He suggests that most people continue to experience life in a national frame, rendering transnational history marginal to the expectations and desires of all but those cosmopolitan agents – 'connected nomads' – for whom transnationalism reflects their own (privileged) reality.[80] This is, I think, a welcome reminder of the need to reflect on the extent to which global connections intersect with everyday lives and the ways in which people might imagine their lives as 'being global'. Moreover, global and transnational histories need to monitor the extent to which they replicate rather than challenge worldwide inequalities: do transnational histories liberate the Global South from histories determined by frameworks of Western colonialism, capitalism and cultural imperialism, or do they fix local histories permanently within this framework? It is important to remain mindful of the extent to which 'going global' might be considered a privilege in the neoliberal university, whose methodologies of control limit capacity for extensive work in multiple archives separated by long distances. These questions demonstrate that global and transnational histories have been, are and will continue to be open to challenge, but they do not, in themselves, mean that we should abandon such approaches to history. Global and transnational histories will continue to offer new understandings of the past.

In conclusion, this broad overview suggests that global and transnational histories do not simply bolt on to existing forms of research, but instead shape the historical questions we might ask. Histories that have been positioned as fundamentally South African experiences and part of an exceptional history of struggle might be reexamined in ways that attend to their interconnections with global processes and developments. If we can recognise the small ways in which 'sites of struggle' were in fact local places enmeshed in 'broader' networks of change – and not simply through those international and transnational networks that conjure narratives of 'solidarity' – then we can begin to compose our collective histories in terms that more fully connect locality and globality.

Notes

1 These connections also play a part in shaping historical research. The original version of this chapter was developed and drafted whilst being a visiting researcher at the History Workshop at the University of Witwatersrand. I am very grateful for their support.
2 See for example N. Lazarus, 'The South African Ideology: The Myth of Exceptionalism, the Idea of Renaissance', *South Atlantic Quarterly*, 103 (4) 2004, 607–28.
3 J. Adelman, 'Is Global History Still Possible, or Has It Had Its Moment?', *Aeon*, Mar. 2017, https://aeon.co/essays/is-global-history-still-possible-or-has-it-had-its-moment (accessed 12 Dec. 2019).
4 D.A. Bell, 'This Is What Happens when Historians Overuse the Idea of the Network', *New Republic*, 26 Oct. 2013, https://newrepublic.com/article/114709/world-connecting-reviewed-historians-overuse-network-metaphor (accessed 12 Dec. 2019); E.S. Rosenberg (ed.), *A World Connecting, 1870–1945: A History of the World* (Cambridge, MA: Belknap Press of Harvard University Press, 2012).
5 R. Drayton and D. Motadel, 'Discussion: The Futures of Global History', *Journal of Global History*, 13 (1) 2018, 1–21, quotes at 15.

6 On the latter, see M. Brown, 'The Global History of Latin America', *Journal of Global History*, 10 (3) 2015, 365–86; G.L. Paz, 'Global History and Latin American History: A Comment', *Almanack*, 14, 2016, 118–24.
7 P. Larson, 'African Slave Trades in Global Perspective', in R.J. Reid and J. Parker (eds), *The Oxford Handbook of Modern African History* (Oxford: Oxford University Press, 2013).
8 A. Klotz, 'Borders and the Roots of Xenophobia in South Africa', *South African Historical Journal*, 68 (2) 2016, 185–6; R.I. Rotberg, *The Founder: Cecil Rhodes and the Pursuit of Power* (Oxford: Oxford University Press, 1988), 238–87.
9 On 'border thinking', see W. Mignolo, *Local Histories/Global Designs: Coloniality, Subaltern Knowledges, and Border Thinking* (Princeton, NJ: Princeton University Press, 2012).
10 B. Anderson, *Imagined Communities: Reflections on the Origin and Spread of Nationalism* (London: Verso, 1991).
11 K. Grant, P. Levine and F. Trentmann (eds), *Beyond Sovereignty: Britain, Empire and Transnationalism, c. 1860–1950* (Basingstoke: Palgrave Macmillan, 2007); A. Nützenadel and F. Trentmann (eds), *Food and Globalization: Consumption, Markets and Politics in the Modern World* (Oxford: Berg, 2008); A. Thompson, *The Empire Strikes Back? The Impact of Imperialism on Britain from the Mid-nineteenth Century* (Harlow: Pearson Longman, 2005).
12 J. Darwin, *The Empire Project: The Rise and Fall of the British World-System, 1830–1970* (Cambridge: Cambridge University Press, 2009), 217–54.
13 A.M. Burton, *Empire in Question: Reading, Writing, and Teaching British Imperialism* (Durham, NC: Duke University Press, 2011), 279–80.
14 R.E. Karl, *Staging the World: Chinese Nationalism at the Turn of the Twentieth Century* (Durham, NC: Duke University Press, 2002), 140–1.
15 C.A. Bayly, *The Birth of the Modern World, 1780–1914: Global Connections and Comparisons* (Oxford: Blackwell, 2004), 231–3, 439–47, quote at 439.
16 J. Belich, *Replenishing the Earth: The Settler Revolution and the Rise of the Anglo-World, 1783–1939* (Oxford: Oxford University Press, 2009).
17 J. Osterhammel, *The Transformation of the World: A Global History of the Nineteenth Century*, translated by Patrick Camiller (Princeton, NJ: Princeton University Press, 2014), 483–7.
18 Osterhammel, *Transformation*, 490. Space precludes a full list of works presenting the twentieth-century racial order in South Africa as something *other* than a consequence of 'frontier values', but those most pertinent include S. Dubow, *Racial Segregation and the Origins of Apartheid in South Africa, 1919–36* (Basingstoke: Macmillan, 1989); M. Legassick, 'British Hegemony and the Origins of Segregation in South Africa, 1901–14', in W. Beinart and S. Dubow (eds), *Segregation and Apartheid in Twentieth-Century South Africa* (London: Routledge, 1995); T.J. Keegan, *Colonial South Africa and the Origins of the Racial Order* (Cape Town: David Philip, 1996).
19 S.J. Potter and J. Saha, 'Global History, Imperial History and Connected Histories of Empire', *Journal of Colonialism and Colonial History*, 16 (1) 2015.

20 F. Cooper and A. Stoler, *Tensions of Empire: Colonial Cultures in a Bourgeois World* (London: University of California Press, 1997), 4; C. Hall, *Civilising Subjects: Metropole and Colony in the English Imagination, 1830–1867* (Oxford: Polity Press, 2002).

21 A. Lester, *Imperial Networks: Creating Identities in Nineteenth-Century South Africa and Britain* (New York: Routledge, 2001); E. Elbourne, *Blood Ground: Colonialism, Missions, and the Contest for Christianity in the Cape Colony and Britain, 1799–1853* (Montreal: McGill-Queen's University Press, 2002).

22 Lester, *Imperial Networks*.

23 D. Lambert and A. Lester (eds), *Colonial Lives across the British Empire: Imperial Careering in the Long Nineteenth Century* (New York: Cambridge University Press, 2006).

24 B. Everill, 'Freetown, Frere Town and the Kat River Settlement: Nineteenth Century Humanitarian Intervention and Precursors to Modern Refugee Camps', in B. Everill and J.D. Kaplan (eds), *The History and Practice of Humanitarian Intervention and Aid in Africa* (Basingstoke: Palgrave Macmillan, 2013), 23–42, quote at 38.

25 J. Comaroff and J.L. Comaroff, *Of Revelation and Revolution*, vol. 1, *Christianity, Colonialism, and Consciousness in South Africa* (London: University of Chicago Press, 1991), and vol. 2, *The Dialectics of Modernity on a South African Frontier* (London: University of Chicago Press, 1997).

26 I. Hofmeyr, *The Portable Bunyan: A Transnational History of 'The Pilgrim's Progress'* (Princeton, NJ: Princeton University Press, 2004).

27 M.E. Keck and K. Sikkink, *Activists beyond Borders: Advocacy Networks in International Politics* (Ithaca, NY: Cornell University Press, 1998).

28 A. Klotz, *Norms in International Relations: The Struggle against Apartheid* (Ithaca, NY: Cornell University Press, 1995).

29 C.A. Bayly, *Remaking the Modern World 1900–2015: Global Connections and Comparisons* (Hoboken, NJ: John Wiley, 2018), 142, 176.

30 S. Pedersen, *The Guardians: The League of Nations and the Crisis of Empire* (Oxford: Oxford University Press, 2015); M. Mazower, *No Enchanted Palace: The End of Empire and the Ideological Origins of the United Nations* (Woodstock: Princeton University Press, 2009).

31 J. Eckel and S. Moyn (eds), *The Breakthrough: Human Rights in the 1970s* (Philadelphia: University of Pennsylvania Press, 2014); S. Moyn, *The Last Utopia: Human Rights in History* (London: Belknap Press of Harvard University Press, 2010); R. Burke, *Decolonization and the Evolution of International Human Rights* (Philadelphia: University of Pennsylvania Press, 2010).

32 S. Stevens, 'Why South Africa? The Politics of Anti-apartheid Activism in Britain in the Long 1970s', in Eckel and Moyn, *Breakthrough*, 202–24; S. Dubow, *South Africa's Struggle for Human Rights* (Athens: Ohio University Press, 2012); R. Skinner, 'The Dynamics of Anti-apartheid: International Solidarity, Human Rights and Decolonization', in C. Jeppeson and A.W.M. Smith (eds), *Britain, France and the Decolonization of Africa: Future Imperfect?* (London: University College London Press, 2017), 111–30.

33 Bayly *Remaking the Modern World*, 141.
34 J. Allman, 'Nuclear Imperialism and the Pan-African Struggle for Peace and Freedom: Ghana, 1959–1962', *Souls*, 10 (2) 2008, 83–102; R. Skinner, 'Bombs and Border Crossings: Peace Activist Networks and the Post-colonial State in Africa, 1959–62', *Journal of Contemporary History*, 50 (3) 2015, 418–38. On African Americans and anticolonialism, see, for example, B.G. Plummer, *Rising Wind: Black Americans and U.S. Foreign Affairs, 1935–1960* (Chapel Hill: University of North Carolina Press, 1996); B.G. Plummer (ed.), *Window on Freedom: Race, Civil Rights, and Foreign Affairs, 1945–1988* (Chapel Hill: University of North Carolina Press, 2003); P.M. Von Eschen, *Race against Empire: Black Americans and Anticolonialism, 1937–1957* (Ithaca, NY: Cornell University Press, 1997).
35 Bayly *Remaking the Modern World*, 156.
36 *Times* (London), 26 Apr. 1994.
37 *New York Times*, 27 Apr. 1994.
38 J. Hyslop, 'The Imperial Working Class Makes Itself "White": White Labourism in Britain, Australia, and South Africa before the First World War', *Journal of Historical Sociology*, 12 (4) 1999, 399.
39 J. Hyslop, 'The World Voyage of James Keir Hardie: Indian Nationalism, Zulu Insurgency and the British Labour Diaspora, 1907–1908', *Journal of Global History*, 1 (3) 2006, 361; J. Hyslop, *The Notorious Syndicalist JT Bain: A Scottish Rebel in Colonial South Africa* (Johannesburg: Jacana, 2004).
40 P. Bonner, J. Hyslop and L. van Der Walt, 'Rethinking Worlds of Labour: Southern African Labour History in International Context', *African Studies*, 66 (2–3) 2007, 137–67.
41 I. Hofmeyr, *Gandhi's Printing Press: Experiments in Slow Reading* (Cambridge, MA: Harvard University Press, 2013).
42 A. Thompson and G. Magee, 'Remittances Revisited: A Case Study of South Africa and the Cornish Migrant, c. 1870–1914', *Cornish Studies*, 13, 2005, 256–87.
43 Bonner *et al.*, *Rethinking Worlds of Labour*, 150.
44 R. Skinner, 'Struggles on the Page: British Antiapartheid and Radical Scholarship', *Radical History Review*, 119, 2014, 216–31.
45 University of Bristol Special Collections, The Penguin Archive, Penguin Africa Library Editorial files, DM 117-AP9, R. First, 'Editor's Preface [draft]' (n.d.).
46 D.R. Culverson, *Contesting Apartheid: U.S. Activism, 1960–1987* (Boulder, CO: Westview, 1999); R. Fieldhouse, *Anti-apartheid: A History of the Movement in Britain* (London: Merlin Press, 2005); C. Jennett, 'Signals to South Africa: The Australian Anti-apartheid Movement', in C. Jennett and R.G. Stewart (eds), *Politics of the Future: The Role of Social Movements* (South Melbourne: MacMillan, 1989), 98–155.
47 South African Democracy Education Trust, *The Road to Democracy in South Africa*, vol. 3, parts 1 and 2, *International Solidarity* (Pretoria: Unisa Press, 2008).
48 Culverson, *Contesting Apartheid*.

49 H. Thörn, *Anti-apartheid and the Emergence of a Global Civil Society* (Basingstoke: Palgrave Macmillan, 2006).
50 C. Gurney, '"A Great Cause": The Origins of the Anti-apartheid Movement, June 1959–March 1960', *Journal of Southern African Studies*, 26 (1) 2000, 123–44; A. Lissoni, 'Transformations in the ANC External Mission and Umkhonto We Sizwe, c. 1960–1969', *Journal of Southern African Studies*, 35 (2) 2009, 287–301; R. Skinner, *The Foundations of Anti-apartheid: Liberal Humanitarianism and Transnational Activism in Britain and the United States, c. 1919–64* (Basingstoke: Palgrave Macmillan, 2010); W. Goedertier, 'The Quest for Transnational Authority, the Anti-apartheid Movements of the European Community', *Revue belge de philologie et d'histoire*, 89 (3–4) 2011, 1249–76.
51 R.M. Resha, 'Paper on Apartheid', presented on behalf of the ANC of South Africa to the UN Human Rights Seminar on Apartheid, Brasília, 1966; see also Skinner, 'Dynamics of Anti-apartheid'.
52 A. Konieczna and R. Skinner (eds), *A Global History of Anti-apartheid: 'Forward to Freedom' in South Africa* (Basingstoke: Palgrave Macmillan, 2019).
53 R. Skinner, 'Humanitarians, Human Rights and Anti-Apartheid', in Konieczna and Skinner, *Global History of Anti-apartheid*, 19–20.
54 J. Collins, 'Unite in Action for Liberation of Southern Africa: A Plea to All Nations', paper presented to the World Conference for Action against Apartheid, UN Centre against Apartheid, Lagos, 24–26 Aug. 1977.
55 On criticism of global history's tendency to reproduce global inequalities, see, e.g., Adelman, 'Global History'. Although histories of antiapartheid and international solidarity have generally focused on movements in Europe and the West, work has begun to emphasise other national movements – e.g., A. Lissoni, 'Yusuf Dadoo, India and South Africa's Liberation Struggle', in Konieczna and Skinner, *Global History of Anti-apartheid*, 203–38, and K. Makino, 'Afro-Asian Solidarity and the Anti-apartheid Movement in Japan', in Konieczna and Skinner, *Global History of Anti-apartheid*, 265–90.
56 S. Dubow, 'New Approaches to High Apartheid and Anti-apartheid', *South African Historical Journal*, 69 (2) 2017, 304–29.
57 *Guardian* (London), 22 Aug. 1977.
58 Dubow, 'New Approaches', 325–7.
59 R.M. Irwin, *Gordian Knot: Apartheid and the Unmaking of the Liberal World Order* (Oxford: Oxford University Press, 2012).
60 H. Sapire and C.C. Saunders (eds), *Southern African Liberation Struggles: New Local, Regional and Global Perspectives* (Claremont: University of Cape Town Press, 2013), 1.
61 C. Saunders, 'Anti-apartheid, Decolonization and Transnational Solidarity: The Namibian Case', in Konieczna and Skinner, *Global History of Anti-apartheid*, 317–38.
62 C.A. Williams, *National Liberation in Post-colonial Southern Africa: A Historical Ethnography of SWAPO's Exile Camps* (Cambridge: Cambridge University Press, 2015); S.R. Davis, *The ANC's War against Apartheid: Umkhonto We Sizwe and the Liberation of South Africa* (Bloomington: Indiana University Press, 2018).

63 L. White and M. Larmer, 'Introduction: Mobile Soldiers and the Un-national Liberation of Southern Africa', *Journal of Southern African Studies*, 40 (6) 2014, 1271–4.
64 J. Alexander, J. McGregor and B. Tendi, 'The Transnational Histories of Southern African Liberation Movements: An Introduction', *Journal of Southern African Studies*, 43 (1) 2017, 12; see also O.A. Westad, *The Cold War: A World History* (New York: Basic Books, 2017).
65 J. Hyslop, 'German Seafarers, Anti-fascism and the Anti-Stalinist Left: The "Antwerp Group" and Edo Fimmen's International Transport Workers' Federation, 1933–40', *Global Networks*, 19 (4) 2019, 499–520; K. Braskén, 'Making Anti-fascism Transnational: The Origins of Communist and Socialist Articulations of Resistance in Europe, 1923–1924', *Contemporary European History*, 25 (4) 2016, 573–96; P. Cole, *Dockworker Power: Race and Activism in Durban and the San Francisco Bay Area* (Urbana: University of Illinois Press, 2018).
66 Irwin, *Gordian Knot*; J. Miller, *An African Volk: The Apartheid Regime and Its Search for Survival* (Oxford: Oxford University Press, 2016).
67 F. Devji, *Muslim Zion Pakistan as a Political Idea* (Cambridge, MA: Harvard University Press, 2013); Bayly, *Remaking the Modern World*, 155.
68 Dubow, 'New Approaches', 327–9.
69 Bayly, *Birth of the Modern World*, 2.
70 J. Allman, 'Between the Present and History: African Nationalism and Decolonization', in Reid and Parker, *Oxford Handbook of Modern African History*', 237.
71 Adelman, 'Global History'.
72 Drayton and Motadel, 'Futures of Global History'.
73 Q. Slobodian, *Globalists: The End of Empire and the Birth of Neoliberalism* (Cambridge, MA: Harvard University Press, 2018).
74 D. Posel, 'Races to Consume: Revisiting South Africa's History of Race, Consumption and the Struggle for Freedom', *Ethnic and Racial Studies*, 33 (2) 2010, 157–75, and 'Getting Inside the Skin of the Consumer: Race, Market Research and the Consumerist Project in Apartheid South Africa', *Itinerario*, 42 (1) 2018, 120–38.
75 L. Schumaker, A. Brooks, M. Msiska, E. Pollard, and D. Potts, 'Situating the BRICS Phenomenon within the Histories and Cultures of Southern Africa', *Journal of Southern African Studies*, 43 (5) 2017, 856. See also articles by Wilmsen, Pikirayi, and Nikis and Livingstone Smith in the same issue.
76 One exception has been the effort undertaken to chronicle the role of Cuba in Angolan – and by extension South African – histories of liberation. See P. Gleijeses, *Conflicting Missions: Havana, Washington, and Africa, 1959–1976* (Chapel Hill: University of North Carolina Press, 2002); P. Gleijeses, *Visions of Freedom: Havana, Washington, Pretoria and the Struggle for Southern Africa, 1976–1991* (Chapel Hill: University of North Carolina Press, 2013); C. Hatzky and M. Edmunds-Harrington, *Cubans in Angola: South-South Cooperation and Transfer of Knowledge, 1976–1991* (Madison: University of Wisconsin Press, 2015); C. Saunders, 'South Africa's War, and the Cuban Military, in Angola', *Journal of Southern African Studies*, 40 (6) 2014, 1363–8.

77 S. Sparks, 'Crude Politics: The ANC, the Shipping Research Bureau and the Anti-apartheid Oil Boycott', *South African Historical Journal*, 69 (2) 2017, 251–64.
78 D. Brown, 'National Belonging and Cultural Difference: South Africa and the Global Imaginary', *Journal of Southern African Studies*, 27 (4) 2001, 757–69.
79 Drayton and Motadel, 'Futures of Global History'.
80 P. Saunier, *Transnational History* (Basingstoke: Palgrave Macmillan, 2013).

Bibliography

Adelman, J. (2017) 'Is Global History Still Possible, or Has It Had Its Moment?', *Aeon*, Mar. 2017, https://aeon.co/essays/is-global-history-still-possible-or-has-it-had-its-moment (accessed 12 Dec. 2019).
Alexander, J., J. McGregor, and B. Tendi (2017) 'The Transnational Histories of Southern African Liberation Movements: An Introduction', *Journal of Southern African Studies*, 43 (1).
Allman, J. (2008) 'Nuclear Imperialism and the Pan-African Struggle for Peace and Freedom: Ghana, 1959–1962', *Souls*, 10 (2).
Allman, J. (2013) 'Between the Present and History: African Nationalism and Decolonization', in Reid and Parker, *Oxford Handbook of Modern African History*.
Anderson, B. (1991) *Imagined Communities: Reflections on the Origin and Spread of Nationalism*. London: Verso.
Bayly, C.A. (2004) *The Birth of the Modern World, 1780–1914: Global Connections and Comparisons*. Oxford: Blackwell.
Bayly, C.A. (2018) *Remaking the Modern World, 1900–2015: Global Connections and Comparisons*. Hoboken, NJ: John Wiley.
Belich, J. (2009) *Replenishing the Earth: The Settler Revolution and the Rise of the Anglo-World, 1783–1939*. Oxford: Oxford University Press.
Bell, D.A. (2013) 'This Is What Happens when Historians Overuse the Idea of the Network', *New Republic*, 26 Oct. 2013, https://newrepublic.com/article/114709/world-connecting-reviewed-historians-overuse-network-metaphor (accessed 12 Dec. 2019).
Bonner, P., J. Hyslop and L. van Der Walt (2007) 'Rethinking Worlds of Labour: Southern African Labour History in International Context', *African Studies*, 66 (2–3).
Braskén, K. (2016) 'Making Anti-fascism Transnational: The Origins of Communist and Socialist Articulations of Resistance in Europe, 1923–1924', *Contemporary European History*, 25 (4).
Brown, D. (2001) 'National Belonging and Cultural Difference: South Africa and the Global Imaginary', *Journal of Southern African Studies*, 27 (4).
Brown, M. (2015) 'The Global History of Latin America', *Journal of Global History*, 10 (3).
Burke, R. (2010) *Decolonization and the Evolution of International Human Rights*. Philadelphia: University of Pennsylvania Press.

Burton, A.M. (2011) *Empire in Question: Reading, Writing, and Teaching British Imperialism*. Durham, NC: Duke University Press.
Cole, P. (2018) *Dockworker Power: Race and Activism in Durban and the San Francisco Bay Area*. Urbana: University of Illinois Press.
Collins, J. (1977) 'Unite in Action for Liberation of Southern Africa: A Plea to All Nations', paper presented to the World Conference for Action against Apartheid, UN Centre against Apartheid, Lagos, 24–26 Aug.
Comaroff, J., and J.L. Comaroff (1991) *Of Revelation and Revolution*, vol. 1, *Christianity, Colonialism, and Consciousness in South Africa*. London: University of Chicago Press.
Comaroff, J., and J.L. Comaroff (1997) *Of Revelation and Revolution*, vol. 2, *The Dialectics of Modernity on a South African Frontier*. London: University of Chicago Press.
Cooper, F., and A.L. Stoler (1997) *Tensions of Empire : Colonial Cultures in a Bourgeois World*. London: University of California Press.
Culverson, D.R. (1999) *Contesting Apartheid: U.S. Activism, 1960–1987*. Boulder, CO: Westview.
Darwin, J. (2009) *The Empire Project: The Rise and Fall of the British World-System, 1830–1970*. Cambridge: Cambridge University Press.
Davis, S.R. (2018) *The ANC's War against Apartheid: Umkhonto We Sizwe and the Liberation of South Africa*. Bloomington: Indiana University Press.
Devji, F. (2013) *Muslim Zion Pakistan as a Political Idea*. Cambridge, MA: Harvard University Press.
Drayton, R., and D. Motadel (2018) 'Discussion: The Futures of Global History', *Journal of Global History*, 13 (1).
Dubow, S. (1989) *Racial Segregation and the Origins of Apartheid in South Africa, 1919–36*. Basingstoke: Macmillan.
Dubow, S. (2012) *South Africa's Struggle for Human Rights*. Athens: Ohio University Press.
Dubow, S. (2017) 'New Approaches to High Apartheid and Anti-apartheid', *South African Historical Journal*, 69 (2).
Eckel, J., and S. Moyn (eds) (2014) *The Breakthrough: Human Rights in the 1970s*. Philadelphia: University of Pennsylvania Press.
Elbourne, E. (2002) *Blood Ground: Colonialism, Missions, and the Contest for Christianity in the Cape Colony and Britain, 1799–1853*. Montreal: McGill-Queen's University Press.
Everill, B. (2013) 'Freetown, Frere Town and the Kat River Settlement: Nineteenth Century Humanitarian Intervention and Precursors to Modern Refugee Camps', in B. Everill and J.D. Kaplan (eds), *The History and Practice of Humanitarian Intervention and Aid in Africa*. Basingstoke: Palgrave Macmillan.
Fieldhouse, R. (2005) *Anti-apartheid: A History of the Movement in Britain*. London: Merlin Press.
Gleijeses, P. (2002) *Conflicting Missions: Havana, Washington, and Africa, 1959–1976*. Chapel Hill: University of North Carolina Press.
Gleijeses, P. (2013) *Visions of Freedom: Havana, Washington, Pretoria and the Struggle for Southern Africa, 1976–1991*. Chapel Hill : University of North Carolina Press.

Goedertier, W. (2011) 'The Quest for Transnational Authority, the Anti-apartheid Movements of the European Community', *Revue belge de philologie et d'histoire*, 89 (3–4).

Grant, K., P. Levine, and F. Trentmann (eds) (2007) *Beyond Sovereignty: Britain, Empire and Transnationalism, c. 1860–1950*. Basingstoke: Palgrave Macmillan.

Gurney, C. (2000) '"A Great Cause": The Origins of the Anti-apartheid Movement, June 1959–March 1960', *Journal of Southern African Studies*, 26 (1).

Hall, C. (2002) *Civilising Subjects: Metropole and Colony in the English Imagination, 1830–1867*. Oxford: Polity Press.

Hatzky, C., and M. Edmunds-Harrington (2015) *Cubans in Angola: South-South Cooperation and Transfer of Knowledge, 1976–1991*. Madison: University of Wisconsin Press.

Hofmeyr, I. (2004) *The Portable Bunyan: A Transnational History of 'The Pilgrim's Progress'*. Princeton, NJ: Princeton University Press.

Hofmeyr, I. (2013) *Gandhi's Printing Press: Experiments in Slow Reading*. Cambridge, MA: Harvard University Press.

Hyslop, J. (1999) 'The Imperial Working Class Makes Itself "White": White Labourism in Britain, Australia, and South Africa before the First World War', *Journal of Historical Sociology* 12 (4).

Hyslop, J. (2004) *The Notorious Syndicalist JT Bain: A Scottish Rebel in Colonial South Africa*. Johannesburg: Jacana.

Hyslop, J. (2006) 'The World Voyage of James Keir Hardie: Indian Nationalism, Zulu Insurgency and the British Labour Diaspora, 1907–1908', *Journal of Global History* 1 (3).

Hyslop, J. (2019) 'German Seafarers, Anti-fascism and the Anti-Stalinist Left: The "Antwerp Group" and Edo Fimmen's International Transport Workers' Federation, 1933–40', *Global Networks*, 19 (4).

Irwin, R.M. (2012) *Gordian Knot: Apartheid and the Unmaking of the Liberal World Order*. Oxford: Oxford University Press.

Jennett, C. (1989) 'Signals to South Africa: The Australian Anti-apartheid Movement', in C. Jennett and R.G. Stewart (eds), *Politics of the Future: The Role of Social Movements*. South Melbourne: Macmillan.

Karl, R.E. (2002) *Staging the World: Chinese Nationalism at the Turn of the Twentieth Century*. Durham, NC: Duke University Press.

Keck, M.E., and K. Sikkink (1998) *Activists beyond Borders: Advocacy Networks in International Politics*. Ithaca, NY: Cornell University Press.

Keegan, T.J. (1996) *Colonial South Africa and the Origins of the Racial Order*. Cape Town: David Philip.

Klotz, A. (1995) *Norms in International Relations: The Struggle against Apartheid*. Ithaca, NY: Cornell University Press.

Klotz, A. (2016) 'Borders and the Roots of Xenophobia in South Africa', *South African Historical Journal*, 68 (2).

Konieczna, A., and R. Skinner (eds) (2019) *A Global History of Anti-apartheid: 'Forward to Freedom' in South Africa*. Basingstoke: Palgrave Macmillan.

Lambert, D., and A. Lester (eds) (2006) *Colonial Lives across the British Empire: Imperial Careering in the Long Nineteenth Century*. New York: Cambridge University Press.

Larson, P. (2013) 'African Slave Trades in Global Perspective', in Reid and Parker, *Oxford Handbook of Modern African History*.
Lazarus, N. (2004) 'The South African Ideology: The Myth of Exceptionalism, the Idea of Renaissance', *South Atlantic Quarterly*, 103 (4).
Legassick, M. (1995) 'British Hegemony and the Origins of Segregation in South Africa, 1901–14', in W. Beinart and S. Dubow (eds), *Segregation and Apartheid in Twentieth-Century South Africa*. London: Routledge.
Lester, A. (2001) *Imperial Networks: Creating Identities in Nineteenth-Century South Africa and Britain*. New York: Routledge.
Lissoni, A. (2009) 'Transformations in the ANC External Mission and Umkhonto We Sizwe, c. 1960–1969', *Journal of Southern African Studies*, 35 (2).
Lissoni, A. (2019) 'Yusuf Dadoo, India and South Africa's Liberation Struggle', in Konieczna and Skinner, *Global History of Anti-apartheid*.
Makino, K. (2019) 'Afro-Asian Solidarity and the Anti-apartheid Movement in Japan', in Konieczna and Skinner, *Global History of Anti-apartheid*.
Mazower, M. (2009) *No Enchanted Palace: The End of Empire and the Ideological Origins of the United Nations*. Woodstock: Princeton University Press.
Mignolo, W. (2012) *Local Histories/Global Designs: Coloniality, Subaltern Knowledges, and Border Thinking*. Princeton, NJ: Princeton University Press.
Miller, J. (2016) *An African Volk: The Apartheid Regime and Its Search for Survival*. Oxford: Oxford University Press.
Moyn, S. (2010) *The Last Utopia: Human Rights in History*. London: Belknap Press of Harvard University Press.
Nützenadel, A., and F. Trentmann (eds) (2008) *Food and Globalization: Consumption, Markets and Politics in the Modern World*. Oxford: Berg.
Osterhammel. J. (2014) *The Transformation of the World: A Global History of the Nineteenth Century*, translated by Patrick Camiller. Princeton, NJ: Princeton University Press.
Paz, G.L. (2016) 'Global History and Latin American History: A Comment', *Almanack*, 14.
Pedersen, S. (2015) *The Guardians: The League of Nations and the Crisis of Empire*. Oxford: Oxford University Press.
Plummer, B.G. (1996) *Rising Wind: Black Americans and U.S. Foreign Affairs, 1935–1960*. Chapel Hill: University of North Carolina Press.
Plummer, B.G. (ed.) (2003) *Window on Freedom: Race, Civil Rights, and Foreign Affairs, 1945–1988*. Chapel Hill: University of North Carolina Press.
Posel, D. (2010) 'Races to Consume: Revisiting South Africa's History of Race, Consumption and the Struggle for Freedom', *Ethnic and Racial Studies*, 33 (2).
Posel, D. (2018) 'Getting Inside the Skin of the Consumer: Race, Market Research and the Consumerist Project in Apartheid South Africa', *Itinerario* 42 (1).
Potter, S.J., and J. Saha (2015) 'Global History, Imperial History and Connected Histories of Empire', *Journal of Colonialism and Colonial History*, 16 (1).
Reid, R.J., and J. Parker (eds) (2013) *The Oxford Handbook of Modern African History*. Oxford: Oxford University Press.
Resha, R.M. (1966) 'Paper on Apartheid', paper presented on behalf of the ANC of South Africa to the UN Human Rights Seminar on Apartheid, Brasília, 1966.

Rosenberg, E.S. (ed.) (2012) *A World Connecting, 1870–1945: A History of the World*. Cambridge, MA: Belknap Press of Harvard University Press.

Rotberg, R.I. (1988) *The Founder: Cecil Rhodes and the Pursuit of Power*. Oxford: Oxford University Press.

Sapire, H., and C.C. Saunders (2013) *Southern African Liberation Struggles: New Local, Regional and Global Perspectives*. Claremont: University of Cape Town Press.

Saunders, C. (2014) 'South Africa's War, and the Cuban Military, in Angola', *Journal of Southern African Studies*, 40 (6).

Saunders, C. (2019) 'Anti-apartheid, Decolonization and Transnational Solidarity: The Namibian Case', in Konieczna and Skinner, *Global History of Anti-apartheid*.

Saunier, P. (2013) *Transnational History*. Basingstoke: Palgrave Macmillan.

Schumaker, L., A. Brooks, M.-H. Msiska, E. Pollard and D. Potts (2017) 'Situating the BRICS Phenomenon within the Histories and Cultures of Southern Africa', *Journal of Southern African Studies*, 43 (5).

Skinner, R. (2010) *The Foundations of Anti-apartheid: Liberal Humanitarianism and Transnational Activism in Britain and the United States, c. 1919–64*. Basingstoke: Palgrave Macmillan.

Skinner, R. (2014) 'Bombs and Border Crossings: Peace Activist Networks and the Post-colonial State in Africa, 1959–62', *Journal of Contemporary History*, 50 (3).

Skinner, R. (2014) 'Struggles on the Page: British Antiapartheid and Radical Scholarship', *Radical History Review*, 119.

Skinner, R. (2017) 'The Dynamics of Anti-apartheid: International Solidarity, Human Rights and Decolonization', in C. Jeppeson and A.W.M. Smith (eds), *Britain, France and the Decolonization of Africa: Future Imperfect?* London: University College London Press.

Skinner, R. (2019) 'Humanitarians, Human Rights and Anti-apartheid', in Konieczna and Skinner, *Global History of Anti-apartheid*.

Slobodian, Q. (2018) *Globalists: The End of Empire and the Birth of Neoliberalism*. Cambridge, MA: Harvard University Press.

South African Democracy Education Trust (2008) *The Road to Democracy in South Africa*, vol. 3, parts 1 and 2, *International Solidarity*. Pretoria: Unisa Press.

Sparks, S. (2017) 'Crude Politics: The ANC, the Shipping Research Bureau and the Anti-apartheid Oil Boycott', *South African Historical Journal* 69 (2).

Stevens, S. (2014) 'Why South Africa? The Politics of Anti-apartheid Activism in Britain in the Long 1970s', in Eckel and Moyn, *Breakthrough*.

Thompson, A. (2005) *The Empire Strikes Back? The Impact of Imperialism on Britain from the Mid-Nineteenth Century*. Harlow: Pearson Longman.

Thompson, A., and G. Magee (2005) 'Remittances Revisited: A Case Study of South Africa and the Cornish Migrant, c. 1870–1914', *Cornish Studies*, 13.

Thörn, H. (2006) *Anti-apartheid and the Emergence of a Global Civil Society*. Basingstoke: Palgrave Macmillan.

University of Bristol Special Collections, The Penguin Archive, Penguin Africa Library Editorial files, DM 117-AP9, R. First, 'Editor's Preface [draft]' (n.d.).

Von Eschen, P.M. (1997) *Race against Empire: Black Americans and Anticolonialism, 1937–1957*. Ithaca, NY: Cornell University Press.

Westad, O.A. (2017) *The Cold War: A World History*. New York: Basic Books.
White, L., and M. Larmer (2014) 'Introduction: Mobile Soldiers and the Un-national Liberation of Southern Africa', *Journal of Southern African Studies*, 40 (6).
Williams, C.A. (2015). *National Liberation in Post-colonial Southern Africa: A Historical Ethnography of SWAPO's Exile Camps*. Cambridge: Cambridge University Press.

Index

#Black Lives Matter 67, 153
#Fees Must Fall *see* Fees Must Fall movement
#Rhodes Must Fall *see* Rhodes Must Fall movement

1914 Rebellion 149

Adelman, Jeremy 227
African Americans 67, 234
African National Congress 7, 9, 87, 145, 147, 148, 151, 153–4, 157, 160, 198, 213, 234, 237
Afrikaans 1, 11–15, 63–4, 66, 102, 135, 148, 149, 156, 188, 202, 206–7, 214
Afrikaner Weerstandsbeweging 14
Afrikaners and Afrikaner nationalism 12–14, 16, 61, 126, 142–3, 146–52, 161, 178, 186–7, 190, 202–3, 206–8. 210, 213–14
Agar-Hamilton, J. A. I. 12
agriculture 4, 25, 29, 32–5, 130, 132, 210, 230
Alan Paton Book Prize 150, 155–6, 158, 160
Alexander, Jocelyn 239
Algeria 238
Althusser, Louis 4, 130, 180, 185
animal history 25–44, 242
Annales School 13
Anthropocene 15, 27, 28
anthropology 1, 42, 105, 122, 185, 187

antiracism 17, 65, 177–9, 185, 191, 232
antislavery 231
apartheid x–xii, 3, 6–8, 10, 13, 16–17, 28, 35, 37, 55, 58, 62–4, 67–8, 78, 81, 86, 95, 103, 106, 108, 119–20, 129, 131–2, 142, 145–52, 154–5, 157–9, 161, 177–81, 184–90, 198–201, 203–6, 208–12, 215, 230, 232–4, 236, 238–43
archaeology 1, 2, 9, 15, 29–30, 119, 121–3
archives 9–11, 13, 16, 29, 31, 41, 62–4, 77–8, 80–1, 89, 95, 102–5, 110–12, 131–2, 144–6, 161, 188–9, 192, 240, 244
art history 65
Atmore, Anthony 2, 120–1, 129–30
Australia 235–6
autobiography 85, 142–3, 147–8, 152, 154, 156, 192
Azania, Malaika wa 153

Badat, Hussein 67
Bain, J. T. 235
Baldwin, James 191
Ball, Jonathan 152
Bambatha, Chief 106
Bantustans 61, 123
Bayly, Christopher 229, 232, 234, 240
Beinart, William 119–20, 131
Beit, Alfred 60
Beit, Otto 60
Belich, James 229

Index

Bell, David 227
Bell Pottinger 153
Benians, E. A. 122–3
Bergh, Johan 14
Berning, J. Michael 124
Beukes, Lauren 156
Bhattacharya, Neeladri 10
Biko, Steve 147, 184, 190–1
Biography 8, 10, 16, 81, 89, 142–5, 147–8, 150–2, 154–6, 158–61
biology 28, 42, 44
Black Consciousness 66, 79, 132
Black Power 243
Blommaert, Willem 11
Blood River, Battle of 13–14
Boer War (First, 1880–81) 126
Boer War (Second, 1899–1902) 126, 148–9, 181, 229
Boers *see* Afrikaners
Bonner, Phil 4
Boraine, Alex 148
Border War, South African (1966–1989) 150
Bosman, Isak 12
Bozzoli, Belinda 4–5, 79, 130
 Class, Community and Conflict (1987) 202
Bradford, Helen 103
Brand, Christo 192
Braskén, Kaspar 239
Brazil 242
Breckenridge, Keith x, 132
Breytenbach, Breyten 148, 150–1
Bridgland, Fred 159–60
Brink, André 151
Brookes, Edgar Harry (E. H.) 123
Bundy, Colin 128, 147
Bunyan, John 232
Burton, Antoinette 80–1, 229
Bushmen *see* San
Buthelezi, Mbongiseni 112

Callinicos, Luli 4
Cambridge History of South Africa, The (2010, 2012) x, 65, 119, 131–2
Cambridge History of the British Empire, The (1936, 1963) 1, 122, 128
'cancel culture' 67

cannabis 189
capitalism 79, 87, 153, 180, 182, 192, 199, 201–4, 210, 235–6, 241
Chakrabarty, Dipesh 192
Changuion, Louis 13
Chatterjee, Partha 185–6, 192
Chibber, Vivek 185, 192
China 25, 229, 242
Christian National Education 149
Christianity 103–4, 113, 189, 233
clan genealogies/histories 102, 107–13
'Clash of Civilizations' 203
class 5–6, 8–10, 12, 15, 17, 38, 55–7, 59–61, 66–7, 79, 84–5, 94, 131–2, 144, 149, 177, 179–82, 185–92, 198–215
Clingman, Steven 150
Clynick, Tim 181
Cobbing, Julian 111
Coghlan, Timothy 121
Cold War, the 203, 237, 239, 240, 242
Cole, Peter 239
Collins, Canon John 237
Collins, Patricia Hill 94
Colonialism x, 1, 2, 9–10, 15, 17, 28–9, 31, 33, 55, 57, 60, 62–8, 80, 103–5, 107–9, 111, 113, 119, 121–2, 128, 129–30, 132–3, 145, 153, 178, 209, 228–32, 234–5, 233–9, 242, 244
'Coloureds' (South African) 55, 57, 61, 63, 66, 122, 134, 205
communism 13, 148, 234
Congress of Democrats 179
Congress of South African Trade Unions 198
consumerism 15, 55, 241–2
Cooper, Frederick 177–8, 230
Cory, George 16, 124–5, 128, 132–4
Council on Higher Education 77
course evaluations 56, 68
Couzens, Tim 4, 145
COVID-19 xii, 15, 25–8, 42
Croce, Benedetto 125, 135
Cronje, Geoffrey 187–8
Culverson, Donald 236
Curry, Dawne xii

dagga see cannabis
Dakar meeting (1987) 148–50

Danielson, Larry 111
Dart, Raymond 37
Darwin, John 229
Darwinism *see* Social Darwinism
Davenport, Rodney 11, 119
Davies, Robert 201, 203
Davis, Rebecca 157
De Beers Consolidated Mines 60
De Kiewiet, Cornelis Willem (C. W.) 103, 121–2, 127–9, 134–5
De Kock, Eugene 154–157
De la Rey, Koos 149
decolonisation xi, 16, 65–6, 77, 135, 153, 177–9, 184–6, 190–1, 228, 237, 240
Degenaar, Johan 151
Delius, Peter 131
Democratic Alliance 199
Devji, Faisal 239
Dhlomo, Herbert Isaac Ernest (H. I. E.) 16, 111
Die Antwoord 207
Die Stem 147
District Six Museum 9–10
Dlamini, Jacob 66, 154–5, 158, 160
domestic servants *see* maids
Drayton, Richard 227, 243
Du Bois, W. E. B. 177, 184, 190–2
Du Plessis, Irma 212–13
Du Preez, Max 155
Du Toit, André x
Dube, John 145, 161
Dubow, Saul 187, 238
Duly, Leslie 121
Dutch Reformed Church 148

ecology 28, 30, 42–3
Economic Freedom Fighters 199
Eersterust 63, 67
Eichmann, Adolf 155
Eley, Geoff 186, 192
'End of History' 203
environmental history 15, 28–30, 38–9, 41–3, 79, 242
epistemology 10, 62–3, 105, 108, 177, 228, 241
ethnoprimatology 15, 29, 42
ethology 28, 42
Eurocentrism 120, 241
European Community, the (EU) 237

Facebook 40, 67
'Fallists' *see* the Fees Must Fall movement
Fees Must Fall movement 66, 153–4, 184
feminism 76–9, 94, 148, 158–61, 203, 207, 213
fiction (literary) 76, 80–2, 88, 94–5, 143
Fieldhouse, Roger 236
First, Ruth 148, 236
Fischer, Abraham 148
Fischer, Bram 148–51
folklore 29, 102, 104–5, 111, 113, 124
Fouché, Leo 12
'Fred' the baboon 40–1
Freedom Park 147
Freund, Bill 208–9
Frontier, the (South Africa) 3, 5, 28, 33–4, 119, 125, 128, 230
Fuze, Magema 102, 113, 145

Gandhi, Mohandas K. 234–5
Gcaleka, Nicholas Tilana 9, 62, 107
Geduld, Allison 59
gender 10, 15, 37–8, 55–9, 66, 76–81, 84–7, 89, 92, 94–5, 158, 160, 185, 188, 203–4, 213
Genovese, Eugene 180
Giliomee, Hermann 119, 148, 150–1
Gilroy, Paul 68
global history and globalisation 14, 17, 26–8, 42, 86, 132, 146, 154, 177, 188, 199–200, 204, 208, 210, 212, 214, 227–44, 241, 243
Gobodo-Madikizela, Pumla 155–6
Godeé-Molsbergen, Everhard C. 11
Goosen, Jeanne 207
Gordon, David 131
Gqoba, William 103–4, 107
Gramsci, Antonio 130, 180, 185
Great Britain *see* United Kingdom
Great Trek, the 126
Grundlingh, Albert 181
Guy, Jeff 109

Haffajee, Ferial 183
Hall, Catherine 231
Hammond-Tooke, W. D. 33, 108–9

Hardie, Keir 235
Harries, Patrick 131
Harris, Verne 78, 81
Hey, Douglas 39
Hintsa (king) 9–10, 62–3
Historical Association of South Africa 78
History Workshop (Ruskin College, Oxford) 4
History Workshop see Wits History Workshop
Hobsbawm, Eric 180
Hofmeyr, Isabel 232, 235
homosexuality 86–7, 92, 95, 187
hooks, bell 191
Hoskins, Lewis 121
human rights and humanitarianism 17, 177, 184, 231, 233, 237–8, 241–2
Hyam, Ronald 120, 129
Hyslop, Jon 146, 181–2, 204, 210, 235, 239

imperial history and imperialism 10, 60, 102, 104, 127, 130, 178, 181, 204, 228–32, 235, 242
India 25, 80, 185, 188, 235, 242
Indians (South African) 57, 61, 66, 122, 205
industrialisation 3–4, 17, 25, 60, 109, 119, 126, 129, 132, 135, 146, 199–201, 203–4, 206–15, 230, 241
Inskeep, Ray 123
Instagram 67
International Defence and Aid 237
intersectionality 55, 59, 67–8, 79, 84, 89, 94–5, 178, 199, 210, 214–15, 233
Izibongo 108, 112–13
Iziduko 108, 110–13
Izithakazelo 108–10, 112–13

Jack Parow 207
Jameson, Leander, S. 60
Jansen, Annemari 154–7
Jennet, Christine 236
'Jimmy' the baboon 41
Johnstone, Frederick 3, 130–1, 201
Jonker, Ingrid 151

Jordan, Archibald Campbell (A. C.) 16, 103, 111
Joubert, Elsa 151

Kallaway, Peter 4
Kannemyer, John 151
Kawa, Richard 111
Kenya 39, 57, 231
Khoe 33
Klotz, Audie 232
Krikler, Jeremy 181, 204
Krog, Antjie 150, 155
Kros, Cynthia 7
Kuzwayo, Ellen 148
Kuzwayo, Fezekile 153, 157–8

Labour 3, 59–60, 66–7, 78–80, 83, 88, 92, 130, 132, 187, 199–206, 211–14, 235–6, 241–2
Lalu, Premesh 8–10, 15, 62–3, 64
Lambert, Alan 231
Larmer, Miles 239
League of Nations 233
Legassick, Martin 2–6, 8, 130–1
Leroke, Windsor 15, 62, 63–5
lesbian 76, 86–7
Lester, Alan 231
LGBTIQ (lesbian, gay, bisexual, transgender, intersex and queer) 76, 78, 80, 85, 88, 94–5
liberal historiography and South African liberalism 2, 4, 6, 11, 59–61, 64–5, 105–6, 119–21, 124–31, 135, 151, 199, 201, 203, 208
liberalism see liberal historiography and South African liberalism
Lipton, Merle 121, 203
Literary Studies and criticism 16, 65, 76, 80, 81–2, 85, 88, 94–5, 102–6, 108–9, 111–12, 147, 151, 153, 155–6, 179, 203, 206–7
Luthuli, Albert 147

Macmillan, William Miller (W. M.) 119, 124–8, 131, 134–5
'Madams' 82–5, 89–90, 92
Madikizela-Mandela, Winnie 148, 159–61
Mafeje, Archie 106

Mager, Anne Kelk x–xi, 110, 131
Magona, Sindiwe 16, 76, 81–6, 94
Magubane, Bernard 106
Magubane, Zine 58, 60–1
Mahabeer, Pryah 59
Maharaj, Mac 147
'maids' 81–5, 88–93
Maine, Kas 7–8, 11, 145–6
Makhanya, Mondli 143
Malan, D. F. 142–3, 154
Malema, Julius 152
Mandela, Nelson 7, 147–8, 152, 159, 161, 192
Marais, Eugène 38
Marks, Shula 2–4, 106, 120–1, 123, 131
Marxism 6, 8–9, 12, 79, 105, 120, 130–2, 144, 179–80, 182, 185, 188, 192, 201, 203
masculinity 148, 153, 213
Mashinini, Emma 148
Masilela, Ntongela 16, 104
Maxengana, Nomalungisa 111
Mazower, Mark 233
Mbeki, Govan 236
Mbeki, Thabo 148–50, 152
Mbenga, Bernard 119
McGregor, JoAnn 239
Meer, Fatima 148
Mfecane 110–11, 241
Mgqwetho, Nontsizi 103
Miller, Jamie 243
Mineworkers' Union (MWU) 211, 213–14
mining 60, 130, 132, 201, 203, 206, 211, 213
Minkley, Gary 7–11
Mirzaei, Abas 67
missions and missionaries 103–4, 119, 124–5, 145, 231–2
Mokhele, Matseliso 59
Mokoena, Hlonipha 10–11, 145–6
Moleko, Anne-Gloria Sengkane 58
Mompati, Ruth 87
Mooney, Katie 189
Morrell, Robert 181, 203
Morudu, Palesa 157
Motadel, David 227, 243
Mouton, Alex 150–1
Mqhayi, Samuel 103

Msimang, Sisonke 159–61
Muholi, Zanele 16, 76, 77, 85–95

Naidu, Sam 104
Namibia 39, 57, 239
Nasson, Bill x–xi, 131
National Party (NP) 61, 148, 181, 186–7, 199, 204–5, 206, 208, 210–11, 213
Naudé, Beyers 148–9
Ndebele 35
neoliberalism 68, 214–5, 241–2
Newton, A. P. 122–3
Nguni, the 2, 32–3, 108–9, 123
Nigeria 238
Nkosi Sikelel' iAfrika 147
Norval, Aletta 187
Nyamnjoh, Francis 185
Nzimande, Nomkhosi 59

O'Meara, Dan 202, 206
Omer-Cooper, John 1
Opland, Jeff 103, 105
Opperman, G. O. 189
oral history 2, 4, 7–10, 16, 29, 31, 33, 80, 95, 102, 104–5, 108, 110, 113, 123–4, 145–6, 202, 212
Organisation of African Unity 238
Orkney Snork Nie! 206–7
Osterhammel, Jurgen 230
Oxford History of South Africa, The (1969, 1971) 2–3, 105, 119–23, 129–30, 201

Painter, Nell Irvin 190
Pakistan 239
palaeontology 15, 30, 42
paleoecology 30, 42
Pan-Africanism 66, 79, 234
Peires, Jeff 103, 105, 107–10
Pelzer, A. N. 12
'people's history' 7–8, 11–12, 111
Phadi, Mosa 64
Phakade, Nomancotsho 64
Phalo (king) 107–8
Phaswana, Edith 59
Philip, John 125
Pienaar, Schalk 151
Pirie, Gordon 132
Plaatje, Sol 145, 161, 191

Pohlandt-McCormick, Helena x
Posel, Deborah 181–2, 186, 198, 241
postcolonialism 10, 65, 79, 179, 203, 207, 213, 238
Potgieter, Cheryl-Ann 58
Poulantzas, Nicos 4, 130, 180, 185
poverty 3, 78, 90, 125, 153, 198, 206–7, 209, 211
praise poems 102, 108, 111
precolonial 2, 15, 28–9, 31, 79, 107–8, 120–2, 132, 145, 178

Qichao, Liang 229
Qotole, Msokoli 103

race and racism 3, 6, 8–9, 15, 38, 55–7, 59, 64–5, 68, 77–9, 84, 92, 100, 119, 127, 132, 153, 155, 179–92, 198–205, 210–13, 233–4, 241
radical/revisionist historiography x–xi, 4–6, 8–9, 14, 17, 64–5, 119–20, 129–32, 135, 186, 191, 201–3, 212, 234–6
Rand Afrikaans University 61
Rand Revolt, the 3, 181, 201, 235
Ranger, Terence 178
rape 66, 87, 91, 153, 158
Rassool, Ciraj 7–11
Rees, Wyn 121
religion 14, 34, 189
revisionist historiography *see* radical/revisionist historiography
Rhodes, Cecil John 60–1, 66, 153, 228
Rhodes Must Fall movement 66, 153
Rhodes Trust 60
Rhodes University 56–7, 59–62, 66
Rhodesia *see* Zimbabwe
Rivonia Trial, the 148
rock art 29–31, 33–4, 42
Rodriguez, Ileana 183
Roediger, David 181, 191–2, 204
Ross, Robert x–xi, 131
Rubusana, Walter 102, 105
Russia 27, 135, 242

San, the 31–4
Sapire, Hilary 238
Sarkar, Sumit 188

Saunders, Chris 121, 128, 134, 238–9
Saunier, Pierre-Yves 243
Schapera, Isaac 123
Sedibe, Glory 154
Segal, Ronald 236
segregation 3, 17, 127, 132, 179–80, 184, 188, 198, 201, 230, 234
Seipei, Stompie 159
Seme, Pixley ka Isaka 145
sex, and sexism 77, 78, 80, 85, 87, 88–9
Shaik, Schabir 152
Shaka (king) 104–5
Sharp, John 213
Sharpeville massacre 232, 234
Shell, Robert 124
Shell, Sandra 133
Shoba, Makhosi 59
Shona totemism 35
Simons, Jack and Ray 236
Sisulu, Albertina 147–8
Sisulu, Walter 147
Slabbert, Frederik van Zyl 148, 151
slavery 128, 198, 228
Slobodian, Quinn 241
Smith, Ken 133–4
Smith, Scotty 40
Smuts, Jan 178
Smuts, Johan 213
Social Darwinism 35–7
social history 4–5, 7–9, 11, 15, 17, 62–3, 88, 105, 144, 179–86, 188–9, 191–3, 199, 202–3, 210, 212
'Societies of Southern Africa in the Nineteenth and Twentieth Centuries' Seminar 2–3
sociology 63, 65, 77, 182, 187, 241
Solidarity/Solidariteit (social movement) 213–14
Soske, Jon xi, 65
Sotho, the 2–3, 61
South African Communist Party 198
South African Democracy Education Trust (SADET), *Road to Democracy* series 236
South African Historical Journal 1, 13
South African School of Mines (Kimberley) 60
South West Africa *see* Namibia

Southern African Historical Society 77–8
Soviet Union 6, 27, 242
Soweto Uprising, the (1976) 13
Spanish Flu, the 26
Sparks, Stephen 131
Spies, Francois du Toit 12–14
Springbok Legion 179
Stander, André 40
'State Capture' 153
Steyn, Jaap 151
Steyn, Melissa 182
Stoler, Ann 230
Stolten, Hans Eric x
Subaltern Studies 9, 17, 183, 185, 188

Tambo, Oliver 147
Tanzania 39
Tendi, Blessing-Miles 239
Teppo, Annika 209
Terre'Blanche, Eugene 14
Theal, George McCall 16, 103–4, 107, 119–20, 123–4, 132–4
Thlabi, Redi 158, 160
Thom, H. B. 11–12
Thomas, Kylie 87
Thompson, E. P. 180, 186, 202
Thompson, Leonard 1–2, 119, 121–4
Thörn, Håkan 236–7
Tisani, Nomathamsanqa 16, 104, 107–8, 112
Transgender 76–80, 86, 94
Transkei 60
transnational history 132, 146, 200, 204, 215, 227–8, 230–44
transphobia 92
Transvaal University College (later, the University of Pretoria) 12
Trapido, Stanley 4
Trump, Donald 177
Truth and Reconciliation Commission 81, 150, 154, 158
Tsonga, the 61
Tswana, the 2, 61
Turner, Richard 184
Tutu, Desmond 152
Twitter 67

Umkhonto we Sizwe 154
United Kingdom 4, 181, 236–7
United Nations 233, 237–8
United States of America 26, 67, 81, 153, 236, 239
University of Cape Town (UCT) 4, 36, 59, 60, 61, 66, 153
  African Studies Library fire (18 April 2021) 78, 145
University of Durban Westville 61
University of Fort Hare 61, 77
University of Johannesburg 77, 182
University of Natal 4, 59, 61, 104
University of Port Elizabeth 61
University of Pretoria xii, 12, 61, 63, 66, 67, 77, 187
University of South Africa 1, 12–13, 61
University of Stellenbosch 11–12, 26, 61, 66
University of the North 61
University of the Orange Free State 61
University of the Western Cape 7, 61–2, 77
University of the Witwatersrand 4, 7, 12, 59, 77, 180
  see also Wits History Workshop

Van der Merwe, Carel 146
Van Jaarsveld, Floors 1, 13–14
Van Niekerk, Marlene 151, 207
Van Onselen, Charles 4–5, 8, 10–11, 145–6, 181, 202
Van Riebeeck, Jan 149
Van Wyk, Stephan 213
Van Wyk Louw, N. P., 151
Venda, the 61
Verhoef, Grietjie 130
visual arts 85–6, 94, 182
Volkgeskiedenis 11–15
Volksmoeder 149
Voortrekkers, the 126, 146
  Voortrekker Monument, the 147

Walker, Eric 103, 134–5
Walzer, Michael 150–1
Webster, Alan 111
Webster, Eddie 4, 203
Welsh, Sharon 64
Wernher, Julius 60
Westlake, Nancy 129–30

White, Luise 239
'whiteness' 17, 59, 65, 177–93, 204
Wiehahn, Nic 211, 213
Wilson, Monica 1–2, 105, 121–3
Wits History Workshop 4–5, 7–9, 63, 144, 180–2
Witz, Leslie 7–8
Wolpe, Harold 3, 6, 8
'wokeness' 55, 65–8
women 57–9, 61–2, 64, 66, 68, 76–80, 83–9, 92–5, 144, 148, 150, 157–61, 179, 187–90, 203
womxn *see* women
Woolf, Daniel 113
Worden, Nigel 119
workers 5, 6, 12, 58, 61, 76, 80, 82, 85, 88–9, 92, 94–5, 144, 149, 180–2, 184, 186–8, 190, 198–215, 235, 242

World Campaign for the Release of South African Political Prisoners 237
World War One 26, 36, 204, 235
World War Two 37, 43, 200
Wright, Harrison 120
Wright, John 106–7, 109

xenophobia 67, 92, 214
Xhosa, the 9, 16, 62, 82, 103–5, 107–8, 111–12, 147
Xingwana, Lulu 87

Yudelman, David 203

Zimbabwe 39, 57, 122
Zulus, the 104–7
Zuckerman, Solly 36–8, 44
Zuma, Jacob 152–3, 157–8